Steven Rg̲
mpls   15 XII 88

The Wonderful World of Succulents

Cultivation and Description of Selected Succulent Plants Other Than Cacti
Second Edition, Revised

by Werner Rauh
Translated by Harvey L. Kendall

Smithsonian Institution Press
Washington, D.C. 1984

Originally published as Die groBartige Welt der Sukkulenten, 2nd (revised) edition
©1979 Paul Parey Publishers, Berlin/Hamburg
Translated with permission of Paul Parey Publishers
First printing in English in the United States
©1984 Smithsonian Institution Press. All rights reserved.

Library of Congress Cataloging in Publication Data

Rauh, Werner.
The wonderful world of succulents.
Translation of: Die grossartige Welt der Sukkulenten.
Includes index.
1. Succulent plants. I. Title.
SB438.R313 1984 635.9'55 83-20148
ISBN 0-87474-780-5

Editor: Donald C. Fisher

Dedicated in grateful respect to the late Mr. Hans Herre, former curator at the Botanical Garden at Stellenbosch and tireless researcher of the plants of South Africa.

FOREWORD TO THE SECOND EDITION

Twelve years have passed since the appearance of the first edition. Reviews in professional journals and conversations with serious admirers of succulents have shown the author that the book has found wide acclaim, although many fans have been deterred by the high price.

In the meantime the author and others, especially his friend LAVRANOS, Johannesburg, have undertaken numerous research expeditions in little-known succulent areas and have returned with an abundance of new, interesting succulents. It would not have been difficult to expand the book to twice its size; unfortunately costs restrain us.

Thus the original concept of the first edition was maintained. In some places the text was expanded, some photographs have been replaced, and the nomenclature has been brought up to date.

It is hoped that the second edition will contribute to increasing the steadily growing number of succulent admirers.

Heidelberg, spring 1979 WERNER RAUH

FROM THE FOREWORD TO THE FIRST EDITION

The succulents belong without a doubt to the most bizarre and striking phenomena of the plant world. These are plants with thick, fleshy leaves or shoots that are often bristling with a thick array of thorns and barbs.

In lay circles such plants are commonly taken for cacti, which is erroneous, because this designation can be given to only a very specific group of plants, the members of the family *Cactaceae*. For example, even though a euphorbia may resemble a cactus, it is not a cactus but a succulent.

This latter designation is of a more general and broader significance and comprises all of those plants equipped with juicy, fleshy organs, and such plants do not belong to one but to many plant families. If one wishes to make a distinction, then one should really speak of "cacti and other succulents," as has become common usage.

Although numerous books large and small have appeared in recent years on cacti, which occupy the interest of admirers and collectors, the "other succulents" have been treated rather miserly. In cactus books they are usually mentioned only in an addendum, and so the admirer can hardly get a proper idea of their beauty and variety. With the exception of the great work by H. JACOBSEN: *Handbook of Succulent Plants,* 3 vols., and the book by H. KRAINZ: *Sukkulenten* (Silvia-Verlag, Zürich, 1958), there is no newer, better work specifically on the "other succulents" in either German or English literature. I have therefore responded to the wish and encouragement of the PAUL PAREY publishing house to fill this gap and have done so all the more enthusiastically because I have undertaken extensive trips through the succulent areas of South America, Africa, and Madagascar and I am acquainted with this group of plants from personal observation in their natural habitats. Throughout the years I have assembled an abundance of living plants and a rich collection of pictures, which in the work at hand could be exploited only partially, because of its enormous size. This book on succulents does not pretend to be a handbook—even handbooks cannot be complete—it is only to stimulate interest and to give interested plant fans an idea of the natural living areas, an overview of the variety of the "other succulents," and a guide to their care in our less sunny climate. Therefore only a selection can be discussed, and any selection, of course, must be personal. Many fans will miss such familiar plants as Agavaceae, but in their place they will find species which, until now, have been totally unknown in collections. I have tried to introduce at least some typical representatives for each major succulent group in words and pictures and in doing so place special emphasis on showing many plants in their natural habitat.

May the book serve to intensify the love for succulents and to draw new friends into the circle of succulent collectors.

Heidelberg, summer 1966 WERNER RAUH

CONTENTS

9

Instructions for the Use of the Book:

In the plate references in the text the first number refers to the plate number; the second, italicized number refers to the corresponding illustration in the plate. In the plate legends the following abbreviations are used: (ul) = upper left, (um) = upper middle, (ur) = upper right, (ml) = middle left, (mm) = middle middle, (mr) = middle right, (ll) = lower left, (lm) = lower middle, (lr) = lower right.

GENERAL

What are succulents?

Hardly any group of plants has found so many admirers in the past several decades than the succulents. Interest in these bizarre plants is constantly increasing; in almost every country there are societies in which succulent fans get together, report on their cultivation experiences at conventions and meetings, organize the exchange of plants and seed, and publish their own journals. Nurseries and importers who have specialized in the cultivation and introduction of these plants can barely meet the demand.

Of course there are also fans of other plant groups. Let me just mention the orchids, which again and again inspire one with their beautiful shapes and colorful flowers, and the remarkable bromeliads. Compared to the great number of succulent admirers, however, orchid and bromeliad fans are far fewer, for orchids and bromeliads require very careful care. For them one should at least have an indoor garden, if not a small greenhouse, in order to create the proper growing conditions. Only a few orchids and bromeliads can tolerate the dry air of our living rooms. Not so with succulents! They are happy with a bright window sill and require far less care—one of the main reasons for their popularity. Since many succulents stay small and also grow very slowly, one can accommodate a rather large variety of widely differing types even on a window sill. One can set them out on a south-facing balcony in full sunlight in the summer and even place them in the ground around a doorstep. Because succulents, as inhabitants of semi-deserts and deserts, are extraordinarily tough and can survive with little water, they can be left to themselves (for example, during a vacation period) for two weeks without drying out. Of course, to enjoy plants one must not neglect their care completely. Care, of course, means time and work, but the lover of succulents does not shy away; such work in the helter-skelter of today means a far greater relaxation and recuperation than many other pastimes. Just the fact that succulents grow slowly demands patience, and patience

is a healing medicine to treat the bustle of everyday life. If the plants thrive and one day unfold their beautiful flowers, then the admirer is rewarded a thousandfold for all the effort spent on the collections. The continual busying with the plants, even if it is only a few minutes a day, binds hobbyists with their plants; the owner gets to know their growing habits and thereby penetrates daily deeper and deeper into the secrets of nature.

Let me now define what succulents are. First, they belong to the biological category of the so-called xerophytes; these are inhabitants of low-precipitation areas, deserts, semi-deserts, dry cliffs, and grasslands which are subjected to long dry periods. The plants must thus be able to withstand these periods without harm and therefore have a series of structural characteristics which make life possible for them under these extreme conditions. Sufficiently fast water absorption must be assured. Therefore most xerophytes have a many-branched root system that frequently extends only a few centimeters below the surface of the ground; they are furthermore equipped with devices to prevent evaporation of the absorbed water; and finally, many xerophytes are able to store for long dry periods moisture that sometimes falls only on a few days a year. They thereby experience morphological transformations and become fat, fleshy, and juicy—succulent. In Latin "succus" means "juice"; succulents are therefore plants which to a high degree store juice, i.e., water. In German and French they are erroneously called "fat plants" ("Fettflanzen" or "plantes grasses"). This expression refers only to their lushness, because they do not, of course, store fat.

In essence all of the basic organs of a plant can serve as water reservoirs—roots, leaves, and stems. Accordingly we distinguish between root succulents, leaf succulents, and stem succulents. The root succulents are relatively rare and are of little interest to the hobbyist, because the appearance of the succulent quality as such is not visible.

Considerably more common and more sought after are the leaf and stem succulents. In the stem succulents either the whole stem system—the main stem with its lateral branches—comprises the water storage area or the swollen area is limited to the main stem, which becomes fat and knotty, while the side branches remain thin. The result is a growing habit typical of certain relatives of the pumpkin (Cucurbitaceae), e.g., *Gerrardanthus* (Plate 52), *Momordica* (Plate 52), *Melothria,* etc. We call these caudiciforms. Of course various succulent types are not always clearly distinguishable from one another and are connected by transitional forms. For example, plants with fleshy main stems could also have succulent leaves.

The interior tissues, the parenchyma, serve as water storage. In the leaf succulents it is the well-developed leaf parenchyma (Figure 1,*1*), in the stem succulents it is the cortex or the core tissue (Figure 1,*2–3*). The parenchyma cells are large, bladder-shaped, and thin walled; woody cell elements are barely present in a microscopic picture. Succulent stems can therefore be so soft that one can easily cut them with a knife. Even in South Africa we find common names such as "butter tree" (*Cotyledon paniculata,* Plate 59,*3* and *4)* or "lard tree" (*Portulacaria afra,* Plate 82,*4),* whose main stems are as soft as butter or lard. Only the stem bases are somewhat wooden, which give the plants a firm anchor.

The phenomenon of succulence is not limited to one single family, but is found in no less than about 50 different plant families not related to one another but which all inhabit the same locations and whose representatives under identical environmental conditions often take on the same appearance, the same shape. This remarkable phenomenon is called "convergence."

The best-known succulents are the cacti, which exist in a multitude of species more numerous than in almost any other plant family. The lay person, without thinking, places all plants with a similar appearance into the category of cacti. Indeed professional botanists also often have trouble, upon superficial examination, in distinguishing a cactus from a euphorbia in its non-blooming stage, because the two are often characterized by the same shape and thorn arrangement (Plate 1,*1* and *2*).

Let me digress for a moment. On the window sill of my home I am growing two plants of approximately the same size and with the same amount of thorns. They are pictured in Plate 1 at the top. The one to the left is a euphorbia (*Euphorbia horrida);* to the right is a cactus

(*Lobivia ferox).* They are both rather young plants and still have a spherical shape. Later, however, they will become columnar. It is fun to ask friends to tell me which is which. In about half of the cases I am told that both

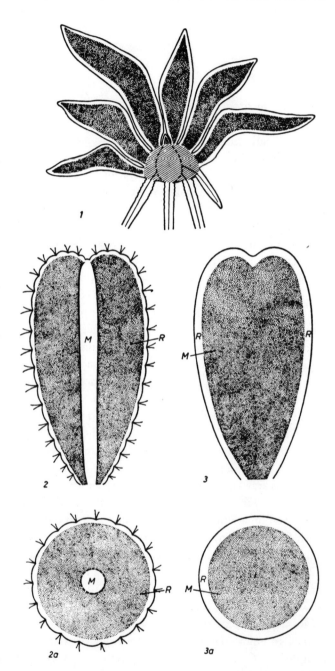

Figure 1. *1,* Longitudinal section of a leaf succulent (*Gasteria).* Axis tissue hatched. *2–3,* Longitudinal sections of stem succulents. Water storage parenchyma stippled. In *2* the cortex tissue (R) stores water, in *3* the core tissue (M); stores water; *2a* and *3a* are the corresponding latitudinal sections of *2* and *3.* Water tissue stippled.

plants are of course cacti. Only experienced hobbyists can rescue themselves and know the difference between a euphorbia and a cactus; they will stick both of them with a knife. If one yields a milky sap, it must be a euphorbia. (There are, however, cacti with milky sap, e.g., a number of tubercle cacti (mammillarias)). The experienced hobbyist also knows that the thorns of cacti are altered leaves, belong to a so-called areole, and are perched on a downy cushion that the euphorbias do not have. One will see later that the euphorbia thorns are altered bracts or inflorescences.

It is almost a miracle of nature that the growth forms of cacti, indigenous exclusively to the New World, under similar climatic conditions are duplicated as convergents in plant groups of the Old World. This is true not only of the common columnar forms but also of the considerably rarer extreme-spherical forms. The spherical form of the sea urchin cactus *(Astrophytum asterias)* is repeated convergently in the South African *Euphorbia obesa* and *E. symmetrica* (Plate 1,3). Therefore one also speaks of the so-called cactus shape, which however is not found solely in the family of Cactaceae but also in other plant groups. Plate 1,4 illustrates a small selection of these.

The typical cactus is characterized by the following features:

a. Formation of a succulent main axis.
b. Extreme reduction of the leaves; their function is taken over by the main axis itself, which thereby retains its green color for many years (only in the case of a woody main axis can cortex formation and brown coloration occur).
c. Frequent formation of thorns; they are modified leaves or parts thereof.

Also within the leaf succulents there are many convergences, and the similarities in form are so frequent that only a specialist can readily tell from their non-flowering state to which family the plants belong.

The above discussion indicates that the phenomenon of succulence is not limited to the cactus family alone; therefore, in order to make a distinction, one speaks of "cacti and other succulents." While the former, with the single exception of one genus *(Rhipsalis)*, are exclusively inhabitants of the New World, the habitat of 90% of the "other succulents" is the Old World. In the present work I will limit myself to the latter.

The habitats of succulent plants

I have already made mention of the fact that by far most succulents inhabit areas with little precipitation, so-called arid zones, deserts, semi-deserts and dry bush areas. They are the main component of the very sparsely, often meagerly developed and completely xerophytic vegetation.

Arid zones comprise about 35% of the total surface of the earth. They are located along both sides of the tropics and therefore belong to the subtropic zones of the Northern and Southern hemispheres. In Asia and North America, however, they extend far into the moderate climate region (Figure 2).

Although all dry areas receive very little precipitation, there is, according to WALTER,[1] no uniform arid climate, but rather a series of varying types that can be distinguished. "It can be said that almost every arid zone has its own climatic peculiarities and in one way or another differs from the others."

Thus WALTER makes these distinctions:
Arid areas with winter rain and a dry summer period.

Arid areas with summer rain and a dry winter period.

Arid areas with two rain periods or with no clearly distinguishable rain period.

Extreme arid areas (full deserts), in which rain falls only sporadically or not at all.

The so-called fog deserts comprise a special type of arid zone—for example, the Peruvian-Chilean coastal desert and the Namib Desert in Nambia (formerly South-West Africa). These are deserts completely without rain, i.e., full deserts, but which are characterized by frequent and lengthy periods of fog, whose formation can be traced to a cold sea stream running parallel to the coast. In Peru, for example, lies a thick, well-confined fog layer of the desert-like coastal strip. The upper limit of this fog layer lies between 600 and 800 m. Although it never rains, the moisture from the fog suffices to keep alive a considerable number of plants, primarily succulents, xerophytic

[1] WALTER, H.: *Die Vegetation der Erde in öko-physiologischer Betrachtung.* Vol. I. *Die tropischen und subtropischen Zonen.* Gustav Fischer, Jena, 3rd edition, 1973.

bromeliads, and many annuals. For these plants the fog is the only source of moisture. A similar situation exists in the Namib Desert, the scene of a great number of remarkable and rare succulents.

A peculiarity of many arid zones is the great amount of salts in the soil released by erosion of the existing rock. Among these, sodium chloride (table salt) plays an important role; also we find magnesium chloride and sulfates (sodium sulfate and magnesium sulfate). The build-up of salts causes the soil to become briny. This is especially the case in areas where WALTER says sedimentary stone appears. Salty soils are unknown in arid zones that have crystalline rock or primordial rock. The sedimentation contains large amounts of the salts, which are eroded from the rock by rains and are transported into low places and hollows that have no run-off. Slopes are accordingly less salty than low places, in which the rich build-up of salt following evaporation of the water can even "bloom." So-called salt pans form, which can be distinguished from surrounding areas even from a great distance because of

their white color, but these salt soils are not completely without vegetation; salt-loving plants, so-called halophytes, establish themselves here, distinguished by strong succulence, predominantly in their leaves. Plate 2,3 shows such a salt pan with a mass of leaf-succulent Zygophyllaceae, *Augea capensis*. Also, interesting mesembryanthemums such as *Muiria hortenseae* (Plate 92,6), *Diplosoma leipoldtii,* etc., grow only on very briny soil. All these plants, because they are halophytes, cause great problems in cultivation and cannot be kept for long; they perish after just a short time.

In addition to lack of rain in the arid zones, other climatological factors affect the vegetation. As a result of little cloud cover, all dry areas are subject to an intensive and long radiation from the sun.

According to MARLOTH[2] the interior of South Africa,

[2] MARLOTH, R.: "Das Kapland, in Sonderheit das Reich der Kapflora, das Waldgebiet und die Karroo." In: *Wissenshaftl. Ergebnisse der Deutschen Tiefsee-Expedition 1898–1899.* Vol. II/III, Jena, 1908.

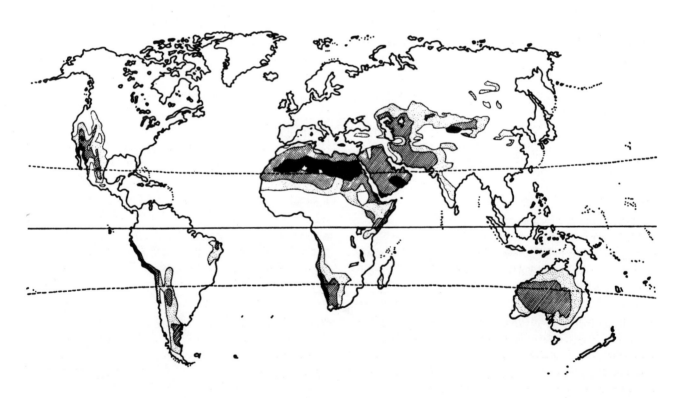

Figure 2.   Distribution of the dry areas of the earth. Black: full deserts. Hatching: semi-deserts. Stippled areas: semi-arid zones (adapted from WALTER).

the major distribution area of most succulents, is one of the sunniest areas on earth. "Don't think that the intensity and long duration of the light has stunted the plants; we find exactly the opposite; the succulents, especially in their vegetative organs as well as in their inflorescences, are most surprisingly sensitive to differences in the intensity of the light." (MARLOTH, 1908, p. 346). That is also the reason that many asclepiads such as *Trichocaulon, Hoodia,* etc., which grow in extremely sunny habitats, also present such great difficulties in cultivation, since one simply cannot give them sufficient light.

Especially sensitive to lack of light are rosette- and semi-rosette-forming *Crassula* species, which in their native habitat have charming beauty, but in cultivation, especially in dim winter months, completely lose their typical form. Many thorny euphorbias in cultivation lose their stiff thorns and can hardly be recognized.

Although the majority of succulents are definitely sun plants, there are exceptions. A number of species even shun direct sunlight and prefer semi-shady locations; they grow under brush or in the shadow of boulders. Chiefly among these are many haworthias but also conophytes. Other succulents, such as *Fenestraria, Lithops, Ophthalmophyllum,* and the rare *Haworthia maughanii* and *H. truncata,* thrive in very sunny locations but protect themselves against intensive sun in a very special way: they completely bury their vegetative bodies in the earth and present only the blunt leaf tips to the light (see Plate 4,3). However, as one will see later in more detail, these leaf tips are equipped with a window with no chloroplasts (Plate 4,4). Light can reach the water tissues and the assimilation parenchyma only in a roundabout way and thus loses much of its effect. Light intensities that are too high destroy the chlorophyll.

The arid zones are also characterized by great temperature changes between day and night. On hot, cloudless days the ground surface temperature may reach +50° C (112° F) during the mid-day hours; bare rocks, the habitat of many ultra-succulent species, can become even hotter. At night, however, the temperature can drop to freezing and below, so a dew or even frost forms. Some euphorbias, especially those of the high mountains (e.g., *Euphorbia clavarioides* var. *truncata, E. pulvinata,* etc.) as well as the rare *Aloe polyphylla,* which may be found as high as 3000 m, can even withstand rather long frost periods and snow without damage.

A further hazard to the vegetation in many dry zones is the wind, which blows constantly over long periods of time and which, as a result of its parching effect, has a very unfavorable influence on the plant life.

When it does rain in the dry areas, the valuable precipitation comes in the form of violent downpours; one rain can comprise a third of the annual precipitation. In the arid zones with rainfall of 50 to 300 mm per year, it rains for only a few days. In just a few hours after a storm, at the most after one or two days, there is hardly any indication of the rain. The earth is often as hard as cement. This hard ground crust and the sparse growth cause the water to run off so fast that only slight amounts are absorbed by the plants' root systems. Not just the macroclimate, the overall climate distribution (rain, temperature, light, and wind), but also the micro-climate, climate in its most limited space, plays a role in the distribution of plant life. As a result of the mountainous geography of desert and semi-desert areas, they have a large variety of environments. The shadow sides of mountain chains are exposed to different climatic conditions than are the sunny slopes; different temperature and wind conditions prevail in deep, narrow valleys than in regions of the peaks. Therefore the vegetation in a very small area can be subject to a great variety of conditions.

Because of the extreme climatic conditions described above, there is also a variety of plants in these areas; only those plants that can adapt to these conditions can thrive here, and those are the succulents. In addition to them there are a few bushes and trees of stunted growth-form, which prefer to live along the water runs, a few other xerophytes, and some annuals in great number, whose seeds can stand drought for years but following a rain can germinate within 24 hours. The young plants grow quickly and after a short vegetative development bloom and then just as quickly disappear again. For a tourist in the dry zones it is always one of the most impressive experiences to see how the desert changes overnight into a blooming garden. You simply must divorce yourself from the lay conception that desert areas are completely without vegetation. Of course there are vast desert areas, especially sand deserts (great parts of the central Sahara, Saudi Arabia, and the Central Asian Gobi Desert) which are completely without vegetation. These are the so-called full deserts (Figure 2), whereas the semi-deserts (Plate 2) support a considerable number of plants.

There are two primary distribution areas for succulent plants on the earth; the first comprises the dry areas of the New World, Baja California, Arizona, Mexico, Central and South America. This is primarily the realm of cacti. Also there are here a number of leaf succulents, agaves, and Crassulaceae (*Echeveria, Sedum, Pachyphytum*), etc., while stem succulents (except cacti) are represented only by a few euphorbias and representatives of a few uncommon families.

The second great distribution area is the Old World and here especially the dry areas of Africa and the coastal islands of Madagascar, Socotra, and the Canary Islands, as well as southern Arabia. In India there are a few euphorbias and stapeliads. With the exception of the rare *Sarcostemma australis, Anacampseros australiana,* and some annual mesembryanthemums, the gigantic dry areas of Australia have no succulents at all; that is not to say that they do not have xerophytes—these are just not in succulent form.

The greatest number of different species of succulent plants is found undoubtedly in South Africa and Namibia, while to the north and east one encounters a gradual diminishing in the number of species as well as in individual specimens. Additionally the islands of Madagascar and Socotra are rich in unusual plant forms.

The South African dry zones stretch approximately from the 18th to the 30th degree of latitude south. They comprise the western Cape Province, the Southern and the Great Karroo, the Northern Karroo highlands, Bushman Land, the Kalahari, the western coastal area of the Little and the Great Namaland (Namaqualand) along with the Namib Desert (Figure 3), and areas of the highlands of Transvaal.

Especially rich in succulents is the Karroo,[3] a system of basins, which is separated from the rainy coastal area by the Langeberg and the Zwarteberge mountain ranges running parallel to the coast at altitudes up to 2000 m. The land between these two mountain ranges is called the Southern Karroo; the land stretching north of the Zwarteberg range belongs to the Great Karroo, which gradually merges into the northern Karooian Highlands (Figure 3), which is touched by the summer rains. The yearly precipitation in the Karroo proper is less than 200 mm (somewhat more in the east, though); the temperatures in the summer are high. During the winter months nighttime frosts are no rarity.

Typical for the Karroo is the yellowish or reddish (see Color Plate 1,2) soil resulting from the so-called Dwyka conglomerate and which would be quite fertile if it would

get sufficient precipitation. It is precisely this heavy Karroo soil, though, that is agreeable to many succulents. Thus the Karroo is the native habitat for most shrubby mesembs,[4] and the predominant plant form is consequently a dwarf bush. Areas more than a square kilometer are covered with bushes 30 to 60 cm high (Plate 2,1), which during the dry season appear dull gray-brown, but in the rainy season are densely covered with thousands of red, violet, or white flowers and present a splendidly colorful picture (Color Plate 1). In sandier places a host of annuals, predominantly Compositae, flourish along with numerous bulb plants.

Frequently mixed in with the plants are extensive "quartz fields," in which clumps of quartz of various size are strewn over the red Karroo soil. Here we find no bushy mesembryanthemums; instead there are highly succulent species of the same family, such as *Gibbaeum* (Color Plate 1,1), *Argyroderma, Stomatium,* etc., and many stapeliads (*Stapelia, Caralluma, Hoodia, Trichocaulon,* etc.). The genera *Lithops* and *Conophytum* are represented in the Karroo by only a few species. Dry slate cliffs are the habitat for numerous *Aloe,* great, bushy *Crassula,* and *Cotyledon* species.

The eastern part of the Karroo is the habitat of many euphorbias; for example, in the Jansenville District *Euphorbia coerulescens* forms stands as big as a square kilometer (Plate 3,6). Also the favorite columnar euphorbias *E. horrida* and *E. polygona* and the spherical euphorbias (*E. obesa, E. valida, E. meloformis*) are found in the eastern Karroo, as well as the majority of haworthias and gasterias.

The northwestern Ceres Karroo and Bushman Land are the locations of many beautiful *Lithops* species and other mesembryanthemums.

Little Namaqualand up to the Orange River is a treasure trove of rare succulents; parts of this area receive winter rain. It is a mountainous land in which gneiss, granite, slate, and quartz mountains alternate colorfully. Mixed in are vast stretches of sand and quartz fields. The dry, primitive rock cliffs are the habitats of the large, tree aloes (*A. dichotoma,* Plate 3,1; *A. pillansii,* Plate 3,2;

---

[3] "Karroo" in the Hottentot language means "dry area."
[4] Plants from the family of Mesembryanthemaceae or Aizoaceae are referred to by hobbyists as "mesembs."

Color Plate 1.

1 (u)   Quartz field in the Great Karroo
        with a mass stand of *Gibbaeum*
        pubescens

2 (m)   The Karroo in flower with mounds
        of *Drosanthemum*

3 (l)   A section of the flower meadows of
        the Little Namaqualand with stands
        of *Dorotheanthus bellidiformis*

Plate 1.

No layman will be able to distinguish the youth stage of

(ul) *Euphorbia horrida* from that of the cactus

(ur) *Lobivia ferox!*

(m) Examples of convergences and of plant symmetry. Left: *Euphorbia obesa* (Euphorbiaceae); right: *Astrophytum asterias* (Cactaceae).

(l) Examples of cactus forms in members of various families. From left to right: *Cerus* species (Cactaceae), *Euphorbia heterochroma* (Euphorbiaceae), *Stapelia grandiflora* (Asclepiadaceae), *Senecio stapeliiformis* (Compositae), *Cissus quadrangularis* (Vitaceae)

Plate 2.

1 (u) Mesembryanthemum steppes (Grea Karroo near Beaufort West)

2 (m) Succulent-rich sand desert at the mouth of the Orange River near Grotderm (Richtersveld)

3 (l) Salt pan with the Zygophyllaceae *Augea capensis* between Brakfontain and Kliprand (Little Namaqualand

Plate 3.

1 (ul) Semi-desert with specimens of *Aloe dichotoma* (northern Ceres Karroo) about 4 m tall.

2 (um) Specimens of *Aloe pillansii* about 6 m tall in the rock desert of the Richtersveld near Kuboes

3 (ur) *Pachypodium namaquanum* on a quartz slope near Hangpaal (Little Namaqualand)

4 (ml) Specimen of *Trichocaulon alstoni* about 70 cm tall. Hangpaal (Little Namaqualand)

5 (mr) Forest of *Didierea madagascariensis* in the coastal sand desert near Morombé (southwestern Madagascar)

6 (ll) Mass vegetation of *Euphorbia coerulescens* near Jansenville (eastern Karroo)

7 (lr) A forest of *Euphorbia nyikae* at the foot of the Taita Hills in Kenya

Plate 4. (facing page)

(ul) *Haworthia setata*, rosette during the dry period

(ur) Rosette of *Haworthia setata* in the rainy period

(ml) *Fenestraria aurantiaca* buried in a sand dune (near Alexander Bay)

(mr) Longitudinal section of a rosette of *Fenestraria aurantiaca*. The windows of the club-shaped leaves appear white.

(ll) *Adromischus poellnitzianus*, stem with air roots

(lr) *Crassula pyramidalis*

Plate 5. Examples of devices for absorbing rain or dew by above-ground organs (see page 20)

(ul) *Crassula hystrix*

(ur) *Delosperma pruinosum*

(ml) *Trichodiadema densum*

(mr) *Anacampseros filamentosa*

(ll) *Crassula deceptrix*

(lr) *Anacampseros papyracea* (in the middle of the shoot some of the papery bracts have been removed to show the actual foliage)

Plate 6.

1 (u) Succulents in the house:
The pots are sunk into pumice gravel and
set in a plastic box on a window sill. The
plants are (from left to right): *Pachypodium
geayi, Trichocaulon alstoni, Didierea madagascariensis, Pachypodium lamerei*

Succulents in the greenhouses of the
Botanical Garden of the University of Heidelberg:

2 (m) View into the Madagascar house with a
stand of *Pachypodium geayi.* The long, thin
shoots on the right are *P. rutenbergianum.*

3 (l) View into the Africa house with predominantly euphorbias. Note the fluorescent
tubes on the ridge for extra light.

Plate 7.

1 (ul) *Kalanchoe daigremontiana* with brood plants

2 (ur) Leaf cutting of *Adromischus* species with a developing plantlet

3 (ll) A straight graft of *Caralluma ramosa*

4 (lr) Oblique graft of *Caralluma pruinosa* (The carallumas are grafted onto tubers of *Ceropegia woodii*)

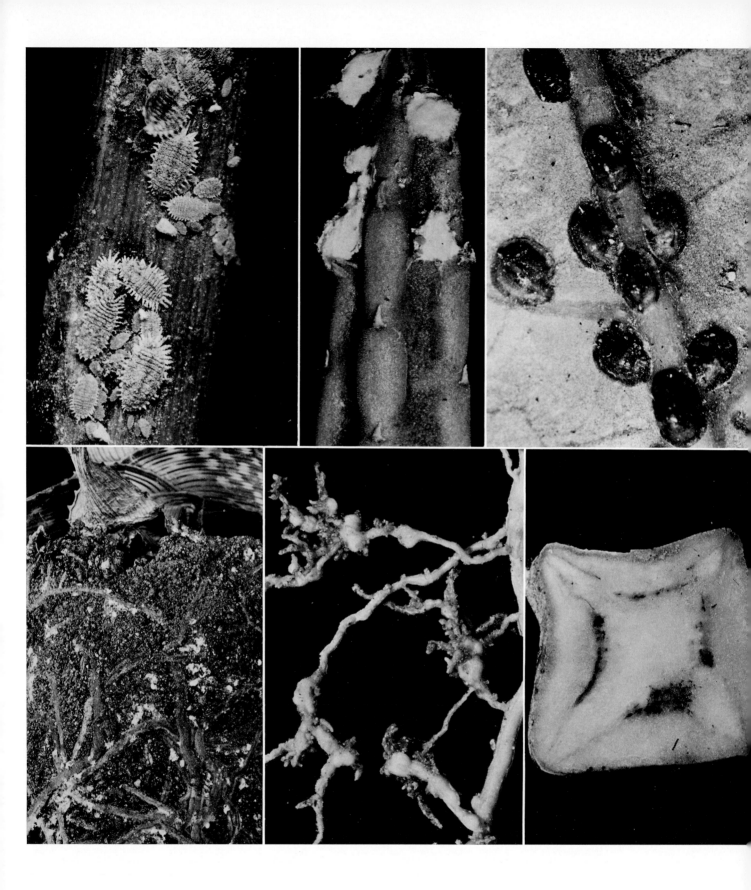

Plate 8. Pests and Diseases

1 (ul) Mealy bugs running free
2 (um) Mealy bugs in a woolly covering

3 (ur) Scale
4 (ll) Root scale on the root ball of an *Aloe*
5 (lm) Nematode swellings on the roots of a *Cucurbitaceae*

6 (lr) Cross section of the stem base of a *Caralluma*. The black places indicate infection by the "black death"

Plate 9. Growth forms of some euphorbias

1 (ul) A tree of *Euphorbia candelabrum* ca. 10 m
tall in the dry bush of Kenya

2 (ur) *Euphorbia dregeana* (Little Namaqualand)

3 (ll) A bush of **Euphorbia didiereoides** 2 m tall
in central Madagascar

4 (lr) Columns of *Euphorbia horrida* ca. 1.2 m
tall in eastern Cape Province area (Willowmore District)

Plate 10. Growth forms of some euphorbias

1 (u) Medusa head euphorbia *Euphorbia esculenta* (eastern Cape Province)
2 (m) Mound of *Euphorbia aggregata*, eastern Cape Province (Willowmore District)
3 (l) Female plant of *Euphorbia symmetrica* (Kruidfontain Farm, eastern Cape Province)

Plate 11. (facing page). Examples of leaf and thorn formation on euphorbias

1 (ul) *Euphorbia undulatifolia*
2 (um) *Euphorbia ingens*
3 (ul) *Euphorbia aphylla*
4 (ml) *Euphorbia grandicornis*
5 (mm) *Euphorbia didiereoides*
6 (mr) *Euphorbia graciliramea*
7 (ll) *Euphorbia knuthii*
8 (lm) *Euphorbia subsalsa*
9 (lr) *Euphorbia venenifica*

Plate 12.

Shoot thorns of:
1 (ul) *Euphorbia stenoclada*
2 (um) *Euphorbia enopla*
3 (ur) *Euphorbia stellaespina*
4 (ml) *Euphorbia valida*

Mamilla formation in euphorbias:
5 (mm) *Euphorbia dregeana*
6 (mr) *Euphorbia weberbaueri*
7 (ll) *Euphorbia tuberculata*, lateral branch
8 (lr) *Euphorbia clava*

Plate 13. (facing page). Examples of mamilla and rib formation in euphorbias

1 (ul) *Euphorbia bupleurifolia*
2 (ur) *Euphorbia mammillaris* with inflorescence thorns
3 (ml) 2-ribbed shoot of *Euphorbia antiquorum*
4 (mm) 3-ribbed shoot of *Euphorbia trigona*
5 (mr) *Euphorbia resinifera* with 4-ribbed shoots
6 (ll) Multi-ribbed shoot of *Euphorbia officinarum* var. *beaumieriana*
7 (lr) *Euphorbia xylophylloides* (= *enterophora*) (undescribed form from Ihosy with fuzzy-brown shoot tips)

Plate 14.

1 (ul) *Euphorbia atripurpurea* in the Teno area
        of Teneriffe (Canary Islands)
2 (um) Flowering shoot of *Euphorbia atripurpu-
        rea*
3 (ur) Flowering shoot of *Euphorbia bravoana*

4 (ml) *Euphorbia balsamifera*. Foreground: *Cer-
        opegia dichotoma*. Near Buenavista on
        Los Frailes (Teneriffe, Canary Islands)
5 (mm) Fruit-bearing *Euphorbia balsamifera*,
        Gran Canaria (Canary Islands)
6 (mr) *Euphorbia clandestina* in habitat in the

        Ladysmith Karroo
7 (ll)   Flowering *Euphorbia clandestina*
8 (lm)   *Euphorbia clavarioides* var. *truncata*
         young mound from below
9 (lr)   Young cluster of *Euphorbia clavar*
         var. *truncata* from above

Plate 15.

1 (ul) *Euphorbia fasciculata*, near Vanrhynsdorp (Cape Province)
2 (ur) Shoot tip of *Euphorbia fasciculata* with inflorescence and pseudo-thorns
3 (ml) *Euphorbia schoenlandii* with emerging thorn shoots
4 (ll) *Euphorbia schoenlandii* with leafless thorn shoots; at their base the inflorescence is just emerging.
5 (lr) Flowering specimen of *Euphorbia schoenlandii*

Plate 16.

1 (ul) *Euphorbia loricata* on the Olifant River near Citrusdale (Cape Province)
2 (um) Seedlings of *Euphorbia loricata* in cultivation
3 (ur) *Euphorbia oxystegia*
4 (ml) *Euphorbia hamata*, segment of a rather large stand near Grotderm (the Richtersveld)
5 (mm) Single plant of *Euphorbia hamata*
6 (mr) *Euphorbia longetuberculosa*
7 (ll) *Euphorbia monteiroi* near Vivo (Zou᷈ Mountains, Transvaal)
8 (lm) *Euphorbia monteiroi* in cultivation
9 (lr) *Euphorbia pseudograntii*, in bloom

A. ramosissima, etc.) and bushy and succulent euphorbias. Mats of numerous *Conophytum* species grow hidden in cracks in the rocks.

Quartz mountains are populated with *Pachypodium* (Plate 3,3), *Trichocaulon* (Plate 3,4), *Conophytum, Crassula,* and *Cotyledon* species; quartz fields on the other hand are the habitats of many highly succulent mesembs.

On the sand fields, especially around Springbok, a great mass of colorful, annual Compositae and mesembs stretches out during years with sufficient precipitation. These are the famous flower fields of the Namaqualand, which again and again attract thousands of visitors (Color Plate 1,3).

Also Great Namaqualand and many parts of Namibia are the home of rare succulents such as *Lithops, Conophytum, Dinteranthus, Fenestraria,* etc., which grow here in sandy or greatly eroded primordial rock soils.

Except for the extreme south, Namibia lies in the area of summer rains (November to March). The annual precipitation ranges between 100 and 300 mm, while the actual desert zone, the Namib, gets only 15 to 25 mm of rain.

The highlands of Transvaal, with the exception of specimens of the genera *Aloe* and *Euphorbia* and some stapeliads, has for the most part few succulents. Their habitats are primarily the mountains.

Another distribution area for succulents is the dry regions (savannas and semi-deserts) of east Africa (Kenya and northern Tanzania). Here the vegetation is dominated not only by forests of tree euphorbias (Plate 3,7), but one also finds a great number of small euphorbias, numerous representatives of the genus *Monadenium,* found only in east Africa, a series of remarkable *Caralluma* species, and the so-called caudiciforms, knot-stemmed succulents with odd-shaped stems that look like rocks; they are of the genera *Pyrenacantha, Gerradanthus, Adenia,* and *Adenium.* The distribution area for *Adenium* stretches into southern Arabia and to the island of Socotra.

In North Africa only southern Morocco is relatively rich in succulents. There are, to be sure, only a few species (especially euphorbias), but these do appear to dominate the vegetation of the landscape (see Plate 24,2).

Among Africa's neighboring islands especially Madagascar has a number of striking succulents. Here are primarily Didiereaceae, of which some species appear as forests in the dry southwestern part of the island (Plate 3,5), but also the genera *Aloe, Euphorbia, Pachypodium, Kalanchoe,* etc., are represented by many interesting species. Also the island of Socotra, because of its isolated location, is rich in remarkable succulents, e.g., the tree Cucurbitaceae *Dendrosicyos socotrana* (see Figure 13) and the caudiciform *Dorstenia gigas* (see Figure 14).

The Canary Islands are the home of bushy and succulent euphorbias, but especially of leaf-succulent Crassulaceae from the genera *Aeonium, Greenovia, Monanthes,* etc.

The morphology of succulents

As I have shown in the previous section, succulents for the most part are inhabitants of hostile areas. They are forced to suffer from a lack of water. In many areas the sparse precipitation can be absent for years. The plants are exposed to great ranges in temperature, a strong and long-lasting radiation from the sun, and sometimes stormy winds. These extreme living conditions are reflected in the exterior shape of these plants. They are equipped with numerous devices that not only permit them to live but also permit growth and propagation. As mentioned briefly above, the plants must be able to absorb quickly the water at their disposal, to store this water in the various organs, and limit water loss (transpiration) as much as possible.

I have already mentioned the various means of storing water and related morphological changes in the plant.

Fast water absorption is made possible by a very-much-branched root system, which in many succulents stretches out flat under the earth surface, so that the fine absorption roots are able to take up the slightest trace of moisture, not just rain but also settled dew and fog. Others have immense, fleshy roots or carrot-shaped roots which thrust deep into the soil to water-bearing layers. In addition to absorbing water they also store water.

The devices for preventing evaporation are especially numerous. Evaporation occurs primarily through the leaf pores (stomata). Plants from a rainy, humid area typically have leaves of a large surface with many stomata. Since water is plentiful and the atmosphere is saturated with moisture, any limitation of evaporation would be superfluous. The situation is different for the inhabitants of extremely arid zones. Because these plants have only a

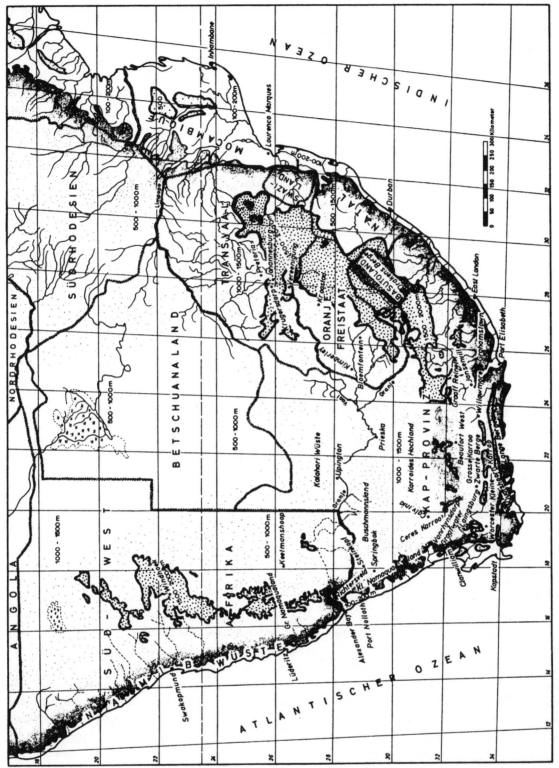

Figure 3. Map of South Africa. Mountain and river areas simplified. (Drawing by Peter Raub.) [Atlantischer Ozean = Atlantic Ocean; Basutoland = Lesotho; Buschmannsland = Bushman Land; Gr. Namaqualand = Great Namaqualand; Grosse Karroo = Great Karroo; Indischer Ozean = Indian Ocean; Kalahari Wüste = Kalahari Desert; Kap-Provinz = Cape Province; Kl. Karroo = Lesser Karroo; Kl. Namaqualand = Little Namaqualand; Lourenco Marques = Maputo; Mocambique = Mozambique; Namib Wüste = Namib Desert; Nordrhodesien = Zambia; Oranje Freistaat = Orange Free State; Südrhodesien = Zimbabwe; Süd-West Afrika = Namibia.]

limited amount of water at their disposal, transpiration must be kept at a minimum.

I divide succulents into the following groups and characteristics:

Stem succulents

1. When normal, large-surface leaves are formed, they are relatively short lived. They appear at the beginning of the rainy period and are cast off as the dry season starts. Therefore during the greater part of the year, the plants are leafless. There are few stem succulents with evergreen foliage.

2. The leaf surfaces are greatly reduced (see Plate 11,2) and the leaves have mostly lost their actual function.

3. The plants appear completely leafless during the whole year. Sometimes rudimentary leaves sprout, but these are so tiny and so short lived that the plants are to be considered leafless (see Plate 11,3).

The loss of leaves in a number of succulents, especially many euphorbias and stapeliads, may be compensated for by an enlarging of the stem surface and by the formation of mamillae and ribs. More will be said about this subject in the introductory chapter to the genus Euphorbia (see p. 34 ff.).

The limiting of water evaporation, however, is not accomplished solely by a reduction of the foliage, but also by a reduction of the stem surface itself—in extreme cases into a sphere, because a sphere has the greatest storage volume for the smallest surface area. Among the stem succulents, the spheroid form is most beautiful in some euphorbias, as in E. obesa (Plate 1,3, left) and E. symmetrica (Plate 10,3).

With reduction or complete disappearance of leaves, leaf function is transferred to the stem itself. Therefore the stem in all stem succulents is always green; even if it is enveloped in a cork layer, there is green tissue underneath.

The stem takes over not only the function of assimilation but also that of transpiration. In order for the stem to limit transpiration, the stomata are set deep in crevices, so that they are not directly exposed to the drying effect of the wind; the stem epidermis may furthermore be covered by a layer of wax, and finally the whole axis can be enveloped in a thick cork layer. As an example of this let me cite the interesting Sarcocaulon species (see page 100 ff.), small succulent dwarf bushes from extremely dry habitats, foliated only for a few weeks, and otherwise giving the impression of being completely dead. Their axes are wrapped in a cork layer several millimeters thick, whose cells are so heavily impregnated with wax that even living plants can be set afire and will burn like candles. This characteristic has caused it to be called "candle bush."

A further characteristic of the stem succulents is the occurrence of thorns, which can have various morphological origins. In rare cases whole lateral branches can be covered with thorns, e.g., in Euphorbia stenoclada (Plate 12,1) from Madagascar. The simple or branched thorns can correspond to inflorescences. Examples of this are many euphorbias, some pelargoniums, Compositae, and Crassula species. But much more common are leaf thorns. Either complete leaves or leaf parts (stems or stipules) may be transformed into thorns.

Leaf succulents

The leaf succulents also have many devices that serve to mitigate the loss of water during dry periods:

1. The most frequent behavior is a diminishing of the leaf surface itself. The leaves may take on a scoop-like shape and press tightly against the axis, as is the case in many Crassulaceae. The leaf may also be spherical. Examples of this are Pachyphytum oviferum (Plate 77,2), Senecio herreianus (Plate 80,3), S. citriformis (Plate 78,2), etc.

2. Frequently the leaves are arranged in tight rosettes, in which the blades for the most part overlap. If sufficient moisture exists, the rosette leaves are spread out flat; in a long drought they bend inwards and lie tightly on one another like an onion. An example of this behavior is Haworthia setata (Plate 4,1).

Noteworthy in this regard is also Crassula pyramidalis, a plant whose stem up to 10 cm tall is densely covered with small leaves. As a result of extreme shortening of the internodes, the leaves lie so tightly packed on top of one another that they expose only their margins to the light and the wind. Since the leaves also cross over one another, the whole growth takes on a four-cornered shape (Plate 4,6) found otherwise in many stem succulents. Crassula pyramidalis also corresponds to stem succulents physiologically, because only the leaf margins are green and only here does one find chloroplasts and stomata.

3. Another device for adapting to the aridity is the diminishing of the number of leaves. In extreme cases

only two leaves are formed per year, which are connected except for a narrow cleft and expose only their upper margin to the light, as in *Conophytum, Lithops,* etc. (Figure 4). During the dry period this leaf pair shrivels to a paper-like hull on top of the young leaf pair of the coming year protecting it from drying out (see Figure 15).

4. Also, anatomically the leaves show many devices for limiting evaporation. Just like the stems, they also have a thickened epidermis, which may be covered with a waxy layer or with thick hairs. The stomata are frequently set in deep crevices.

A remarkable phenomenon of many leaf succulents from the family of Mesembryanthemaceae *(Fenestraria, Lithops, Ophthalmophyllum, Conophytum),* but also of some Liliaceae *(Haworthia),* is the formation of "windows," as mentioned above. In these plants the end of the leaves is characterized by a lack of chloroplasts, and the central water-storage tissue extends right up to the epidermis. Thus the end of the leaf appears glassy and transparent just like a window (Figure 4).

The assimilation tissue is located exclusively on the surface of the leaf, the upper side as well as the lower. Since in habitat the leaves are covered by the soil up to the tips (Plate 4,2), the sunlight can reach the chloroplast layers only by passing through the window and the central water-storage tissue and, according to SCHMUCKER,[5] is thus greatly weakened. MARLOTH considers the window to be protection against too much sun, a concept shared by SCHMUCKER, but TROLL[6] had already raised the justifiable objection to the protection theory by stating that among the mesembs "there are also forms very similar to the window types in which the assimilation tissue is in the strongly illuminated parts, i.e., at the point where the window would be."

Instead of having a large window, many species have just small, translucent spots *(Conophytum, Lithops, Cheiridopsis)* that frequently flow together and thus produce a marbled effect that is suggestive of the surrounding rocks. In such a case one speaks of protective coloring or mimicry (see page 136 ff.).

In addition to devices that serve to reduce water evap-oration, many succulents also have devices for capturing moisture from the air.

I have already mentioned that in many succulent areas the nighttime cooling is so great that dew is formed and, comparable to the fogs in the fog deserts, the dew often provides the only source of moisture for the plants for months. One must therefore ask whether succulents, like bromeliads, have devices for absorbing this moisture. According to MARLOTH (1908) this is indeed supposed to be the case, and he outlined the following possibilities for water absorption:

a. Leaf hairs. Examples are all the hairy *Crassula* species and some shrubby mesembs. In *Crassula hystrix,* for example (Plate 5,1), and *Delosperma echinatum* (Plate 5,2) the entire leaves and sometimes the main axis are covered with hairs that take moisture out of the air. In *Trichodiadema densum* and other species the leaves resemble the mamillae of many cacti (e.g., *Dolichothele).* These leaves are round and have at their tip a

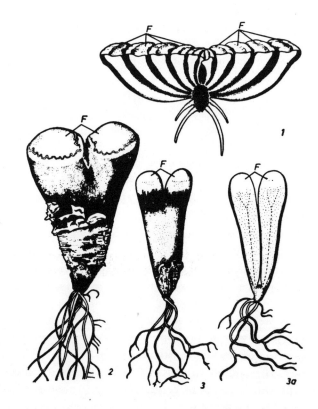

Figure 4. Window-leaf plants. *1,* Longitudinal section of a rosette of *Haworthia truncata. 2, Lithops olivacea. 3, Ophthalmophyllum australe; 3a,* longitudinal section. F = window. Assimilation tissue in the cross sections stippled.

[5] SCHMUCKER, TH.: "Ökologie der Fensterblätter." *Planta,* 13 (1913).
[6] TROLL, W.: *Vergleichende Morphologie der Höheren Pflanzen.* Vol. I, Part 2. Gebr. Borntraeger Verlag, Berlin, 1939.

bundle of hairs (Plate 5,3) on which moisture, dew, and fog condense. MARLOTH writes: "As soon as you put a drop of water on the hair tips of a withered leaf, a stream of activity begins in the cells, and in a short time the cells are again turgid. Gradually you can see that the leaf has again begun to regain its turgor" (1908, p. 307).

b. Expandable epidermis cells which unite into groups and project over the environment and appear to have an uneven upper surface (*Crassula deceptrix;* Plate 5,5).

c. Hygroscopic stipules (secondary leaves). Examples are *Anacampseros* species from section Avonia. In *A. papyraceae* and other species of section Avonia (see page 132) the large stipules are skin-like or papery and completely envelop the small, green leaves (Plate 5,6) and are capable of absorbing moisture. In the species of section Telephiastrum the stipules have been transformed into hair bundles (Plate 5,4), which, however, have the same function.

d. Air roots. In many *Adromischus* species, e.g., *A. cristatus, A. poellnitzianus,* etc., the stems are enveloped in a thick coat of air roots (Plate 4,5), which serve to absorb water. Also in many *Kalanchoe* species, air roots can be observed if the plants are grown in a humid environment.

e. Many succulent plants belong to the so-called CAM-plants. CAM means *Crassula*-acid-metabolism, for this physiological process was first discovered in *Crassula* species. All CAM-plants close their stomata during daytime, when the sun is shining and the air is dry; they reduce therefore their transpiration; however the stomata are open at night; the plants produce organic-acids, especially malon-acid, which is reduced during daytime to CO_2. This however cannot escape into the atmosphere, because the stomata are closed, but is transformed into sugar and starch. The ecological advantage of the *Crassula*-acid-metabolism is that the assimilation of CO_2 takes place through the stomata, opened at night, so that the plants lose, in consequence of the lower night-temperature and higher air humidity, less water and can therefore exist in regions with low precipitation (see also p. 13).

Although the devices mentioned here are capable of absorbing water, research and observations in the natural habitats have not been conducted extensively enough to determine whether the amount of water absorbed is sufficient to keep the plants alive. During trips in the dry areas one observes again and again that after long dry periods such as those happening now from time to time in South Africa and Namibia, many highly succulent plants lie as withered corpses in the desert sand or among boulders. Where masses of succulents were present a few years ago, now the land is bare. Even these plants cannot exist completely without water.

The cultivation of succulents

I have shown that succulents are inhabitants of hot, dry areas of intense light and therefore need warmth and light. These criteria are the prerequisites for successful growing, even if it is impossible to imitate natural conditions completely. First of all the latitude (Germany) lacks the intensive sun light that is almost even throughout the year.

One should also not forget that the plants are being taken out of the natural rhythm of their native habitats. There, summer and winter, i.e., rainy and dry seasons, which are synonomous with growth and dormant periods, are directly opposite from the seasons of the Northern Hemisphere. Therefore, especially when dealing with imported plants, one must always be concerned with acclimating the plants to our seasonal rhythm. For many plant groups this is no problem, even within a few years; a few, however, cannot be persuaded to adjust and they maintain their habitat rhythm. *Conophytum* blooms here in the fall and early winter; that corresponds to the native seasons, i.e., the spring and early summer. At this time of year the plants must be watered, while the closely related *Lithops* species must be kept dry. This adherence to the proper watering schedule requires from the hobbyist some precise knowledge of the growing conditions and an additional portion of "feel" for the plants' requirements; otherwise the hobbyist is wasting money and will lose the joy of growing succulents.

Only a few succulents, except for some Crassulaceae, are so winter hardy that they can be grown outdoors year round in central Europe; only around the Mediterranean Sea is this possible. Therefore the plants, especially in the winter months, must be placed in a protected area. This applies also to those species that experience night frosts or even prolonged snow cover in their habitats, but during the summer months all succulents can be put outside without worry, provided that they are protected against severe rain storms.

The beginner just starting a collection will have only a modest number of plants and should begin with the less sensitive varieties, in order to become acquainted with the methods of cultivation.

As long as one is dealing with just a few plants, they can be kept in a room in the house. Choose a south window (Plate 6,1), for as inhabitants of bright areas succulents need the most possible sunlight during the dim winter months. To avoid one-sided and uneven growth, the plants should be turned occasionally. Drafty locations are to be avoided at all costs; if windows are opened even for a short time in the winter, the plants should not stand in the draft.

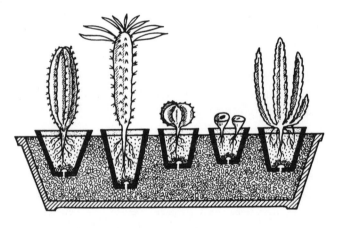

Figure 5. Cross section of a flower box with the pots set in pumice gravel.

For species that need winter rest, especially those that drop their leaves, a room with central heating is usually too warm. In order to avoid too much shrinking of the plants, one could water a little now and then, but the plants may be forced to grow too soon. One can somewhat soften the effect of the dry, heated air by squirting them occasionally with a water atomizer available from any flower shop. It is better, however, to winter such species in an unheated but bright living room.

To display a large number of plants well, the narrow window sills in most modern homes are insufficient, but with a few materials one can increase the window space. The pots should not be placed directly on the sill but in pumice gravel or sand. For this purpose one can buy flower boxes of plastic (styrofoam). These are not only light but also retain heat so that the plants do not get "cold feet," which is important for many species. Fill the boxes with fine pumice gravel into which the pots are set (Plate 6,1; Figure 5). This medium has the advantage that one does not have to water the plants themselves, but one waters the pumice, which holds the moisture for a long time; also in the summer the boxes can be placed outside on a protected balcony or on a covered patio.

The dream of every plant hobbyist, however, is to own a greenhouse, no matter how small. Any greenhouse manufacturer will gladly supply information on the structure and style. Basically any greenhouse is suitable for cultivation of succulents, provided it is bright and easy to ventilate, for in addition to light, succulents also need much fresh air. Shading is usually superfluous; a thin application of whitewash on the roof during the summer months provides sufficient protection for sun-sensitive plants such as haworthias and many stapeliads.

Since succulents must not be allowed to freeze, attention must be given to heating. The winter temperatures should not fall below 10°–12° C (50°–54° F). Therefore it is not advisable to winter "the other succulents" in the same house with cacti, since the latter on the average require considerably lower temperatures (5°–8° C or 40°–46° F).

The benches that come with the greenhouse are covered with marine board; a 15 cm layer of coke gravel, sand, or pumice gravel is added, in which the pots are sunk (Figure 6)—as in the flower boxes—in order to prevent the vessels from drying out, on the one hand, and to avoid direct watering of the plants, on the other hand, because sensitive succulents tend to rot right at the soil line.

Although most succulents are grown in pots, which have the advantage of being able to be placed outdoors easily in the summer, most of them do better planted directly on the open benches, in unconfined soil (see Plate 6,2 and 3). In so doing, one can to a certain degree imitate the natural environment and by using various rocks one can create charming effects. For planting in unconfined soil, if the greenhouse has enough room, a center bench is desirable (Figure 6), because it would be accessible from all sides, making tending the plants easier and allowing the plants to be grouped in an aesthetically pleasing way. Planting on the open benches has the disadvantage that the plants cannot be put outside in the summer months.

Every plant hobbyist knows from experience that no greenhouse is large enough, for plant collecting can and does usually become a passion sooner or later. If one is not in a position to build a larger greenhouse, one can gain additional space by adding hanging shelves (Figure 6), but be aware that the lower plants may get too much shade and will collect water dripping from above. In the winter the hanging shelves should be reserved for sun-loving plants such as *Trichocaulon, Hoodia,* and rosette-shaped, white-waxy *Crassula* species.

It is still debatable whether succulents have to be given extra light during the winter months. Being from tropical and subtropical areas these plants are exposed to the sun for nearly 12 hours a day the whole year; in our latitude (Germany), however, they get about 15 hours of sun in the summer, while during the winter they get only about 7 hours, often even less. Therefore the dim, short autumn and winter days are not sufficient for growth, especially

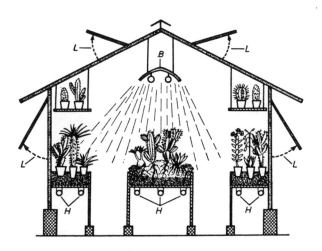

Figure 6. A small greenhouse in cross section. L = vents; H = heating tubes; B = lighting.

when the growth period is in the winter months. Additional, artificial light, as used in the Botanical Garden in Heidelberg, has thus proven to be very beneficial. Common commercial fluorescent tubes are used here because they generate little heat and have a predominance of red

and blue light. Experiments have shown that this spectrum promotes plant growth. Recently the Osram Company has developed a fluorescent tube (L-Fluora) that emits the red as well as the blue-green spectrum and is therefore especially beneficial to plant growth.

Watering

One of the most important aspects of cultivation is watering. A lot of damage can be done in this respect. As a rule more plants are watered to death than die of thirst. One must always remember that succulents demand far less water than plants from wet, tropical areas. One must also consider that many succulents have a dormant period and a growth period, which from group to group fall in different times of the year. I have already indicated that some species do not adjust to central European seasons. When, for example, conophytes and other mesembs shrivel their leaves in the spring, that is no sign that they have been kept too dry, but it is a quite natural process. The plants are simply entering their vegetative rest stage and one must simply withhold water, but when the dry leaf hull is broken open in the fall and new, green leaves appear, one must begin to water. If the leaves of euphorbias, pachypodiums, and other leafy stem succulents become yellow and drop off, this also may be a sign of the beginning of the dormant stages. Here, too, one must stop watering; but as soon as the first leaves unfold again, the plants need water. Try as one may, there is no general rule for watering, since every collection is made up of different succulent groups. In displaying your collection you should keep in mind from the beginning the various dormant stage and growth periods and keep plants from the two groups separated.

As a basic rule for watering one should commit the following statement to memory: water thoroughly or not at all. Watering thoroughly means giving so much water that not only is the soil moist but also that the lowest roots in the pot get sufficient water. Then wait until the soil is almost dry for the next watering; especially make sure that the pot drains.

Plants with waxy leaves or leaves covered with white hairs should not get their leaves wet, because they will become spotted and lose their beauty; also, they should not be misted but watered only with a watering can with a narrow spout. If possible you should use rain water or boiled water. Although many succulents are not harmed

Watering Schedule

for all the genera from this book. The schedule is valid
for central Europe.

Month	1	2	3	4	5	6	7	8	9	10	11	12
Adenia			○	○	○	●	●	●	○	○	○	
Adenium		○	○	○	○	●	●	●	○	○	○	
Adromischus			○	○	○	●	●	●	○	○	○	
Aeonium		○	○	○	●	●	●	●	○	○		
Alluaudia			○	○	●	●	●	●	○	○	○	
Alluaudiopsis		○	○	○	●	●	●	●	○	○		
Aloe				○	○	●	●	●	●	○		
Aloinopsis			○	○	○	●	●	●	●	○		
Anacampseros[1]				○	○	●	●	●	○	○		
Argyroderma			○	○	○	●	●	●	○	○	○	
Astroloba			○	○	●	●	●	●	○	○	○	
Bergeranthus				○	●	●	●	●	●	○		
Brachystelma				○	●	●	●	●	○	○		
Caralluma				○	○	●	●	●	○	○		
Ceraria				○	●	●	●	●	●	○		
Ceropegia				○	○	●	●	●	●	○	○	
Chamaealoë				○	○	●	●	●	○	○		
Cheiridopsis			○	○	●	●	●	●	○	○		
Cissus[2]			○	○	●	●	●	●	○	○	○	
Conophyllum					○	●	●	○				
Conophytum	●	●	○						○	○	●	●
Cotyledon			○	○	●	●	●	○	○	○		
Crassula			○	○	●	●	●	○	○	○		
Crassula mesembry-anthemopsis	●	●	○						○	○	●	●
Dactylopsis	●	●	○					○	○	●	●	●
Decaryia				○	●	●	●	●	○	○		
Delosperma			○	○	○	●	●	●	○	○	○	
Didierea				○	○	●	●	●	○	○		
Didymaotus			○	○	○				○	○	○	
Dinteranthus				○	○	○	○	○	○	○		
Diplocyatha				○	○	●	●	●	○	○		
Dorstenia				○	●	●	●	●	●	○	○	
Drosanthemum				○	○	●	●	●	●	○		
Duvalia			○	○	○	●	●	●	●	○		
Echeveria				○	○	●	●	●	●	○	○	
Echidnopsis				○	○	●	●	●	○	○		
Edithcolea				○	○	●	●	●	○	○		

Month	1	2	3	4	5	6	7	8	9	10	11	12
Euphorbia[3]			○	○	●	●	●	●	●	○	○	
Faucaria				○	○	●	●	●	●	○	○	
Fenestraria				○	○	●	●	●	○	○		
Fockea					○	●	●	●	○	○		
Frerea					○	●	●	●	○	○	○	
Frithia	●	●	○						○	○	●	●
Gasteria				○	○	●	●	●	○	○	○	
Gerrardanthus				○	○	●	●	●	●	○	○	
Gibbaeum	●	●	○						○	○	●	●
Glottiphyllum				○	○	○	●	●	○	○	○	
Graptopetalum				○	○	●	●	●	●	○		
Greenovia				○	○	●	●	●	●	○		
Haworthia				○	○	●	●	●	○	○	○	
Hoodia				○	○	○	●	●	○	○	○	
Hoodiopsis				○	○	●	●	●	○	○	○	
Huernia				○	○	●	●	●	●	○	○	
Huerniopsis				○	○	●	●	●	○	○		
Idria				○	○	●	●	●	●	○	○	
Jatropha				○	○	●	●	●	●	○		
Kalanchoë			○	○	●	●	●	●	○	○	○	○
Lampranthus				○	○	●	●	●	●	○	○	
Lapidaria				○	○	○			○	○	○	
Lithocaulon (=Pseudolithos)				○	●	●	●	●	●	○		
Lithops					○	●	●	●	●	○	○	
Lomatophyllum				○	○	●	●	●	○	○		
Mitrophyllum	○	○							○	○	●	●
Momordica				○	○	●	●	●	○	○		
Monadenium				○	●	●	●	●	●	○		
Monilaria	○	○							○	○	○	●
Muiria						○	●	○				
Neoalsomitra				○	○	●	●	●	○	○		
Odontophorus				○	○	●	●	●	●	○	○	
Oophytum	●	○	○						○	○	○	●
Ophthalmophyllum	●	●	○							○	○	●
Othonna				○	○	●	●	●	●	○	○	
O. euphorbioides O. herrei	●	●	○						○	●	●	●
Pachyphytum			○	○	●	●	●	●	○	○		

24

Simplified table for families

Watering table (genera)

Month	1	2	3	4	5	6	7	8	9	10	11	12
Pachypodium			○	○	●	●	●	●	●	○	○	
Pectinaria			○	○	●	●	●	●	○	○		
Pedilanthus			○	○	●	●	●	●	○	○		
Pelargonium	●	●	○	○					○	●	●	●
Piaranthus				○	●	●	●	●	○	○		
Pleiospilos			○	○	●	●	●	●	●	○	○	
Poellnitzia			○	○	●	●	●	●	●	○		
Portulaca			○	○	●	●	●	●	●	○		
Portulacaria			○	○	●	●	●	●	●	○		
Psammophora				○	●	●	●	●	○	○		
Pterodiscus	●	●	○						○	○	●	●
Pyrenacantha			○	●	●	●	●	●	○	○		
Rhombophyllum				○	●	●	●	●	○			
Ruschia			○	○	●	●	●	●	○	○		
Sarcocaulon	○	○	○					○	○	○	○	○
Schwantesia			○	○	●	●	●	○	○			
Sedum			○	○	●	●	●	●	●	○		
Senecio			○	○	●	●	●	●	○	○		
Sesamothamnus	○	○			○	○	●	●	○	○		
Seyrigia			○	○	●	●	●	●	○	○		
Sinocrassula			○	○	●	●	●	●	●	○	○	
Stapelia			○	○	●	●	●	●	●	○	○	
Stapelianthus			○	○	●	●	●	●	●	○	○	
Stomatium			○	○	●	●	●	●	●	○	○	
Sultitia			○	○	●	●	●	●	●	○		
Synadenium			○	●	●	●	●	●	●	○	○	
Tavaresia			○	○	○	○	○	○	○	○		
Teschleria			○	○	●	●	●	●	○	○		
Titanopsis			○	○	○	○	○	○	○	○		
Trichocaulon			○	○	○	●	●	●	○	○		
Trichodiadema			○	○	●	●	●	●	○	○		
Vanheerdia				○	●	●	●	●	○	○		
Uladia				○	●	●	●	●	●	○		
Xerosicyos			○	○	●	●	●	●	●	○		

Simplified table for families

Month	1	2	3	4	5	6	7	8	9	10	11	12
Apocynaceae			○	○	●	●	●	●	●	○	○	
Asclepiadaceae			○	○	●	●	●	●	○	○		
Compositae*			○	○	●	●	●	●	○	○		
Crassulaceae*			○	○	●	●	●	●	●	○	○	
Cucurbitaceae			○	○	●	●	●	●	○	○		
Didiereaceae			○	○	●	●	●	●	●	○	○	
Euphorbiaceae			○	○	●	●	●	●	●	○	○	
Fouquieriaceae			○	○	●	●	●	●	○	○		
Geraniaceae	●	○	○						○	●	●	●
Icacinaceae				○	●	●	●	●	○	○		
Liliaceae			○	○	●	●	●	●	●	○	○	
Mesembryanthemaceae*	○	○	○	○	●	●	●	●	○	○	○	○
Moraceae				○	●	●	●	●	○	○		
Passifloraceae				○	●	●	●	●	○	○		
Pedaliaceae	●	○	○					○	●	●	●	●
Portulacaceae			○	○	●	●	●	●	●	○		
Vitaceae			○	●	●	●	●	●	●	○	○	

* Exceptions:

Month	1	2	3	4	5	6	7	8	9	10	11	12
Fam.: Crassulaceae												
Crassula mesembryanthemopsis	●	●	○						○	○	●	●
Fam.: Compositae												
Othonna euphorbioides	●	●	○						○	●	●	●
Othonna herrei	●	●	○						○	●	●	●
Fam.: Mesembryanthemaceae												
Conophytum	●	●	○						○	○	●	●
Dactylopsis	●	●	○						○	●	●	●
Frithia	●	●	○						○	●	●	●
Gibbaeum	●	●	○						○	●	●	●
Ophthalmophyllum	●	●	○						○	○	●	●

□ do not water (dormant period)

○ little water (once a month at the most)

● much water, but not every day (at least once a week)

...pecies from section Avonia get less water.
...eafed species get water also in winter.
...eafed species more than the leafless ones.

by water that has a high calcium content, tap water, normally high in calcium, causes the soil to "sour" and form a crust; also the plants are marked by water spots.

Many succulents benefit from the "dew" formed in the greenhouse. This can be accomplished by using misters, preferably in the evening; thus the night dew of the natural habitats is imitated to a certain degree. On very hot and sunny days sufficient humidity can be created by wetting the paths in the greenhouse. It is also important to keep the greenhouse ventilated, because succulents do not like damp, stale air.

In conclusion I can only add about watering: use moderation! Better too little than too much. If you work with your plants a lot, you will soon learn to recognize when they need water and how much.

Soil

As is the case with watering no comprehensive rule can be made about soil mixes.[7] Each grower has a personal recipe he or she swears to.

Most succulents in their native habitat live in porous, although more or less heavy soil. Unlike plants that specifically prefer an alkaline soil, succulents require a neutral to slightly acid medium. For the main component we should use old, well-rotted compost or leaf mold mixed with one part each of loam and sand. Since this mix is generally too porous, we should add a little peat or pumice; either will hold the moisture for a while. Typical gypsum-loving plants (e.g., *Titanopsis calcarea*) require some lime; powdered wall plaster is especially good for this.

Growers must rely on their intuition and experience to know what mix is best for their plants. Humus-loving plants, e.g., many crassulas, require more humus than plants that grow in heavier soil, such as most euphorbias, which require calcareous, nutritious, but porous soil. Plants from sandy habitats (many asclepiads such as *Hoodia, Trichocaulon, Tavaresia,* etc.) like a coarse, porous, sandy-loamy mix. The least demanding in terms of soil are the many leaf succulents such as *Echeveria, Aeonium, Aloe,* etc., which are happy in any porous soil that is not too lean in nutrition.

The highly touted, all-purpose soils frequently used by nurseries have not proven beneficial to succulents. In the beginning the plants show good, fast growth, but eventually become too soft and therefore susceptible to diseases.

It is recommended that you "steam" (sterilize) the mix before using it, in order to destroy any possible pests, especially soil nematodes.

In general succulents should be grown "hard," i.e., without much nutrition; this has the advantage that they not only keep their typical growth shape but also are for the most part protected from pests.

Thus the question of additional fertilizer is partially answered. Fresh soil in its proper mixture contains all the necessary nutrition in sufficient amounts so that we can dispense with additional fertilizer. Plants grown in the same free soil for several years should get a complete fertilizer at least once a year; avoid a high-nitrogen fertilizer.

Pots and potting

In the spring after night frosts have ended, the plants should be brought out of their winter quarters and put outside or into a cold frame; then you can begin re-potting. Fast-growing succulents should be re-potted once a year, at the beginning of their growth period; slow growers get re-potting only every two to three years. If the roots have grown up over the edge of the pot severely, it is better to break the pot than to cut off the roots. The old soil should be carefully shaken off and the root ball loosened with a pointed stick. Old, dead roots should be removed. This is especially true of liliaceous plants, whose roots are short-lived. If any pests are detected (see page 30 ff.), they should be taken care of immediately.

After removing the old, dead leaves the plants should be placed in fresh, slightly damp soil. Special attention should be given to the selection of the proper pot; it should be neither too large nor too small. For plants with a small root system use a small pot; for those with a highly developed root system use a larger pot. For euphorbias with a fleshy root use tall, narrow, so-called tree-nursery pots. If you want to plant several specimens, e.g., *Lithops* or *Conophytum,* in the same pot, a shallow container is best. To save space in your display area, the pots should be square or rectangular rather than round. For re-potting it is always best to use new pots; old, used pots should be thoroughly cleaned and boiled in water for a while to sterilize them before re-use.

---

[7] Special attention is given to soil mixes in the Specifics part of this book.

More and more, especially for growing cacti, we see the use of plastic pots, which are available in several forms. Many growers have already converted completely to the use of plastic pots and swear that their plants grow better in these than in traditional clay pots.

Certainly the plastic pot has an advantage in that the non-porous sides prevent the soil from drying quickly. This lack of evaporation also prevents much cooling of the soil and the plants thus do not get "cold feet." With evaporation in porous pots, as BUXBAUM specifically mentions in his book *Cactus Culture Based on Biology,* nutriments are absorbed by the pot wall causing the fine roots to adhere to the walls, and because the root tips are very sensitive, they dry out when the pot evaporates too much water and when watering is infrequent. On the other hand, in a non-porous pot the fine absorption roots are always found in the interior of the root ball and only a few of them reach the sides of the pot.

The greatest advantage of the plastic pot is that, as a result of less evaporation, one does not need to water as much, which is undoubtedly a great saving for large nurseries.

By the way, the problem of porous vs. non-porous pots is not nearly so new as the current literature would have one believe. In subtropical, dry, hot areas plants have long been grown in old tin cans and gasoline containers which, of course, have been provided with drainage holes. This is done on the one hand out of necessity because clay pots are not available, and on the other hand because clay pots would dry out too fast in the hot climate.

I will not advocate one type of pot over the other, especially since experiments have not yet been extensive enough. My investigation has shown that cacti and robust succulents thrive very well in plastic pots, whereas "touchy" and difficult species show better growth in clay pots, especially when they are set in pumice gravel or sand.

In the process of potting, be sure that the pot will drain well. Place a pot shard over the drainage hole (Figure 7,T) and cover it with a layer of sand, fine coke gravel, or charcoal 1–2 cm thick (Figure 7,K). Then fill in with the planting mix. The surface, especially in the case of water-sensitive plants such as stapelias, should be covered with a layer of sand 1–2 cm thick (Figure 7,S), so that the water will drain through quickly and the base of the plant will not rot. For special effects, especially with mimetic plants (*Lithops, Conophytum,* etc.), one can embed the surface with pebbles that in shape and color resemble the plants.

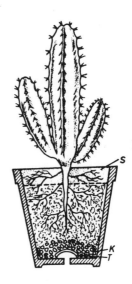

Figure 7. Cross section of a pot. T = shards over the drainage hole; K = charcoal; S = layer of sand.

When the potting is finished, water thoroughly; then the plants should be kept at a relatively high temperature and high humidity for a few days so that they can begin to build new roots as quickly as possible; re-potting always means a radical upset in the life rhythm of the organism.

It is important to "identify" the plants, i.e., give them a label with the proper scientific name, because you will not be able to keep in mind all the names in a large collection, and you will also want to avoid confusion with similar species, which is especially important when trading with other growers. For labelling you can use durable plastic labels, which are available in all sizes; when written on with a water-proof ink these labels will last for many years. Also you should keep an index catalog in which you note the name of the plant and its origin, because only a carefully documented collection can be useful in research.

Importation of wild plants

It is the goal of every grower to own a collection of especially beautiful, healthy plants that resemble the plants in shape and color in their native habitats. Today this is

27

relatively easy to achieve, with a considerable outlay of money, by importing plants. It is not possible for all of us to travel to the sometimes quite remote succulent habitats to gather plant species ourselves and become familiar with their native growing conditions; instead there are many nurseries today that specialize in the importation of succulents and also have the necessary experience to acclimatize them. A prerequisite for successful growing of imports is a precise knowledge of the growing conditions and habitats. No amateur should buy plants that come directly from the native habitat, but should acquire only plants that have been cultivated for a while. The author has collected numerous succulents during his study trips in a great variety of areas of the world and has had them sent to Europe, where they were subsequently grown in the Botanical Garden of the University of Heidelberg. Of course when importing one must also always count on a certain amount of loss, but losses should not exceed more than 10%.

The following points should be taken into consideration when importing plants directly. The imports should not be mixed in with the existing collection right away, but should be grown for some months away from the old collection—they are put into quarantine, so to speak. Even if the plants are accompanied by a phytosanitary certificate from the country of origin and have also passed inspection in the import country, they should be thoroughly examined for pests. As a preventive measure every plant should be treated with a pesticide. The roots should be trimmed in order to remove rotted parts. If the rot is far advanced perhaps parts can still be saved and can be grown as cuttings. Non-branching euphorbias such as *E. obesa, E. schoenlandii,* etc., which are affected by rot are unusable and should be thrown away immediately.

The treated plants should stay for a few days in semi-shade protected from direct rays from the sun, so that any possible injuries can dry well. Larger cuts and injuries should be powdered with pulverized charcoal. To promote new root growth I use a light mix: with stapelias, mesembs, etc., pure, washed sand is recommended; for new rooting of euphorbias, pachypodiums, aloes, haworthias, etc., the following mix has been proven useful here at the Botanical Garden: ⅓ sand, ⅓ peat, ⅓ composted leaf mold, with an addition of styrofoam pellets. The styrofoam has no direct effect on the plants, absorbs no water, but does loosen the mix, thus encouraging new root development. Newly potted import plants should

not be watered immediately, but must be kept for a while in high humidity. New root growth is recognizable by the plants becoming plump and firm again; also the top shows new growth. Only then should the plants be put in their prescribed soil and added to the collection.

Growing imported plants requires a great deal of instinct but is a lot of fun, but—let me re-emphasize—only an experienced grower, not a novice, should get involved in the importation of plants.

Growing succulents from seed

A second—although slower—way to increase a collection is to grow from seed. It provides perhaps even more pleasure than growing import plants, because the owner sees the plants grow and can better study their habits.

Under cultivation most succulents bloom and form fruit; therefore, it is possible to get viable seed. Many nurseries offer seed, at least of the most common species; for the rarer species you must produce the seed yourself or have them sent to you from the native lands. In trying to get your own seed, it must be noted that many species are self-sterile, i.e., the pollen of a flower placed on the pistil of a second flower from the same plant will not produce seed. This is true for example for the mesembs. Therefore you must have at least two plants, preferably from widely separated areas, because even the pollen from plants of the same clone[8] will not produce seed. In euphorbias it must be noted that many species are single sexed and dioecious, i.e., one plant produces only male, another only female flowers (e.g., *Euphorbia obesa*). Thus, in order to get seed, you must have both sexes in bloom at the same time.

In order to avoid undesired pollination and consequent hybrids (many species tend to cross-pollinate easily), pollination should not be left up to insects but should be undertaken personally. Use a fine, clean artist's brush and transfer the pollen from one flower to the pistil of another on a second plant. After use, the brush should be cleaned in high-percentage alcohol.

The fruits sometimes take a long time to ripen. In pachypodiums and mesembs this process takes almost a year; in aloes and other Liliaceae, on the other hand, it

---

[8] By "clone," I mean the plants resulting from vegetative reproduction of one plant.

takes only a few weeks. Give special attention to the fruits of the euphorbias. These are dry capsules, whose maturity can be judged by the brown color. On dry, hot days these will explode suddenly with an audible pop, sending the seeds flying far into the air. To prevent this, the capsules must be covered with a wad of cotton. A considerably surer way is to wrap the fruit in loose gauze or a piece of nylon stocking, since the cotton wad will get wet and the fruits could then mold.

In general the viability of succulent seed is good. The length of time that they remain viable, though, varies among the individual species. Whereas stapelia seed loses its viability after just a few days, the seed of mesembs, euphorbias, crassulas, etc., remain viable for many years.

Sowing of the seed generally occurs from March to April. As a planting medium I use well-composted leaf mold that has been mixed with approximately twice as much washed sand. To prevent algal growth it is advisable to sterilize the soil. Fungus spores on the seed can be killed by disinfecting with a dilute solution of Chinosol, Physan, or other available fungicide. Use small pots or shallow dishes for sowing the seed. After the seed has been put down, the container is not watered from above but is set in a flat pan of water so that it can absorb water from below. Thus the seed is prevented from being washed away.

If the seed is kept at a temperature of 30°–35° C (86°–95° F) and at a humidity of 80%–90%, germination often takes place within 24 hours. It is best to have a small wooden box with a glass lid for seed sowing. As soon as germination takes place the box must be aired during the day by lifting the glass slightly for a few hours.

The soil must not be allowed to dry out. Once the seedlings have reached a certain height and have become sturdy, they must be put into other pots, a process which a gardner calls "pricking out." Using a pointed stick lift the seedlings carefully from the soil without damaging them and set them individually into a nutritious medium. The distance between the seedlings will depend on their growth. In any case select a planting distance so that the young plants can stay in the same pot at least a year without crowding. For the first few days the newly pricked-out plants should be kept in high humidity, but then they should be acclimatized to the air and light in order to harden them off soon. For species with a distinct dormant period, the dormancy should be observed in the

first year in order to get the plant adjusted to its natural rhythm, but watering should not be entirely forgotten during the dormant period, because seedlings are much more sensitive to drying out than are older plants. Many plants require several re-pottings into community pots before planting them in individual pots and giving them a definite place in the collection.

Vegetative propagation

Along with cultivation from seed, which may not always be possible, vegetative propagation plays an important role. It is usually the faster way of achieving adult plants. Almost 90% of all succulents can be propagated easily vegetatively, with the exception of non-branching species such as *Euphorbia obesa*. Succulents with a swollen base, such as *Adenia globosa, Gerrardanthus,* etc., can be propagated from cuttings, but then the typical swelling may not form; also lateral cuttings of euphorbias of the Medusa head type (see page 43) do not generally develop the growth habit of a seedling.

In general, however, propagation of stem succulents is not difficult. Cut off a lateral branch at its narrowest point and let the cut surface dry thoroughly. With plants that have a milky sap (Euphorbiaceae) let the cutting "bleed," i.e., the milky sap must drain completely; the cut is then powdered with pulverized charcoal, because a crust of sap will lead to inferior root formation.

Even highly succulent mesembs, *Lithops* and *Conophytum,* etc., can be propagated easily from cuttings if you are careful to leave a short piece of the main stem on the cutting.

In addition to propagation from stem cuttings, propagation from leaves also is significant. Some *Kalanchoe* species from the section Bryophyllum naturally form sprouts on their leaves (Plate 7,1) which take root while still on the mother plant, fall to the ground, and become new plants. Thus they can become a nuisance weed. *Kalanchoe rhombopilosa,* many *Adromischus* species, *Sedum stahlii,* etc., drop their leaves at the slightest touch. Just let them lie, and in a short time roots and new sprouts will appear at the point where the leaf was attached (Plate 7,2).

In other species, especially Crassulaceae (*Echeveria, Cotyledon, Pachyphytum,* etc.) and Liliaceae (*Haworthia, Gasteria*), just carefully tear off the leaves from the main stem and they will root and form sprouts in a short time.

Rooting of all cuttings—stem succulents or leaf succulents—is done in a special cutting bed, for which a wooden box like that used for sowing seed is best, as long as sufficient bottom heat is supplied. The medium should consist of a mixture of sand and peat in a ratio of 2:1. To lighten the soil you can use styrofoam pellets. The cuttings are placed 1–2 cm deep in the soil and the soil firmed around them so that they will not fall over; leaves are put in at an angle with the upper side of the leaf upwards.

In the beginning the propagation bed must be kept closed, moderately moist, and somewhat shaded. Rotting pieces should be removed immediately so that fungus will not form. Rooted cuttings are carefully lifted from the medium and planted in the appropriate soil.

Propagation by cuttings can be carried out basically at any time of year; the best time, however, is in the spring just before the beginning of the growth period or in the summer just after the growth period. Frequently you will find that because of sudden decay you will have to undertake propagation even in the winter, but root formation will take considerably longer at that time of year.

Grafting

Grafting is becoming more and more important in the growing of succulents, because importation of plants from the native areas is becoming more and more difficult. In addition there are many species of succulents as well as cacti that do not grow well on their own roots but do better when grafted. Also many normally unbranched species begin to branch when grafted. You can then remove the lateral branches and graft them in turn or try to root them in order to grow them on their own roots.

Until now the favorite succulents for grafting have been the difficult stapeliads that come from extremely dry areas and on their own roots either wither away when they are kept dry or rot when they are grown moist. These are species that are known to be especially "ticklish" among growers. Among them are some *Stapelia* and *Caralluma* species and *Trichocaulon, Hoodia, Tavaresia,* etc.

As a base I use especially the tubers of *Ceropegia woodii* (see page 91) or other tuber-forming ceropegias; but one can also use fast-growing, thick-stemmed *Stapelia* species (e.g., *Stapelia hirsuta, S. gigantea,* etc.) or *Ceropegia dichotoma.* Grafting is carried out as with cacti. With a sharp knife make a horizontal cut through the base and then cut a thin slice which is at first left on the cut surface until the graft scion is ready. Depending on the thickness of the axis, the scion is cut either horizontally (for thick axes, Plate 7,3) or diagonally (for thin axes, Plate 7,4). After removing the thin slice from the base, place the scion onto the base in such a way that at least some of the vascular tissues match up with those of the base. By using special grafting aids such as those used for cacti or by using rubber bands, press the scion firmly onto the base and maintain pressure until the two are firmly united. This will take about 2–3 days. Grafting should be done only on warm, sunny days, when the scion and the base grow together quickest.

Practically speaking, almost all stem succulents can be grafted. For details on the method see W. RAUH and W. DINKLAGE: "Grafting Succulents," in *U.S. Cactus and Succulent Journal,* Vol. XVIV, 1972.

Diseases and pests

At this point I will make only a few general comments; special diseases will be discussed in the commentary on the individual plant groups.

With the proper care, i.e., the appropriate soil mix, moderate watering at the right time, bright, sunny, and airy location, succulents in general are little afflicted by pests. Nevertheless the rule to be followed here is "An ounce of prevention is worth a pound of cure." Therefore it is important to be able to recognize the pests and, better yet, not to allow them to get at the plants at all. The most harmful animal pests are:

Aphids. These little, soft-shelled, green, yellow, or blackish, zig-zagging, sucking insects seldom appear on succulent plants. You find them now and then on crassulas or on the flower heads of composites. One or two sprayings with an appropriate pesticide will soon eliminate them.

The little, white "mealy bugs" look like woolly sow bugs and like to nestle in inaccessible places like the axils of leaves or amid the newly forming leaves and protect themselves against moisture by emitting a fine, mealy wax. They multiply extraordinarily fast into a thick, woolly mat (Plate 8,2) and cause a lot of damage by sucking the plant juices, especially at the growing tip, which can completely stunt its growth. Since they love dry conditions, they appear mostly during dormancy on plants with low new shoots, usually on the under side or at the base of the main shoot. Their eradication may be accomplished with contact poisons or with nicotine solutions.

"Scale" is also a sucking insect. In its juvenile stage it moves about freely, but as an adult it covers itself with a strong, 1–3 mm, brownish or yellowish shield (Plate 8,3), under which the animal produces eggs and raises the young brood. Combat it with repeated sprayings of Malathion.

"Root mealy bug" is by far more dangerous than the types mentioned above, because its presence is noted only by the advanced damage to the plant (withering and failure to produce new growth), and the fine absorption roots are by then destroyed. The bluish white pests resemble mealy bugs but are much smaller (Plate 8,4). They suck directly on the roots and thrive especially well on plants that are kept very dry. You will recognize them most easily by dumping the plant out of the pot in the spring. Often the root ball is snow white with them. Wash the root system carefully and dip it in a solution of contact pesticide. In the fall you can prevent attack if you water the roots weekly with a contact poison, but you must be careful to drench the soil thoroughly in order to eradicate all the brood.

Also dangerous is the pest known in gardening as "red spider"; it is, however, not a spider but a mite from the genus *Tetranychus*. It is about 0.5 mm long and of varying color depending on the stage of development (whitish, yellowing, or reddish brown). Its damage is seen in a gray coloration or in the appearance of specks resulting from sucking, because mites suck out the plant juices. They spread quickly during warm, dry weather and in a short time can attack an entire collection. Today there are a number of good sprays for red spider, but it is advisable to alternate from one to another so that the pests will not develop resistant strains.

The most dangerous animal pests are the "root nematodes," which live in the soil and for which there is unfortunately no 100% effective chemical cure. These microscopic pests, sometimes called "root eels," penetrate the roots, cause gall-like bulges up to the size of a pigeon egg (Plate 8,5), and destroy the whole root tissue so that

finally the plant may die from the bottom up. As a permanent stage the nematodes form cysts, which are extraordinarily resistant to drought, to high temperatures, and to chemical treatment.

Especially vulnerable to nematodes are cacti, euphorbias, Cucurbitaceae, kalanchoes and many others. If you find the typical swellings on the roots when you are repotting, then only a radical cure will help, namely, to remove all the roots and re-root the plants in a nematode-free soil. The infected soil must be thrown away or sterilized for a long time at very high temperatures. There is probably no botanical garden, no nursery, nor any collection that is completely free of nematodes.

Botanical pests

Powdery mildew. Some succulent groups, especially euphorbias, crassulas, etc., are attacked by powdery mildew when they are kept too crowded, in high humidity, and with too little air movement. Its appearance is recognized by a white, mealy coat on the stricken organs.

One must distinguish between the false and the true powdery mildew. False mildew is the fungus from the family Peronosporaceae, which lives in the interior of the afflicted plant parts and sends out tree-like, branched, spore-bearing mycelia through the pores. Eventually the spore bearers form a mealy coat, which, depending on the location of the pores, usually is found on the underside of the leaf. Treatment consists of repeated sprayings with copper solutions such as Maneb, Zineb, Zitram, or Captan. The true powdery mildew belongs to the family Erisyphaceae. It lives only on the surface of the plant tissue and sends short suction tubes through the epidermis into the parenchyma. Its treatment consists of spraying or dusting with powdered sulfur or other sulfur preparations.

"Black death." In the stapeliads, especially in the fall and winter, one of the most feared diseases appears, "black death." It is not a virus, but a fungus, for which there is no known cure. It is recognized by a black coloration of the epidermis. When these spots appear it is already too late; the plant has been given a death sentence. The fungus enters through the roots and spreads through the veins in the plant tissue (Plate 8,6). Especially vulnerable are the top of the root and the parts of the main shoot that touch the ground, since the fungus evidently needs moisture in order to develop. Precious little is known about its life cycle.

An effective treatment is simply to cut away the affected shoots and burn them, then root the healthy parts anew or graft them. As a preventive measure you can brush or pour on a dilute fungicide solution, but on the basis of my own experience I can say that this method is no sure thing.

Damp rot. Highly succulent mesembs (*Lithops, Conophytum,* etc.) suffer from so-called damp rot during the dark winter months: the plants become weak, turn dark, and collapse. This is a bacterial disease brought about by poor watering technique. The same is true of dry rot. It causes reddish brown spots that penetrate the plant tissue and kill it. As soon as the central, water-bearing tissue becomes affected the plant dies. Victims should be removed from the collection, so that the disease cannot spread.

In addition to the mentioned diseases there are still a number of fungus diseases, especially in the aloes and euphorbias, which cause a brown coloration and hardening of tissues in the stricken parts. Treatment is extraordinarily difficult, because the fungus lives in the interior of the tissue and the usual treatment is not effective.

The variety of the mentioned pests, however, should not keep us from pursuing the cultivation of succulent plants. Proper care makes them almost immune to many diseases. If one discovers a pest—there are hardly any collections that do not have them—then one must fight it immediately. The chemical industry in recent years has given us an abundance of effective treatments; but all of them are poisonous and extreme care must be given when using them.

Building a collection

Love for and interest in succulents is often based on chance, usually not on a studied decision. Someone gives you a plant, you enjoy its bizarre form, and from visits to botanical gardens, flower shows, and nurseries you become inspired to buy more. Larger flower shops offer a broad assortment not only of cacti but also of other succulents. From one plant you get two; from two you get several, and thus a collection slowly forms. At first a window sill is sufficient for holding the plants, but if the collection becomes a passion, as is usually the case, that may lead to the desire to have a heated planter or a small greenhouse, in which you can house your little charges properly. As a rule the beginner should stick to species that are undemanding. If you then go on to putting together a larger collection, you should get advice from experienced hobbyists and have a look at the literature, in which you can find a selection of beautiful and easily grown plants described and depicted.

Most of them can be bought in specialty nurseries, or you can trade with other collectors. As was already emphasized, you should wait to import plants until you have had sufficient experience. Frequently people will decide to specialize in certain groups and find that this can be more attractive than growing a superabundance of various species.

In general, hobbyists should not try to collect a wide variety of species; only botanical gardens should consider owning specimens from every family and genus in order to show the enormous variety of forms; for the hobbyist the beauty of the plants should be the only determining factor. You should enjoy them and let the extent of your collection be determined by how much time you have to spend on it and how much room you can give your plants.

Color Plate 2.

1 (ul) *Euphorbia mammil-laris* in the Lesser Karroo

2 (ur) Mound of *Euphorbia pulvinata,* Zout-pansberge (Trans-vaal)

3 (mul) *Euphorbia fusca* near Prieska (Bushman Land)

4 (mur) *Euphorbia woodii* (eastern Cape Prov-ince)

5 (mll) *Euphorbia hottentota* near Kuboes (the Richtersveld)

6 (mlr) *Euphorbia stellaespina* in the Great Karroo near Beaufort West

7 (ll) *Euphorbia pubiglans*

8 (lm) *Euphorbia coerulescens* near Jansenville, eastern Cape Prov-ince

9 (lr) *Euphorbia ramiglans*

SPECIFICS

A selection of the most beautiful succulents

Introduction. Because this book is not really a handbook, only a selection from the enormous number of succulent plants can be given. Along with generally known species I also present less well-known, sometimes even rare species, in order to give the hobbyist an idea of the variety of forms and bizarre beauty of these remarkable plants. Nearly all of the plants shown here are grown in the Botanical Garden of the University of Heidelberg.

The grouping of the material is based on the type of water retention, i.e., the plants are divided between stem succulents and leaf succulents. Since many families contain both types, these therefore appear at two different places. The order of the families does not follow a botanical system nor are they in alphabetical order; the families with the largest variety of succulents come first.

Even if botanical details in general have little interest for the hobbyist, it nevertheless seems justified to preface each of the larger genera with a short chapter on the morphology and the variety of forms of the various organs in the genus.

Unfortunately we can not dispense with using the scientific names of the plants, because in many cases there are no common names and also because lists and catalogs from the nurseries give only the Latin names. And finally these names are used internationally, and collectors can thus correspond with foreign collectors.

A further word on nomenclature, which is based on certain rules in the international nomenclature code: biology, botany, and zoology use so-called binary nomenclature. The first name is that of the genus, the second is the species within that genus. The latter name is usually such that it describes a certain feature of the vegetative organ, the flower, or the fruit. Frequently a plant is named after the person who discovered it; sometimes it is named after the place where it was found. The choice of name is also identified with the person who first described the plant. The person's name is added, usually abbreviated, at the end of the species name.

If in re-examining a genus, a species has to be transferred to a different genus; this is shown in the nomenclature by placing the name of the original describer in parentheses, and the name of the person who made the transfer follows.

As a general orientation I give here an overview of all the families (in alphabetical order) from which representatives are discussed and illustrated.

Aizoaceae:	see Mesembryanthemaceae
Apocynaceae:	stem succulents
Asclepiadaceae:	stem succulents
Asteraceae	
(= Compositae):	stem and leaf succulents
Crassulaceae:	stem and leaf succulents
Cucurbitaceae:	stem and leaf succulents
Didiereaceae:	stem succulents
Euphorbiaceae:	stem succulents
Fouquieriaceae:	stem succulents
Geraniaceae:	stem succulents
Icacinaceae:	stem succulents
Liliaceae:	leaf succulents
Mesembryanthemaceae:	predominantly leaf succulents
Moraceae:	stem succulents
Pedaliaceae:	stem succulents
Portulacaceae:	stem and leaf succulents
Vitaceae:	stem succulents

Not considered in the book are the "onion" forms, the agaves and their close relatives, or the xerophytic bromeliads.

FAMILY EUPHORBIACEAE

One of the plant groups extremely rich in stem succulents is the family Euphorbiaceae with its genera *Euphorbia*, *Monadenium*, *Synadenium*, *Pedilanthus*, and *Jatropha*. The common name "wolf's milk" refers to the white, gum-like, often bitter and **poisonous** milky sap present in all the organs of the plant in special cells, the milk tubes, and which flows freely when the plant is wounded. If this sap gets into open wounds or in the eyes, it causes a severe burning pain; take extreme care when digging out a specimen or when taking cuttings! The milk dries in the air and hardens into a brown, gummy substance, which has been traded since antiquity as *Euphorbium* and is used medicinally, but this drug is obtained only from a few species, e.g., from the north African *E. resinifera* (Plate 13,5).

The poisonous qualities of this milk sap in many species has resulted in the fact that they are not eaten by the grazing animals and therefore appear in mass stands in their native habitats (Plate 3,6–7); on the other hand, other forms do not produce a poisonous milk sap and provide the farmers with valuable animal feed in times of drought.

Of the above named genera the one having by far the most species (over 2000) is

Euphorbia L.

Several hundred of them are succulents and resemble cacti so closely in their non-blooming stage that the amateur simply considers many euphorbias as cacti. It is not too wrong to call the succulent euphorbias the "cacti of the Old World," although the two plant groups have nothing in common systematically. Although cacti are exclusively inhabitants of the dry areas of the New World, euphorbias belong to the characteristic plants of the arid areas of the Old World. Their arena stretches from the southern tip of Africa through the whole continent (with the exception of the ever-wet rain forests) and from here across Arabia to India. Smaller habitats are the Canary Islands, Madagascar, and Socotra, while the New World is poor in strictly succulent species.

THE MORPHOLOGY OF EUPHORBIAS

Considering the size of the native area, the variety of habitat and living conditions, and the great number of species, it is no wonder that succulent euphorbias, like cacti, appear in a great variety of forms. Plates 9–10 and Color Plate 2 are intended to give a little impression of this variety.

One encounters gigantic "trees" up to 10 m tall with a thick woody stem and a mighty crown of succulent branches (e.g., *E. candelabrum;* Plate 9,1). The scrubby growth-form is widespread: the primary shoot is hardly visible and branches right from the base. The individual side branches also tend to branch at their base, which causes the scrubby growth-form in the course of years. The plants themselves may be of various types: they may be highly succulent, as *E. avasmontana* (see Plate 23,1), *E. hottentota* (see Color Plate 2,5), they may also be cylindrical and rod-shaped *(E. dregeana,* Plate 9,2), or they may be more or less wooden and armed with thorns. This is the case with many Madagascar species, of which we picture *E. didiereoides* as an example (Plate 9,3; 11,5).

Of special interest, especially for the hobbyist, are the columnar euphorbias, which usually have very thick, branched or unbranched, often extremely thorny, columnar shoots and most closely resemble the cactus form. Examples are *E. horrida* (Plate 9,4), *E. polygona* (Plate 22,3), *E. stellaespina* (Color Plate 2,6), and many others.

The so-called Medusa head types are remarkable forms of euphorbias. From a short primary shoot buried almost to the tip in the soil spring numerous, snake-like lateral branches that lie on the ground or stand upright *(E. caput-medusae, E. fusca,* Color Plate 2,3; *E. esculenta,* see Plate 10,1). Also we find the growth type known as "runners"; the shoots are fleshy runners that creep over the soil and rise above the earth with short air shoots *(E. stapelioides, E. cylindrifolia,* see Plate 29,1 and 2).

Cushion-forming growth, such as is found in high-mountain cacti, is also common among euphorbias. The richly branching shoots emerge from a fleshy main root and gather into a compact cushion, whose top seems to be sheared. The most striking example of this type is the high-mountain spurge *E. clavarioides* var. *truncata* (see Plate 14,8 and 9), but other species such as *E. aggregata*

(Plate 10,2), *E. pulvinata*, *E. mammillaris* (see Color Plate 2,1–2) tend to form massive cushions.

Of special beauty, however, are the spherical euphorbias *E. obesa* (Plate 1,3, left) and *E. symmetrica* (Plate 10,3), whose usually unbranched, flattened ball shapes are prime examples of plant symmetry.

There is also a great variety in the "foliage" of euphorbias. Many species have normal, sometimes broad leaves, which develop at the beginning of the rain period and fall off as the dry season begins, so the plants are leafless during most of the year and only the new growth has leaves (Plate 11,1,5 and 9); in other species the leaf blades are small and short-lived (Plate 11,2 and 7), or they are reduced to tiny scales, visible only with a magnifying glass, and the plants appear to be completely leafless (*E. aphylla* (Plate 11,3), *E. obesa*, etc.). Only the blade, however, is affected by this stunting, whereas the leaf base develops normally—but it runs along the shoot axis and is fused with it (Plate 12,5–7). The basal segments of the leaves, also referred to as leaf cushions (pulvinus) or podarias form a kind of "coat," which, because it remains green, assumes the function of the fallen leaf blades. Often the leaf base becomes very succulent and rises wart-like or like a mamilla above the stem.

In addition to "thornless" varieties (Plate 11,3) there are also species that are known for their thorns, as are cacti. These can be of varying morphological origin. Basically there are two forms of thorns, leaf thorns and stem thorns.

Leaf thorns

One finds rudimentary stages of leaf thorns in *E. hamata*, *E. susannae*, etc. They develop when the persistent leaf base elongates markedly, hardens after the leaf blade falls, and remains on the plant as a pseudo-thorn. Although the leaf blade in *E. hamata* is well developed, in *E. susannae* it is extremely reduced and appears only as a hair-like appendage. Consequently the leaf tip ends in a thin point (Plate 20,4).

By far more common are the "stipular" spines or thorns that appear alongside the main leaves. Many species have stipules, small appendages alongside the main leaves, which soon harden, and after the leaf blades fall, the stipules remain as thorns. Normally these appear in pairs on both sides of the leaf stem. All of the double-thorned euphorbias are grouped in the section Diacanthium, which

includes many species. The thorns themselves are of varying length and thickness. The largest ones are to be found on *E. grandicornis* (Plate 11,4), where they can reach a length in excess of 5 cm. At the base of the two thorns is a so-called shield or plate, which is frequently woody and fused with the axis (Plate 11,6 and 8). In ribbed euphorbias (see page 37) all of the shields may be united into a continuous "horny ridge."

According to recent research, however, the large thorns are not actually stipulary thorns—these are usually very small and inconspicuous—but are secondary appendages of the leaf base. Therefore, H. UHLARZ calls them "dorsal spines," which, as mentioned, in *E. grandicornis* can reach a length of up to 5 cm, whereas the real stipular thorns are small and inconspicuous (Plate 11,4). In the specimens of section Tetracanthae PAX, the thorns appear in the fours and are often formed alike, as in the case with *E. isacantha* (Plate 26,9). The two upper thorns are homologous to the stipules; the two lower ones are considered to be dorsal spines (see also *E. subsalsa*, Plate 11,8). Occasionally the two dorsal spines will be raised on a "foot," as is the case with *E. glochidiata* (see Plate 26,4 and 5). In the specimens of section Triacanthae PAX, the thorns appear only in threes (e.g., *E. graciliramea*, Plate 11,6; *E. monacantha*, Plate 26,7). The two real stipules are very strongly reduced, but the single dorsal spine (pointing downward) has a middle position and is large. The members of section Monacanthae behave in a similar way. These are one-thorned species (with the west African species *E. unispina*, Plate 26,1; *E. venenifica*, Plate 11,9; *E. poissonii*), in which the thorns appear to be single, but there are very close relationships with the Tetracanthae or the Triacanthae, namely in the manner in which the median dorsal spine is the product of two lateral spines growing together. This behavior can be shown, however, only in seedling plants. Additionally there are still two true, stipular thorns, even if they are extremely small and inconspicuous.

In the Madagascar species from section Splendentes BERGER (*E. milii*, Color Plate 3,5), the two stout thorns are actually homologous to stipules; they seldom flank just the leaf base but are accompanied by dorsal spines, which are especially numerous in *E. didiereoides* (Plate 11,5), thus giving the plant its name, because the dense thorns bear a certain similarity to those in the genus *Didierea* (Plate 58,8).

In a number of Madagascar euphorbias (e.g., *E. neo-*

humbertii, Color Plate 3,4; *E. viguieri,* Color Plate 3,7; *E. lophogona,* Plate 28,3, etc.) from section Goniostema BAILL., we find the formation of so-called stipular ribs. According to UHLARZ this is not a matter of widened and branched stipules but mere ridge formation.

Literature: UHLARZ, H: ["Developmental-Historical Research on the Morphology of Basal Leaf Configurations of Succulent Euphorbias from Sub-sections Diacanthium BOISS. and Goniostema H. BAILL."] In: *Tropische und Subtropische Pflanzenwelt,* 9 (1974), W. RAUH, editor. [In German.]

Stem thorns

These are not homologous to leaves, stipules, or thorns, but represent transformed stems. Madagascar's *E. stenoclada* is distinguished by an especially rich formation of stem thorns. In its habitat it is a bushy or tree-shaped, very-much-branched plant, in which every lateral branch ends in a sharp thorn (Plate 12,1).

Of a different nature are the thorns of all the species that are compiled in section Anthacantha *(Florispinae),* the "Thorn Flowers." Here we find *E. enopla* (Plate 12,2), *E. pentagona, E. heptagona, E. aggregata* (Plate 10,2), *E. polygona, E. horrida* (Plate 1,1, Plate 9,4), *E. mammillaris* (Plate 13,2), *E. stellaespina* (Plate 12,3). In these plants the thorns appear in the axils of small, short-lived leaves. Thus they are axil shoots that are either distributed over the whole length of the stem or often appear in patches *(E. stellaespina,* Plate 12,3; *E. mammillaris,* Plate 13,2). Before they become woody they bear small, rudimentary, deciduous scale leaves. On young plants they are sterile and end in a sharp, pointed tip; on blooming size plants they end their growth by forming a tip inflorescence, a cyathium (see page 37), as can be seen clearly in Plate 12,2, *Euphorbia enopla.* Such thorns are also called "inflorescence thorns," because they are homologous to sterile or fertile inflorescences or to their withered and retained stems. If they are sterile, they morphologically represent true thorns, because the vegetative point becomes a sharp, hardened tip. Fertile inflorescence thorns, however, are actually "pseudo-thorns"; they have a blunt tip because their vegetative point ends with the formation of a cyathium.

In most euphorbias of section Anthacantha, the inflorescence thorns appear singly and unbranched in the axils of the deciduous leaves. *Euphorbia polygona* (see Plate 22,3 and 4) and *E. horrida* are exceptions to this behavior. In the leaf axils of older plants are found whole groups of thorns of various lengths. If one studies the development of these thorns, one finds that only one thorn corresponds to the thorns of other species of the section—the primary thorn, which is always sterile and differs from the others in length and thickness. At its base, however, shorter secondary thorns develop, which are henceforth sterile and after the cyathia fall remain in place as pseudo-thorns.

Of special interest are the thorn formations of *E. stellaespina,* a favorite and widely cultivated plant. In contrast to *E. polygona* and *E. horrida* the primary thorn splits not at its base but in the tip region. It ends its length growth with a terminal cyathium (on young plants it may be missing). Below this, in the axils of scale leaves, short, sterile thorns develop into star-like shapes, giving rise to the common name, "star-thorn spurge," and giving it a truly bizarre appearance (Plate 12,3).

Branched thorn systems also appear on blooming size plants of other euphorbias, e.g., *E. valida* (Plate 12,4), *E. meloformis, E. pillansii;* but in these plants the thorns are hardened remainders of multi-branched inflorescence stems, i.e., pseudo-thorns.

Mamilla euphorbias

The similarity of many euphorbias to cacti is not based solely on the formation of spines, but also on the shape of the stem axis itself. Here one thinks primarily of the mamillae, those wart-like bumps that, as in cacti, cover the whole stem surface. As stated briefly above, they are formed from the leaf bases spreading downward on the stem to which it is fused. This can be seen clearly in the piece of *E. dregeana* pictured in Plate 12,5. The leaf base, although very short, is clearly delineated by a lighter line against the rest of the stem tissue. In South American species from section Pteroneurae (see page 40) such as *E. pteroneura, E. sipolisii, E. weberbaueri* (Plate 12,6) the leaf base is very long and reaches down to the next node. Because of its rib-like, protruding leaf veins the stem axes seem narrow and angularly winged (Plate 12,6).

In *E. dregeana* and in *E. weberbaueri,* as the axis grows thick, the leaf pads stretch considerably onto the surface, and do not grow directly inward into the stem but remain flat. We speak of mamillae or podaria only when the leaf pads grow not only onto the surface but also inward into the stem, take on a succulent appearance, and give the surface of the stem a warty look (Plate 12,7–8, Plate 13,1 and 2). Since the podaria frequently become thicker in their upper portions than at the base, they take on a hooked appearance, as can be seen in the lateral shoots of *E. tuberculata* (Plate 12,7). Such hooked or recurved mamillae are found also on *E. fasciculata, E. schoenlandii* (Plate 15,3,4 and 5), *E. hamata* (Plate 16,4 and 5), etc. Because the leaves are pressed tightly one on the other, the podaria cover the axis completely but are delineated clearly from one another. In species with a spiral arrangement of the leaves, they are usually hexagonal; if the leaves are arranged in straight lines, as in *E. stellaespina* (Plate 12,3) or *E. mammillaris* (Plate 13,2), they are rather square or rectangular. They always show the scar of the fallen leaf blade for a long time in the top portion of the stem, and in their axils one finds the vegetative points, which can develop into vegetative lateral branches or into flower buds or thorns.

Of special interest are the mamillae of the favored *E. bupleurifolia,* which in its native habitat forms a 30 cm long, cylindrical main stem that branches at the base, and which at the beginning of every growing season sends out a rosette of long-stemmed leaves. As dormancy begins, the leaves fall and leave their swollen leaf bases, which cover the whole length of the stem in "diagonal lines" (spirostiches) (Plate 13,1). In contrast to the mamillae of all other species, these begin to lignify very early, and so they become water retainers rather than act as an aid to assimilation.

Ribbed euphorbias

Besides mamilla euphorbias there are also ribbed euphorbias, which bear a strong resemblance to cacti. As far as the ribbing is concerned they are like cacti only in the species in which the leaves are not arranged diagonally but in "straight lines" (orthostiches): all the podaria of the leaf row are raised on a common base and blend with one another into a more or less raised rib. *E. stellaespina* and *E. mammillaris* (Plate 13,2) show rudimentary rib formations. In these the leaves are arranged in straight lines, but the mamillae are still clearly delineated by sharp indentations, and the ribs themselves are still flat. In the typical ribbed euphorbias, however, these are more or less raised, the boundaries between the mamillae frequently blurred, and only recognizable by their thorns (Plate 13,6).

The number of ribs is dependent on the type of leaf arrangement. If the plant has a two-row leaf arrangement, i.e., if there are only two orthostiches, then the stem has two ribs. This is the case of the lateral shoots of *E. antiquorum* (Plate 13,3); the stems of *E. trigona* are 3-ribbed (Plate 13,4) as are those of *E. triangularis; E. resinifera* is an example of a 4-ribbed stem (Plate 13,5); *E. officinarum* (Plate 13,6), *E. horrida, E. polygona,* and *E. fruticosa* are multi-ribbed, as are many others.

It often happens that the axes of many species in their juvenile stage have only two ribs or just a few, but as the plant ages and becomes stronger, the number of ribs on the individual stems can increase.

In this regard, note the remarkable Madagascar species *E. xylophylloides (= E. enterophora)*. In their native habitat they form large bushes or trees up to 5 m high with a thick, round stem; the lateral branches, however, are not round, but flattened; but the broadening does not come about because of rib formation, but because of a flattening of the axis itself (Plate 13,7). In this case one speaks of "flat stems." Even the primary stem of young plants is at first flattened and does not take on a round appearance until it is older. The leaves themselves are small and deciduous, and the function of assimilation, as in other species, is taken over by the green axes.

The flowers of euphorbias

Whereas euphorbias have a seemingly unending variety of forms in regard to their growth habits and shapes, the structure of the fertile organs is characterized by great simplicity. But what the amateur mistakes for a simple flower is in reality a highly complicated inflorescence known as a "cyathium" and consists of numerous, highly simplified, single-sexed, individual flowers. Thus one finds "male" and "female" "flowers"; the former consist of a single stamen perched on a short stalk (Figure 8,1a, St); the boundary between this stem and the filament of the stamen is marked by a slight indentation where later the whole stamen will drop off. The female flower consists of a glabrous (naked), stalked, 3-carpel ovary with three simple or divided, sometimes vividly colored stigma branches (Figure 8,3,F).

The structure of the flower determines whether the flower has "unisexual" or "hermaphroditic" cyathia: the former is usually found in dioecious situations, i.e., where one plant produces only female cyathia while another plant of the same species produces only male cyathia. As an example of this behavior I choose *E. bupleurifolia.*

First look at a male cyathium as depicted in cross section in Figure 8,1. A large number of stipitate, male flowers arranged in five groups are surrounded by a cup-shaped hull, the involucrum, which consists of 5 fused leaf organs, whose free tips, often slit at the top, are bent inwards. These are called involucral leaves or interglandular bracts (Figure 8,2, Jb).

Among these are four or five nectar glands of various shapes, the "glandulae" (Figure 8, D), which secrete a honey-like substance for the pollinating insects (flies). The form of the glands is so typical for some species that they serve as identification characters. In *E. bupleurifolia,* as in many other species, the glands are small and insignificant, diagonally oval and yellowish green. Below the cyathium cup there are two rather large leaf organs (bracts), called cyathophylls (Figure 8, Cy). In *E. bupleurifolia* they are greenish; in other species they are sometimes vividly colored. These are what we first notice about the whole inflorescence. The female cyathium is shaped identical to the male, with the exception that instead of 5 stamen groups it has only a single, female flower consisting of a stalked, glabrous ovary (Figure 8,2–3, F).

Not all euphorbias have unisexual cyathia; there are many species with two-sexed or hermaphroditic cyathia. In these, the central female flower is surrounded by five groups of male flowers (Figure 8,5). Such a cyathium is pre-female, (proterogynic), i.e., the female flower pushes out of the hull by lengthening its stalk and unfolds the ripe stigma before the male flowers (stamens) are visible. Later the ovary hangs far out of the hull (Figure 8,5). This proterogyny prevents self-pollination.

Even though cyathia are "inflorescences" (LINNAEUS considered them dioecious flowers) they are functionally the same as dioecious flowers and are pollinated accordingly.

In *E. bupleurifolia* the cyathia are on long stalks but otherwise unbranched. In other species branching can occur when two (sometimes more) lateral shoots emerge from among the axils of scale-shaped, usually green bracts. These lateral shoots in turn end with a cyathium and can branch again. Thus we find multi-forked inflorescences such as those that are typical for the Madagascar species from the *E. milii (= splendens)* group (see Color Plate 3,5). The cyathophylls do not always appear in flower-

like formation with brilliant coloring. Frequently they are reduced to insignificant scales. Then one speaks of "naked" (glabrous) cyathia. This phenomenon is extraordinarily widespread. As examples for this I have pictured the east African species *Euphorbia taitensis* and *E. uhligiana* (see Color Plate 3,1,3). The relatively small cyathia appear usually in groups of 3, but occur in large numbers at the tip of the stem. Their nectar glands are olive-green and yellow, respectively.

For the missing cyathophylls, which make the cyathium attractive, there are many substitutes. In American spe-

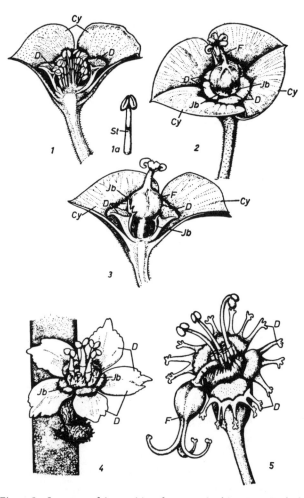

Figure 8. Structure of the cyathias of some euphorbias. *1–3, Euphorbia bupleurifolia. 1,* Longitudinal section of a male cyathium; *1a,* individual male flower; St. = staminal column. *2,* Female cyathium; *3,* the same in longitudinal section; F = female flower; Jb = involucral leaf (interglandular bract); D = nectar gland; Cy = the two cyathophylls. *4,* Cyathium of *Euphorbia antisyphilitica.* The nectar glands (stippled dark) are equipped with petal-like appendages. *5,* Cyathium of *Euphorbia monteiroi;* the nectar glands bear slit appendages (D).

cies such as *E. antisyphilitica* and *E. cereiformis,* the glands have flower-like appendages that make the cyathium at its peak look like a radial flower (Figure 8,4). In other species the glandulae possess a great variety of appendages, frequently vividly colored, which also lend the cyathia attractiveness. As an example of this phenomenon I have pictured *Euphorbia monteiroi* (Figure 8,5). Also *E. pseudograntii* (Plate 16,9) and *E. ramiglans* (Color Plate 2,9) can be mentioned in this regard.

The fruit of the euphorbias is a three-chambered, woody capsule, which explodes at maturity with an audible noise, scattering the seeds far afield. Each capsule chamber contains only one large seed equipped with an appendage that contains oil and protein.

THE CULTIVATION AND PROPAGATION OF EUPHORBIAS

Many of the following euphorbias are well suited to living-room cultivation; larger ones, however, should be planted in unconfined soil in a greenhouse in order to allow them to develop completely; the winter temperature should be kept above + 12° C if possible (+ 54° F).

All species prefer a well-drained, sandy, nutritious soil; water during the summer months. The leafy species require more water than the highly succulent, leafless varieties. Use caution in watering during the darker winter months; most species, especially in their leafless stage, withstand rather long periods of drought without harm, whereas too frequent watering can soon lead to rot. Deciduous euphorbias absolutely need winter rest.

Propagation is accomplished either by seed or by cuttings. Species that do not branch can be propagated only by seed (e.g., *E. obesa*), but because most of them are dioecious you must have a male and a female plant and pollinate the flowers yourself, provided that both sexes bloom at the same time. Cover the ripening fruits with a cotton pad or wrap the plant in a thin nylon cloth in order to prevent the seeds from being lost.

Most branching species can be propagated easily from cuttings; take the cutting in the late spring and separate the branch at its thinnest point, i.e., at the point of attachment to the main stem. (Be careful of the poisonous, milky sap!). Then dip the cutting in water, sand, or powdered charcoal in order to stop the milky sap from running, which would otherwise form a crust on the wound and prevent roots from forming. Let the cuttings

dry for a few days and plant them in a light medium of sand and peat; with good air circulation they will form roots relatively quickly.

Although the majority of euphorbias can be propagated this way, not all cuttings will take on the growth form of the mother plant. That is true especially of the fleshy-rooted species, whose lateral stems when treated as cuttings seldom form a thick root; also problematical are all the plants from the "Medusa head" group. As mentioned above, these have a short, central, thick stem, the so-called head, from which emerge the elongated lateral stems (Plate 10,1). If you treat these as cuttings, they usually grow unbranched without forming a new head.

Like cacti, euphorbias can be grafted; for a stock we usually use *E. resinifera, E. mamillaris,* etc., but this method is rarely used, because most species grow true from their own roots and can be rooted easily.

PESTS AND DISEASES

In general, euphorbias are relatively seldom attacked by diseases and pests. Leafy species are often plagued by red spider; leafless, highly succulent forms are susceptible to mildew when kept in constantly high humidity. When the plants grow too slowly, especially in the winter months, the stems tend rapidly to become woody. Although this is a natural process and not a disease, the plants become unattractive and weak, since they cannot assimilate properly.

Euphorbias are especially vulnerable to root nematodes (see page 30). If they are detected, all infested roots must be cut off and the plant re-rooted in sterile soil.

Anyone who becomes involved with euphorbias and takes care of them properly will enjoy them every bit as much as cacti, even if the "flowers" in general are rather insignificant and can not compete with the beauty of cactus flowers.

THE SYSTEMATIC GROUPING OF THE GENUS *Euphorbia*

It is not the intent of this book to present a detailed systematic of the genus *Euphorbia,* especially since research in this area is by no means complete. Whereas A. BERGER[9]

[9] BERGER, A.: *Sukkulente Euphorbien.* In: *Illustrierte Handbücher sukkulenter Pflanzen.* Verlag E. Ulmer, Stuttgart, 1907.

divides succulent euphorbias into 12 sections, WHITE, DYER, and SLOANE[10] group the South African species alone into 19 sections based on their growth habits and the structure of their cyathia. Here follows a short overview of the most important species.

Euphorbias without stipular spines

If thorns are present, they are stem or inflorescence thorns, i.e., suberized inflorescences that have remained on the plant for several years.

Section TITHYMALUS BOISS.

Shrubs with stems that are succulent in the beginning but suberize with age; leaves well developed, periodically deciduous; cyathia in multi-radial, simple or branched cymes (false umbel).

Section ARTHROTHAMNUS BOISS. (including section TIRUCALLII BOISS.)

Shrubs or trees with reed-shaped, cylindrical or flattened, multi-branched stems that sometimes end in thorny tips; leaves small, deciduous. African, Madagascar, Canary Island, and American species.

Section PTERONEURAE BRGR.

Low shrubs with angular branches; angular edges formed by the bases of deciduous leaves that trail down the stem axis; species found in America only.

Section TREISIA HAW. (including PSEUDEUPHORBIUM PAX)

Miniature shrubs or unbranched stem succulents with stems covered by succulent leaf bases arranged in spirals; leaf blades sometimes very large, deciduous; inflorescence stalk frequently remaining on the plant for a long time as a pseudo-thorn. African species.

Section MEDUSEA HAW. (Medusa heads)

Plants of the "Medusa head" type; numerous, snake-like, elongated branches drooping to the ground emerge from the top of a stout central stem; cyathia with short or rather long stems, one or two ovary chambers usually at the end of the lateral branches. African species.

Section PSEUDOMEDUSEA BRGR. (pseudo-Medusa heads)

Similar to the above but with cyathia sessile or short-stemmed, hermaphroditic, predominantly on the main stem, seldom on the lateral branches.

Section DACTYLANTHES HAW. (finger-flower euphorbias)

Miniature plants often in large clusters with more or less spherical or stubby cylindrical, finger-like, separate stems; cyathia sessile or long-stalked. African species.

Section MELEUPHORBIA BRGR. (melon-shaped euphorbias)

Miniature, dioecious species that are spherical or stubby columnar; cyathia single or in branched inflorescences that are sometimes woody after ripening of the fruit. African species.

Section ANTHACANTHA LEM. (= FLORISPINAE HAW., euphorbias with inflorescence thorns)

Species of cactoid habit, with axes covered by succulent leaf pads; inflorescence thorns frequently found in the axils of the leaves.

Species with leaf (stipular) thorns (= STIPULACANTHAE JACOBS)

Section DIACANTHIUM BOISS. (= section EUPHORBIA)

Here one finds the majority of succulent euphorbias whose foliage has thorned stipules with simple or branched dorsal thorns. Within this section, BERGER as well as WHITE, DYER, and SLOANE distinguish several sub-groups.

Section GONIOSTEMA BAILL.

Spines arranged in straight lines and fused into wing-like thorn strips. Only Madagascar species.

Section MONACANTHAE CHEV.

Shrubby species with round, succulent branches. Dorsal spines always single below the insertion of the usually large, deciduous foliage. Known from tropical west Africa.

Section TRIACANTHAE PAX

Dwarf species with ribbed stems; thorns in threes: in addition to a stout dorsal spine there are two weaker lateral stipular thorns.

Section TETRACANTHAE PAX

Dwarf species with ribbed stems; thorns in fours: above the two true stipular spines there are two smaller dorsal spines.

SHORT DESCRIPTION OF SPECIES RECOMMENDED FOR HOBBYISTS

African species

(Including Arabia and the Canary Islands)

Section TITHYMALUS BOISS.

From this group I choose the following, indigenous to the Canary Islands: E. atropurpurea BROUSS., E. bourgeana J. GAY, E. bravoana SVENIT, E. balsamifera AIT. (also in southern Arabia), E. dendroides L. (also widely distributed in the coastal region of the Mediterranean), and E. obtusifolia POIR. var. regisjubae WEBB et BERTH. (also in northern Africa [Morocco]).

---

[10] WHITE, A., R. DYER, and B.L. SLOANE: The Succulent Euphorbieae (Southern Africa). 2 volumes, Abbey Garden Press, Pasadena, California, 1941.

They are all multi-branched, spherical scrubs 1–2 m high with a short, branched stem, woody at the base. The lateral stems ramify into branches during every flowering period. They are round and spineless. During the growing period they have a rosette of long-oval leaves that fall at the beginning of the dry period. The cyathia are either single, as in *Euphorbia balsamifera* (Plate 14,4), or unite into more or less richly branched cymes *(E. atropurpurea* (Plate 14,1–2), *E. bravoana* (Plate 14,3), *E. bourgeana, E. dendroides). E. atropurpurea* and *E. bravoana* are especially beautiful at flowering time. The leaves below the terminal inflorescences become iridescent purple-red. Even the cyathophylls of these two species are dark purplish red; in *E. bourgeana,* on the other hand, they are pale yellowish.

None of these species are recommended to hobbyists with limited space. Planted in unconfined soil, however, they develop into attractive, free-blooming scrubs within a few years.

Section ARTHROTHAMNUS BOISS. (including TIRUCALLII BOISS.)

The species of this section, too, at least the African species, are of lesser interest to the hobbyist. (The Madagascar species in this group will be discussed later.) These are unattractive scrubs or trees with round, reed-shaped stems with tiny, deciduous leaves. The stems branch sympodially after the flowering period. The cyathia appear in multiples in terminal cymes.

As examples I select:

Euphorbia aphylla BROUSS.

A spherical dwarf shrub up to 1 m high, it has grayish green, round stems that end their growth with terminal inflorescences and continue to branch in whorls. Its leaves are very small, scale-shaped, and deciduous; 3 to 5 small cyathia, on short stalks at the ends of the branches (Plate 11,3). *Habitat:* Canary Islands.

An unattractive species, it becomes rather imposing when planted in unconfined soil; in a pot it remains small.

Euphorbia dregeana E. MEY. (Plate 9,2)

A multi-branched, reed-like scrub from 1 to 1.5 m high and just as wide, this plant has round, short-haired stems 1 to 5 cm thick, which become barky near the leaf bases that trail down the stem (Plate 12,5). The leaf blades are up to 0.5 cm long, visible only on new growth; the cyathia are small and insignificant and appear in terminal cymes. *Distribution:* western Cape Province (Namaqualand).

E. dregeana prefers to grow on primordial rock, where it often appears in large stands. In cultivation it is rewarding only when it is repeatedly cut back and forced to branch; otherwise it becomes thin and unattractive.

Other species of this section are:
E. mauritanica L. (widely distributed in South Africa)
E. schimperi PRESL. (southern Arabia)
E. stapelioides BOISS. (South Africa–Namaqualand)
E. tirucalli L. (tropical eastern and southern Africa, today planted in all tropical areas. Considered to be very poisonous.)
The Madagascar species from this section, *E. enterophora* and *E. stenoclada,* will be discussed on page 56.

Section TREISIA HAW. (including PSEUDEUPHORBIUM PAX)

Euphorbia bupleurifolia JACQ. (Plate 13,1)

The stem is up to 20(–30) cm long, up to 7 cm thick, and covered with spirally arranged, succulent, but quickly suberizing and thus brown leaf bases. In cultivation it is usually unbranched; in the native habitat, subterranean stem segments send up axil buds causing the primary stem to be surrounded by numerous shorter side branches. At the beginning of the rainy season a rosette of light green to blue-green leaves develops; they are lanceolate, up to 7 cm long and 2 cm wide. They have the same shape as those of the plant known as "rabbit-ears" (*Bupleurum,* family Apiaceae), which explains the name "rabbit-eared spurge."

Along with the leaves appear the long-stalked, single-sexed, dioecious cyathia (Figure 8,1–3), whose structure was discussed on page 37. Occasionally one finds plants with two-sexed cyathia. At the end of the rainy season the leaves fall, and the plant spends the dry period in dormancy. *Habitat:* southeastern Cape area and Natal (near Durban).

E. bupleurifolia is a favorite and much sought-after plant. It requires a humus-like, well-drained soil, more warmth and humidity than the other species and a semi-shady location. During the dormant stage the plant must be kept absolutely dry. In cultivation it usually does not branch; therefore, propagation is only possible from seed.

Euphorbia clandestina JACQ. (Plate 14,6 and 7)

This plant usually forms unbranched columns, rarely sending up offshoots at the base, 30–80 cm tall, up to 6 cm thick, cylindrical or club-shaped. The columns are covered with mamilla-like, elongated leaf bases arranged in spiral rows. The leaves, which are lineally long to oval and ca. 4 cm long, are in a terminal rosette and are always shed at the end of the rain period; cyathia are single, sessile, and surrounded by large, green cyathophylls; nectar glands are small, yellow. *Distribution:* southeast Cape Province.

E. clandestina is a pretty, easily grown species, which, because of its columnar shape, is called "soldier" in its native habitat.

Closely related to this is *Euphorbia clava* JACQ. (Plate 12,8), whose cylindrical body can grow up to 1 m tall; the mamillae are not raised so much as in the above species; the leaves are much longer and the cyathia, which also appear singly and are surrounded by green cyathophylls, are on stalks up to 10 cm long that persist after the capsules ripen.

Also related to the above two species is

Euphorbia pubiglans N.E. BR. (see Color Plate 2,7).

whose simple or slightly branched cylindrical stem, covered by the succulent leaf bases, can grow up to 30 cm long. *E. pubiglans* has a rosette of naked leaves 2–4 cm long, whose blades are usually folded upwards; cyathia appear singly, on hairy stalks 2–6 cm long and are surrounded by 3–5 large, green, plate-shaped, splayed cyathophylls; nectar glands are hairy on the upper side, which gives it its species name "hairy gland." *Distribution:* eastern Cape Province.

E. pubiglans is a pretty succulent that is seldom seen in collections.

Euphorbia clavarioides BOISS. (Plate 14,8 and 9)

This is a cushion-type euphorbia: from a short, thick primary shoot equipped with a stout, fleshy root emerge numerous, initially spherical, later stubby-cylindrical stems up to 7 cm long, which in turn branch so that finally a cushion is formed, which is compact, up to 50 (–100) cm in diameter, flat or semi-spherical and whose stem tips all end in a common surface. Leaves are only 1–2 mm long and deciduous. The sessile, male or two-sexed cyathia (both on the same plant) are found in the axils and appear in such large number that the surface of the cushion appears yellow from the greenish-yellow nectar glands, which are slightly serrate on their edges.

Var. *truncata* (N.E. BR.) WHITE, DYER et SLOANE differs from the type by having considerably shorter branches, more branching, and the resulting much more compact cushions (Plate 14,8 and 9); also the nectar glands are more prominently serrate. *Distribution* of the species: eastern Cape Province, Orange Free State, Lesotho, Transvaal, and Natal; var. *truncata* is found mostly in Transvaal. *E. clavarioides,* especially var. *truncata,* is especially a mountain plant and prefers to grow in high altitudes between 1500 and 2500 m, usually in grassy or rocky areas. In cultivation it requires a bright, sunny location and cool winter temperatures; otherwise the stems will elongate and the plant will lose its typical growth. In its habitat *E. clavarioides* grows even in frost and snow.

Euphorbia fasciculata THUNG. (Plate 15,1 and 2)

has an unbranched, columnar stem up to 30 cm high and up to 15 cm thick. It is covered with hexagonal, sharp, close leaf pads, which elongate into hooked tips that are pointed downward. Their small, deciduous blades are detectable only at the top of the column. The podaria have a trough on their upper side, which houses the axil meristem in its base. This meristem is not exhausted with the formation of one inflorescence, but from the same meristem come new inflorescences (ca. 10 cm long) in the following year. The inflorescences have cymes of 3–7 long-stalked, hermaphroditic cyathia with small, greenish yellow or brownish nectar glands. After the fruit ripens the inflorescence stalks lignify and are retained for a long time as pseudo-thorns (Plate 15,2). Since the leaf-axil meristem stays active for several years, several pseudo-thorns may be found in the axil of each podarium. *Distribution:* Cape Province: Little Namaqualand (Vanrhynsdorp District).

E. fasciculata is a very handsome and much sought-after species. It is, however, very sensitive to over-watering. It can easily be confused with *Euphorbia schoenlandii* PAX, which grows in the same area.

Euphorbia schoenlandii PAX (Plate 15,3–5)

This plant's unbranched columns can reach a length of up to 1.3 m. The differences from *E. fasciculata* are seen especially in the formation of off-shoots and in the structure of the inflorescences. The podaria of *E. schoenlandii* are exactly like those of *E. fasciculata.* They are elongated mounds and show the same troughs on the upper side. At their bases are the axil meristems. But this one first forms an axil shoot that bears foliage, is purely vegetative, has a thorn tip, and is about 5 cm long and up to 5 mm thick (Plate 15,3). After the leaves fall, this shoot lignifies and persists as a "true" thorn for many years (Plate 15,4). It is homologous to the primary inflorescence of *E. fasciculata.* Not until successive years do inflorescences appear at the base of the thorns from the same axil meristem; these are then considerably shorter than the thorns, up to only 2.5 cm long, and have 1–3 male or hermaphroditic cyathia (Plate 15,5). The formation of these inflorescences may occur for several years at the same podarium.

E. schoenlandii is also a favorite plant, and in comparison to *E. fasciculata* it is somewhat more robust and therefore is easier to grow in cultivation.

Euphorbia hamata (HAW.) SWEET (Plate 16,4 and 5)

This plant is a dwarf shrub up to 45 cm high, richly branched, forming rather large clumps. It has a stout, fleshy root. Its 1.5 cm thick, vaguely triangular stems are covered by long, thorn-like, elongated, hooked leaf bases, which turn downwards; their broadly oval blades up to 1.7 cm long fall as the rest period begins. Cyathia are single at the end of the stalks, with a usually 3-leafed, cup-like whorl of bracts (cyathophylls), which are initially yellowish green and later vivid red. *Distribution:* western Cape Province (Little and Great Namaqualand).

E. hamata is an attractive and interesting species, which in its native habitat, because of its often mass growth and its non-poisonous sap, provides valuable cattle feed. Therefore, you will seldom find specimens that have not been partially eaten.

Euphorbia loricata LAM. (Plate 16,1 and 2)

E. loricata is a richly branched dwarf shrub, woody at the base, with long, lanceolate leaves up to 7 cm long, in whose axils appear thorns, which are 5 cm long, gray or reddish brown, and covered with scale-leaves; in young plants these thorns are sterile, but in older plants they each bear a terminal cyathium, which is encased in three yellowish green, later reddish, leafy cyathophylls. After the fruit falls the stalk of the inflorescence persists for several years as a pseudo-thorn. *Distribution:* Cape Province: Clanwilliam District, common on the Olifants River and in the Poison Mountains.

E. loricata is a splendid species, sometimes with starry thorns, but it is not easy to cultivate. Even seedlings, because of their thorns, are very pretty.

Euphorbia monteiroi HOOK. f. (Plate 16,7 and 8)

forms thornless, unbranched or branched, cylindrical stems usually up to 50 cm, sometimes up to 4 m high. During the growth period numerous, leafy shoots with terminal cyathia at their tips develop from the upper segments of the stems. Below the cyathia is a whorl of 2–3 leafy bracts, from whose axils emerge lateral branches, which again end in a cyathium, etc. The cyathia themselves are rather large and are attractive because of the purplish red, serrate nectar glands (Figure 8,5). After the fruit ripens, the whole inflorescence is usually cast off except for the base, but in its native habitat it can remain for several years. *Distribution:* Transvaal up to Namibia and Angola.

E. monteiroi is a widely spread plant that grows quickly in cultivation. Its closest relative is probably *E. longetuberculosa* HOCHST. (Plate 16,6), common in southern Arabia. It has the same general appearance, but it becomes at the most 20 cm tall; the dorsiventral cyathia are small and insignificant.

E. pseudograntii PAX (Plate 16,9),

from east Africa, shows a certain similarity to *E. monteiroi* and *E. longetuberculosa* in regard to the structure of the cyathia, especially the form of the nectar glands with their tattered appendages. It is a deciduous shrub up to 2 m high with weedy, woody branches at the base; the leaves are without stipules, arranged in a spiral, gathered near the tip of the stem in a rosette; the blade is naked on both sides, shiny green, nerved in white, lanceolate, up to 20 cm long and 8 cm wide, ending in a sharp, thorny tip. The blade is attached with a broad, short petiole. Inflorescence terminals are in cymes, with large oval-elliptical, long-tipped, sessile, light-green bracts heart-shaped at their base, from whose axils emerge branches; the cyathia are very large with attractively shaped and colored nectar glands. These sit on narrow, violet bases, widen into a wedge, are green when young, but become yellow as they age and have several yellow or red-violet, fork-tipped appendages on their edge; fruit buds on long stems, stretching far out of the cyathium cup, bright purplish red and with a waxy coating. Of all euphorbias, probably *E. pseudograntii* has the prettiest and largest cyathia.

Easily grown and closely related to *E. grantii* OLIV.

Euphorbia oxystegia BOISS. (Plate 16,3)

is a dwarf shrub up to 20 cm high with a fleshy root. The cylindrical, gray-green branches have leaves 2.5 to 10 cm long and up to 1.4 cm within a terminal rosette. The long-stalked inflorescences end with a terminal cyathium, below which is a whorl of 2–5 bracts, from whose axils further branching can occur. The inflorescence stalks later suberize and persist on the plant for several years. *Distribution:* Namaqualand.

E. oxystegia is a rare species, closely related to *E. clava,* from which it is especially distinguished by its fleshy main root.

A species differing from all other African euphorbias and placed by BOISSIER into section Rhizanthium is

Euphorbia tuberosa L.,

which belongs to the type called fleshy-rooted geophytes, i.e., the plant consists essentially of a big, unbranched, napiform (turnip-shaped) root, which terminates in a very short stem-axis, completely covered by the soil. Every year this stem forms a rosette of large, long-petiolate leaves, which are shed at the end of the growing period, and so during dormancy nothing of the plant can be seen. The cyathia gather into a cyme of long-stalked inflorescences ca. 5 cm long. They are encased in 2 larger, yellow-green cyathophylls. *Distribution:* southern Cape Province.

I have found *E. tuberosa* only in places that are damp and swampy but dry up during the dry season. The plant is not difficult to cultivate, provided that it is kept completely dry during its leafless stage.

E. crispa (HAW.) SWEET and *E. silenifolia* (HAW.) SWEET are similar. The former has distinctly wavy leaves that are pleated on the top; the latter has narrow, lineal leaves and in comparison to *E. tuberosa* has strikingly long-stalked (up to 12 cm) inflorescences. It is considerably more widespread in the southern Cape area than is *E. tuberosa*.

Section MEDUSEA BRGR.

A typical representative of this growth-form is

Euphorbia caput-medusae L., the "Medusa head" spurge (Plate 17,1).

Numerous stems lying on the ground or arched upward and covered by succulent leaf pads emerge from a short, almost subterranean, stout main stem that merges into a fat, fleshy root. The root is up to 30 cm thick; the stem is 3–5 cm thick, up to 70 cm long, and has small (up to 5 mm long), lineal foliage, which soon drops off. The short-stalked cyathia arise singly in the axils of the leaf pads, but appear in great numbers at the ends of the stems. Its attractiveness comes about because of the large, white or pink-edged, serrate nectar glands. *Distribution:* near Cape Town on the Tafelsberg (Table Mountain) and Lionshead.

E. caput-medusae requires a sunny, warm location and a winter temperature of $+12°$ to $+14°C$ ($+54°$ to $+57°$ F). Propagation only by seed, because cuttings of side branches usually continue growing as side branches and seldom form a new "head," i.e., a central stem. Planted in the open ground it is a very attractive species.

Very similar to the above in growth-form is

Euphorbia bergeri N.E. BR.,

but its stems are much shorter (up to 25 cm long) and thinner (up to 2 cm); the leaf blades are much more reduced and the cyathia are smaller. Also the appendages to the nectar glands are not white but greenish white. Nothing is known about the origin and distribution of *E. bergeri.* BERGER was the first to recognize this species as different from *E. caput-medusae,* but he attributed it to *E. parvimamma* (BOISS.) BRGR., which differs from *E. caput-medusae* by its very short (up to 5 cm) lateral branches.

Euphorbia esculenta MARL. (Plate 10,1)

is a very attractive species. The main stem is club-shaped, is up to 20 cm thick, and is buried in the ground almost up to the top. From it emerges a rosette of shoots 5 to 20 cm long and up to 2 cm thick. The plant can reach a diameter of 0.5 m. The tiny, deciduous leaves sit in the middle of slightly swollen, hexagonal leaf pads. The cyathia appear singly in the leaf-axils and only on the tips of the stems; their 5 to 8 mm long stalks have 3 to 5 white, woolly bracts; the nectar glands are greenish brown, diagonally oval, irregularly toothed or with deep cuts. The flower bracts of the stigma groups are covered with thick, white wool and completely fill the cyathium. *Distribution:* eastern Cape Province.

E. esculenta, not difficult to cultivate, is called "Vingerpol" in its native habitat, which means "finger pad." Because it is quite common in places and its milky sap is not bitter, it is a valuable animal feed, which in turn has caused it to be extinct in many places.

Very closely related is *E. inermis* MILL., which differs from the above by its shorter stalks of the cyathia, whose dark green nectar glands have two appendages in the shape of a reindeer antlers.

Also related to the two species described above is

Euphorbia fortuita WHITE, DYER et SLOANE (Plate 17,3),

which is known only from the Lesser Karroo (Ladysmith District). It differs from *E. esculenta* and *E. inermis* by the fact that the primary shoot is not set off clearly from the fleshy main root but is a continuation of it. Also the glands of *E. fortuita* are dark purple and have up to 7 entire-edged, recurved appendages.

Euphorbia tuberculata JACQ. (Plate 17,4 and 5)

is a "Medusa head" type that is widely distributed in the western Cape area. From a short, stout, and almost completely buried primary shoot that merges into a fleshy root arise numerous, upright or reclining shoots up to 50 cm long and up to 4 cm thick, which are covered with rhomboid, spirally arranged, succulent leaf pads (Plate 12,7). The long-stalked cyathia appear in a large number on the tips of the shoots and owe their attractiveness to the large, brownish green nectar glands, which have creamy white or reddish teeth on their edges (Plate 17,5). The old cyathia stalks persist on the plant for a long time.

E. tuberculata in its habitat grows on sandy, brackish ground; in cultivation it requires conditions similar to *E. caput-medusae* but less water.

The following species, which in a broad sense belong to the section Medusea, are placed in their own group by WHITE, DYER, and SLOANE because their normally short, sometimes very thick and almost spherical primary stem, for the most part, grows above ground and is not hidden in the soil, as is the case with the true Medusa heads.

A typical representative of this growth-form is

Euphorbia decepta N.E. BR.,

a dwarf species with a spherical main stem up to 8 cm long and up to 10 cm thick covered with large, hexagonal, flat podaria. From the tip emerge short, more or less upright, cylindrical lateral branches, on which the little cyathia appear, whose 2-cm-long stalks later harden and persist for several years. *Distribution:* Great Karroo (Beaufort West District).

E. decepta prefers, as do all species of this group, a warm location and requires only a little water.

Of the same dwarf growth-form is

Euphorbia maleolens PHILLIPS (Plate 18,5).

Numerous lateral branches, up to 10 cm long and 1 cm thick and covered with rhomboid leaf pads, emerge from a short stem, which is up to 9 cm thick at the top and which merges into a thick, fleshy root. Leaves are about 1 cm long, narrowly lineal, deciduous. The cyathia appear singly near the tip of the shoot on 1 to 2 cm long stems, which persist for a long time

after the fruit ripens. The nectar glands are dark green with 2 to 3 appendages up to 2 mm long. *Distribution:* Transvaal (Zoutpansberge and near Lydenburg). Cultivation is the same as for the above.

Of considerably larger size is

Euphorbia fusca MARL. (Color Plate 2,3).

Its spherical main stem can reach a diameter up to 30 cm and a length up to 20 cm and merges into a long root. From the "head" arise numerous lateral branches, which die off from the base of the main stem upward. They are 2 to 15 cm long, up to 1 cm thick, cylindrical, and are covered by rhomboid, hexagonal podaria. In the habitat these lateral branches are brownish red. The small cyathia appear singly, generally at the tips of the lateral branches, on stalks about 2 cm long, which harden after the seed is ripe and remain on the plant. Nectar glands are brown, toothed on the edge. *Distribution:* Karroo (Britstown District) to Namibia (Warmbad).

Having a somewhat different growth-form is

Euphorbia braunsii N.E. BR.

From a short main stem that merges into a fleshy primary root, originate several upright, lateral shoots up to 3 cm thick. These are initially unbranched but later branched and, with increasing age, result in compact clusters up to 25 cm in diameter. Cyathia appear singly or in groups of 2 to 3 in the axils of the flat podaria at the end of the shoots on stalks about 2 cm long, which persist on the plant for several years. Nectar glands are dark green with 2 to 5 reddish teeth. *Distribution:* Great Karroo.

One of the most remarkable South African euphorbias of this group is

Euphorbia multiceps BRGR. (Plate 20,1),

the "many-headed euphorbia," which earns its name because the succulent primary stem, which is up to 60 cm long and has a thick main root, produces numerous short lateral branches that are compacted into spiral lines and decrease in length toward the tip. Their tips form a common surface, resulting in a many-headed, spherical to pyramidal body (Plate 20,1). On the primary shoot as well as on the side branches appear sterile inflorescences 1 to 7 cm long, which are homologous to thorns. The cyathia appear singly on short stalks in the leaf axils of the lateral shoots, but there are many of them. With their yellow-green nectar glands, which have fine, white teeth on their edges, they give a splendid appearance to the plant at flowering time. *Distribution:* not uncommon in the Great and the Southern Karroo and in Namaqualand.

E. multiceps is not very easy to cultivate; it requires a warm, sunny location and very little water.

Another species in this group is

Euphorbia filiflora MARL.,

whose cylindrical main stem up to 30 cm high produces a large number of short-lived lateral branches in its apical part. Its leaves are narrowly lineal, up to 3 cm long; cyathia appear singly on stalks up to 7 cm long; and nectar glands have greenish yellow, thread-shaped appendages; thus the name "thread-flowered spurge." *Distribution:* Cape Province (Namaqualand).

This is a pretty species that is easily grown.

Euphorbia ramiglans N.E. BR. (Color Plate 2,9)

is an attractive species of the Medusa head group that is especially pretty at flowering time. The short, club-shaped stem is up to 5 cm thick and merges into a stout, fleshy root. It produces numerous upright, short, bluish green shoots that are 2 to 4 cm long (in cultivation up to 6 cm). They are about as thick as a finger and are covered by the spirally arranged podaria that run longitudinally into the tooth-like leaf scar. Leaf blades are deciduous and few are found in a terminal rosette. They are only 5 to 8 mm long, lanceolate, blunt at the tip, bluish green. The cyathia appear singly just under the tip of the shoot on thick, 1 to 1.5 cm stalks and are very attractive because of the nectar glands. These are diagonally elliptical, olive green to reddish and have white, fork-tipped appendages arranged in a star-burst of 4 to 6 rays. Interglandular bracts are green with reddish, tattered edges.

WHITE, DYER and SLOANE indicate Little Namaqualand as the distribution area with no exact localities given. I found the plant in rather large populations in the dunes in the back land of Alexander Bay, where it appears together with *Fenestraria aurantiaca.* Its stems are completely buried in the sand, from which only the attractive cyathia peeked through; otherwise I would have completely overlooked the plant.

Section PSEUDOMEDUSEA BRGR.

The species of this section are closely related in form to those of the previous section, i.e., they, too, have central primary shoots, often buried to the top in the ground, from which emerge wreaths of lateral branches. The lateral branches are short lived. While the older, basal shoots die after just a few years, new shoots are continuously formed in the apical region of the main stem. The fleshy root contracts, causing the stem to be drawn so far into the earth that the youngest lateral branches lie on the surface of the soil and barely rise above it. The sessile or short-stalked cyathia, in contrast to those of the species of section Medusea, are found on the lateral branches as well as on the main stem.

A typical representative of this growth-form is

Euphorbia gorgonis BRGR. (Plate 18,*1*).

It has a main stem 5 to 10 cm thick buried in the ground, which gradually merges into a fleshy root and produces offshoots; it is covered with spherical podaria arranged in a spiral. Just below the submerged tip emerges a wreath of short, cylindrical lateral branches 0.8 to 5 cm long. The short-stalked cyathia appear singly at the tip of the primary shoot as well as on the lateral branches; its nectar glands, with teeth on their edge, are dark red to brownish red. When young the fruits have hair; when old they are naked. *Distribution:* eastern Cape Province, in meadows.

E. gorgonis is a very pretty species that even in cultivation keeps its growth-form and whose lateral branches, in contrast to the closely related

Euphorbia pugniformis BOISS. (Plate 18,*2,3* and *4*),

do not elongate. In the latter, however, they can reach a length of up to 20 cm (in its native habitat only up to 3 cm); by doing so the plant loses some of its bizarre beauty. Furthermore, it differs from *E. gorgonis* by its yellowish green, entire-edged or slightly toothed nectar glands; the fruits are usually pubescent, seldom glabrous.

E. pugniformis is an extremely variable species that can easily be confused with

Euphorbia woodii N.E. BR. (Color Plate 2,*4*).

There are probably few collections in which both species are exactly identified. Indeed the morphological differences between the two species are not very significant; in *E. woodii* the nectar glands are not green but bright yellow and the fruit capsule has only scattered tufts of long hairs.

In their distribution areas, however, the two species do not overlap. *E. woodii* is found in the coastal area of Natal (in the vicinity of Durban); *E. pugniformis,* on the other hand, is found in the southeastern Cape area.

Both species are easy to grow and as coastal plants require more humidity than most other succulent plants.

Closely related to the two species described above and not easily distinguished from them are:
Euphorbia gatbergensis N.E. BR. (closely related to *E. pugniformis*) and *Euphorbia franksiae* N.E. BR. (closely related to *E. woodii*).

Occasionally one finds crested forms of *Euphorbia pugniformis* in cultivation. They appear in two forms, the so-called "leaf crests" and "stem crests." In the former the lateral branches are fasciate and flattened into "leaves" (Plate 18,*2*); in the stem crests, on the other hand, the main shoot is fasciate and equipped with normal lateral branches (Plate 18,*4*). Both forms can easily be propagated.

At this point, a few remarks should be made about crests in general. They are also known by the name "cockscomb forms." These are monstrose forms, which are characterized by the fact that the normally round axes broaden into a band. This process takes place when the normally single vegetation point of a growing shoot continuously divides into a large number of vegetation points, which are all arrayed in one plane, whereby a band-shaped flattening of the tip occurs. This kind of cockscomb also forms in certain cultivated plants, e.g., *Celosia argentea* var. *cristata,* but especially in cacti. There are many hobbyists who specialize in collecting only crests.

Also in euphorbias crests are not rare, but are much less common. In Plate 18,*6* one can see another crest of *E. lactea* (see p. 55).

The cause of this fasciation is completely unknown. People have often tried to create it artifically, but up to now without success.

Fasciation occurs suddenly on healthy plants that for years have grown normally. On the other hand, crests can disappear again, and completely or partially normal shoots may be produced. In any case, "comb formation" is not a disease but occurs in completely healthy plants in which vegetative growth is vigorous. Crested forms therefore flower much less often than normal forms, a fact which is known to any cactus fancier.

Section DACTYLANTHES HAW.

comprises a group of miniature euphorbias with spherical or short-cylindrical, phallus-like, separate shoots. Because of the characteristic form of the nectar glands, the plants can also be called "finger flowers." The glandulae have two lips: a short upper lip and a longer lower lip equipped with finger-shaped appendages that are warty (Plate 19,2,4,6).

All five species of this section are difficult to distinguish from one another, because their growth-form may be greatly changed in cultivation, with inappropriate care, causing them to resemble one another to a great extent.

One of the most beautiful species of this group is

Euphorbia globosa (HAW.) SIMS (Plate 19,1 and 2),

the "ball spurge," a mat-forming species whose shoot system consists of numerous spherical bodies equipped with roots that send up shoots. The forming of such a mat happens when the short-lived primary shoot, equipped with a fleshy root, sends out spherical, lateral branches that, by contracting their roots, are pulled into the ground. At the tip of these primary lateral branches appear new offsets (off-shoots), which begin with a thin base, become stouter, and then assume a spherical shape. These, too, are pulled into the ground by their roots and branch farther on in the same manner. Because this process is repeated annually, in the course of many years mats up to 0.5 m in diameter occur that are made up of off-shoot spheres, of which only the youngest lie on the ground while the older generations are buried in the soil. When new roots are formed, the individual off-shoots become independent of the main root system. They are about 2 to 3 cm thick and covered by flat, broad, hexagonal podaria, in the middle of which the scar from the small, deciduous leaf blade is visible. As the shoots approach flowering time they elongate into a thin inflorescence up to 8 cm long, bearing some scaly leaves. Beneath the rather large terminal cyathium one usually finds two larger bracts, from whose axils branching can occur. The upright nectar glands have a small, white, upper lip and a lower lip split into three to four finger-shaped appendages that have white wart-like bumps on their upper side (Plate 19,2).

E. globosa is an interesting species, common in the eastern Cape area under bushes, and is easy to propagate. In cultivation it requires a bright, sunny, and dry location, otherwise it completely loses its characteristic growth form, because the spherical shoots elongate greatly. If that happens the plant appears in a growth-form that resembles

Euphorbia ornithopus JACQ. (Plate 19,3),

the "bird's foot euphorbia." From a fleshy primary shoot emerge numerous runners, which at first grow underground but later are exposed, producing roots and creeping across the ground. They are stubby and cylindrical, up to 3 cm long and 1 cm thick, but elongate considerably in shady conditions. They start with a thin, stem-like base, become thicker toward the tip and are covered with broad, hexagonal leaf pads. From the

segments near the tip emerge lateral branches, with the result that over a few years chains of shoots are formed. The inflorescences are up to 10 cm long and are composed of stalked cymes. The terminal cyathium normally has 5 nectar glands with 3 to 4 finger-like appendages, which on the top are covererd with small, white-edged, pitted warts (Plate 19,4). *Distribution:* southeastern Cape Province near Grahamstown.

The species name *"ornithopus"* refers to the shape of the nectar gland, which has a five-fingered appendage and indeed resembles a bird's foot (Plate 19,4).

The same growth-form is also represented by the following species:

Euphorbia tridentata LAM. (Plate 19,5) and
Euphorbia wilmanae MARL. (Plate 19,6).

Both plants send out runners, which creep across the ground with short or elongated shoots.

In *E. tridentata* the shoots are spherical or elongated-cylindrical (up to 15 cm), much branched, and covered by hexagonal leaf pads. The cyathia are single or arranged in groups of 3 to 4 on the tip of the shoot, on stems about 4 mm long. The nectar glands have two lips, the upper lip having three to four finger-shaped appendages, which are warty on the upper side.

In *E. wilmanae* the above-ground shoots are elongated cylinders, thin and covered by tooth-like, elongated podaria.

Cyathia appear singly on the shoot tips, sessile or on very short stalks. The nectar glands have two lips as in the above plants; the lower lip has two or three finger-shaped warty appendages (Plate 19,6).

Further species of section Dactylanthus are:
Euphorbia planiceps WHITE, DYER et SLOANE and *E. polycephala* MARLOTH.

Section MELEUPHORBIA BRGR.

In the section of the "melon-like" euphorbias we find two growth types:

a. Types whose primary shoot is almost completely buried in the soil or only the ribbed, columnar, or cucumber-shaped lateral branches peek above the substrate. The stalks of the cyathia fall after the fruit is ripe. Examples are: *E. susannae, E. pseudoglobosa, E. tubiglans, E. jansenvillensis.*

b. Types whose spherical or fat-cylindrical primary shoot grows mostly above the ground. Of these I list: *E. obesa, E. symmetrica, E. meloformis, E. valida.* In the latter two species the persisting inflorescence-stalks remain on the plant several years after the seed is ripe.

Euphorbia jansenvillensis NEL (Plate 20,2).

The subterranean primary shoot forms short runners, which appear above the ground as upright, 5-ribbed shoots up to 16 cm long and up to 2 cm thick. The very short leaf blades up to 2 mm long soon fall, leaving a tooth-like podarium pointed downwards. The cyathia appear singly just under the tip of the shoot on stalks about 1 cm long, which bear a few scape bracts, the uppermost of which are leafy and form a green hull around the cyathium (Plate 20,2). *Distribution:* eastern Cape Province (Jansenville and Uitenhage District).

E. jansenvillensis is actually a very pretty species, whose cortex in cultivation, however, tends to become hard and cork-like, making the plant rather unseemly.

Closely related to this species is *E. tubiglans* MARL., found in the same area and distinguished from the above species especially by its thick, fleshy root, which continues into the cork-line, subterranean main stem. From its tip emerge 2–5 columnar shoots up to 8 cm long and 2 cm thick with 5 ribs and which begin with a thin, stem-like part, which suddenly thickens. The structure of the inflorescences is nearly identical to that of *E. jansenvillensis*.

Also, *E. pseudoglobosa* MARL. (Plate 20,3) belongs to this same growth-form. As in *E. tubiglans* this plant also has a fleshy main root and a short, subterranean stem from which emerge numerous spherical to fat-cylindrical stems with 5 to 6 ribs. The single, short-stalked cyathia do not have the leafy scape bract hulls as in *E. jansenvillensis* and *E. tubiglans*. *Distribution:* eastern Cape Province (Ladysmith Karroo, Riversdale District).

E. pseudoglobosa in cultivation requires much warmth. Under too much humidity it loses its characteristic growth-form and the spherical shoots begin to elongate.

Euphorbia susannae MARL. (Plate 20,4)

is a dioecious, miniature euphorbia, whose shoot system in its native habitat is buried to the tips and therefore is extremely difficult to find. It has a thick primary shoot, which in its youth is unbranched and which has a long fleshy root. At the base of the primary shoot emerge one or more rings of short columnar lateral shoots, 5 to 8 cm long and up to 3.5 cm thick, having 12 to 16 ribs. Its tooth-like podaria elongate into bristly leaf blades, which soon dry and are detectable only on the tips of the shoots. The small, short-stalked cyathia appear singly or in pairs in the axils of the podaria but occur in great number on the tip of the shoots. *Distribution:* only in the Lesser Karroo (Ladysmith District).

E. susannae is easily recognized and cannot easily be confused with any other species; it enjoys a great popularity among collectors. It requires a dry, warm location.

Without a doubt one of the most beautifully shaped and therefore most sought-after species is

Euphorbia obesa HOOK. f.,

an example of botanical symmetry, which has its counterpart only in the "sea urchin" cactus, *Astrophytum asterias* (Plate 1,3). Like the other species of this group, *E. obesa* is dioecious, seldom monoecious, and in its youth forms regularly flat spheres of grayish green with darker diagonal stripes. Its 8 to 10 flat ribs become flat with maturity, the mamillae, are small, and the leaf-blades are extremely reduced. In maturity the bodies can elongate into short cylinders up to 20 cm long and 10 cm thick. The cyathia appear singly or in cymes just below the slightly indented tip. *Distribution:* eastern Cape Province (only in the vicinity of Graaf Reinet).

Natural hybrids of *E. obesa* and *E. ferox* are known; they are distinguished by their elongated bodies that are covered with persistent inflorescence stalks. Cultivated hybrids of *E. obesa*

with *E. valida, E. meloformis,* and *E. mammillaris* are common in collections.

Very closely related to *E. obesa* and difficult for non-specialists to identify is *Euphorbia symmetrica* WHITE, DYER et SLOANE (Plate 10,3), discovered by R.A. DYER in the Willowmore district (East Cape Province). The differences between *E. symmetrica* and *E. obesa* are as follows: the form of *E. symmetrica* remains spherical even as it matures and therefore is wider than it is tall. The "fertile eyes" (vegetation points) are not round but elongated and usually produce several inflorescences. *E. symmetrica* also forms natural hybrids with *E. ferox*.

Both species, the more commonly cultivated *E. obesa* and the rarer *E. symmetrica,* are among the "gems" of the euphorbias; they can be propagated only by seed, because they rarely set off-shoots. Cultivation is not very difficult: loose, well-drained medium, moderate watering during the summer months and a light, warm, dry location in winter will give the plants a healthy look.

The following two species have stronger ribbing and suberization of the encircling inflorescence branches.

Euphorbia meloformis AIT. (Plate 21,1 and 2)

forms spherical or short-columnar shapes up to 10 cm in diameter, usually with 8 ribs, uniformly dark green or with brownish green diagonal bands caused by the intense sun or sometimes with lighter diagonal bands. The plant grows singly or, as a result of off-setting, forms small clusters. The blunt ribs are wider than tall and the podaria of the scale-shaped, deciduous leaves are divided from each other by deep furrows; the cyathia are unisexual and dioecious; they are small and found near the tip of the plant in groups of 2 to 12 on stalked, branched cymes. The nectar glands are elliptical, bright green. *Distribution:* eastern Cape area (Uitenhage, Port Elizabeth and Albany District) in meadows, hidden among the grass.

E. meloformis is a favorite species but variable in form and color. It is very closely related to

Euphorbia valida N.E. BR. (Plate 12,4).

(*Distribution:* eastern Cape Province—Jansenville, Somerset East, Steylerville Districts.) Young plants of *E. valida* are usually spherical with a slightly indented tip (unlike *E. meloformis*), and the gray-green striping of the ribs is much more prominent than in *E. meloformis*. At maturity *E. valida* becomes a stubby column and it can reach up to 20 cm in height and can be up to 12 cm wide. The suberized inflorescences persist on the plant longer than in *E. meloformis*. Also *E. valida* prefers to grow under low bushes and not in meadows.

Cultivation of the two species is similar to that of *E. obesa,* but they require more water during the summer months.

Section ANTHACANTHA LEM.

In this group of "thorn bloomers" are numerous, highly succulent, ribbed species, whose suberized thorns are comparable to simple or branched, sterile or fertile inflorescences. All species are worthy of cultivation.

Euphorbia aggregata BRGR. (Plate 10,2; Plate 21,5)

in its habitat forms compact cushions up to 1 m in diameter;

stems are richly branched, up to 3.5 cm thick, with 8 to 9 blunt ribs and numerous thorns, which at first are reddish, later blackish brown, 1 to 2 cm long; leaves 1 to 2 mm long, deciduous; cyathia single, near the tip, short-stalked with dark purplish red or green nectar glands. *Distribution:* eastern Cape area.

Closely related to the above is

Euphorbia ferox MARL. (Plate 21,3),

which is distinguished from the above by its more numerous thorns. Also the shoots emerging from the short primary stem branch only at the base.

E. ferox also forms clusters up to 60 cm in diameter and up to 50 cm high. Stems have 9 to 12 ribs with very stiff thorns (Plate 21,4). *Distribution:* eastern Cape Province (Willowmore, Jansenville).

Euphorbia mammillaris L. (Color Plate 2,1; Plate 13,2)

forms many-stemmed, almost cushion-shaped shrubs up to 30 cm high and up to 1 m in diameter (see Color Plate 2). The stems are 4 to 6 cm thick and have 7 to 17 ribs divided by the square-to-hexagonal leaf pads, which are sharply delineated (Plate 13,2). Sterile inflorescence thorns are rigid, up to 1.5 cm long, usually arching downwards, and frequently arranged in zones. Cyathia are numerous near the tip; there are 5 nectar glands, diagonally elliptical, dark purple or yellowish green. *Habitat:* eastern Cape area (Oudtshoorn District).

E. mammillaris is a very pretty species that, however, loses some of its typical growth-form in cultivation: the shoots become thinner and longer, and the thorns become weaker. Propagation is easy by means of cuttings.

Euphorbia enopla BOISS. (Plate 12,2)

forms loose, spherical shrubs 30 to 100 cm high with very thorny, gray to vivid green off-shoots up to 3 cm thick, having 6 to 7 ribs; thorns are numerous, stout, 1 to 6 cm long, dark red in youth, blackish purple to gray at maturity; cyathia are unisexual, on stalks 0.5 to 2.2 cm long. *Distribution:* eastern Cape Province (Willowmore District), in rocky places between 600 to 900 meters.

Closely related to the above and difficult to distinguish from it is

Euphorbia heptagona L. (Plate 22,1),

a very thorny species up to 1 m high and sparsely branched. At the base of the primary shoot emerge lateral branches of the 1st order, at first pointing upwards, which branch anew at their tips. Although most have 7 ribs, the number of ribs can vary greatly. The shoots themselves are densely covered with brown inflorescence thorns up to 3 cm long. Cyathia appear singly near the tips of the shoots on stalks about 1.5 cm long, and the nectar glands are glabrous and green. *Distribution:* eastern Cape Province.

E. heptagona is a name commonly found in collections but usually is a mis-labeling of *E. enopla.*

Again very similar to the above is

Euphorbia pentagona HAW. (Plate 22,2),

a shrub up to 3 m high with a protruding main stem, which bears lateral branches curving upwards and arranged in a near spiral; the branches in turn branch in the same way. Shoots are up to 4 cm thick, bright green, usually having 5 sharp ribs; thorns are distributed rather regularly, up to 2 cm long, grayish green to yellowish green; and cyathia are in short-stalked inflorescences of (1–) 3 to 5. Beneath the terminal cyathium, which may be the only one, emerge 3 to 4 additional cyathia from the axils of the bracts, an important point of distinction when compared to *E. heptagona,* in which the cyathia always appear singly. *Distribution:* eastern Cape Province.

Euphorbia pulvinata MARL. (Color Plate 2,2)

is an easily grown and easily propagated species, which appears in sub-alpine regions of rather high mountain chains and grows there in cushions, giving it the name "cushion euphorbia." Its shoots are initially spherical. Later, stubby cylinders having 7 to 10 ribs and richly branched form in the course of a few years large cushions between boulders and are up to 2 m across and up to 80 cm tall. Leaves are linear, sometimes up to 3 cm long, and deciduous, with up to 2 cm long thorns in their axils which bear scale leaves. The unisexual, sessile or short-stalked cyathia appear at the tip of the shoots in such great numbers that at flowering time, the cushions become very beautiful because of the vivid dark purple (seldom yellowish green) nectar glands. The distribution area of *E. pulvinata* ranges from Cape Province (Queenstown District) to the Transkei, Natal, and Lesotho, on into northern Transvaal (Zoutpansberge).

E. pulvinata, as a mountain plant, requires a cool location and little water during the winter months.

Euphorbia submammillaris BRGR. (Plate 21,6)

is a dioecious, dwarf species, which in cultivation forms richly branched, dense cushions 10 to 20 cm high and up to 50 cm in diameter. Its dark green shoots appearing at the base quickly suberize and become up to 2.5 cm thick and have 7 to 10 ribs. The wart-shaped podaria, equipped with tooth-like scars from the fallen leaf blade, are separated from each other by deep rills; thorns are numerous, 1 to 2 cm long; and cyathia are on short stalks with 5 diagonal, brown nectar glands.

E. submammillaris is common in collections; nothing is yet known about its place of origin.

Among the most beautiful ribbed euphorbias with inflorescence thorns, most closely resembling cacti, are *E. horrida* and *E. polygona,* two species cherished by growers.

Euphorbia horrida BOISS. (Plate 9,4),

as a result of basal off-shoots, forms small or moderately large clusters of upright columns. These can reach a height of up to 1.2 m and a diameter of up to 20 cm and have 13 to 20 (on the averge 14) ribs up to 2 cm high, which have star-like thorns. Thus the specific name *horrida,* the "wildly starred one." In the axil of each mamilla emerges a great number of stiff thorns of various lengths; the primary thorn, and at the

Color Plate 3.

1 (ul)   *Euphorbia caput-medusae* on Table Moun-
         tain near Cape Town
2 (ml)   *Euphorbia tuberculata* near Eendekul

(Piketberg, Little Namaqualand)
3 (ll)   *Euphorbia fortuita* in the Lesser Karroo
         near Ladysmith

4 (ur)   *Euphorbia tuberculata*, young plant
5 (lr)   Segment from a flower plant of *Euphor-
         bia tuberculata*

Plate 18.

1 (ul) *Euphorbia gorgonis*

2 (ur) *Euphorbia pugniformis*, "leaf crest"
3 (ml) Normal form of *Euphorbia pugniformis*
4 (mr) "Stem crest" of *Euphorbia pugniformis*

5 (ll) *Euphorbia maleolens*, near Pieter
(Transvaal)
6 (lr) *Euphorbia lactea* var. *cristata*

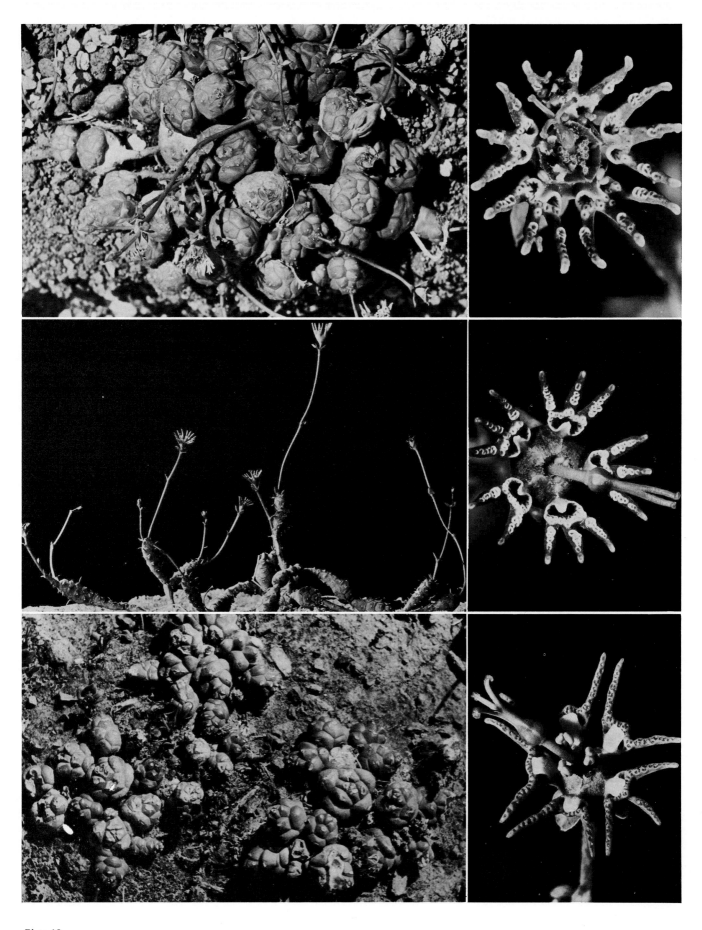

Plate 19.

1 (ul) *Euphorbia globosa* in habitat near Jansenville

2 (ur) Individual cyathium of *Euphorbia globosa*

from above, greatly magnified

3 (ml) *Euphorbia ornithopus* in cultivation

4 (mr) Single cyathium of *Euphorbia ornithopus* from above, greatly magnified

5 (ll) *Euphorbia tridentata* near Willowmore (eastern Cape Province)

6 (lr) *Euphorbia wilmanae*, cyathium from above, greatly magnified

Plate 20.

1 (ul)   *Euphorbia multiceps*

2 (ur)   Flowering shoot of *E. jansenvillensis*
3 (ml)   *Euphorbia pseudoglobosa*
4 (lr)   *Euphorbia susannae* near Ladysmith

Plate 21.

1 (ul) *Euphorbia meloformis* in habitat near Grahamstown (eastern Cape Province)

2 (ur) *Euphorbia meloformis* in cultivation
3 (ml) *Euphorbia ferox* in habitat near Willowmore (eastern Cape Province)

4 (mr) Piece of a mound of *Euphorbia ferox*
5 (ll) *Euphorbia aggregata*
6 (lr) *Euphorbia submammillaris*

Plate 22.

1 (ul)   *Euphorbia heptagona*, young imported plant
2 (um) *Euphorbia pentagona* in cultivation
3 (ur)   *Euphorbia polygona*, a plant ca. 1.8 m tall on a steep slope in the Trapps Valley (southeastern Cape Province)
4 (ml) Fruit-bearing shoot of *Euphorbia polygona;* in the lower part of the picture is the dwarf mistletoe *Viscum minimum*
5 (ll)   *Euphorbia horrida* var. *striata*
6 (lml) *Euphorbia cereiformis*
7 (lmr) *Euphorbia inconstantia*
8 (lr)   *Euphorbia pillansii*

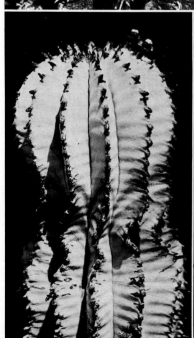

Plate 23.

Plate 24.

1 (ul) Forest with *Euphorbia grandidens* in the
        Fish River Valley near Grahamstown
        (eastern Cape Province)

2 (ur) *Euphorbia resinifera*, on the slopes of the
        Atlas Mountains (Morocco)

3 (ml) *Euphorbia phillipsiae* in rock clefts near
        Moula Matr (high plateau of Mukeiras,
        southern Arabia)

4 (mr) *Euphorbia virosa* in the rock desert o
        Richtersveld near Modderdrift on t
        Orange River

5 (ll) *Euphorbia micracantha*

6 (lr) *Euphorbia decidua*

Plate 25.

(t.l.) Tip of a young plant
of *Euphorbia grandidens*

(t.r.) Young plant of
Euphorbia tetragona

(b.l.) *Euphorbia squarrosa*,
uprooted (Grahams-
town, southeastern
Cape Province)

(b.r.) *Euphorbia stellata*, lateral branch treated as
a cutting

Plate 28.

1 (ul) *Euphorbia capuronii*
2 (ur) *Euphorbia genoudiana*
3 (ml) *Euphorbia lophogona*
4 (mr) *Euphorbia delphinensis*
5 (ll) *Euphorbia durani*
6 (lr) *Euphorbia millotii*

Plate 29.

1 (ul) *Euphorbia cylindrifolia* ssp. *cylindrifolia*
2 (ur) *Euphorbia cylindrifolia* ssp. *cylindrifolia*, showing the formation of
        runners
3 (mu) *Euphorbia decaryi*
4 (mr) *Euphorbia françoisii*
5 (ml) Forest of *Euphorbia stenoclada* on sand dunes in the valley of the
        Fiherenana near Tuléar (southern Madagascar)
6 (ll)   *Euphorbia primulaefolia*, highlands near Tananarive (central Mada-
        gascar)
7 (lr)   *Euphorbia primulaefolia* removed from the ground

Plate 30. (facing page)

1 (ul) *Monadenium lugardae*
2 (ur) *Monadenium yattanum*
3 (ml) *Monadenium guentheri*
4 (mr) *Monadenium schubei*
5 (ll) *Monadenium ellenbeckii*
6 (lm) Leafless shoot of *Monadenium magnificum* (the
inflorescence is not fully
developed)
7 (lr) *Monadenium spinescens*

Plate 31.

1 (ul) *Monadenium echinulatum*
2 (ur) *Synadenium cupulare*
3 (ml) *Pedilanthus smallii*
4 (mr) *Jatropha podagrica*
5 (ll) *Jatropha peltata*
6 (lr) *Jatropha berlandieri*

Plate 32. On the morphology of stapelia[

1 (ul)   Leafy shoot of *Frerea indica*

2 (um)   *Caralluma priogonium* shoot wit▮
          scale leaves

3 (ur)   Shoot of *Echidnopsis* species, wh▮
          mamillae bear tiny leaflets

4 (ml)   *Stapelianthus pilosus;* the mamil▮
          end in hair-like tips

5 (mm)   *Hoodia bainii,* mamillae end in ▮
          thorn tips

6 (mr)   *Caralluma mammillaris* with th▮
          mamillae

7 (ll)   *Tavaresia grandiflora,* mamillae ▮
          3 thorns

8 (lm)   *Trichocaulon meloforme,* shoot ax▮
          with flat podaria

9 (lr)   *Caralluma baldratii,* shoot with▮
          mamillae elongated leaf-like

same time the strongest, is up to 4 cm long and is the actual axil shoot; it corresponds to a sterile inflorescence. The shorter thorns at its base are pseudo-thorns, i.e., they are the suberized inflorescence stalks remaining on the plant and having a terminal male or female cyathium at their tips. Nectar glands are green or purplish red.

I recognize the following varieties of *E. horrida:*

var. *horrida:* nectar glands dark reddish purple.

var. *major:* larger in all parts and more robust than the type; nectar glands dark reddish purple.

var. *striata:* shoots silvery gray, waxy, and with light-green cross-banding (Plate 22,5), the most beautiful of all the varieties!

The distribution area of *E. horrida* is eastern Cape Province (Willowmore, Steytlerville, Jansenville Districts). It grows here usually on rocky plains covered with low bushes, which is in contrast to the closely related

E. polygona HAW. (Plate 22,3 and 4),

the "many-ribbed spurge," which prefers steep slopes and inaccessible cliffs, from which the long columns frequently hang like fat snakes.

E. polygona differs from *E. horrida* in its thinner columns, greater number of ribs (up to 20), and shorter thorns, which on old shoots are sometimes completely absent. Also *E. polygona*, because of its basal off-shooting, forms larger clumps (Plate 22,3) of erect or curved columns up to 1.5 m long and up to 15 cm thick and are unbranched and grayish green; its narrow ribs, up to 1.5 cm high, are often undulate. In regard to thorn formation the conditions here are the same as in *E. horrida*, but the number of thorns is less. The cyathia have dark purple nectar glands. *Distribution:* eastern Cape area (Port Elizabeth, Uitenhage, Albany Districts).

The cultivation of these two beautiful species is not difficult. They require an alkaline, sandy soil and a sunny location; propagation is by seed or cuttings.

E. polygona and *E. horrida* are the only host plants of the parasitic dwarf "mistletoe," *Viscum minimum*, which penetrates the axis tissue with its roots and breaks the surface of the stem with tiny leaf and flower shoots (Plate 22,4). With its large, coral-red berries the parasite makes a splendid decoration on its host plant, which, by the way, is only slightly damaged by it.

Related to the above two species is

Euphorbia inconstantia R.A. DYER,

the "inconstant spurge" (Plate 22,7), which in regard to growth-form, size, and thorn formation bears a great similarity to both *E. polygona* and *E. pentagona*. According to WHITE, DYER, and SLOANE this may be a natural hybrid of the two, because until now it has been found only in areas where the other two grow or only a few miles away. The highly variable growth-form of *E. inconstantia* seems to confirm its hybrid nature: it resembles *E. pentagona* at one time and *E. polygona* at another.

Another multi-ribbed columnar euphorbia with inflorescence thorns is

Euphorbia cereiformis L. (Plate 22,6),

the "cactus spurge." Although it is found in all collections, nothing is known of its origin or distribution. Therefore it is among the questionable species and the grower, according to WHITE, DYER, and SLOANE, "while observing his or her beautiful plants called *E. cereiformis* should always think of the mysterious atmosphere surrounding the name of this plant in the past 200 years." Hardly any spurge has had so many names as *E. cereiformis* L.; it has been known as *E. erosa* WILLD., *E. odontophylla* WILLD., *E. polygonata* LODD., *E. echinata* SALM-DYCK, and *Treisia erosa* HAW. In spite of its uncertain origin, *E. cereiformis* is a very pretty plant resembling the columnar cereus in its growth-form. Its dark-green columns, up to 10 cm thick with 9 to 15 ribs and basal off-sets, have tiny leaves visible only at the tip and numerous thorns up to 2 cm long. These thorns appear in groups of 1 to 3 in the axils of the mamilla, are red-violet when young and gray at maturity, and have tiny scale leaves.

The plant seldom blooms in cultivation; the cyathia are unisexual and dioecious.

Euphorbia stellaespina HOW. (Color Plate 2,6; Plate 12,3)

holds a special position within the section of Anthacanthae, in that the thorns giving it its species name are branched in a star shape. *E. stellaespina*, with its shoots up to 15 cm thick and with 10 to 16 ribs, forms rather compact clumps up to 1 m high and up to 1.5 m in diameter (Color Plate 2). The thorns, which are frequently arranged in patches, are reddish with gray wax when young and are grayish brown when mature. They are found singly in the axils of the broadly hexagonal podaria and bear a terminal cyathium. Below these emerge rather short, sterile thorns from the axils of scale-shaped bracts of the primary inflorescence thorns. These thorns are arranged in a swirl, resulting in star-shaped, branched thorn systems, which give the plant its typical appearance. The "star thorns" appear even on young plants, where, however, the primary thorn is sterile and a cyathium does not form.

E. stellaespina inhabits a rather large area; its distribution area stretches from the Great Karroo eastward into the Willowmore District and north into the dry areas of Little Namaqualand. Because of its bizarre appearance *E. stellaespina* is a favorite and is not difficult to cultivate if you provide a sunny, warm location. Propagation is possible from cuttings.

Euphorbia pillansii N.E. BR. (Plate 22,8)

has branched inflorescence thorns, but in contrast to those of *E. stellaespina* these are pseudo-thorns, i.e., suberized inflorescence branches.

Section DIACANTHIUM BOISS.

Here one finds the majority of all euphorbias. Common to all of them are "stipular thorns" (see p. 35 ff.), which always appear in pairs at the base of the deciduous leaf blade. This explains the section name Diacanthium, the "two-thorned one!" Hereafter, when I speak of thorns, I mean the dorsal thorns, mentioned on page 35. The actual stipular thorns are usually very small.

There is a great variety of growth-form in this group: along with trees of often gigantic proportions *(E. candelabrum,* Plate *9,1)* one finds large scrubs and miniature, creeping species. Although hobbyists are most interested in the latter, the tree and scrub forms are also worthy of cultivation, for their young growth and cuttings are often of special beauty.

In the following paragraphs I can present only a limited selection from the great variety of species in this group.

Euphorbia avasmontana DTR. (Plate 23,1),

named after the Auas Mountains, is a plant with a short, barely protruding main stem, from the base of which emerge numerous, arched, unbranched lateral branches with 5 to 8 ribs and becoming up to 7 cm thick. As the older basal shoots die off, new branches are produced from the tip. The thorns are hard and sharp, 1 to 2 cm long, their shields hardening into a horn-like ridge; the cyathia are near the tip of the shoot, usually in threes, and have short stalks. The nectar glands are yellowish. *Distribution:* South Africa and Namibia, frequently appearing in masses, mostly on granitic rock.

Of the same growth-form is also the "Hottentot euphorbia,"

Euphorbia hottentota MARL. (Color Plate 2,5),

which heretofore has been found only in the mountains in the vicinity of Kuboes in the Richtersveld, where it forms rather large masses on primordial rock. The main stem is short, producing numerous, arched shoots up to 2 m long and strikingly slender—only up to 4 cm thick—with 4 to 5 (−6) angular, gray-green branches. The thorns are short, 3 to 5 mm long, with their shields joined into a continuous horny ridge. The cyathia appear usually in threes in the axis of the mamilla. The central cyathium is male; the other two are hermaphroditic.

Euphorbia cactus EHRENB. ex BOISS. (Plate 23,2)

is a candelabrum-type bush 1 to 3 m high with a short main stem and numerous, arched, usually 3-edged (seldom 4), gray-green (reddish brown at the tip), darkly marbled branches 7 to 10 cm thick. Thorns in the new growth are leather brown; at maturity they are gray, very hard, 1 to 4 cm long, and greatly flared, their shields merging into a continuous, light gray, frequently somewhat undulate, arched horny ridge. The leaves are very small, falling soon, and inflorescences are numerous in the apical region of the shoot. The cyathia appear usually in threes, with yellow, diagonally kidney-shaped nectar glands. *Habitat:* southern Arabia and Ethiopia.

The true *E. cactus,* seldom found in cultivation, is a very pretty species that, because of its dry, hot origins, requires a very warm soil and only a little water.

On trips in southern Arabia (Aden Province), we (J. LAVRANOS and I) found in Wadi Maadin a large mass of *E. cactus* with spiralled lateral branches. Because seedling plants showed the same phenomenon (Plate 23,4), I must assume that it was a mutation.

E. cactus should not be confused with

Euphorbia pseudocactus BRGR. (Plate 23,7),

which comes from Natal and which is common in collections in botanical gardens. It differs from the above by its much thinner, vividly green, more strongly marbled stems with 4 to 5 ribs and by the much shorter thorns that reach only up to 1.5 cm. It is a fast-growing and easily propagated species.

Euphorbia canariensis L. (Plate 23,3),

the "Canary Island spurge," in the course of many years forms gigantic shrubs up to 2.5 m high and several meters in diameters. The shoots usually have 5, seldom 4 or 6 edges, and the fruits are large, and reddish purple. *Habitat:* Canary Islands.

As a small plant it is well suited for pot cultivation.

Euphorbia candelabrum TREM. (Plate 9,1),

the "candelabra spurge," in its habitat is a tree up to 10 m tall with a short stem and a stout, richly branched crown. Its branches usually have 4 ribs and have stiff, brown stipular thorns. The leaves are small with elongated, oval, pointed blades, and the cyathia occur in great numbers, usually at the shoot tip.

According to investigations by P.R.O BALLY (oral communication), *E. ingens* E. MEY. and *E. ammak* SCHWEINF. are the same as *E. candelabrum.* Therefore, its distribution area would stretch from Natal to Somalia and southern Arabia.

As a young plant *E. candelabrum,* with its greenish white striped shoots, is very pretty and promising; it is easy to cultivate and grows fast.

Now and then a strikingly white-marked mutant of *E. candelabrum* with little chlorophyll is found in cultivation (Plate 11,2).

Euphorbia coerulescens HAW. (Plate 3,6 and Color Plate 2,8), (= *E. virosa* BOISS. var. *coerulescens* BRGR.),

forms large, richly branched shrubs up to 1.5 m tall, which often appear in masses several kilometers square (Plate 3,6). Their 4- to 6-edged, 3 to 5 cm thick, greenish blue shoots are divided into rhythmic links, each link representing one growing period. Its thorns are sharp, dark brown, and the cyathia appear in 3-flowered cymes, which occur in great numbers at the ends of the shoots. The nectar glands are large and vividly yellow. *Distribution:* dry areas of southeastern Cape Province.

In times of great drought *E. coerulescens* is fed to cattle. The burning taste of the milky sap is said to disappear when the shoots are cut into pieces and allowed to dry in the sun for several days.

The bluish green color of the shoot epidermis makes *E. coerulescens* a very pretty species; even though it grows slowly it is easy to cultivate.

Euphorbia cooperi N.E. BR. (Plate 23,6).

This is a tree-form, 3 to 7 m tall, with a thick main stem and a broad crown of branches which have 5 to 6 ribs and are clearly divided into yearly growth sections. Its leaves are small, spoon-shaped, and deciduous. The thorns stand out horizontally; in their youth they are brown, later gray. Their shields unite into a continuous horny ridge. The cyathia are in sessile, 3-flowered cymes; the central cyathium is male, and the two lateral ones female. The nectar glands are diagonally oval and yellowish. *Distribution:* Transvaal, Zululand, and Swaziland, almost forming forests. As young plants they are very decorative and fast growing; they pose no special problems in cultivation.

A morphologically interesting spurge is

Euphorbia decidua BALLY et LEACH (Plate 24,6),

which in growth-form is similar to *E. micracantha* (Plate 24,5) but differs considerably from it morphologically. As the name indicates, the branches are deciduous and usually live for only one growth period.

E. decidua is a representative of the fleshy root geophytes. It has a stout, slightly branched, napiform root, which near the tip is reduced to a short, thick shoot axis covered by the scars of the falling branches. From its main stem it develops, each year, a tuft of short, upright or arched, unbranched, lateral, 3-angled shoots up to 12 cm long. Their ribs undulate through the mamilla-shaped podaria. Foliage is minute, barely 2 mm long; at the base of the leaf petioles are two hooked, downward-curving, greatly flared, leather-brown dorsal thorns 2 to 3 mm long. Sometimes just above these is another tiny pair of thorns, visible only through a magnifying glass. Floral initiations are found in the foliage leaf-axils, but these are not developed. At the end of the growing period the foliage is cast off, and from the apical region appear the short-stemmed, single or dual flower buds, which now produce the cyathia. This behavior is unique among euphorbias.

In the closely related Angolan *Euphorbia imitata* N.E. BR., also a fleshy root geophyte, the branches are similarly cast off, but they are also a part of the cyathia-forming system. In it there is no differentiation between purely vegetative and fertile growth.

The distribution of the interesting *E. decidua* stretches from Angola, across Zambia and Zimbabwe, and into Malawi. In its branchless state the plant requires strict rest.

Euphorbia echinus HOOK. f. et COSS. (Plate 23,8)

forms richly branched shrubs up to 1 m tall. From a central stem emerge numerous, 5–8(–13)-ribbed lateral branches 4 to 5 cm thick and arching upwards. Leaves are scoop-shaped and deciduous. The thorns are 1 to 1.5 cm long, reddish in youth, later gray, with merging shields. Cymes are sub-sessile with 4 to 5 male and hermaphroditic cyathia, and the nectar glands are diagonally elongated and brownish red. *Distribution:* southern Morocco.

E. echinus is a fast-growing species suitable as stock for grafting.

Euphorbia fruticosa FORSK. (Plate 23,9)

forms rather compact columnar mounds up to 60 cm in diameter and up to 50 cm tall, with 10- to 13-ribbed, gray-green shoots up to 10 cm thick. Thorns on the new shoots are reddish, later gray, and dense, and the cyathia are numerous at the tip, with yellow nectar glands. *Distribution:* southern Arabia: Yemen and Aden Province near Mukeiras.

Euphorbia grandicornis GOEB. ex N.E. BR. (Plate 11,4)

A slightly branched shrub 1 to 2 m tall, it has a short main stem and ascending lateral branches having 3 broad ribs and is clearly divided into seasonal growth. It is uniformly green or lightly striped, up to 7 cm in diameter. The thorns are very hard, up to 7 cm long, light brown at the tip but a gray at maturity, and their shields are united into a continuous horny ridge. The leaves are small and deciduous. The cyathia are large, in 3-flowered, short-stalked cymes. The two lateral cyathia are female, the middle one is male, and the fruits are dark red. *Distribution:* in coastal forests of Kenya through Tanzania to Natal (Zululand) and Mozambique.

E. grandicornis is a generally well-known and favored species with a bizarre appearance due to its prominent thorns. Seedling plants are very pretty; their shoots are striped a vivid gray-green, whereas the older plants are uniformly gray-green. Propagation by cuttings is possible.

Of the same growth-form and equally beautiful is

Euphorbia grandialata R.A. DYER,

similar to the above but found only in Transvaal (Lydenburg District). In young plants the broad-ribbed (3 to 4 ribs), gray-green shoots are decorated from the base of the ribs to the mamillae with yellow-green cross-bands. The dorsal thorns are, however, considerably shorter than in *E. grandicornis*. Above them are two tiny stipular thorns.

Euphorbia grandidens HAW. (Plate 24,1; 25,1)

is a tree-form plant up to 16 m tall with a thick, round stem and ascending, rather fat, lateral, primary branches. The short, usually 3-angled, lateral secondary and later branches, found deeply seated between the mamillae, are short lived and fall after just a few years, and so they are found only on the apical regions of the stouter shoots and gather there in a swirl (Plate 25,1).

E. grandidens is wide spread in the coastal area of southeastern Cape Province, sometimes appearing as forests (Plate 24,1) and frequently associated with *E. triangularis* DESF. and *E. tetragona* HAW. The former is a tree up to 18 m tall with a thick stem and 3- to 5-ribbed lateral branches. In *Euphorbia tetragona* (Plate 25,2), a tree up to 13 m tall, the last branches are usually 4-ribbed.

In spite of their tree shape, all three species are worthy of cultivation and as small pot plants are bizarrely beautiful.

Euphorbia officinarum L. (Plate 13,6)

forms columns up to 1 m tall that are sparsely branched, with 9 to 13, usually 11 ribs. Its thorns are 5 to 15 mm long and are whitish gray. *Habitat:* unknown, probably Morocco.

Variety *beaumierana* (HOOK. f. et COSS.) MAIRE differs from the type by its more vigorous branching; it forms shrubs up to 1.5 m in diameter and up to 2 m tall.

Euphorbia phillipsiae N.E. BR. (Plate 24,*3*)

is a very rare, small, clustering plant growing in rock crevices and has shoots 2 to 3 cm thick, usually with 9 ribs, gray-green to sharp green. Its foliage is small, triangular, and deciduous, and the thorns are up to 16 mm long, spreading, thin, and brown. The cyathia are small, with yellowish nectar glands. *Distribution:* Somalia and southern Arabia.

E. phillipsiae is a beautiful, small species, which in cultivating requires a warm but somewhat shady location.

Euphorbia resinifera BRGR. (Plate 13,*2;* Plate 24,*2*)

in its habitat forms spherical shrubs up to 2 m high and up to 3 m in diameter; they are much branched and compact and in places dominate the landscape on the slopes of the Antiatlas. Their light-green, 4-angled shoots reveal tiny, deciduous leaves only in the tip region, otherwise they have only brownish thorns that become gray with age. The cyathia usually occur in 3-flowered cymes; the nectar glands are diagonally elliptical or slightly rounded to heart-shaped, yellow. *Habitat:* Morocco, southwest of the city of Marrakesh on the lower slopes of the High Atlas and the Antiatlas mountains.

E. resinifera is common in collections and easy to grow; it is well suited as a stock for grafts. It is the source of the drug "Euphorbium," traded since antiquity. A white milky sap that dries in the air, it is obtained by making cuts in the shoot axis.

Euphorbia squarrosa HAW. (Plate 25,*3*)

is a fleshy-rooted euphorbia; the short, subterranean primary shoot is equipped with a stout carrot-like root. From its top emerges a wreath of creeping or semi-erect shoots 4 to 20 cm long with three edges, whose ribs are deeply delineated by the mamilla-like podaria. The thorns are basally thickened, 1 to 6 mm long, reddish green, later gray, at the tip of the mamillae. The cyathia occur in threes in short-stalked cymes, and the nectar glands are light-green. *Distribution:* southwestern Cape Province.

E. squarrosa is decorative but, like all other napiform-rooted euphorbias, difficult to cultivate. Propagation is best from seed, because branch cuttings rarely form fleshy roots and thus lose their typical growth-form.

Related very closely to the above species is

Euphorbia stellata WILLD. (Plate 25,*4*),

which resembles the former completely in its growth-form; it differs from it, however, in its feathery, whitish marking on the shoots, in the less-pronounced mamillae, and in the dark yellow nectar glands. *Distribution:* southeastern Cape Province (Uitenhage, Port Elizabeth, and Albany Districts).

Related to both of the above is the beautiful

Euphorbia micracantha BOISS. (Plate 24,*5*),

an interesting dwarf euphorbia with a long, fleshy root and a very short, thick primary shoot, at whose tip a wreath of 4 to 14 cm long shoots emerge. These shoots are up to 1.5 cm thick and have 4 ribs. The podaria protrude only slightly; the thorns are short, thin, and greatly flared. The cyathia are small, and the nectar glands are greenish yellow. *Distribution:* rare in southeastern Cape Province.

One of the most interesting South African dwarf euphorbias is

Euphorbia tortirama R.A. DYER,

the "twisted spurge," whose 6 to 30 long and up to 4.5 cm thick, three-angled lateral branches are spirally twisted (Plate 23,*5*). Such contortion is not rare in euphorbias, but is usually an abnormality. In *E. tortirama,* on the other hand, the twisting is normal and is inherited. The lateral branches emerge in great numbers from the head of a large, fleshy root and are covered with long mammary-shaped podaria, which at their tip have two stout, flared, leather-brown thorns, whose shields fuse into a continuous ridge. The cyathia occur in groups of three in the tip region of the twisted shoots. The central cyathium is male, the two on each side are hermaphroditic, and the nectar glands are yellowish green. *Distribution:* Transvaal.

The cultivation of *E. tortirama* is not very difficult. Branches treated as cuttings retain their spiral habit but rarely form a fleshy root.

Euphorbia virosa WILLD. (= *E. dinteri* BRGR.) (Plate 24,*4*),

the "poisonous spurge," is a slow-maturing species, which grows in extremely dry rock deserts of southwestern Africa (Namaqualand). It has a short (30 cm at the most), frequently spiralled main stem, from which emerges a number of thick, irregularly constricted, arched lateral branches with 5 to 8 ribs. The shrubs, when about 1.5 m high, may reach a diameter of 2 m. The thorns are very stiff, greatly flared, up to 1 cm long, and their shields are fused into a continuous horny ridge. The cyathia occur in 3-flowered cymes in the apical region of the shoots.

E. virosa lives up to its name because it has a very poisonous milky sap, which was used by bushmen and Hottentots to make poisonous arrowheads.

Section MONACANTHAE

The species of this group are limited to tropical western Africa. They are succulent shrubs with thick, round shoots that are covered by large scars from the fallen leaf blades. The thorns always appear singly underneath the leaf insertion (Plate 11,*9*) (see page 35). The following species are hard to distinguish from one another.

Euphorbia sapinii DE WILD.

forms slightly branched shrubs up to 1.6 m high, with round, lateral branches, 5 to 10 cm thick with gray cork at the base, and with tips covered by leaf scars and thorns. The latter are leather-brown, the upper side is flattened, and the base is thickened. There are 8 to 15 leaves in a terminal rosette. These leaves are broadly linear, pointed, 8 to 16 cm long, up to 2 cm wide, with a red edge, narrowing to a short stem. The cyathia usually occur in threes. *Distribution:* Zaire.

Euphorbia unispina N.E. BR. (Plate 26,*1*)

is a richly branched shrub up to 3 m high with thick, round shoots covered by spiral leaf pads and short, conical thorns that are flat at the base. The leaves appear in a terminal rosette and are 5 to 10 cm long and up to 2.5 cm wide, frequently serrated at the tip, undulate along the margin, and narrowing into a petiole near the base. Cymes have 3 to 9 flowers, are almost sessile, and appear in the axils of fallen leaves. *Distribution:* dry areas of west Africa (Zaire, northern Nigeria).

Eastern Sudan is the native habitat for the very similar

Euphorbia venenifica TREM. et KOTSCHY (Plate 11,9),

which differs from the above by its thorns, which are not flat at the base, and by its differently shaped leaves. The leaves are broadly lanceolate, rounded at the tip, serrate, and very curly-undulate along the margins.

All three species shed their leaves as the dormant period (winter) begins and then need a strictly observed vegetative rest period. When leaves begin to grow again they need a lot of water.

Section TRIACANTHAE

All the species of this group are of dwarf growth-form and therefore are especially liked by hobbyists. Their main distribution is in the dry areas of northern Africa (including Arabia), and all species are characterzed by the fact that the podaria have 3 thorns, a central, rather stout dorsal thorn and two lateral, rather short stipular thorns (Plate 11,6). The leaves are reduced to small, deciduous scales that are visible only in the newer growth.

Euphorbia graciliramea PAX (Plate 11,6; 16,2 and 3)

is a miniature shrub with a fleshy root, whose numerous, reclining, ascending, or arched, 5 to 10 cm long and 1 cm thick, gray-green or yellowish striped branches appear to be almost quadrangular because of the long, succulent leaf bases (sometimes the shoots are also rather round). Leaves are scoop-shaped and deciduous; thorns in the new growth are brown, later gray; and dorsal thorns are up to 2 cm long, protruding horizontally with elongated shields about 5 mm long. Cyathia occur in the axils, in threes, and are short stalked; the central one is male, the two lateral ones hermaphroditic or female. Nectar glands are diagonally oval, 3 mm wide, fleshy, entire, bright yellow. *Distribution:* eastern Africa (highlands of Kenya).

E. graciliramea is an interesting species, which in growth-form and in coloration is somewhat variable, blooms readily, and is easy to propagate by cuttings. In cultivation the shoots can become as long as 30 cm.

Euphorbia glochidiata PAX (Plate 26,4 and 5)

is a small dwarf shrub with a fleshy root and upright shoots, which are up to 30 cm long, ca. 1 cm thick; the long leaf bases make them appear quadrangular. The shoots are gray-blue-green, lighter between the ribs; leaves are staggered opposite each other, are scoop-shaped, and soon fall. Below the leaf blade is a stout, horizontal "thorn foot" up to 2 cm long and having 2 dorsal thorns and a very long, brown shield (Plate 26,5). At the base of the "foot" are two lateral, fine, horizontal stipular thorns. Cyathia occur in the leaf axils, always in threes, and are very short-stalked; the middle one is male, the two lateral ones are female. Nectar glands are dark purple, the serrated interglandular bracts are vivid carmine red, and fruits

are glabrous with dark red margins. *Distribution:* highlands of Kenya (vicinity of Nairobi, on black soil, ca. 1800 m) and Somalia.

E. glochidiata is one of the most beautiful dwarf euphorbias of eastern and northern Africa, which in cultivation blooms willingly and plentifully. It is distinguished from most others by its vividly purple-red nectar glands. Propagation is easy from cuttings, and in cultivation this plant can attain a length of up to 1 m.

Euphorbia monacantha PAX (Plate 26,7)

is a small, richly or sparsely branched dwarf shrub with cylindrical or slightly angular, gray-green, brightly marbled shoots up to 2 cm thick. Thorns occur in threes (the two lateral ones are sometimes missing, thus explaining the name "monacantha," the "uni-thorn"); the dorsal thorns are horizontal, gray, 1.5 to 2 cm long with a short, gray shield. Cyathia occur in threes, preferably at the tip, with olive-green, diagonally elliptical nectar glands. *Distribution:* Somalia. Slow growing, seldom seen in cultivation.

Closely related to this is

Euphorbia triaculeata FORSK. (Plate 26,6),

the "three-thorned spurge," a small, sparsely branched dwarf shrub with 10 to 15 cm long shoots about 1 cm thick that are gray-green and rounded or with a suggestion of 5 angles; the podaria are slightly protruding. Thorns have a small, 3-cornered shield; the dorsal thorn is 1.5 to 3 cm long, gray-brown on the new growth, later gray, and the two stipular thorns are very tiny. *Distribution:* Arabia (eastern Aden), Ethiopia.

E. triacantha EHRENB. is similar but smaller than the above.

Section TETRACANTHIAE

The species in this group are also of dwarf growth-form. They are all distinguished by the formation of 4 thorns on the podarium (Plate 11, 7 and 8) (see page 36).

One of the most beautiful of this group is

Euphorbia aeruginosa SCHWEICK. (Color Plate 3,2),

a much-branched dwarf shrub with rounded or slightly angular shoots up to 20 cm long and 1 cm thick, often spiralled and of a striking copper-green color. Leaves are scoop-shaped and deciduous. Thorns are reddish brown to golden yellow, appearing in fours; the two larger ones are up to 2 cm long with long, copper-brown shields. Cyathia occur in groups of 3 and are small, with yellowish green nectar glands. *Distribution:* Transvaal (Zoutpansberge).

Because of the remarkable copper-green coloration of its shoot epidermis, in contrast to its yellow thorns, *E. aeruginosa* is one of the most decorative euphorbias. It is propagated easily by cuttings.

Closely related to the above is

Euphorbia schinzii PAX

(named after the Swiss botanist SCHINZ), a dwarf euphorbia with subterranean runners. It has numerous, quadrangular, dark blue-green shoots, 10 to 15 cm long and up to 1 cm thick, that spread across the ground. Thorns occur in fours;

the two basal ones are up to 1 cm long and dark brown, and the two upper ones are small, 1 to 2 mm long. Shields are greatly elongated; cyathia appear in groups of three, almost sub-sessile, with bright yellow nectar glands. *Distribution:* Transvaal (Pretoria), southern Zimbabwe, and Botswana, usually in clefts in the rocks.

Closely related to both of the above is

Euphorbia angustiflora PAX (Plate 27,*1*),

the "sparsely blooming spurge," a richly branched dwarf shrub with quadrangular, dark green shoots, 10 to 30 cm long, ca. 1 cm thick. Its ribs are constricted by greatly mounded podaria between the nodes. The two dorsal thorns are stout, leather brown, with their brown shields running down the stem 5 to 7 mm. Cyathia appear in groups of three, and are short-stalked (differing from *E. schinzii*) and small, with yellowish green glands. *Distribution:* from Tanzania to Mozambique.

Euphorbia isacantha PAX (Plate 26,*9*),

the "equal thorned spurge." A dwarf shrub up to 50 cm tall, it has quadrangular shoots ca. 1 cm thick; its leaves are scoop-shaped and deciduous; thorns are small, reddish brown, occurring in fours. Stipular thorns point upwards and are equal in length to the dorsal thorns, which point downward; their shields are small, barely elongated. *Distribution:* Tanzania.

E. isacantha, because of the four nearly equal thorns, is easy to recognize. It is also a fast-growing plant.

Euphorbia knuthii PAX (Plate 11,*7*),

named for the botanist R. KNUTH, also belongs in the group with *E. schinzii,* but differs from it in its fleshy root and unbranched shoots up to 15 cm long, ca. 1 cm thick, which have 3 to 4 ribs and a dark green epidermis with lighter central stripes. The podaria are greatly mounded. Thorns occur in fours; the two lower ones are longer (4 to 8 mm), and the two upper ones are 1 to 2 mm long. Cyathia appear singly or in groups of 3, with yellowish green nectar glands. *Distribution:* Mozambique (Lourenço-Marques).

Euphorbia nyassae PAX (= *E. tetracantha* PAX) (Plate 26,*8*)

A shrub up to 0.5 m tall, it has slightly angular, gray-green, marbled shoots ca. 1 cm thick; the podaria have 4 thorns, of which the two lower dorsal ones point down and are considerably longer than the two upper stipular thorns; cyathia appear in groups of 3, with yellowish red nectar glands. *Distribution:* Tanzania (Nyassaland).

Euphorbia subsalsa HIERN (Plate 11,*8*)

is a small, richly branched dwarf shrub up to 1 m high with numerous, 4-ribbed branches up to 1.2 cm thick. Thorns appear in fours, up to 1 cm long, dark gray, with long shields; leaves are small, scoop-shaped, and deciduous. Cyathia usually occur in threes, and are small, with upright, yellowish nectar glands.

The specific name *"subsalsa"* (salt spurge), refers to the type-locality of the plant, the Pedra de Sal (salt rocks) in southwest Angola.

Euphorbia ndurumensis BALLY (= *E. taitensis* PAX)[11] (Color Plate 3,*1*)

The plant has a fleshy root and few, upright, more or less richly branched, gray-green shoots up to 30 cm long (in cultivation up to 80 cm). Their margins are usually dirty red. Thorns are thin, the two lower ones ca. 0.5 cm long, the upper ones shorter and weaker; their shields stretch downward as a horny ridge almost to the next node. Cyathia are distributed almost all over the shoot, in groups of three, and are short stalked; nectar glands are diagonally oval, olive green-yellow, with the interglandular bracts reddish violet. *Habitat:* Kenya (near Taita). A very pretty, small, decorative species.

Euphorbia uhligiana PAX (Color Plate 3,*3*)

has a thick, fleshy main root, from which emerge numerous short, upright or arched (downwards), 4-ribbed branches up to 15 cm long and up to 1 cm thick; the leaves are scale-shaped. Mamillae are long, triangular, and flattened, with two hard, flared dorsal thorns, 0.5 cm long at their tip; the gray shields descend far along the podaria. Stipular thorns are small; cyathia appear in groups of three, are short stalked, and are arrayed over the entire length of the shoot. The nectar glands are intense yellow. In var. *furcata* the shoots are stouter, the podaria are longer, and the thorns are much harder. *Distribution:* highlands of Kenya.

Indian euphorbias

All of the following species belong to section Diacanthium; some of them are very common in cultivation.

Euphorbia antiquorum L. (Plate 13,*3*)

A tree or shrub up to 4 m high, it has a stem with 4 to 5 angles and lateral branches that are upright, segmented, and have 2 to 3 ribs that are sinuate. Thorns are separated 2 to 3 cm, with small, roundish shields; leaves are small. Cyathia appear at the ends of the shoots, singly or in groups of three, with diagonally elongated, yellowish glands. *Distribution:* on dry hills, in eastern India.

Similar to the above is

Euphorbia trigona HAW. (Plate 13,*4*),

the "three-ribbed spurge," differing from the above by its low, greatly sinuate ribs. Shoots are mostly 3-angled, with whitish green markings; leaf-blades are 3 to 5 cm long, with a short tip. *Distribution:* eastern India and the Molucca Islands.

E. trigona is a fast-growing species, whose shoot markings

---

[11] According to P.R.O. BALLY, this species must be renamed *E. ndurumensis* BALLY, because BOISSIER has already described a *E. taitensis* from Tahiti.

make it a very decorative species; it is easy to propagate by cuttings.

Belonging to the same growth-form is

Euphorbia lactea HAW. (Plate 27,*2*),

the "milky white spurge." Branches have 3 to 4 angles and are 3 to 5 cm in diameter, dark green with milky white, irregular markings. Ribs are strongly sinuate because of the tooth-like, protruding leaf pads; thorns are ca. 5 mm long, brown; and leaves are small, roundish, and pointed.

In comparison to *E. trigona*, *E. lactea* is relatively slow growing. Cristate forms of *E. lactea* are often cultivated (see Plate 18,*6*).

Euphorbia neriifolia L.,

the "oleander-leafed spurge," is a richly branched, deciduous tree or shrub, 6 to 7 m tall, with a round stem and swirled, light-green lateral branches that are slightly 5-angled, up to 4 cm thick. Thorns are short, black, and flared; leaf blades are 7 to 12 cm long, fleshy-leathery, bright green, obovate, and pointed, narrowing into a short petiole. Scars of the fallen leaves are visible for a long time; inflorescences appear in the axils of the upper leaves, 1 to 7 cyathia.

E. neriifolia, widespread in western India (Bombay Province and on the Dekkan plateau), is frequently used in tropical areas as a hedge plant. When leaves are present *E. neriifolia* requires a lot of water, but after the leaves fall a rest period should be strictly observed.

Similar is

Euphorbia nivulia BUCH.-HAM. (Plate 27,*3*),

a richly branched shrub with almost round shoots; leaf pads slightly protruding and widely separated; thorns short, flared, pointed downwards, and black; cyathia in groups of three. *Distribution:* common on dry hills in western India.

Closely related to the two above is

Euphorbia undulatifolia JANSE,

the "wavy leafed spurge" (Plate 11,*1*), a tree or shrub up to 3 m tall with 5 distinct ribs and lateral branches that are 5 to 7 cm thick. Ribs are sinuate because of the greatly mounded podaria; leaves occur in a terminal rosette with longitudinally oval blades, 15 to 18 cm long, up to 6 cm wide, narrowing into a long petiole, and undulate on the margins (differing from *E. neriifolia*). Leaf scars are visible for a long time after the leaves fall; thorns are small, sharp, and blackish brown.

Although this very decorative plant is common in collections, it is known only in cultivation. It is assumed to be native to India.

Euphorbia royleana BOISS. (Plate 27,*4*)

forms trees up to 8 m high with a stem ca. 50 cm thick and upright. It has segmented branches that have 5 ribs and are up to 7 cm thick. Ribs are almost straight, slightly sinuate; thorns are 4 to 5 cm long, pointed downward. Cyathia occur usually in groups of three and are large, up to 1.5 cm in diameter, with yellow nectar glands. *Distribution:* India, dry hills of the Siwalik mountain chain up to 2000 m.

South American species

In comparison to the Old World, South America has only a few succulent euphorbias. Although some of them have been in cultivation for a long time, they are not very attractive and because of their scrubby growth are ill-suited for the hobbyist. Best known are the species from section Pteroneurae BRGR. (see page 40), from which we list the following:

Euphorbia sipolisii N.E. BR. (Plate 27,*5*)

This is a shrub with segmented branches, which are vaguely 4-angled due to the long leaf base, and are sometimes round. Segments are ca. 10 cm long and 1 cm thick, gray-green to reddish; leaves are small, triangular, pointed, and deciduous. Inflorescences are lateral and terminal, with few cyathia, which are surrounded by the 2 to 3 pale-green scape bracts (cyathophylls). *Habitat:* Brazil (Prov. Minas Gerais).

Similar is

Euphorbia pteroneura BRGR. (Plate 27,*6*),

distinguished from the above by its 5- to 6-ribbed shoots. Its leaves are deciduous, short petiolated, 2 to 3 cm long and 1 to 2 cm wide. Cyathia occur in umbrel-like cymes, surrounded by 2 heart-shaped, greenish cyathophylls. *Habitat:* probably Mexico. An easily grown species, it is easily propagated by cuttings.

Euphorbia phosphorea MART.,

the "phosphorescent spurge," is very similar to the above but with shorter and sharper 6-angled shoots. Its leaves are small, lanceolate, and deciduous; the cyathia have serrate nectar glands.

Like *E. alata* HOOK. (Jamaica) and *E. cassythoides* BOISS. (Cuba), *E. phosphorea* is said to give off a glow on warm nights, probably because of its growing with phosphorescent fungi or bacteria in its habitat.

Euphorbia weberbaueri MANSF. (Plate 12,*6*)

forms richly branched shrubs up to 1 m high with rod-shaped, dark green shoots that are given ribs by the extended leaf bases. The shoots are about 1 cm thick; leaves are small, deciduous, and reddish brown; and the cyathia are terminal and lateral with dark purple nectar glands. *Habitat:* central and northern Peru, at altitudes between 1800 and 2000 m, forming mass populations.

E. weberbaueri is fast growing and easy to propagate, but is not very free-blooming in cultivation.

Euphorbia antisyphlitica ZUCC. (section Arthrothamnus)

is a shrub up to 1 m high with thin, round, rod-shaped branches and small deciduous leaves. Cyathia appear usually in groups of three; their attractiveness is due to flower-like appendages of the 5 reddish nectar glands, whereby each cyathium gives the impression of a radial flower (Figure 8,5). *Distribution:* highlands of Mexico, on dry cliffs.

Very similar is

Euphorbia cerifera ALC. (Plate 27,7),

also from Mexico, the "wax euphorbia," whose round shoots are covered with a gray wax layer. Cyathia are small, with cream-colored nectar glands and white, petal-like appendages.

The euphorbias of Madagascar

Madagascar is the home of a great number of interesting euphorbias, which vary so much in their growth-form from the African species that they are listed separately and compared to one another. Unfortunately, the most beautiful species are so difficult to grow that they are found only in a few collections. There is little agreement on the systematic categorizing of the Madagascar euphorbias. Preliminary work in this area has been accomplished by J. LÉANDRI, Paris.[12]

1. *Euphorbia milii* group

Best known are the forms of the "*milii* group," known to all gardners and hobbyists as "splendens" or "crown of thorns." They below to section Diacanthium and are considered by BERGER in their own group of Splendentes. There is a confusion about the name *E. milii*. It is generally believed that the *E. milii* described by DES MOULIN (1826) is the same as the *E. splendens* published by BOJER (1829), and so the first name is given priority. The characteristics for the whole "milii" group according to J. LÉANDRI are as follows:

Richly branched shrubs with eventual lignified branches covered with stipular thorns; the two stipular thorns are sometimes accompanied by weaker, spiny emergences. The cyathia cups are surrounded by 2 spreading, vividly red, seldom yellow scape bracts (cyathophylls).

Euphorbia milii DES MOULIN var. *milii* (= *E. bojeri* HOOK.; = *E. splendens* BOJ. var. *bojeri* M. DENIS) is a much branched shrub with cylindrical branches 8 to 10 mm thick, and remote thorns thickened at the base; leaves leathery, shiny, oval pointed, narrowing to a petiole; cyathia in slightly branched, long-stalked cymes with shiny red or sometimes yellow cyathophylls of 7 to 8 mm.

Variety *splendens* (BOJ. ex HOOK.) URSCH et LÉANDRI (= *E. splendens* BOJ. ex HOOK.; *E. splendens* var. *typica* LÉANDRI) is larger and more robust overall than the above. It forms a shrub up to 2 m tall with vaguely angular shoots, usually thicker than 1 cm; the podaria have stout thorns up to 2 cm long, frequently branched at the base, initially dark red, later black. Leaves are up to 5 cm long and 2 cm wide, long oval, short tipped, leathery, bright green, and the cyathia occur in groups of 4 to 16, in much branched inflorescences, surrounded by round, shiny red or yellow (forma *lutea*) cyathophylls up to 1 cm across.

E. milii var. *splendens* (Color Plate 3,5) is a favorite euphorbia, which blooms almost the year around and is quite suitable as a house plant. Propagation is by cuttings in the spring, rooted in a light, sandy mix. In all tropical areas var. *splendens*, because of its fast growth and its prolific bloom, is used as a hedge plant.

Two especially robust varieties of *E. milii* are var. *breoni* URSCH et LÉANDRI (= *E. breoni* L. NOISETTE) and var. *hislopii* URSCH et LÉANDRI (*E. hislopii* N.E. BR.). Both are richly branched shrubs, 1 to 2 m tall, with thorny branches more than 2 cm thick. The leaves appear in terminal rosettes and are very large, 10 to 18 cm long and up to 5 cm wide. Inflorescences occur on stalks, 5 to 10 cm long with 4 to 8 (−16) cyathia; cyathophylls are shiny red, in var. *hislopii* 5 to 6 mm long and 8 to 10 mm wide, in var. *breoni* 1–1.5 cm long and as wide.

Both of the above cited varieties are considerably more decorative than var. *splendens* itself and when planted in unconfined soil grow into richly branched shrubs that bloom for the whole summer.

The main distribution area for *E. milii* and its varieties are the gneissic and granitic mountains of the highlands of Madagascar, where the plants frequently appear in great masses.

In many of the mountain areas we find special forms, which because of their growth-form, shape of thorns, and color of the cyathophylls differ to some degree from the generally recognized forms and have thus been described as separate species by URSCH and LÉANDRI. It is still not clear if these are really species or are natural hybrids.

Here are a few examples:

Euphorbia capuronii URSCH et LÉANDRI (Plate 28,1)

Named for the French botanist R. CAPURON, this is a much-branched shrub up to 1 m tall. Its stipular thorns are up to 2 cm long, accompanied by emergences; leaves occur in a terminal rosette, lanceolate, 3 to 5 cm long, 4 to 8 mm wide, and hairy. The cyathia are small, as many as 32 in a richly branched inflorescence, with greenish yellow cyathophylls up to 6 mm long, hairy and sharply pointed. *Distribution:* southwestern Madagascar.

Similar is

Euphorbia genoudiana URSCH et LÉANDRI (Plate 28,2),

a dwarf shrub up to 50 cm tall differing from the above by its simple stipular thorns and naked, narrowly linear leaves. Inflorescence-cymes have 2 to 8 (−16) small cyathia; cyathophylls are greenish yellow and long tipped; and nectar glands are yellow-orange. *Distribution:* southwestern Madagascar.

Euphorbia durani URSCH et LÉANDRI (Plate 28,5)

Forming richly branched, spherical shrubs up to 40 cm high, its branches have a gray bark, up to 2 cm thick, with usually simple thorns up to 16 mm long and thick at the base. Its leaves are longitudinally oval, 3 to 5 cm long, and acute; inflorescences are almost sub-sessile, with only 1 to 2 cyathia;

---

[12] LÉANDRI, J.: "Les Euphorbes épineuses et coralliformes de Madagascar." *Cactus,* 1952–1953. URSCH, E., and J. LÉANDRI: "Les Euphorbes malgaches épineuses et charnues du Jardin Botanique de Tsimbazaza." *Mém. Institut Scientifique de Madagascar, Série B,* Vol. V, 1954.

cyathophylls are round, up to 10 cm long, greenish to reddish yellow. *Distribution:* central Madagascar.

Similar is

Euphorbia fianarantsoae URSCH et LÉANDRI.

It differs from the above by its thinner shoots and shorter thorns, which are not thickened at the base; inflorescences have 2 to 4 cyathia; their cyathophylls are yellowish or reddish yellow. *Distribution:* central Madagascar (mountain range in the vicinity of Fianarantsoa, at 1200 to 1600 m).

The differences between the two species are so insignificant that it would be justified to unit them into one species.

Euphorbia delphinensis URSCH et LÉANDRI (Plate 28,4)

Named for the town of Fort Dauphin in southern Madagascar, this is a richly branched shrub, with downward arching, crooked, reddish gray to gray branches ca. 1 cm thick. Its thorns are usually simple, thin, up to 1.8 cm long; leaves are leathery, dark green, oval, up to 2 cm long, 1.2 cm wide, short acute. Inflorescences have 4 to 8 small cyathia; cyathophylls are pale yellowish green, upright, with recurved tips. *Distribution:* southern Madagascar (Fort Dauphin), in the coastal area.

In spite of the small cyathia, *E. delphinensis* is a very attractive plant that, in contrast to the other species of the *milii* group, has leaves and blooms during the entire year.

Euphorbia didiereoides M. DENIS (Plate 9,3; 11,5)

is one of the most thorny of the euphorbias from Madagascar (Plate 11,5), which in its growth-form resembles a *Didierea* (see page 106). It forms sparsely branched shrubs, 2 to 3 m tall (Plate 9,3) with thick shoots made rigid by the thorns; the long shoots are also covered with short shoots. Leaves are longitudinally oval, up to 4 cm long, and hairy on both sides; inflorescences occur on long stems, with numerous, dense, small cyathia; and cyathophylls are upright and yellowish green. *Habitat:* central Madagascar on gneissic rocks.

E. didiereoides is very attractive also as a young plant, because of the ferocious thorns, but it grows slowly. It requires much soil warmth and a rest period during the winter.

Euphorbia horombensis URSCH et LÉANDRI

is similar in growth habit to *E. milii* var. *breoni* but differs from it in the shape of the thorns, which are flattened and broadened at the base and in the richly branched inflorescences and the considerably smaller, reddish brown cyathophylls. *Distribution:* central Madagascar (Horombe Plateau).

2. *Euphorbia lophogona* group (= section Goniostema BAILL.)

The species of the section Goniostema BAILL., compiled by J. LÉANDRI into the *lophogona* group, are among the most beautiful euphorbias of Madagascar. They are characterized by the formation of so-called stipular ribs (see page 36).

Euphorbia lophogona LAM. (Plate 28,3),

native to the forests of southeast Madagascar, has unbranched or slightly branched, 5-ribbed, winged shoots 20 to 60 cm long; the wings are formed by the modified emergences, which longitudinally widen at the base and appear as leather-brown teeth at the tip. Leaves appear in a terminal rosette rilled on the top with leathery, shiny, dark-green nerves, which are 10 to 15 cm long and 3 to 4 cm wide. The inflorescences, which appear in the axils of the upper leaves, have long stalks and 4 to 8 cyathia with large, white or reddish cyathophylls.

E. lophogona is a very attractive plant, which thrives in light, sandy-humusy soil in semi-shade. It propagates itself by scattered seed.

The species usually incorrectly identified in botanical gardens as *E. lophogona* is in reality

Euphorbia leuconeura BOISS. (= *E. fournieri* hort. ex Rev. hortic.),

differing from the above in the following characteristics: shoots are usually with 4 ribs formed by numerous leather-brown bristles; leaves are soft green on the top; cyathia appear in groups of three and are very short stalked; and cyathophylls are upright, insignificant, and yellowish green.

E. leuconeura requires essentially more humidity and warmth than *E. lophogona*.

Closely related and perhaps only a variety of *E. leuconeura* is

Euphorbia neohumbertii P. BOIT. (Color Plate 3,4).

It differs from the above by its dark green shoots, which are marked by white cross bands. Also it has much longer, bristly emergences, bluish green leaves, and vivid green-red cyathophylls that do not unfold and completely enclose the cyathium. Only the yellow pollen sac and style are visible.

E. neohumbertii blooms in its leafless state and then presents a splendid sight with its numerous, bright-red cyathia; when the bloom fades the leaves appear. *Distribution:* northern Madagascar, on limestone.

Euphorbia viguieri M. DENIS (Color Plate 3,7)

has usually unbranched, columnar, green stems that are 1.5 m tall, up to 5 cm thick, and covered by the large leaf scars. Its rib spines are very large, mounted on broad, flattened bases, branched, and lignified at the tip. Cyathia are similar to those of *E. neohumberti*, in floriferous, dense, sub-sessile or stalked inflorescences; cyathophylls are upright, completely surrounding the cyathium, shiny cinnamon red. As in *E. neohumberti* the large, vivid green, reddish stemmed leaves develop only after the bloom fades. In cultivation the plants may also bloom when leaves are present. *Distribution:* northern Madagascar, on limestone.

E. viguieri has been divided into several varieties according to formation of the thorns and length of the inflorescence stalks. It represents a valuable item in our collections. It is easy to grow, but propagation is practical only by seed. Water sparingly in its leafless state.

3. *Euphorbia ankarensis* group

Euphorbia ankarensis B. BOIT. (Color Plate 3,6)

produces unbranched shoots up to 70 cm tall and 4 cm thick; they have a gray bark, and tiny thorns appear only on the tip and later disappear; cyathia numerous, pendulous, in short-stalked inflorescences, which appear on the tip. Their two acute cyathophylls are skin-like and of a pale flesh-color; after the bloom fades a rosette of 5 to 7 long petiolate leaves appear, which have sparse hair on both sides. *Distribution:* northern Madagascar (Ankara Mountains, on limestone). Culture and propagation as above.

Another species just as endearing to collectors is

Euphorbia millotii URSCH et LÉANDRI (Plate 28,6).

This plant is named for the French zoologist Prof. MILLOT. From the base it forms richly branched scrubs up to 50 cm tall with round, initially greenish red, later gray, lignified branches. Cyathia are pendulous, surrounded by the large, dark, wine-colored cyathophylls, which unfold only slightly. The foliage, which appears after the bloom fades, is purple-red at first. *Distribution:* northeastern Madagascar (Lac Bleu).

E. *millotii* is a charming phenomenon among the euphorbias of Madagascar; because of its basal shoots it is also easily propagated by cuttings.

Among the "dwarfs" of the Madagascar euphorbias are the following two, equally charming species, which are especially desirable because of their small size.

Euphorbia cylindrifolia RAUH et MARN.-LAP. (Plate 29,1–2)

is a small, low-growing species with thin shoots up to 0.5 cm thick and covered by leaf scars and tissue-like, deciduous bristles. The shoots bear a rosette of cylindrical, reddish green leaves that have on the upper side a longitudinal furrow, are up to 3 cm long, and are bent into a hook at the tip. Cyathia appear singly or in 2-flowering cymes in subterminal position, pendulous, enveloped by large, gray-violet cyathophylls.

I distinguish 2 subspecies of *E. cylindrifolia:* ssp. *cylindrifolia* and ssp. *tuberifera.* The former is characterized by the formation of long, subterranean runners, and thereby it forms stands several square meters in size in its habitat. Ssp. *tuberifera,* on the other hand, has an underground caudex up to 10 cm in diameter, from which emerge numerous, short shoots. Both grow easily in cultivation and can be propagated readily from cuttings, but ssp. *tuberifera* will then often not form a caudex. *Distribution:* southern Madagascar, deciduous in forests.

Closely related to the stoloniferous subspecies of *E. cylindrifolia* is

Euphorbia decaryi A. GUILL. (Plate 29,3),

which also has the pendulous cyathia, but differs from the above by the thicker, above-ground, distinctly angular shoot segments. These bear a rosette of lanceolate-ovate, very fleshy, dark green to reddish brown leaves, 3 to 5 cm long and wavy edged. The numerous, suberizing bristles join into narrow, wing-like edges. A very attractive species, it is easy to propagate from runners.

Very similar to this in growth-form is

Euphorbia françoisii LÉANDRI (Plate 29,4).

It differs, however, from the above by the upright cyathia and the spreading cyathophylls. Seedlings have a thick, fleshy main root and rooted, stolon-like, elongated shoots, which bear stiff, leathery leaves, that are extremely variable in shape and lie in a rosette on the ground. Their wavy leaf blade is sometimes narrowly lanceolate, sometimes rhomboid-shaped, 4 to 6 cm long and 2 to 3 cm wide. Leaves produce numerous suberized bristles at the base of the petiole. Inflorescences occur in subterminal position with 2 to 8 upright cyathia, which are enveloped by yellowish green, spreading cyathophylls. *Distribution:* only in the extreme south of Madagascar (near Fort Dauphin), on sand dunes.

Closely related to the southern African species from section Rhizanthium (*E. tuberosa, E. silenifolia, E. crispa,* see p. 43) is

Euphorbia primulaefolia BAK. (Plate 29,6 and 7)

from the central Madagascar highlands. It is widely distributed there and is quite variable. At maturity it has a stout, slightly branched fleshy root up to 15 cm long and up to 7 cm thick, which produces a short axis buried into the ground to its tip. In the rainy season it develops a rosette of large, primrose-like leaves that are pressed to the ground. As the dry period begins they die. The flowers appear in the leafless state. Cyathia occur in groups of 2 to 4 on a short, common scape with white or reddish cyathophylls frequently notched on the edge.

Closely related to *E. primulaefolia* is

Euphorbia quartziticola J. LÉANDRI,

growing only in quartz cliffs of the Itremo Mountains (central Madagascar). Its quite large but multi-tipped root produces a short axis with a tuft of leathery, yellowish green, frequently red-edged leaves, which have at their base two bristly, deciduous bracts. Cyathia appear in short-scaped inflorescences with spreading, lemon-yellow cyathophylls.

Both species can be propagated only by seed; in their leafless state they require a strictly observed rest period.

From the great variety of Madagascar euphorbias I list only the following.

Euphorbia stenoclada H. BAILL. (Plate 12,1; 29,5)

forms shrubs or trees up to 3 m tall with a stem 10 to 20 cm thick covered by a rough bark and a much-branched crown made formidable with thorns; every lateral branch ends in a hard, sharp thorn; leaves are scale-shaped and deciduous.

Even as a cutting plant, *E. stenoclada,* because of its heavy thorn coat and the silvery gray color of the shoots, is one of the most bizarre and, at the same time, easily grown species. In its habitat *E. stenoclada* is quite variable. Along with extremely thorny forms there are also forms that are almost thornless. *Distribution:* southwestern Madagascar, generally on sand dunes near the coast.

Euphorbia xylophylloides A. BROGN. ex LEM. (= *E. enterophora* DRAKE?)

has a special position within the entire range of euphorbias, because all the lateral branches appear as flattened growths (platyclades). They have small, deciduous leaves arranged in two rows (Plate 13,7). In its habitat *E. xylophylloides* forms trees 8 m high, which, with their thick stems and wide-reaching crowns, from a distance resemble pine trees. *Habitat:* southern Madagascar, in dry, deciduous forests. As a cutting plant it is attractive and fast growing!

Other spurges

Stem-succulent spurges are also found in other genera; first I present the close relative to euphorbias,

Monadenium PAX,

of which P.R.O. BALLY (1961)[13] in the most recent study lists 47 species, whose main distribution area is eastern Africa (from Mozambique to Somalia). Only 3 species are native to western Africa. It is remarkable that the genus is entirely missing in the Cape area, which otherwise is so very rich in succulent euphorbias.

Although many monadeniums are very similar in growth-form to the euphorbias, especially in regard to the succulence of the shoot axes covered with leaf pads, the formation of thorns and spines, and the reduction of foliage, there is nevertheless a significant difference between the two genera, which lies especially in the structure of the cyathia. While those of *Euphorbia* have 4 to 5 more or less prominent nectar glands and the whole cyathium is of a radial structure, the cyathia of all *Monadenium* species has a dorsiventral structure. Specifically there is only one (although quite large) nectar gland, which gives the genus its name, the "single gland spurge." The gland itself always points to the dorsal (back) side of the cyathium. From above it resembles a horse shoe (Figure 9,2–3, 4–6 D) and conceals the actual nectarium at its base (N).

As in *Euphorbia* the ovary (female flower) hangs out of the cyathia cup on a long pedicel pointed downwards (Figure 9,2–6,F). As in many euphorbias the cup is surrounded by two bracts (cyathophylls, Figure 9, Cy), in some species very large and prominently colored, which except for a notch are fused together into a shell on one side of the cyathium (Figure 9,3). Their central nerves usually protrude as distinct keels. Branching may occur from the axils of these cyathophylls (Figure 9,1). The inflorescences are usually simple dichasia: in addition to the terminal cyathium (Figure 9,4) only two lateral cyathia (Figure 9,4, E_1 and E_2) develop. Only in a few species (*M. coccineum, M. magnificum,* among others) are the inflorescences, usually on the upper shoot segment, more richly branched.

The usually somewhat fleshy leaf blades, which are sessile or narrowed into a petiole and arranged in a spiral, fall at the end of every growing period; they also have at their base small stipulary thorns, which often appear in threes, of which the middle thorn is the largest. The succulent leaf bases often form mamillae and are united with the shoot axis, which therefore takes on a tesselated appearance similar to that in many euphorbias.

In spite of the relatively small number of species there is an astounding variety of growth forms.

There are species that are tree-like (*M. spinescens, M. arborescens*), shrubs (*M. ellenbeckii, M. magnificum, M. coccineum*), highly succulent forms resembling euphorbias (*M. guentheri, M. schubei, M. lugardae, M. stapelioides, M. yattanum, M. ritchiei, M. heteropodum, M. reflexum,* etc.), and fleshy root-geophytes, i.e., plants with a thick, fleshy root and thin foliage, which is often cast off at the end of the vegetative period (*M. nudicaule, M. simplex, M. oro-banchoides,* etc.).

The genus *Monadenium* is poorly represented in most collections, although many species, especially the highly succulent ones, are extraordinarily decorative, can be propagated easily from cuttings, and, in contrast to the euphorbias, are less susceptible to insect pests and plant diseases. Cultivation is the same as for euphorbias.

I list here only a few species especially recommended for the hobbyist.

Monadenium lugardae N.E. Br. (Plate 30,1)

Stems appear singly or in groups, up to 60 cm long and up to 3 cm thick, cylindrical, covered by large, flat 5- to 6-sided leaf pads, which have leaf scars in their upper third with tiny thorns. Leaves are in a terminal rosette, fleshy, with blades that are 2 to 9 cm long, up to 4 cm wide, oval, acute, with a short, wide petiole, hairy on both sides, uniformly green. Cyathia occur in groups of three; cyathophylls are pale green, keeled on the back; and ovaries have serrate wings. *Distribution:* Botswana, Transvaal, Natal, Zululand.

Monadenium stapelioides PAX

has a fleshy root, from which emerges several shoots, which in cultivation become up to 20 cm long and 2 cm thick and are covered by rhombic or hexagonal, succulent podaria. Thorns are very small or absent; leaves are fleshy, sessile with longitudinally oval, pointed blades 2 to 3 cm long, up to 2 cm wide, and folded inward. Cyathia occur in threes in the upper leaf axils; cyathophylls are greenish white, keeled; nectar glands usually have a reddish edge; and ovaries are green, spotted with red, with serrate margins (Figure 9,4–6). *Distribution:* eastern Africa (Tanzania, Kenya, Uganda).

Very similar and of the same growth-form is

---

[13] BALLY, P.R.O.: *The Genus* MONADENIUM. Benteli-Verlag, Bern, 1961.

Monadenium yattanum BALLY (Plate 30,*2*).

From a thick, fleshy root emerges numerous, usually unbranched stems up to 20 cm long, reclining or ascending, up to 1.5 cm thick, round, which have leaves that are arranged sparsely, thick, lanceolate, acute, on a broad petiole, and whose margins are usually curly. The leaf nerves are lighter and protrude on the upper side. In its habitat in full sun the leaves can take on a deep purple color, contrasting with the white nerves. Thorns are missing; leaf pads are slightly raised, extending far down the shoot axis with three bright nerves. Inflorescences have scapes, numerous in the axils of the upper leaves; cyathophylls are sharply keeled on the back, greenish with purple stripes; and nectar glands are yellowish green. *Distribution:* highlands of Kenya, only on black soil (Machakos District and Yatta plateau).

A very pretty species, it is easily propagated by cuttings, which form fleshy roots.

Another highly succulent species is

Monadenium guentheri PAX (Plate 30,*3*).

From a fleshy root emerges numerous, cylindrical, upright or arching shoots up to 90 cm long and 3 cm thick, covered with very warty, hexagonal leaf pads. Thorns appear usually in threes and are small and sharp; leaves are fleshy, sessile, lanceolate, up to 3 cm long and 2 cm wide, briefly serrate on the margin and wavy. Cyathia occur in threes, cyathophylls have 2 keels, green on the back with reddish dots; and nectar glands have a thick, red margin. *Distribution:* Kenya.

Similar is

Monadenium schubei (PAX) N.E. BR. (Plate 30,*4*).

Shoots are upright, branched from the base, up to 45 cm long and 4 cm thick, dark green, covered by mammary-shaped, elongated leaf pads up to 1 cm long, rectangular or hexagonal. Thorns occur in groups of 3 to 5 around the leaf scar, up to 2 mm long. Leaves are fleshy, lanceolate, up to 6 cm long and 2 cm wide, constricted into a stem near the base, frequently wavy on the margins, with the upper side having lighter colored nerves. Cyathia occur in threes; cyathophylls are green with a white margin; nectar glands have a whitish green or pale-red margin; and ovaries have serrate margins. *Distribution:* Tanzania, Uganda, Zimbabwe.

Var. *formosum* BALLY differs from the type by its always unbranched, thinner, gray-green shoots and its pure white cyathophylls. *Distribution:* Tanzania.

As an example of a shrubby species with succulent, rod-shaped shoots I cite

Monadenium ellenbeckii N.E. BR. (Plate 30,*5*).

Its stems are up to 1 m long and 2.5 cm thick; the podaria are

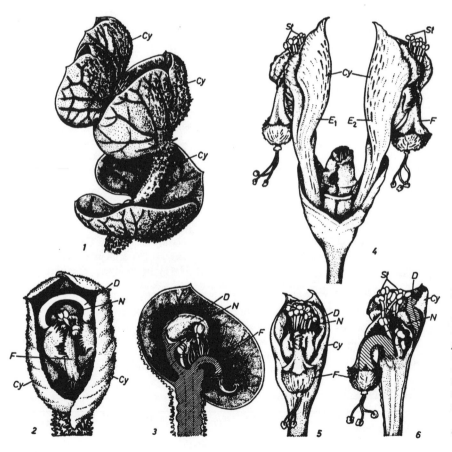

Figure 9. *1–3 Monadenium echinulatum.* 1, Section from the inflorescence; *2,* cyathiun seen from above; *3,* the same in longitudinal section. *4–6 Monadenium stapelioides.* *4,* Dichasium with the already fallen terminal cyathium and the axil cyathias E₁ and E₂; *5,* single cyathium seen from above, *6,* the same in longitudinal section. Labels: Cy = cyathophylls; D = nectar glands with the nectarium (N); F = ovary (on female flowers); St = stamens of the male flowers.

very flat, extending far down the stem, rilled by sunken nerves. Thorns are tiny; leaf blades are broadly oval to round, ca. 1 × 1 cm in size, fleshy, sessile, and soon falling. Cyathia occur in threes and are short stalked; cyathophylls are yellowish green. *Distribution:* from Ethiopia through Somalia to northern Kenya.

M. *ellenbeckii* is an interesting, easily grown species. Closely related to it is

Monadenium virgatum BALLY,

which differs from the above by its thinner, gray-green, barely rilled shoots, its narrower leaves, and its white or reddish cyathophylls. *Distribution:* eastern Kenya (near Mombasa on black soil).

A charming species is

Monadenium echinulatum STAPF (Plate 31,*1;* 9,*1–3*).

Its name is quite justified, because the stem (emerging from a fleshy root, 30 to 70 cm long and up to 1 cm thick), the leaves (mainly on the under side), the inflorescence scapes (up to 6 cm long), the large, reddish green, dark-nerved cyathophylls, and the fruits are heavily covered with stiff, simple or branched thorn bristles. *Distribution:* northern Tanzania.

A very thorny species, which forms a tree up to 6 m tall, is

Monadenium spinescens (PAX) BALLY (= *Stenadenium spinescens* PAX) (Plate 30,7),

whose branches are up to 2.5 cm thick and have a gray-brown bark; they are covered with hard, sharp, recurved thorns. These appear in threes, of which the central one is inserted below the start of the leaf and can reach a length of 1.5 cm. The leaves arranged in a terminal rosette are sessile and have a leaf blade that is up to 9 cm long and 2 cm wide, is usually folded upward, with wavy teeth on the margin, and has both sides naked. Only the central nerve has short spines on the under side. Cyathia occur in long-stalked, richly branched cymes. *Distribution:* Tanzania.

M. *spinescens,* in contrast to all other species, is very slow growing in cultivation and is difficult to propagate.

Monadenium coccineum (PAX) (Color Plate 3,8)

From a fleshy root emerge a few, upright, usually unbranched shoots up to 1.3 m long and 1.5 cm thick, given 5 angles by the long extending leaf bases; blades of the almost sessile, fleshy leaves are up to 9 cm long and 3.5 cm wide, longitudinally oval, pointed, serrate on the margins. Cyathia occur in multi-branched dichasias; cyathophylls and the inflorescence branches are vivid cinnabar red. *Distribution:* Tanzania.

M. *coccineum* blooms freely; it is a very pretty, easily grown species, easily propagated by cuttings. This and the following species are favored by collectors.

Monadenium magnificum E.A. BRUCE (Plate 30,6)

A slightly branched shrub up to 1.5 m tall, its shoots have 4 to 5 angles and are green and up to 1 cm thick; their edges have brown, irregular or regular star-shaped thorns. Leaves are fleshy with a broad base, sessile and bent over, broadly elliptical to oval, acute, naked, up to 15 cm long and 5 to 10 cm wide, with a slightly serrate margin. The central nerve stands out on

the under side like a keel and is thorned; inflorescences appear on long scapes, similar to those of M. *coccineum* but more branched; their axes have 4 sharp angles, are vivid red, and spiny; also the cyathophylls, which have spines on their keels, are vivid red. *Distribution:* Tanzania.

Synadenium BOISS.

This genus differs from *Euphorbia* in its nectar glands not being free but united in a single cup sometimes serrate at the tip or notched (Figure 10,D), to which the genus name refers. The distribution area for the genus runs through all of eastern Africa.

The best known, frequently cultivated species is

Synadenium grantii HOOK. f.,

a thornless shrub, richly branched from the base and in its habitat becoming up to 3 m tall. Young shoots are round, cylindrical, green, up to 2 cm thick; leaves are slightly fleshy, short petiolated with a blade ca. 17 cm long, longitudinally oval, with a short acute tip, up to 6 cm wide, and light green with dark nerves.

The inflorescences appear in the axils of the upper leaves on long stalks and are richly branched cymes, which produce either hermaphroditic or uni-sexed cyathia and which owe their attractiveness to the dark red, hairy gland ring at the base. *S. grantii* is a fast-growing plant, which, when planted in the open, soon becomes a large shrub.

Considerably more attractive, even as small pot plants, are forms with dark red or green-red mottled leaves.

Another, but seldom grown species from Natal is *Synadenium cupulare* (BOISS.) L.C. WHEELER (Plate 31,2). It is considerably smaller than the above, and the nectar glands are yellow; the plant is known to be very poisonous.

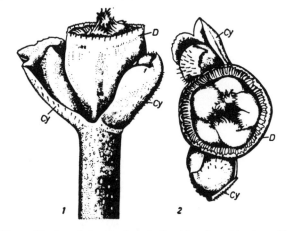

Figure 10. *Synadenium cupulare. 1,* Cyathium in a side view with the cyathophylls (Cy), in whose axes further cyathias are taking shape; *2,* the same seen from above. D = ring-shaped gland. Stamens and ovaries are not visible.

Pedilanthus NECK.

is a New World Euphorbiaceae genus distributed throughout the West Indies, California, and Mexico. Its members have a shrubby growth-form and shoots with milky sap. The distinctly dorsiventral cyathia are especially attractive and are similar in appearance to a small bird's head or a high-top shoe laced tightly at the top. The generic name *Pedilanthus* is from the Greek and means "shoe flower."

The cyathium cup is enveloped by 3 shiny cinnabar or carmine-red bracts of different sizes; they are fused to each other and form a sack-like spur, which enfolds the nectar glands.

All *Pedilanthus* species are easy to grow and easy to propagate by cuttings. Unfortunately they are extremely susceptible to mildew in high humidity conditions.

The most commonly grown species and the one with most forms is

Pedilanthus tithymaloides POIT.,

a richly branched shrub up to 1 m high with upright, cylindrical branches up to 1 cm thick, green, somewhat zig-zag. The longitudinally oval, slightly succulent, green leaves, up to 12 cm long and 6 cm wide, are cast off at the end of the growing period. The bright red cyathia, up to 2 cm across, are found in clusters at the end of the growing shoot. *Distribution:* Mexico to California and on coastal islands.

In tropical countries the plant is frequently used to make a hedge.

Considerably more decorative because of its white-spotted leaves is

ssp. smallii (MILLSP.) DRESSLER (Plate 31,3).

It is very closely related to the above but is more attractive in all parts. Because of the variegation of the leaves, however, it is more susceptible to diseases.

Thin, rod-shaped stems with small, oval, deciduous leaves are the characteristics of *Pedilanthus aphyllus* BOISS. The cyathia, on the other hand, are quite insignificant and have a prominent, spur-like protrusion.

Jatropha L.

The genus *Jatropha,* known in numerous species in the New World (Central and South America) as well as in the Old World (Africa and Arabia), comprises a great number of interesting, succulent species, of which, however, only a few are found in cultivation. In contrast to the already mentioned euphorbian genera, *Jatropha* has complete, sometimes showy flowers with calyx and corolla. The flowers are uni-sexed and gather into richly branched, dichasial inflorescences, in which the terminal flower of a dichasium is female, the lateral flowers male.

The best known species is

Jatropha podagrica J. HOOK. (Plate 31,4)

from tropical Central America, used in all tropical areas today as a garden plant (where sometimes it has escaped), has thick, bottle-shaped, simple or slightly branched, gray-barked stems covered by branched stipular thorns. Foliage occurs on long petioles with large shield-shaped, 3- to 5-lobed, naked, waxy blade, green above and gray-green below. Inflorescences have long scapes and are richly branched. Petals of the 1 cm flower are bright cinnabar red. *Cultivation:* in sandy-loamy soil in a warm place. Flowering time is in the summer. In its leafless state (during the winter) strict rest must be observed.

Of other species worthy of cultivation I list:

Jatropha peltata H.B.K.

(*Habitat:* Brazil, sandy banks of the Amazon, and dry forests of southeastern Peru; Plate 31,5). A branched shrub up to 1.5 m tall, it has thick branches that are green in youth, gray-barked at maturity. Leaves are alternate, long-petioled with shield-shaped, gray-green, 5- to 7-lobed blade that has glandular teeth on the margin. Bracts dissolve into tattered, deciduous gland bristles; inflorescences have long scapes; flowers are vivid red.

J. peltata is also a very decorative plant even when it is not in bloom.

Jatropha macrantha MÜLL. ARG. (Color Plate 3,9)

A slightly branched shrub up to 1 m tall, it has a thick stem and fleshy branches, which are green when young, later with gray bark. Its leaves are long petioled, with a 3-lobed blade that is dark red when young, later shiny green. Stipules are reduced to sessile glands; inflorescences are long stalked and richly branched; and flowers are up to 2.5 cm in diameter with shiny red petals. *Habitat:* cactus areas of the western slopes of the Andes, central Peru, from 1500 to 2400 m.

J. macrantha blooms almost all year, grows fast, and when planted in the open grows into a very pretty bush.

In addition to the above species I should also mention those classified under section Tuberosa PAX, of which, however, only a few are found in cultivation. They are all characterized by their large, subterranean caudices or knotty rhizomes and thin, slightly succulent foliage, which is cast off at the end of the vegetative period. Their distribution area ranges from Mexico to Paraguay and southern Brazil, also from South Africa to western India. As examples of this growth-form I mention the one from Texas and Mexico,

Jatropha berlandieri TORR. (Plate 31,6).

A plant in bloom up to 25 cm tall with a subterranean caudex ca. 10–20 cm in diameter, it is almost round with a gray bark; the caudex shows the stumps of the annually discarded shoots.

Foliage stems are up to 20 cm tall, thin, gray-green, sympodially branched, and emerge from the caudex and produce several inflorescences each season. Leaves are alternate, long petiolated, stippled at the base. The leaf blade is blue-green, appearing as a pinnate shield. The pinnules occur in groups of 5 to 7, and are blue-green, deeply serrate on the edge. Inflorescences are terminal, surpassed by a soon-sprouting axil bud, sympodially branched: terminal flower is female, lateral ones are male. With its carmine-red petals, this is a very attractive plant.

Similar are:

J. baumii PAX. Habitat: Namibia
J. texana MUELL.-ARG. Habitat: Texas
J. tuberosa PAX. Habitat: Sudan

The stem-succulent *Cnidoscolus* species from Mexico, Baja California, on into South America (Peru) should **not** be grown, because their leaves and stems are covered by **stinging** hairs, which can cause severe skin irritations. In their habitat (Mexico and Peru) they are known as "mala mujer" (bad woman).

FAMILY ASCLEPIADACEAE

The family of milkweeds also has noteworthy stem succulents. They are in the group of Stapeliads and belong to the following genera: *Caralluma, Ceropegia, Decabelone* (= *Tavaresia*), *Diplocyatha, Duvalia, Echidnopsis, Edithcolea, Hoodia, Huernia, Huerniopsis, Pectinaria, Piaranthus, Stapelia, Stapelianthus,* and *Trichocaulon.*

THE MORPHOLOGY OF STAPELIADS

All the members of the stapeliads are characterized by the following, common features:
a. Succulence of the stem-axis.

These are of a soft, fleshy consistency and are sometimes slightly woody only at the base. They contain a considerable amount of a colorless, watery sap that flows upon injury. Although the sap is quite bitter, many stapeliads are consumed by natives and also by cattle, sheep, and goats.

The stems are either round or angular, with mamillae or with ribs. The round shoot axes in cross-section show scattered leaf position, whereas the ribbed species, as in euphorbias, have leaves in straight lines (orthostiches).
b. Reduction of leaves.

Nearly all species are characterized by an extreme reduction of foliage. Only the Indian *Frerea indica*, today called *Caralluma frerei* ROWL., has normal foliage (Plate 32,1), which is cast off at the end of the vegetative period; in certain *Caralluma* species (e.g., *C. europaea, C. joannis, C. priogonium*), *Echidnopsis*, etc., the foliage appears in the form of tiny, deciduous scales (Plate 32,2 and 3). In most species, however, the leaf blade dries up immediately after being developed, and seldom does it develop into a soft, hair-like tip or a hard, pricking thorn. Examples of hair-like leaf rudiments are *Huernia pillansii* (Plate 42,4), *Stapelianthus pilosus* (Plate 32,4); species with leaf thorns are *Caralluma* species such as *C. armata, C. mamillaris* (Plate 32,6), *Trichocaulon* species, *Hoodia bainii* (Plate 32,5), *Edithcolea*, etc. Normally the leaf thorns appear singly; in *Tavaresia*, however, they are in threes (Plate 32,7). Whether the two lateral thorns pointing downward should be considered stipule thorns is not yet settled, especially since stipules do not occur on other stapeliads.

Mamilla-like formations

are common in stapeliads. As in many euphorbias these are succulent formations of the leaf pads (podaria) joined to the leaf axis; their axils conceal the vegetative points for lateral shoots. Very flat and hardly raised mamillae are found in *Trichocaulon* species related to *T. meloforme* (Plate 32,8) and in most *Echidnopsis* species (Plate 32,3). In many *Caralluma, Huernia, Stultitia* species, etc., however, the podaria are tooth-like and elongated, and in this case resemble leaves (Plate 32,9).

Rib formations

In those stapeliads whose leaves are arranged in orthostiches, as in euphorbias, ribs are formed when the leaf pads blend in a straight line and are raised. The number of ribs depends on the position of the leaves. If the leaves are in doubly crossed whorls, as in many *Stapelia* and *Caralluma* species, the shoots are four ribbed (Plate 32,2); in *Hoodia, Trichocaulon,* and *Decabelone* (= *Travesia*), however, numerous ribs are present (Plate 32,5 and 7).

Growth-form

The growth-forms of stapeliads are actually quite uniform. Predominant is the shrubby or mat-like growth-form, which arises when lateral, primary branches appear at the base of the primary shoot (Figure 11, P); these lateral shoots in turn branch again at the base, usually on their underside, so that one gets a branching picture as in Figure 11. In the course of many years great shrubs or mats of one to several meters in diameter arise (Plate 33), in which the individual shoots themselves root and become independent of the primary root system. The old shoots in the center of such a mat die in time, while the peripheral ones continue to branch; therefore, many stapeliads in cultivation have a tendency to crawl out of their pots.

In comparison to euphorbias, the stapeliads remain relatively small. The largest ones are probably some hoodias, *Trichocaulon alstoni* and *Caralluma penicillata* (Plate 33,2), whose shoots can become 1 to 1.5 m tall. The majority, however, remain considerably smaller. The shoots either grow upright or arch upwards from reclining bases (Plate 33,1). In addition, however, there are species which crawl, such as *Echidnopsis* and *Duvalia;* few species, e.g., *Caralluma subterranea*, form underground runners.

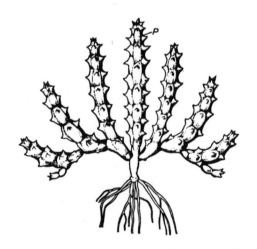

Figure 11. *Stapelia variegata*, a mature seedling showing branching. P = primary (main) shoot.

Flower position

There is great uniformity regarding flower position. Seldom do the flowers appear singly; they usually occur in multiples, and then they are gathered into a cyme or cluster of an inflorescence. As in all milkweeds, the sta-

peliads, too, have the flowers or inflorescences at the tip of the stem; whenever they later appear on the stem axis or even at the base (Plate 34,3), this exceptional behavior can be explained by the fact that the inflorescences were indeed located terminally but surpassed by a lateral branch that started out early (see Plate 35,8). This lateral branch then forms the direct continuation of the flowering shoot and thus pushes the inflorescence into lateral position. Therefore the inflorescences of the stapeliads are never in the axils of the leaves or mamillae, but always between them (Plate 34,4).

One most clearly sees the terminal position of the inflorescences in *Caralluma* species from section Eucaralluma. When a bud is about ready to bloom it begins to elongate considerably and clearly defines itself from the succulent, vegetative shoot (Plate 34,1). The flowers appear on the elongated segment (Plate 35,1). After the seed ripens, the whole blooming part dries up and lateral shoots of the succulent shoot segment take over the continuation of the shoot system. Even the *Caralluma* species from the "umbellata" group clearly show the terminal position of the flowers: in these the inflorescence bud ends with a stout head of numerous individual flowers (Plate 34,2), which correspond to several, cyme-like individual inflorescences at the tip of the shoot. In most species, however, they appear to be in a purely lateral position (Plate 34,3–4).

Flower structure

The flowers of almost all stapeliads are radial (exception: *Decabelone*), occur in five segments, and are always divided into calyx and corolla. The calyx is small and insignificant. The five petals are fused at the base into a short or slightly long tube, and only their upright or flat tips are free. The underside of the petals is usually insignificantly green or reddish; the upper side, on the other hand, has a variety of forms, frequently covered with diagonal weals and furrows or covered with papillae and hairs. Frequently the petals have, at their tips and on the margins, dark violet to blackish purple, clavate (club-like) hairs (Plate 35,4), which are set into motion by the slightest breeze and probably serve to entice insects.

The size of the flower is extraordinarily variable and ranges from a few millimeters to ca. 30 cm in *Stapelia gigantea* (Color Plate 4,8). Regarding color, browns and violets, i.e., the colors of excrement predominate. The

olor Plate 4.

(ul)	*Brachystelma barberiae*	3 (mul) *Duvalia sulcata*	6 (mlr) *Piaranthus punctatus*
(ur)	*Brachystelma foetidum*	4 (mur) *Huerniopsis atrosanguinea*	7 (ll) *Stapelia ambigua*
		5 (mll) *Frerea indica*	8 (lr) *Stapelia gigantea*

Plate 33. Growth forms of some stapeliads in their habitat

a) A mat of *Caralluma retrospiciens* var. *tombuctuensis* ca. 1 m in diameter in the succulent steppes at Lake Magadi (Kenya)

b) *Caralluma penicillata* in the succulent bush of Lodar (southern Arabia)

c) A large specimen of *Hoodia bainii* dying from extreme drought (near Upington, Bushman Land)

Plate 34.

1 (ul) *Caralluma priogonium* in fruit (dry forest near Voi, Kenya)

2 (um) *Caralluma retrospiciens* var. *tombuctuensis*

in flower (dry bush at Lake Baringo, Kenya) (see 5)

3 (ur) *Stapelia ambigua* shoot with inflorescence

4 (ll) *Caralluma hottentotorum* flowering shoot

5 (lm) *Caralluma retrospiciens* var. *tombuc* in fruit (habitat see 2)

6 (lr) *Caralluma*, sprung fruit capsule seed

Plate 35.

Plate 36.

1 (ul)   *Caralluma aperta*
2 (um)   *Caralluma dummeri* (the
         flower is being visited by a
         hopper *(Muscidae)*.
3 (ur)   *Caralluma luntii*
4 (ml)   *Caralluma armata*
5 (mm)   *Caralluma marlothii*
6 (mr)   *Caralluma pruinosa*
7 (ll)   *Caralluma subterranea*
8 (lm)   *Caralluma umdausensis*
9 (lr)   *Caralluma piaranthoides*

ul) *Diplocyatha ciliata* (= *Orbea ciliata*)
       (Photo: J. Marnier-Lapostolle)

2 (ur) *Duvalia compacta*
3 (ml) *Duvalia modesta*
4 (mr) *Duvalia radiata* var. *hirtella*

5 (ll) *Duvalia procumbens*
6 (lr) *Duvalia tanganyikensis*

Plate 38.

1 (u) *Echidnopsis repens* in the dry bush
        near Loitokitok (Kenya)
2 (m) *Echidnopsis watsonii*
3 (l)   *Edithcolea grandis* in the dry bush
        near voi (Kenya)

Plate 40.

1 (ul)   and
2 (um)   *Hoodia gordonii* in the Ceres Karroo
         (Calvinia District). The pick is 90 cm
         long.
3 (ur)   *Hoodia currori*
4 (ml)   *Hoodia ruschii* (from the collection of the
         Jardin Botanique "Les Cèdres")
5 (mr)   *Huernia aspera*
6 (ll)   *Huernia keniensis*
7 (lm)   *Huernia barbata*
8 (lr)   *Huernia bicampanulata*

Plate 41.

	2 (ur) *Huernia pendula*	5 (ll) *Huernia levyi*
	3 (ml) *Huernia namaquensis*	6 (lr) *Huernia whitesloaneana*
1) *Huernia guttata*	4 (mr) *Huernia primulina*	

Plate 42.

1 (ul) *Huernia confus*
2 (um) *Huernia macrocarpa*
3 (ur) *Huernia marnieriana*
4 (ml) *Huernia pillansii*
5 (mr) *Huernia reticulata*
6 (ll) *Huernia leachii*
7 (lm) *Huernia oculata*
8 (lr) *Huernia verekeri*

tion of the Jardin Botanique "Les Cèdres")

Huerniopsis decipiens

Pseudolithos cubiformis (from the collec-

3 (ml) Pectinaria arcuata

4 (mr) Pectinaria saxatilis, flower from above

(left) and from the side (right)

5 (ll) Piaranthus pulcher

6 (lr) Piaranthus ruschii

Plate 44.

1 (ul) *Piaranthus mennellii*
2 (um) *Piaranthus parvulus*
3 (ur) *Stapelia asterias* var. *lucida*
4 (ml) *Stapelia gettleffii*
5 (mr) *Stapelia hirsuta*
6 (ll) *Stapelia wilmaniae*
7 (lm) *Stapelia engleriana*
8 (lr) *Stapelia herrei*

5.

Stapelia erectiflora, flowering plant (see 3)
Stapelia glanduliflora, single flower
Stapelia erectiflora, magnified single flower (see 1)
Stapelia jucunda
Stapelia arenosa
Stapelia rufa
Stapelia kwebensis
Stapelia longipes var. *namaquensis*, characteristic form and single flower

Plate 46.

1 (ul)   *Stapelia semota* var. *lutea*
2 (um) *Stapelianthus decaryi*
3 (ur)   *Stapelianthus montagnacii*
4 (ml) *Stapelianthus pilosus*
5 (mr) *Stultitia cooperi*
6 (ll)   *Stultitia tapscottii*
7 (lm)   *Stultitia conjuncta*
8 (lr)   *Tavaresia grandiflora* (grafted to *Cerope-
         gia dichotoma*)

e 47.

l) *Trichocaulon flavum*
m) *Trichocaulon piliferum* (Great Karroo near Beaufort West)
r) *Trichocaulon pedicellatum*
l) *Trichocaulon columnare*
r) *Trichocaulon cactiforme*
) *Trichocaulon keetmanshoopense*
n) *Trichocaulon truncatum*
) *Brachystelma pygmaea*

Plate 48.

1 (ul)   *Ceropegia ampliat*
2 (um)   *Ceropegia ballyan*
3 (ur)   *Ceropegia robynsia*
4 (ml)   *Ceropegia stapelia*
5 (mm)   *Ceropegia distinct*
6 (mr)   *Ceropegia elegans*
7 (ll)   *Ceropegia radican*
8 (lm)   *Ceropegia woodii*
9 (lr)   *Ceropegia rendall*

smell is also that of excrement or of carrion. It is therefore not without justice that these plants are sometimes called "carrion flowers." A single flower can often fill a whole room or greenhouse with its "aroma," whereby it entices hordes of pollinating insects, predominantly blow flies and dung-flies. But quite in contrast to the often penetrating smell is the bizarre beauty of the flowers, sometimes referred to as starfish flowers (Color Plate 4). Hobbyists should not deny themselves the pleasure of these plants just because of the smell.

Extremely interesting and quite complicated is the pollination process. In order to understand it, it is first necessary to give a brief explanation of the structure of the sexual organs. At the base of the corolla tube, frequently surrounded by a wall-like ring or annulus (Figure 12,1A), is the very complicated sex "column" (gynostegium): the ovary itself is formed from two carpels (Figure 12,3, F_1 and F_2), which are joined only at their tip to a massive, stigma-head (N), which in top view looks like a pentagon (Figure 12,4) and resembles a stigma without really being one. The actual stigmas are on the underside of this stigma-head, between the pollen sacs. The five stamens are united into a "staminal column," which

surrounds the ovaries and the stigma-head; their anthers lie on the stigma-head (Figure 12,3, St). A further peculiarity is that the pollen masses of each pollen sac are stuck together, forming a "pollinium." Every pollinium is connected to a pollinium of a neighboring stamen by bow-shaped "translators" (Figure 12,5, T), which are held together by special "adhesion bodies" (Figure 12,5, K). These are hardened secretions of a gland at the margin of the stigma-head; this gland itself later hardens and takes the place of the adhesion bodies. The two pollinia, united by translators and adhesion bodies, therefore belong to the pollen pockets of two neighboring stamens and to the anthers of the same stamen. The adhesion body thus comes to rest precisely between the anthers and on one of the five protruding corners of the stigma-head (Figure 12,4). If an insect visits a flower, it searches for nectar and gets its proboscis or legs caught in the rill of the adhesion body and when flying away pulls the pollinia out of the pollen sacs and carries them to another flower.

There is also an appendage to the staminal column; it bears nectar and is called the "corona." It is usually divided into an "outer" and an "inner" corona: the tips of the outer corona, frequently deep violet, are usually

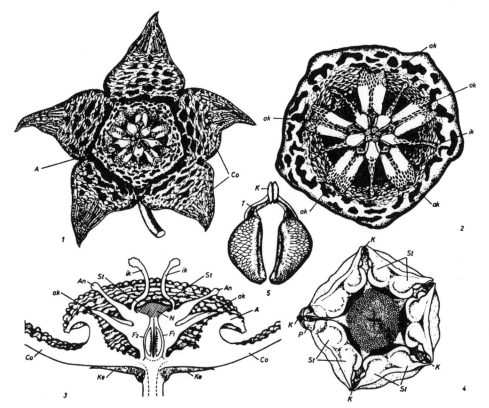

Figure 12. *Stapelia variegata*. 1, Flower seen from above with the annulus (A) and the corolla (Co). 2, Annulus magnified and the sex column seen from above; 3, the same in longitudinal section. 4, Stigma head seen from above with the stamens (St) and the visible adhesion bodies (K). At the left is a pollinium (P) already out of the pollen bag folds. 5, Individual pollinium greatly magnified with the two translators (T) and the adhesion bodies (K). Other labels: Ke (in 3) = calyx; A = annulus; ak = outer corona; ik = inner corona; An = its appendages; St = stamens.

larger than those of the inner corona, upright or spreading, and frequently so deeply cut that the outer corona appears to have 10 tips (Figure 12,2–3, ak), but it may also be so much reduced that it makes the viewer think that only the inner corona is present. The tips of the latter are usually smaller than those of the outer corona; they are fused to the outer corona and often lie across the stigma-head (Figure 1,3, ik). In certain stapeliads the inner corona tips also have variously shaped appendages (Figure 12,3, An). The form of the corona is so typical for the members of the different genera that it provides an important diagnostic character.

Most stapeliads bloom in our (European) climate in the summer months, while the fruits usually do not reach their full size until the next year. After the bloom fades the corolla, the corona, and the stigma head fall, and the two free carpels develop into flaring, horn-like, round, dehiscent fruits growing from the tips (Plate 34,5). When they are ripe they split along a seam and release a large amount of flat, brown seeds with tassels (Plate 34,6). These are carried away by the wind and develop at sites favorable to them. If there is sufficient moisture and warmth, they begin to germinate within 24 hours. But since the seeds in their native habitats often are subjected to long dry periods, they retain their ability to germinate for a long time.

In nature, stapeliads seldom grow in open areas but usually under dense shrubs or squeezed between rocks; however, these locations probably represent only protection against grazing animals, since here they cannot easily be found.

DISTRIBUTION OF STAPELIADS

As water-storing stem succulents the stapeliads are residents of arid and semi-arid areas exclusively in the Old World. Highly succulent species such as *Hoodia* and *Trichocaulon* are found in dry places where precipitation may not occur for years.

The main distribution area is nearly identical with that of succulent euphorbias; i.e., the majority of the species belong to the dry areas of southern Africa. On the west side of the continent stapeliads stretch from Angola to the highlands of Nigeria; on the east side they appear along the mountain ranges over Tanzania, Kenya, Ethiopia, and Somalia, to southern Arabia and the off-shore islands of Socotra. On Madagascar they are represented by only one genus, *Stapelianthus*.

From Ethiopia the distribution area stretches westward to Morocco, and with *Caralluma europaea* in southern Spain, this plant group even reaches European soil. In the east the area stretches over Arabia, southern Iran, Pakistan, and Afghanistan to northern India, and from here southward to Sri Lanka and eastward to eastern India.

THE CULTIVATION OF STAPELIADS

Because of their bizarre, although usually unpleasant smelling blooms, stapeliads are an extremely attractive plant group, which, because of their slight size, are well-suited to indoor cultivation, especially since propagation is not difficult. Most species, besides the highly succulent ones such as *Trichocaulon, Hoodia,* and *Decabelone,* can easily be propagated from cuttings. Separate them at their branching point, let them dry well, and plant them in a sandy, initially dry medium. Only when new roots form may they be watered. The cuttings are best made in spring when repotting. All species that develop turf-like growth can be propagated very easily this way. Species such as *Trichocaulon, Hoodia,* and *Decabelone* can be propagated from seed. The seed is sown in sandy soil; the seedlings must be transplanted as soon as possible to well-drained containers, because otherwise they "succumb," i.e., they rot at ground level.

The late E. LAMB, who successfully occupied himself with the cultivation of many stapeliads, including rare species,[14] recommended a medium consisting of three layers:

Bottom layer: ⅓ gravel, ⅔ leaf mould
Middle layer: 1 part gravel, 1 part leaf mould
Top layer: ca. 2 cm gravel

The topping of gravel is to assure a rapid run-off of water and thus prevent rot at the bases of the shoots. Extreme care is advised in watering stapeliads. Water only enough to keep the shoots from withering. Also the plants should be shaded on very sunny days. During the winter months reduce water considerably. You can even remove the plants from the soil completely and over-winter them completely dry.

[14] LAMB, E.: *Stapeliads in Cultivation.* Blandford Press, London, 1957.

Regarding watering of stapeliads we recommend experimenting—rather too little water than too much! If you are growing stapeliads in a greenhouse, I recommend misting them several times a day during hot weather. Winter temperatures should be kept between +5° and +10° C (+40° to +50° F). Slow-growing species and species subject to diseases should be grafted. As a stock, the tubers of *Ceropegia woodii* (see Plate 7,3–4) and fast-growing stapeliads such as *S. gigantea, S. ambigua,* etc., have proven valuable.

Among the difficult species are *Hoodia* and *Trichocaulon.* They require a lot of sun and soil warmth and need very little water. They thrive best when grafted and put under glass.

PESTS AND DISEASES

In less than ideal conditions stapeliads are sometimes very susceptible to pests and diseases. If kept too dry they are attacked by root-mealy bugs, which are, however, easily controlled. Stapeliads are also frequently attacked by scales, but these can be eliminated with the proper treatment. Much more dangerous, however, is a disease known as "black death" or "black rot." It can wipe out whole collections in a short time (see also p. 31). The damage is manifested by the appearance of pitch-black spots and a yellowing of the shoots. If you cut these apart you will see a blackishness in the whole vascular tissue and to some extent of the epidermis (see Plate 8,6). Such plants should be considered as being dead. Especially susceptible are seedlings.

For a long time it was believed this disease was a virus; only recently has it been determined that this disease is the result of a fungus which enters the shoot tissue through the roots. There is currently no chemical treatment for the disease. There is nothing to be done but to cut out the infected pieces, throw them away, and re-root the healthy shoots in a sterile soil (sand). This disease appears primarily during the dim winter months. It is usually brought in with imported plants. As a preventive measure, not a cure, I recommend application of a fungicide in weak solution every 4 weeks. Above all, seedlings should be treated right from the beginning with fungicide. Not all species are susceptible to "black death." The fast-growing, large stapeliads such as *S. hirsuta, S. ambigua,* and *S. gigantea* are usually safe from it.

Only a small selection from the multi-species group of stapeliads can be listed here. The hobbyist who wants more information about these interesting plants should refer to the standard work of WHITE, A., and B. SLOANE *The Stapelieae,* 3 vols., Pasadena, 1937.

Frerea DALZ., known today as *Caralluma frerei* ROWL.,

is represented by a single species, *F. indica* DALZ. (Plate 32,1; Color Plate 4,5), from India (Concan, Bombay District), where it grows on hills at about 1000 m.

Among stapeliads *Frerea* occupies a special position since the reclining, round, soft shoots bear normal, short-petiolated leaves (Plate 32,1), which, however (in cultivation), are cast off in the winter months. Flowers are single with spreading, 5-pointed corolla; tips are broadly triangular, velvety brownish red with a yellow spot on each.

Frerea, with its pretty flowers, can be called a "gem" among stapeliads. It is seldom seen in cultivation; but once you get one, it is not easily lost, because the plant grows well and is easy to propagate. It requires relatively high humidity. It hybridizes easily with *Caralluma europaea.*

Caralluma R. BR.

is a genus with many species that demonstrate a variety of growth-forms, flowers, and inflorescences. The flower corolla is either a wide bell, wheel-shaped, or divided almost to the base; the corona has multiple forms and is usually double, the outer part is ring-shaped or cup-shaped, more or less deeply split into 5 lobes, with each lobe again divided. The inner corona lobes are fused to the outer ones, lying on the anthers or often extending beyond them and frequently having an appendage on the back. After inflorescences form, one can distinguish the two sections: Eucaralluma K. SCH. and Boucerosia K. SCH.

In the members of section Eucaralluma the stems begin to send out many off-shoots at flowering time and also begin to elongate; a segment of each shoot is sharply set off from the vegetative system and represents the beginning of the inflorescence-shoot (Plate 35,*1*), which dies completely after distributing seed. Renewal of the shoot system comes from the basal, succulent shoot segments.

In the members of section Boucerosia the elongation of the flowering shoots does not take place, nor does the rejuvenation of the stem tip. The flowers, usually arranged in umbel-like cymes, are found in terminal position, but immediately surpassed by a lateral branch emerging early, directly below the inflorescence (see Plate 35,*8*). Only in the species categorized in the "umbellata" group (see p. 64) does the rejuvenation of the shoot system occur from lower axil buds.

Section EUCARALLUMA

Its distribution area stretches from east Africa (Kenya) across Somalia to India; it is not found in southern Africa. All species are rare in cultivation and are somewhat difficult to propagate. The plants require a warm, dry location; the shoots frequently die at the base and must constantly be re-rooted in dry sand.

Caralluma gracilipes K. SCHUM. (Plate 35,*2*)

Stems are numerous, branching at the base, 15 to 30 cm long, 6 to 8 cm thick, vaguely quadrangular, with small, deciduous leaves. Inflorescence shoots are up to 20 cm long, thin, with about 15 pendulous flowers; the corolla is ca. 9 mm long, with a short tube and narrow, brownish red, hairy corolla-lobes (Plate 35,*4*); the corona is high above the base of the staminal column. *Distribution:* Kenya (Mutomo Hills).

Caralluma priogonium K. SCHUM. (Plate 32,*2; 34,1; 35,5*)

Forming tufts richly branched at the base, it has shoots 30 to 45 cm long, 1 to 3 cm thick, quadrangular, sharply serrate by virtue of the protruding leaf pads, gray or reddish green, with reddish spots and stripes. Its leaves are small and deciduous (Plate 32,*2*); inflorescence shoots are up to 30 cm long, upright or arched; and flowers appear in groups of 1 to 5, with a very short tube. Corolla lobes are narrowly lanceolate, star-shaped, spreading, ca. 1.5 cm long, rolled back at the margins, deep dark brown, spotted yellow at the base; upper side is velvety with hairs, and blackish violet hairs appear on the margin, especially at the base, with a few club-shaped hairs at the tips (Plate 35,*5*). *Distribution:* Tanzania (succulent-steppes on the north slope of the Usambara Mountains) and Kenya (backlands of Mombasa).

Very closely related to the above in growth-form is the Kenyan species

Caralluma turneri (BRUCE et BALLY) E.A. BRUCE (Plate 35,*1*)

It differs from the above in its pendulous flowers. Its corolla lobes are only slightly unfolded, folded distinctly backwards, strongly acute, and limber; the tips have a yellowish base color with dark brown to violet diagonal stripes (Plate 35,*3*); on the edges, especially near the base, are long, brown hairs.

Further species from section Eucaralluma are

Caralluma adscendens R. BR. (India)
Caralluma dalzielii N.E. BR. (northern Nigeria)
Caralluma edulis BENTH. et HOOK. f. (India, Pakistan)
Caralluma subulata (FORSK.) DECNE. (southern Arabia)
Caralluma arachnoidea BALLY (Kenya).

Section BOUCEROSIA

In this section, WHITE and SLOANE distinguish a series of groups, of which only the umbel-flowered ones (Umbellata group) are singled out and discussed as a special group. The species of all other groups are listed in alphabetical order.

The umbel-flowered carallumas are characterized by the umbel-like flower cymes being at the tip of the shoot, which stops growing as soon as the flowers appear (Plate 34,*2*). In *C. europaea* and *C. burchardii,* on the other hand, a continuing axil shoot very early resumes growth, and so the flower cymes later appear laterally near the shoot tip.

The main distribution of this group is almost identical to that of section Eucaralluma. Except for a few exceptions, their members have quadrangular shoots, some of which grow to a considerable size *(C. penicillata* up to 1.2 m; see Plate 33,*2*).

Most species are rare in collections, since their cultivation affords similar difficulties to that of the eucarallumas. As examples we list the following species:

Caralluma adenensis (DEFL.) BRGR. (Plate 35,*6*)

forms tufts 20 to 30 cm high, up to 50 cm in diameter; shoots are upright or nearly so, irregularly branched, flatly quadrangular, gray-green. Flowers are up to 25 or 40 in an umbel; the corolla has a warty tube 10 mm long, whose exterior is glabrous and greenish yellow, and whose interior is dark purple. Corolla lobes are triangular, 6 to 9 mm long, dark purple. The outer corona is pale pink, hairy, cup-shaped at the base, with its 5 lobes upright and divided deeply into two teeth; inner corona lobes are shorter than the outer ones and are lying on the anthers. *Distribution:* southern Arabia (Aden Province), predominantly on limestone.

Caralluma retrospiciens (EHRENB.) N.E. BR.

is a large, stout species, which often forms clusters up to 2 m in diameter (Plate 33,*1*). Stems are thick, gray-green, irregularly branched, quadrangular, with hooked teeth pointing downwards. Flowers are numerous, in cymes, which form a spherical head up to 12 cm in diameter; the tube is bell-shaped, ca. 6 mm long, with broadly triangular, hairy lobes, which are reddish on the bottom, dark violet on the top, and have dark-violet, undulating club hairs on the margin. *Habitat:* Red Sea (the island of Dalac), Ethiopia, Somalia, Sudan.

Var. *tombuctuensis* (CHEV.) WHITE et SLOANE

has a somewhat wider distribution. It is found all around the Sahara from Sudan to Mauritania and Senegal and goes southeastward to the dry areas of Kenya and Tanzania, where it is predominant in the so-called succulent-steppes (Plate 33,*1*). The differences from the type are slight: the teeth of the stems are not pointed downwards but are straight, a characteristic that does not seem to be reliable; the blackish purple corolla lobes are warty above and have thin, mobile hairs on the margin (Plate 34,2 and 5).

The largest species of the Umbellata group is

Caralluma penicillata (DEFL.) N.E. BR. (Plate 33,2),

which is distributed in southern Arabia and Yemen, often appearing there in masses up to 2000 m or as individuals. Its shoots are richly branched at the base, up to 5 cm thick, quadrangular and bluntly toothed, light gray-green and can reach a length of up to 1.2 m. Flowers are numerous in terminal cymes; the corolla has a short tube and flat, triangularly oval lobes that are leather-yellow on the upper side and brightly spotted. At the ends of the lobes is a dense, brush-like tuft of mobile, purple-red hairs (Plate 35,8), thus the name "paint brush" caralluma.

Caralluma europaea (GUSS.) N.E. BR.,

as the name suggests, is a species of special interest, because its var. *confusa* FONT-QUER reaches into European territory in southern Spain (Capa de Gata near Almeria).

The type-locality is the island of Lampeduse near Malta. *C. europaea* is an extremely variable species, whose numerous varieties are spread along the coastal area of northern Africa.

C. europaea has reclining or upright, partially subterranean, irregularly branched, quadrangular stems with deciduous, small leaves. Flowers appear in groups of 10 to 13, in cymes (Plate 35,9), with a very short tube and radial, spreading corolla lobes. These are egg-shaped but pointed and are greenish yellow to whitish in basic color, with hairs in the center around the corona; it has concentric, slightly wavy, brown cross-bands near the corolla tube. Lobes of the corolla are uniformly brown.

The plant grows quickly in cultivation; it blooms freely and is easy to propagate. In its habitat it is eaten by natives.

Similar in growth-form is

Caralluma munbyana (DECNE.) N.E. BR.

Its flowers differ from those of the above species by their narrowly linear, satiny brown corolla lobes, which are bent backwards (Plate 35,7).

C. munbyana is the second stapeliad found in Europe (var. *hispanica* (DE COINCY) MAIRE).: in southern Spain near Caravaca (Prov. Murcia).

To the same group also belongs the Canary Island (Fuerteventura) species

Caralluma burchardii N.E. BR. (Plate 35,10).

Its flowers resemble those of *C. europaea* but are not spotted, and the corolla lobes are densely covered with white hairs. Further *Caralluma* species from section Boucerosia are:

Caralluma aperta (MASS) N.E. BR. (Plate 36,1),

the "wide-open caralluma," with its blunt-edged, barely serrate, gray-green shoots and its long-stemmed flowers, very much resembles *Stapelia pedunculata*, but the structure of the corona clearly indicates its membership in the genus *Caralluma*.

Flowers have a short, cup-shaped, densely papillous tube, which is dark green on the inside; corolla lobes are spreading, broadly triangular, with the upper side wrinkled, and basically yellowish white with a dense, irregular network of purple-brown lines and spots. *Distribution:* from Little Namaqualand to the Richtersveld.

Caralluma baldrattii WHITE et SLOANE (Plate 32,9)

Stems are quadrangular, gray-green with dark spots, with long, pointed mamillae. Flowers occur singly or a few together, near the tip of the shoot, and are sub-sessile or short petiolated; corolla lobes are mahogany brown on the upper side, partially cream-colored, and then tipped with red, with fine hairs. *Distribution:* Ethiopia to Kenya.

Caralluma dummeri (N.E. BR.) WHITE et SLOANE (Plate 36,2)

Stems are reclining to upright, indistinctly quadrangular with teeth ca. 15 cm long, gray-green, with reddish stripes. Flowers appear in groups of 2 to 6, ca. 4 cm in diameter, with olivegreen corolla lobes having white bristles on the upper side. *Habitat:* Kenyan dry forests.

This is a very pretty and free-flowering species!

Caralluma hottentotorum (N.E. BR.) N.E. BR.

A plant of shrubby growth-form, it has upright shoots up to 15 cm tall and 2.5 cm thick, gray-green or dark purple, quadrangular, sharply dentate. Flowers are small, appearing in groups up to 10, arranged on the surfaces of the shoot in rows (Plate 34,4). The corolla is ca. 6 mm wide, bell-shaped, deeply cut into 5 parts with pale yellowish green, naked lobes that are only slightly hairy in the throat. *Distribution:* western Cape Province (Little Namaqualand).

Caralluma lugardii N.E. BR.

Stems are reclining to upright, sometimes extended like stolons, quadrangular with wide-spreading teeth that are hard at the tips, gray-green, with dark-brown spots. Flowers occur in bundles of 3 to 7, near the shoot tip, up to 3 cm long, with a short tube, narrowly lanceolate, rolled, chocolate-brown or greenish yellow at the tips; upper side is papillous, with hairy tips rolled onto the margin. *Habitat:* Botswana, western Cape Province, Namibia.

The extremely pretty flowers are distinguished by a terrible smell.

Caralluma luntii N.E. BR. (Plate 36,3)

Stems are upright, 10 to 20 cm high, gray-green with reddish dots, glabrous, quadrangular with wide-spread, sharply triangular teeth. Flowers appear in groups of 1 to 3 near the tip of the shoot. The corolla is deeply split into 5 lobes, with narrowly linear tips that are ca. 18 mm long, upright, and rolled back on the margins; the upper side has short hairs, greenish yellow at the base, dark brown in the upper half. *Habitat:* southern Arabia.

A very pretty species, whose flowers, however, smell strongly like rotten fish, is

Caralluma lutea N.E. BR.,

the "yellow caralluma," which is widespread from Transvaal to northern Cape Province, on grassy slopes. It forms mats with shoots 5 to 10 cm long, quadrangular, coarsely dentate. Flowers are numerous at the base of the shoot, 3 to 7 mm in diameter, with narrowly lanceolate, golden yellow lobes with vibrant, violet club-hairs.

Caralluma mammillaris (L.) N.E. BR. (Color Plate 5,*1* and Plate 32,6),

the "mammilla caralluma." A plant of scrubby growth-form, it has thick, 5- to 6-ribbed, bright green shoots up to 40 cm tall. The podaria and mounded like mamillae, ending in a hard thorn tip (Plate 32,6). Flowers occur in groups of 3 to 20 near the tip of the shoot, with the corolla deeply split into 5 lobes; these are upright to flared, rolled back on the edge, and are blackish purple, with the upper side having fine hairs. The corolla tube is very short and is dotted with white and blackish purple (Color Plate 5). *Distribution:* western Cape Province.

WHITE and SLOANE compiled all "thorned" species into the *Mammillaris* group, to which the following two species also belong:

Caralluma armata N.E. BR. (Plate 36,4),

the "thorny caralluma," is also a very sturdy, shrubby plant up to 40 cm high. Its stems are up to 3 cm thick, quadrangular, with long mamillae ending in a thorny tip. Flowers are numerous, near the tip of the shoot, with a short, greenish yellow, purple-dotted tube; corolla lobes are flared, bent back on the edge, greenish yellow with purple dots at the base, and at the tip uniformly purple-brown. *Distribution:* from Little Namaqualand to Namibia.

Very similar to the above and hardly distinguishable from it in its vegetative state is

Caralluma winkleri (DTR.) WHITE et SLOANE.

The German botanist, Prof. DINTER, who undertook extensive trips in Namibia, placed this plant, as well as *C. armata,* into its own genus, which he named after the type-locality, the Sarcophagus Mountain near Klinghardt (Namibia); he called it *Sarcophagophilus,* but according to N.E. BROWN it is a typical *Caralluma.*

All heavily thorned species are slow growing and do best when grafted.

Caralluma marlothii N.E. BR. (Plate 36,5)

Stems are branched at the base, 8 to 10 cm tall, up to 2 cm thick, dusky dark violet, clearly quadrangular, with pointed teeth 2 to 4 cm long. Flowers are very small, only up to 7 mm across; corolla lobes are bent back, light green, dotted with red, with red hairs on the top and on the edges. *Habitat:* Cape Province, growing under bushes.

This plant is a very heavy bloomer, although the blooms are small; it is easy to grow.

Caralluma nebrownii BRGR.

This plant forms mats with upright stems up to 18 cm long and 4 cm thick, quadrangular, with teeth deeply sinuate, gray-green, with wine colored spots. Flowers appear in groups of 15 to 30 in an umbel with a radial, spreading corolla up to 10 cm. Its tips are dark brown, up to 4 cm long, with purple, vibrating club-hairs on the margins. *Distribution:* Namibia.

C. nebrownii is common in collections; even in its vegetative state it is very decorative.

Caralluma piaranthoides OBERM. (Plate 36,9)

Stems are reclining to upright, up to 10 cm tall, with 4 ribs, with long, sharp teeth. Flowers appear in groups of 2 to 5 near the tip of the shoot, with flatly spread corolla; corolla tips are triangular, acute, yellow with wine-red spots, and upper side is papillous. *Habitat:* Zimbabwe.

Caralluma pruinosa (MASS.) N.E. BR. (Plate 36,6),

the "frosted caralluma," is shrubby, branched with upright stems up to 30 cm long, gray-green, with reddish streaks, quadrangular. Mamillae are flat, extended, with short teeth; flowers are small, in groups of 1 to 3, on the upper segments of the stem, with a radial, spread corolla up to 14 mm across. Corolla lobes are dark blackish brown, with a frosted appearance caused by fine, white, adpressed hairs. *Habitat:* Cape Province (Little Namaqualand).

A heat-loving species, it grows best when grafted (Plate 7,4).

Also among the hard-to-grow species that grow in cultivation only when grafted is

Caralluma ramosa (MASS.) N.E. BR. (Plate 7,3).

This plant is large and richly branched (thus the name *ramosa*), forming tufts up to 30 cm tall. Its shoots are gray-blue-green, in full sunlight purple, up to 2.5 cm thick, quadrangular, with extended, slightly raised mamillae. Flowers occur in bundles between the ribs and are relatively small. Corolla lobes are narrowly linear, pointed, and glabrous, with the upper side blackish purple. *Distribution:* southwestern Karroo.

Caralluma subterranea BRUCE et BALLY (Plate 36,7)

A plant with subterranean runners, it has upright shoots up to 10 cm long, quadrangular, with sharp teeth. Flowers appear singly or in bundles near the tip of the shoot, with dark brown, sometimes yellow corolla lobes, whose upper side has dense, white hair. *Habitat:* Kenya, between 1500 and 1800 m.

This is a very pretty and easily grown species.

Caralluma umdausensis NEL (Plate 36,8)

This plant is small, forming shrubs branched at the base, with upright stems up to 10 cm tall, bluntly quadrangular, dark gray-green. Flowers appear singly, and are long stalked, up to 2.5 cm in diameter. The corolla tube is broadly bell-shaped, ca. 5 mm deep, densely papillous at the base, and reddish purple with a regular white ring around the corona, from which ca. 20 yellowish green stripes radiate and from which three enter the base of the corolla tips. These are long, pointed, greenish yellow, irregularly spotted and warty toward the tip. *Distribution:* western Cape Province (Little Namaqualand–Richtersvelde). It produces beautiful blooms, but is very sensitive, and grows best grafted.

Diplocyatha (Thunb.) N.E. Br [= *Orbea*][15]

has only one species, *D. ciliata* (Thunb.) N.E. Br [= *Orbea ciliata* (Thunb.) Leach]. The old name refers to the fact that the flowers have a double corolla, i.e., at the base of the bell-shaped corolla tube there is a second corolla, which, however, should be seen as merely a distinctly raised ring (annulus) (Plate 37,*1*).

Plants form mats with reclining to upright stems that are 3 to 5 cm long and quadrangular, with sharp, spherical, acute teeth. Flowers appear singly at the base of the stem; the corolla tube is 7 to 8 cm in diameter, inside ash gray, with fine, brown-tipped papillae. The ring (= second corolla tube) is raised into a funnel shape, with a thick, bulging, distinctly warty edge; corolla lobes are ca. 2.5 cm long, broadly triangular, acuminate, spreading or reflexed, and the upper side is distinctly warty, with long, mobile, white club-hairs on the edge. *Habitat:* Cape Province, (Ceres Karroo, Great Karroo).

D. ciliata is a very attractive plant, whose cultivation is like that of *Stapelia*.

Duvalia Haw.

The genus was named by Haworth after the French botanist and succulent researcher, H. Duval. It includes plants of mat-like growth with reclining or diagonally upright, usually short, seldom elongated shoots with 4 to 6 ribs and short teeth. Flowers appear singly or in multiples and structurally differ from those of other stapeliads:

The short corolla tube forms a thick, frequently hairy cup (= ring) that is completely filled by the outer corona, which is developed into a fleshy configuration called a coronal disk. On top of it sit the egg-shaped to spoon-shaped inner corona tips (Plate 37,*2*); corolla lobes are broadly triangular, frequently, however, narrowly linear and then distinctly folded backwards.

The genus contains very decorative, easily grown species, whose distribution stretches from South Africa and Namibia over eastern Africa (Tanzania and Kenya) into southern Arabia.

Duvalia compacta Haw. (Plate 37,*2*)

gets its name from short, fat stems, which are covered by dense leaf pads. Flowers appear in groups of 1 to 5, near the middle of reddish stems that are 15 to 20 mm long. The corolla is ca. 2 cm in diameter, deep brown, with separated, sharp corolla lobes, which point distinctly backward and are reflexed at the tip, glabrous, hairy only at the base. The annulus ring is low, short, slightly hairy; the coronal disk is dark wine-red, vaguely pentagonal; and the inner corona horns are dusky orange. *Habitat:* Cape Province (Little Namaqualand).

D. compacta, a fast-growing, free-blooming species, is related to *D. reclinata* (see p. 72), but differs from it by its smaller flowers.

Duvalia corderoyi (Hook. f.) N.E. Br.

Its stems form tufts that are reclining to upright, short cylindrical, 4 to 5 cm long, ca. 2 cm thick, gray-green or made reddish by the sun, and 4 to 5 angled, with short, fleshy, triangular teeth. Flowers occur in groups of 2 to 4, near the base of the young shoot, on stems 2 to 2.5 cm long, and are 3.5 to 4 cm in diameter. The corolla has a raised, pale-violet annulus covered with soft, purple, separated hairs; corolla lobes are reflexed in the upper segment, olive-green, dark reddish brown near the tip, almost half covered with purple club-hairs. The coronal disk is quadrangular and dark brick red; the inner corona lobes are pale red. *Distribution:* Cape Province, growing under bushes.

Duvalia elegans (Mass.) Haw.,

the "elegant duvalia," differs from the other species by its heavy coat of hairs on the flat and seldom reflexed corolla tips; sometimes in var. *seminuda* N.E. Br. these are glabrous in the apical region. Stems are decumbent to ascendant, longitudinal with 4 to 5 indistinct ribs, dark purple-green. Flowers appear in groups of 2 to 3 at the base of the stem; the outer corona is almost round, dark reddish brown, almost filling the ring; and the inner corona tips are pale yellowish brown. *Distribution:* Great Karroo.

Duvalia maculata N.E. Br.

is a very pretty species in regard to its flower color. It gets its name from the spotted flower annulus that is covered with short hairs. It is basically white with violet spots. Contrasting to this are the chocolate-colored, glabrous, distinctly folded corolla lobes with hairs on the margins. The coronal disk is yellow; the plant forms mats, with short, 4 to 5 angular shoots with strikingly acuminate teeth. *Habitat:* eastern Cape Province and Namibia.

---

[15] [L.C. Leach, Hon. Botanist, Nat. Herbarium Salisburg, Rhodesia (Zimbabwe), has given a new classification of the Stapelieae (literature below). The old genus *Orbea* Haw. and the genus *Tridendata* Haw. are reviewed.

Leach, L.C.: "A Contribution towards a New Classification of Stapelieae (Asclepiadaceae) with a Preliminary Review of *Orbea* Haw. and Descriptions of Three New Genera." *Excelsa,* Taxonomic Series No. 1, pp. 1–75.

Leach, L.C.: "A Second Contribution towards a New Classification of Stapelieae (Asclepiadaceae) with a Review of *Tridendata* Haw. and Miscellaneous Notes on *Stapelia* L." *Excelsa,* Taxonomic Series No. 2, pp. 1–73. Published by Aloe, Cactus and Succulent Society of Rhodesia (Zimbabwe), No. 1 (1978), No. 2 (198).

Diplocyatha N.E. Br. is taken by L.C. Leach into the synonymy of *Orbea.*]

Duvalia modesta N.E. Br. (Plate 37,3),

the "modest duvalia," is of mat-like growth-form. Its stems are briefly egg-shaped with 4 to 5 indistinctly hooked ribs; flowers occur in groups of 2 to 3, in the middle of the younger stems. Corolla lobes are dark chocolate, broad and spreading at the base, reflexed back toward the tip, and bent into a hook; up to half of its length has dense, long, purple hairs on the edge. The annulus is naked; the coronal disk is bluntly pentagonal and flesh colored. *Distribution:* eastern Cape Province.

Duvalia polita N.E. Br. (Plate 39,1)

differs from most other species by its usually upright, cylindrical, 6-angled stems with long, sharp teeth; at the base of the shoot, subterranean stolons are sometimes formed. Flowers are ca. 2.5 to 3 cm in diameter, with a purple-red, papillous ring and broad, pointed, dark reddish brown, shiny tips with purple club-hairs at the base. In var. *transvaalensis* these are basically yellowish green with purplish brown spots; the coronal disk is dark red to chocolate brown. *Distribution:* Namibia to Transvaal.

Duvalia procumbens R.A. Dyer (Plate 37,5),

today known as *Huernia procumbens* Leach, has long, creeping stems that hang from boulders. These stems are dark green, frequently with reddish dots, and bluntly pentagonal, with a mantle of leaf pads that are 1 to 2 cm long and have tiny, soon withering blades. Flowers appear in inflorescences of 1 to 2 flowers, at the base of the young shoots; the corolla is 1 to 3 cm in diameter, with a brownish red, glabrous annulus and narrowly lanceolate, sharply acuminate, earth-colored tips that are edged in red, with the upper side finely and densely hairy and folded upwards somewhat at the tip. The coronal disk is chestnut brown and slightly puffed at the edge. *Distribution:* eastern Transvaal (Krüger Park).

To the same growth-form also belong *D. tanganyikensis* Bruce et Bally and *D. andreaeana* Rauh. In both, which Leach places into the genus *Huernia,* the shoots, sometimes a meter long and indistinctly pentagonal, creep along the ground.

In *D. tanganyikensis* the inflorescences have many blooms (Plate 37,6); the flowers have a diameter of 2 to 2.5 cm; their annulus is raised, glabrous or with short hairs, dark wine red, and shiny. The pale flesh-colored corolla lobes are completely glabrous. *Distribution:* Tanzania (Mont Legido, ca. 1800 m).

All three species are easy to grow in cultivation and are free bloomers; they do, however, take up a lot of room because of their creeping growth-form.

Duvalia radiata (Sims.) Haw.

Its stems are reclining to upright, spherical to cylindrical, 4 to 8 cm long, indistinctly 5-ribbed, with sharp, acute mamillae. Flowers appear usually in twos, near the tip of the shoot, and are dark chocolate colored, with a glabrous or hairy annulus. Corolla tips are glabrous, flaring, and reflexed; the coronal disk is indistinctly pentagonal and reddish brown. *Distribution:* western Cape Province.

D. radiata is a variable species, of which var. *obscura* (N.E. Br.) White et Sloane, var. *hirtella* (Jacq.) White et Sloane,

and var. *minor* (N.E. Br.) White et Sloane have been described. Especially pretty is var. *hirtella,* in which the annulus is densely covered with purple hairs (Plate 37,4).

Very closely related to the above and perhaps only a subspecies thereof is

Duvalia reclinata (Mass.) Haw.

It differs from *D. radiata* by the deep dark chocolate flowers and the more distinctly folded corolla lobes, which have dark purple club-hairs at their base. *Distribution:* eastern Cape Province.

The most beautiful, large-flowered duvalia, and at the same time the only species from southern Arabia (Aden Province) is

Duvalia sulcata N.E. Br. (Color Plate 4,3).

Its shoots are reclining to upright, up to 6.5 cm long, branching into runners at the base, gray-green, with reddish spots, and long, acute teeth. Flowers occur in groups of 1 to 3, on stems that are ca. 3 cm long, opened to 4.5 cm in diameter; the annulus is brownish red, dense with long, white or pale reddish hairs. Corolla lobes are spreading, up to 1.8 cm long and up to 1.2 cm wide at the base, and brownish red; the upper side has 5 deep nerves, is glabrous, long, and mobile, with purple club-hairs at the base. In var. *seminuda* Lavr., however, the annulus is glabrous, and the corolla tips are hairy.

D. sulcata differs from the African species by its quadrangular stems and very large flowers. It might belong to its own growth-form group, and thus it would be the only species of the group.

Echidnopsis Hook. f.

The generic name, not to be confused with the cactus genus *Echinopsis,* means "snake-like" and refers to the growth-form of most of the species, whose round shoots divided into patterns by the oblong leaf pads, look like snakes crawling on the ground (Plate 38,1). The flowers are very small and resemble those of *Trichocaulon;* however, they show relation to the genus *Caralluma* in their corona structure.

The distribution area stretches from South Africa across eastern Africa to Socotra and southern Arabia.

The best known and most commonly cultivated species is

Echidnopsis cereiformis Hook. f. (Plate 39,2).

Its stems are reclining to upright, rooted on the under side, round, with 8 to 10 rows of broadly hexagonal, flat podaria. Flowers appear in groups of 2 to 4 in the furrows with corollas split deeply into 5 lobes; its egg-shaped to lanceolate tips are brownish yellow, with the upper side light yellow and bell-shaped.

In var. *obscura* Brgr. the flowers are vividly brown. *Habitat:* southern Arabia (Yemen), Ethiopia, and Somalia.

This plant is fast growing, free flowering, and easy to propagate.

Echidnopsis bentii N.E. BR.

Its stems are upright, branched at the base, with 7 to 8 ribs, with short, hexagonal mamillae that extend into a dry leaf rudiment. Flowers appear usually in 2-flowered inflorescences near the tip of the shoot, with a broadly bell-shaped, almost radial corolla, whose lobes have velvety wine-red tips. *Distribution:* southern Arabia (probably Hadramaut).

Echidnopsis ciliata BALLY

This plant has reclining, creeping, few-branched stems. The podaria occur in 8 rows and are elongated, bearing the scars of the tiny, soon-falling blades in the upper part. Flowers appear singly or in twos, between the ribs, and are ca. 1 cm in diameter, with a short, bell-shaped tube and spreading corolla lobes that are uniformly deep purple on the upper side, with short papillae, and with hairs on the margin. *Distribution:* Somalia to Kenya.

Echidnopsis dammanniani SPRENG. (Plate 39,3)

In growth-form it is similar to *E. cereiformis;* its stems have 8 to 10 ribs; and the ribs are divided by irregularly shaped mamillae. Flowers appear in groups of 2 to 5 and are almost sessile, with a radial corolla and brown lobes that are papillous on both sides. *Habitat:* Ethiopia, Somalia, and northern Kenya.

Echidnopsis framesii WHITE et SLOANE (Plate 39,4)

Its stems are reclining to upright, up to 10 cm long, 1 to 3 cm thick, with blunt, hexagonal mamillae arranged in longitudinal rows, and scoop-shaped leaves. Its flowers appear in bundles of 2 to 5 near the tip of the shoot, on stems 4 to 5 mm long, and are ca. 9 mm in diameter. Corolla lobes are dark purple, 3 to 4 mm long, and spreading, and the upper side, with the exception of the somewhat reflexed tip, is papillous. *Distribution:* western Cape Province (Vanrhynsdorp District).

Echidnopsis repens DYER et VERDOORN (Plate 38,1)

This is a reclining to creeping plant, with little branching, is easily broken, and is rooted on the underside. Its shoots are round, ca. 1 cm thick, and green or reddish; the podaria are long, in 8 to 10 rows, bearing the dentate scar of the tiny, deciduous leaf blade in the upper segment. Flowers occur usually singly, and are small, with flatly spread, dark-purple corolla lobes and with scattered hairs at the base of the corolla tip. *Distribution:* Tanzania, at the foot of the Vulkanes Meru.

Our examples, collected from the arid bush of Loitokitok (borderland between Tanzania and Kenya), differ from the type by their intensively yellow corolla tips (Plate 38,1).

Echidnopsis serpentina (NEL) WHITE et SLOANE

Its stems are reclining, creeping, irregularly branched, and roundish, with 8 rows of hexagonal, dark-green to reddish violet mamillae. Flowers appear in groups of 8 to 9 near the tip and are ca. 8 mm in diameter; their tips are dark purple on the upper side and are covered with short, stiff bristles; and the corolla tube is yellowish inside. *Distribution:* southwestern Cape Province (Vanrhynsdorp District).

Echidnopsis sharpei WHITE et SLOANE

This plant has shoots that are reclining, creeping, or upright, up to 14 cm long, and cylindrical, with 8 rows of mamillae and small, deciduous leaves. Flowers occur in groups of 1 to 2, slightly below the tip, ca. 1 cm in diameter with velvety red corolla lobes, which have some reddish hairs on their margins and on the tips. *Distribution:* northern Kenya.

Echidnopsis squamulata (DECNE.) BALLY

is a very striking species, whose long-tubed flowers differ from those of other *Echidnopsis* species. The plant was collected by the French botanist BOTTA (1837) in southern Arabia and was described by DECAISNE as *Ceropegia squamulata.* According to investigations by BALLY, however, it belongs to the genus *Echidnopsis.*

Its shoots are reclining, with 7 to 8 ribs, and are gray-green or reddish brown. Flowers have cup-shaped, reddish brown tubes ca. 14 cm long and 5 short, triangular lobes that are greenish yellow at the recurved tips, with red spots. *Distribution:* Yemen and southern Arabia (Dhala and Mukairas Plateau).

Echidnopsis urceolata BALLY

also has long, tubular flowers. Its growth-form resembles a small, thorny *Trichocaulon,* but, regarding the flower structure, it must be placed in the genus *Echidnopsis.*

Stems are single or branching at the base, up to 8 cm long, 2.5 cm thick, and cylindrical, with 18 to 20 ribs; the mamillae are very dense, ending in a short, thin thorn. Flowers appear usually singly near the tip of the shoot, with a tube ca. 10 mm long, urn-shaped, with a pale-green exterior and a purple base; the interior is warty and uniformly purple. The corolla lobes are short, broadly triangular, unfolding only a little, and pale-green. *Distribution:* Kenya (Northern Frontier Province).

This is a very pretty, although rare and difficult to cultivate species.

Echidnopsis watsonii BALLY (Plate 38,2)

Its stems are reclining to upright, slightly branched, up to 20 cm long, and cylindrical, with 8 to 12 indistinct ribs. The podaria are almost rectangular, retaining the soon-withering leaf blades for a long time. Flowers occur usually singly, near the tip of the shoot, with a distinct, dark purple tube up to 7.5 mm long. Corolla lobes are up to 7.5 mm long, very much flared, with a dark purple-red under side and a yellow upper side with recurved edges. *Distribution:* Somalia.

This is a pretty and decorative species.

A remarkable genus is

Edithcolea N.E. BR.,

named for its discoverer EDITH COLE, an English succulent grower, who lived for a long time in Kenya. The distribution area for the genus is Somalia, Kenya, Tanzania, and the island of Socotra.

Edithcolea grandis N.E. Br. (Plate 38,3)

is surely one of the most charming stapeliads; its flowers, up to 15 cm in diameter, are real works of art, to be compared in their markings and color to the beauty of a Persian rug.

In the dry forests of eastern Kenya, *E. grandis* forms square meters of reclining to upright, irregularly branched shoots of a brownish red color, covered with thorny leaf pads. The extremely large flowers appear singly or in twos, just below the shoot tip on short, thick stems. The flowers have a flat, plate-shaped corolla with a short tube and five wide lobes that end in long, usually recurved tips. The basic color of the flower is pale yellow, which is overlaid with a beautiful pattern of purplish brown spots that partially flow together. From the sunken center of the flower up to the sinuses of the corolla lobes run 5 rows of long, purple club-hairs. The edges of the uniformly purple or olive-green points are—with the exception of their yellowish green tips—covered with dark-violet hairs.

Although widely distributed in its habitat, *Edithcolea* is very rare in collections. It is not exactly easy to grow and requires great sensitivity in regard to watering. During the dim winter months it must be kept absolutely dry; in a bright, sunny location it blooms even in cultivation.

Edithcolea sordida N.E. Br.

(habitat: Socotra and northern Kenya), differs from the above by its smaller, uniformly dark-purple flowers; today it is united with *E. grandis* into one species.

Among the sought-after stapeliads are also the members of the genus

Hoodia Sweet,

named for the succulent grower Hood. It is a highly succulent plant with a shrubby growth-form with columnar, multi-ribbed, thick shoots, branching from the base. Their leaf pads end in a sharp thorn (Plate 39,5; Plate 40,1–4). The flowers of most of the species are very large and have a flat, spreading or dish-shaped, usually reddish, lobed corolla (Plate 39,5).

The distribution area for *Hoodia* stretches from southern Cape Province over Namibia to Angola and Botswana. Here it inhabits the driest, most arid areas—stony and sandy-loamy semi-deserts with sparse growth (Plate 40,1–2).

On the basis of the conditions in its habitat (hot and dry), hoodias are also difficult to cultivate. They require a warm, sunny location and absolute dryness during the winter months; even during the summer, caution is advised in regard to watering.

Propagation is usually done from seed, which germinate very quickly, but the seedlings must be grafted onto *Ceropegia woodii*, for they are very susceptible to "black death." Propagation by cuttings is possible, but the cuttings need nearly a year to form roots. Put them in pure sand and place a glass closely over them. Keep them completely dry.

During the summer months the plants can be put in a covered but well-aired vitrine. Only under optimal cultural and climatic conditions can they be made to bloom.

White and Sloane list 16 species; in H. Jacobsen's handbook there are 18. When the genus is re-examined, some of them will surely have to be combined, because they have only the value of varieties. On his trips through the dry areas of South Africa the author himself could see that the variability of flowers, size, and color of *H. gordonii* or *H. bainii*—two quite common species—is so large that I could easily describe several more varieties.

Hoodia bainii R.A. Dyer (Plate 32,5; 33,3; 39,5)

These are richly branched shrubs with gray-green shoots 15 to 40 cm high, ca. 3.5 cm thick, and with 12 to 15 ribs. The dense mamillae are divided by a sharp, diagonal furrow and end in a sharp, pale-brown thorn; flowers appear singly or in twos, up to 7 cm in diameter, with a deep dish shape, are completely glabrous (even in the center), bright yellow, reddish or pale purple, with a short-lobed corolla. *Distribution:* common and widespread from Karroo to Namibia.

Very similar is

Hoodia gordonii (Mass.) Sweet (Plate 40,1 and 2).

It is a splendid sight at flowering time, when the shrubs, which are up to 1 m tall and richly branched at the base, are covered by hundreds of large flowers—a picture of indescribable beauty in the midst of the nearly barren desert.

In contrast to *H. bainii* the flowers are up to 10 cm in diameter and have a flat dish shape, their color is flesh to brownish with green stripes, and they are slightly papillous in the center.

A species with a quite large flower is

Hoodia currori (Hook.) Decne. (Plate 40,3).

Its stems are up to 60 cm tall and 5 cm thick, multi-ribbed, and heavily thorned. Its flowers appear near the tip of the shoot with dish-shaped, reddish brown corollas ca. 10 cm in diameter and having sparse hairs on the upper side; the petals end in sharp tips. *Distribution:* from Angola to Namibia.

This plant blooms freely in cultivation.

An example of a species with very pubescent flowers is the charming

Hoodia dregei N.E. BR. (Color Plate 5,4),

a plant that blooms well even in cultivation and remains small, with stems ca. 30 cm long, with many thorns and 20 to 24 ribs. The relatively small flowers, only up to 3.5 cm in diameter, appear in multiple cymes just below the tip of the shoot; their flat dish-shaped, flesh-colored to brownish red, short-lobed corolla is covered with long, white hairs on the upper side. *Distribution:* Cape Province (southern Great Karroo).

Pubescent flowers are also found on *H. macrantha* DTR., *H. lugardi* N.E. BR., *H. husabensis* NES, *H. rosea* OBERM., *H. parviflora* N.E. BR., and *H. longii* OBERM.; but the pubescence is less prominent on these than on *H. dregei.*

One with very small flowers and hard to grow is

Hoodia ruschii DTR. (Plate 40,4).

Its stems are only up to 50 cm tall and 4 cm thick, with 22 to 24 irregular ribs and thorny mamillae. Flowers are numerous near the tip, with a broad bell-shaped corolla ca. 2 cm in diameter; the upper side has white hairs and is dark reddish brown, yellow in the center. Their petal points are broadly triangular, ending in a short tip. *Distribution:* only in Namibia, near Aus.

A controversial genus is

Hoodiopsis LUCKH.,

which is represented by only one species, *H. triebneri* LUCKH., in Namibia. It is probably a bi-generic hybrid between *Hoodia* and *Stapelia* or *Caralluma,* because the plant shows characteristics of all three genera. The multi-ribbed (up to 9 ribs), heavily thorned shoots and the very large flowers resemble those of *Hoodia,* although the corolla is 5-lobed as in *Stapelia.* The structure of the corona, however, shows certain characteristics of the genus *Caralluma.* Only experimentation with crossing, which can only be done in the habitat area, can settle the question of the hybrid nature of *Hoodiopsis.*

Huernia R. BR. [16]

is a genus with many species that are distinguished by the following characteristics: stems are richly branched from the base, reclining or upright, with 4 to 5 ribs (exception: *H. pillansii*); flowers appear usually on the base of the stem, with bell-shaped, 5-lobed corolla; in the sinuses of the 5 larger lobes are usually smaller, incidental lobes (therefore HAWORTH referred to the genus

as *Decadontia,* the "10-lobed" flower); with few exceptions the upper sides of the corolla lobes have papillae or hairs; the corona is usually double. K. SCHUMANN and A. BERGER used the structure of the inner corona lobes as the basis for their categorizing of the many species.

In the members of section Plagiostelma K. SCHUM., the inner corona lobes are bent over the anthers and not elongated.

In section Orthostelma K. SCHUM. the inner corona lobes are spread outward at the tips; in the species of section Calostelma BRGR. they are thickened at the tip; and in section Podostelma BRGR. the inner corona horns have a thick, recurved appendage resembling an upside-down shoe.

Most *Huernia* species grow fast and are beautiful plants, whose cultivation affords fewer difficulties than most other stapeliads.

The following selection of the approximately 50 known species can give only a slight impression of the beauty of this plant group.

Huernia aspera N.E. BR. (Plate 40,5).

Its stems are reclining to upright, up to 15 cm long, and have 5 to 6 ribs, with flat, elongated podaria ending in a short tooth. Flowers appear in groups of 3 to 5 at the base of the young shoots; the corolla is wide bell-shaped, ca. 12 mm long and 20 to 25 mm wide, with a reddish brown exterior made rough by numerous white papillae. Their recurved lobes are acute-triangular, the lower side has 5 raised nerves, and the upper side is deep purplish brown with papillae of the same color. Intermediate lobes are short; the exterior corona has wide, blunt, satiny, papillous, blackish purple lobes, which are joined in a notched ring. The lobes of the inner corona are dark yellow, lanceolate, bending inward over the stigma head, and geniculate. *Distribution:* Tanzania, Kenya, and Zanzibar.

Similar is

Huernia keniensis R.E. FR. (Plate 40,6),

which grows on the western slopes of Mt. Kenya at 2000 m, but also in many other places in Kenya in the underbrush of the dry forests, where succulents abound. It differs from *H. aspera* in its more sharply toothed shoots and the larger, more bell-shaped flowers, whose tips are only slightly recurved. Its dark-purple inner side is densely covered with club-hairs of the

---

[16] The genus should actually be called *"Heurnia,"* as it is called by K. SCHUMANN and A. BERGER, because the name was created to honor JUSTUS HEURNIUS, one of the first plant collectors in the Cape area, and through whose drawings the stapeliads became known in Europe. The name *Huernia* has become so ingrained that it is retained here, too.

same color; the inner corona lobes are not yellowish as in *H. aspera* but blackish purple, as are the outer tips.

H. aspera and *H. keniensis* bloom freely during almost the entire summer.

A special, large-flowered form of *H. keniensis* is var. *nairobiensis* WHITE et SLOANE, in which the upper side of the corolla is covered with very small papillae.

Huernia barbata (MASS.) HAW. (Plate 40,7)

Its stems are richly branched at the base, upright, up to 6 cm long and up to 2 cm thick, gray-green, with 4 to 5 edges and long, pointed teeth. Its flowers occur in groups of 2 to 3 at the base of young shoots, with a long, bell-shaped tube and triangular, acuminate, spreading lobes; the upper side is a dirty yellow with blood-red spots. From the middle of the tube into the lower third of the corolla tip are long, stiff, purple club-hairs, which sit on a purplish brown foot.

The dense hairs of the corolla tube, which give the plant its name, make the flowers especially charming and exclude any confusion with any other species. *Distribution:* eastern Cape Province, with var. *griquensis* N.E. BR., on into western Griqualand (South Africa).

A splendid species is

Huernia bicampanulata VERD. (Plate 40,8),

the "double-bell," which gets its name from the remarkable form of the large, prominent flowers. The tube, a narrow bell-shape at the base, is ca. 2 cm long and 1.5 cm in diameter, expands into a dish shape, and ends in 5 upright, acute, triangular main lobes and 5 small intermediate tips. The upper segment is ca. 3.5 cm in diameter and yellow inside with wine-red spots; the base is deep purple and heavily papillous; and shoots up to 12 cm long, sharply quadrangular, with separated triangular teeth. *Distribution:* Transvaal.

Closely related to *H. bicampanulata* is

Huernia kirkii N.E. BR.,

whose splendid flowers differ from those of *H. bicampanulata* especially in their spreading corolla lobes and the non-uniformly dark-brown tube as well as the lesser size. Both species have now been combined into *H. kirkii* N.E. BR.

Huernia brevirostris N.E. BR.

This plant is tufted with clumps of short (up to 4 cm long), upright, thick, quadrangular, sinuate, gray-green shoots. Its flowers appear in groups of 2 to 6, with waxy, fleshy, broad bell-shaped corollas; the tubes are short, ca. 6 mm, with large, broadly triangular, acute tips, which are yellow on the upper side with red flecks and are finely papillous. The tubes are reddish white inside, glabrous, with shiny blood-red spots, uniformly blood red at the base.

The plant gets its name from the very short-acute inner corona lobes. *Distribution:* eastern Cape Province.

H. brevirostris is an extremely variable species, of which a number of varieties can be distinguished. In var. *immaculata* the corolla is of a uniformly reddish yellow color; in var. *parvipuncta* the spots are small and numerous; in var. *scabra* the corolla is characterized by a distinct annulus; and in var. *ecornuta*

the inner corona horns are very short and barely extend over the anthers, while in var. *longula* they are especially elongated and reach almost into the tube entrance.

Huernia concinna N.E. BR.

This plant grows in tufts with reclining to upright shoots up to 5 cm long, with 5 edges, with long, sharp teeth. Its flowers appear in groups of 3 to 5 at the base of the young stems, with a bell-shaped corolla that is ca. 2 cm wide and has a yellow interior with fine red dots and yellowish papillae pointed downwards. The lobes are triangular, acute, somewhat wider than long, barely separated, and the intermediate lobes are small. *Distribution:* Ethiopia and Somalia.

Huernia confusa PHILLIPS (Plate 42,1)

has blue-green glabrous shoots with 4 (–5) ribs and are up to 6 cm long. Leaf pads are triangular, ending in a sharp, thorny tip; flowers occur in multiples at the base of the stem, and are up to 3 cm in diameter, with a short, yellowish red, cup-shaped tube and a thick, naked, yellowish red, sometimes greenish spotted annules. Corolla lobes are broadly triangular, acute, greenish-white, with irregular spots and stripes. *Distribution:* Transvaal.

H. confusa has decorative flowers similar to *H. zebrina* (see p. 78), with which it can easily be confused.

Huernia guttata (MASS.) R. BR. (Plate 41,1)

These plants form tufts with upright, thick, toothed, 4- to 5-angled stems. Its flowers appear in groups of 2 to 4 at the base of new shoots, with a bell-shaped tube somewhat narrowing below the neck and with broadly flared, 10-tipped, sulphur-yellow lobes with red dots and a finely papillous edge, which in the center mounds up into a broad, spotted annulus; the tube entrance has warty papillae. *Distribution:* southwestern Cape Province.

Without a doubt the most bizarre flowers are on

Huernia hystrix (HOOK. f.) N.E. BR. (Color Plate 5,2),

whose corolla, up to 4 cm across, is so densely covered on upper side with long, fleshy, thorn-like, yellowish red, striped papillae that a certain similarity to the coat of a hedgehog cannot be denied; thus the name *hystrix* ("hedgehog huernia"). The corolla itself is sulphur yellow dotted with red spots and bands; the shoots are reclining to upright, thin, up to 6 cm long, with 5 angles and sharp teeth that end in a thorny tip. *Distribution:* Natal, Zululand, Orange Free State.

H. hystrix is easy to grow and blooms almost all summer. Its flowers even smell good.

Similarly long-papillate petaled flowers are found on

Huernia volkartii GOSSW. and H. nigeriana LAVR.[17]

but the red-zoned papillae of the upper side of the corolla are considerably shorter than on *H. hystrix*.

A huernia with considerably different flowers is

---

[17] *Huernia nigeriana* LAVR. is believed to be only a variety of *H. volkartii* GOSSW.

Huernia levyi OBERM. (Plate 41,5)

The flowers are distinguished by their strikingly elongated (up to 3 cm), short-lobed corolla tubes. This flower form might be said to be an exaggerated form of the flower of *H. keniensis,* because in *H. levyi,* too, the exterior of the reddish tube is roughly papillous with raised nerves. At the base of the dark-brown tube is a densely papillous, ring-shaped mounding (annulus); above this the tube is densely set with hair-like, pointed papillae 1 mm long, whose length diminishes toward the entrance. The color also changes: the dark brown becomes a red-spotted yellow. Stems are upright, up to 7 cm tall and 4- to 5-angled, with sharp teeth up to 1 cm long. *Distribution:* Zambia and Zimbabwe.

H. levyi in cultivation needs somewhat more water than most other species.

Huernia longituba N.E. BR.

Its stems are richly branched, upright, 2 to 5 cm long, 4- to 5-angled light green, with short teeth. Flowers appear singly or in groups of 2 or 3, with a bell-shaped tube ca. 2 cm long, and with triangular, sharply acute corolla lobes. The exterior of the tube is glabrous, with 20 protruding nerves, and the interior is creamy yellow with red spots and spherical warts. The base of the tube is glabrous, smooth, and whitish, with diagonal, dark-red lines. *Distribution:* Cape Province (Griqualand and Botswana).

This plant is easy to grow and is a free flowerer.

Huernia macrocarpa (A. RICH.) SPRING. (Plate 42,2)

This plant develops tufts with sharply toothed stems ca. 10 cm long, with 5 ribs. Flowers occur singly or in groups of 2 to 4 at the base of new stems, with broadly bell-shaped corollas; the lobes are broadly triangular, acuminate, cream-colored with purple, interrupted, concentric rings and small, air-like papillae, that get smaller toward the tip of the corolla. *Distribution:* Ethiopia, Sudan, and southern Arabia.

Huernia macrocarpa is a collectors' plant of many varieties.

Huernia marnieriana LAVR.

Until recently, with the exception of *H. macrocarpa* var. *arabica,* there were no huernias known from Arabia. J. LAVRANOS, on a trip to southern Arabia (1962), was able to discover two new species, *H. marnieriana* and *H. hadhramautica,* which are related to *H. macrocarpa* but differ distinctly from it.

H. marnieriana (Plate 42,3) grows in tufts and has short, gray-green shoots up to 5 cm long with 5 ribs and sharp teeth. Its flowers appear in multiples on new shoots and are short-peduncled, with a flat, dish-shaped corolla ca. 2.5 cm wide and a greatly reduced tube. The corolla, on the bottom, is pale green with prominent nerves; the top is pale flesh-colored with wine-red papillae. The lobes are broadly triangular and acuminate, with a red, cartilaginous margin; intermediate lobes are very small and barely visible. The exterior corona is fused into a fleshy, pale flesh-colored, 5-lobed disk, which fills the very short corolla tube; inner corona lobes are elongated over the stigma head, leaning into each other, and are pale flesh-colored with papillous, darker, geniculate tips. *Distribution:*

southern Arabia (Audhali Plateau).

This plant is easily grown and is free flowering.

Similar and, in my opinion, only a variety of the above is

Huernia hadhramautica LAVR.,

whose blooms differ from the above in the uniformly dark-red corolla lobes, which are covered with papillae. *Distribution:* southern Arabia (Mula-Mater).

Huernia namaquensis PILLANS (Plate 41,3)

This plant forms thick mats with upright shoots up to 6 cm long, with 4 to 5 angles and teeth. Flowers appear in groups of 2 to 6 at the base of the shoots, with whitish yellow, papillous corolla that are dotted with red. The corolla lobes are upright, triangular, and acuminate, ca. 5 mm long; the intermediary lobes are small. *Distribution:* Little Namaqualand (on rocks near Holgat).

A charming plant is

Huernia oculate HOOK. f. (Plate 42,7),

the "eye-flowered huernia," an easily grown, freely blooming species easily recognized by its bicolored flowers. The margin of the corolla and the triangular lobes are dark purple, which makes a wonderful contrast to the white tube. *Distribution:* Namibia (Hereoland).

A species that differs from all others in its growth-form is

Huernia pendula E.A. BRUCE (Plate 41,2),

whose irregularly branched shoots recline, creep, or hang down from cliffs and can reach a length of 45 to 150 cm. They are gray-green to reddish and more or less cylindrical or bluntly quadrangular; flowers appear singly or in groups of 2 to 4 on short lateral branches at the end of long shoots, similar to those of *H. macrocarpa.* The corolla has a broadly bell-shaped tube, with a dark brown, densely papillous interior; the lobes are triangular, acuminate, and somewhat recurved. *Distribution:* Cape Province (Bola Native Reserve).

Also of the same growth-form is

Huernia leachii LAVR. (Plate 42,6),

from Mozambique. It has stems that reach up to 150 cm long and are cylindrical or bluntly quadrangular. Its flowers have a broadly bell-shaped corolla and broadly triangular, acute, papillous, yellowish white lobes with interrupted red cross-bands; the tube base is usually uniformly dark brown.

Both *H. pendula* and *H. leachii* are suitable for hanging baskets.

One of the most beautiful species, described by WHITE and SLOANE as the "aristocrat" among huernias is

Huernia pillansii N.E. BR. (Plate 42,4),

which differs completely from the others in growth-form. Whereas the stems of most huernias have 4 to 5, seldom more ribs, those of *H. pillansii* have up to 24. They are frequently spiralled, and their dense leaf pads end in a long, hair-like tip. In shady locations the shoots are vivid green; in full sun they take on an intensive dark purple-red coloration. With its multi-ribbed stems and hair-like elongated mamillae, *H. pillansii* resembles a *Trichocaulon* or the Madagascan *Stapelianthus pilosus* (see p. 84). Flowers appear singly or in groups of 2 to 3 on the base of the new growth, and are bell-shaped, with a tube ca. 8 mm long, whose interior is glabrous and reddish cream-colored with red spots and has 5 long, recurved, pale-yellow, reddish flecked lobes, which have dense, red-tipped papillae on the upper side. *Distribution:* western Cape Province growing under shrubs.

H. pillansii is slow growing and sensitive to high humidity. During the winter it needs complete dry conditions and rest; but look out for mealy bug and root mealy bug!

One of the most common and most easily grown species is

Huernia primulina N.E. BR. (Plate 41,4),

which blooms untiringly from early summer into fall. Its stems are richly branched from the base, pressed tightly together, upright, 3 to 8 cm long, with 4 (−5) edges, and regular, sharp teeth, and are gray-green. Flowers appear in groups of 2 to 10 in cymes, with a bell-shaped tube that is 4 to 6 mm long and has a flattened, fleshy, pale yellowish, non-spotted, smooth corolla edge (in var. *rugosa* N.E. BR. warty). *Distribution:* eastern Cape Province (Grahamstown).

Also a charming plant is

Huernia quinta (PHILLIPS) WHITE et SLOANE.

With a tuft-like growth-form as the above, it has shoots 7 cm long, thick, upright, and quadrangular, with teeth that end in a sharp thorn. Flowers have a broadly bell-shaped, papillous tube with red bands; the outer edge is flattened out widely, and is yellowish white and papillous, with 5 short tips; the intermediate tips are clearly developed. *Distribution:* Transvaal.

Huernia reticulata (MASS.) HAW. (Plate 42,5)

produces flowers that are true works of art; its name means the "net flower." The flowers have a broadly bell-shaped tube that is shiny, dark blood-red inside with long club-hairs pointed downward; it also has a flattened corolla margin that is mounded up into a broad annulus in the center. The yellowish basic color is overlaid with irregular, large, frequently merging spots, giving the flower the look of a cleverly knotted net. This plant has a tuft-like growth-form, and its shoots are upright, glabrous, and spotted with red, up to 10 cm long, with 5 edges, sharp teeth. *Distribution:* eastern Cape Province (Little Namaqualand).

Just as decorative are the flowers of

Huernia zebrina N.E. BR. (Color Plate 5,3),

which with their distinctly raised ring resemble a chocolate wreath cake served on a yellow paper napkin decorated with irregular purplish red stripes. Of all the huernias, *H. zebrina* may have not only the most beautiful but also the largest flowers, which in var. *magniflora* PHILLIPS can reach a diameter of up to 7.5 cm. The greatly mounded ring is either uniformly chocolate colored, or the flecking of the broadly triangular, acuminate corolla tips may extend somewhat into the ring. *H. zebrina* differs from the similar *H. confusa* by its much more regular marking of the corolla lobes; its stems are upright, 5

to 8 cm high, up to 1.5 cm thick, gray-green, frequently flecked with red, 5-angled, with prominent, separated teeth.

Huernia verekeri STEN. (Plate 42,8)

Its stems are 3 to 5 cm long, with 5 to 7 ribs, with very long, acuminate leaf teeth. Its flowers appear singly or in groups of 2 to 3 at the base of the stems, with a broadly cup-shaped, whitish tube reddish in the throat; the corolla edge is narrow, with 5 long and narrow, yellowish green corolla lobes that are densely covered with small, purple hairs. *Distribution:* Zimbabwe.

This is an easily grown and free-flowering species.

Huernia whitesloaneana NEL (Plate 41,6)

This plant grows in dense mats with upright, glabrous, greenish red stems with 4 to 5 ribs; the flowers occur at the base of the new shoots with broadly bell-shaped corollas, which are papillous above and sharply ribbed on the outside. The corolla lobes are upright and broadly triangular, with reddish flecks and are covered with long papillae; the corolla tube has blood-red, concentric, interrupted rings on the inside. *Distribution:* Transvaal (Zoutpansberge).

Huerniopsis N.E. BR.

is a small genus, whose 4 species resemble huernias (a fact implied in the name) but whose flower structure is considerably different from that of *Huernia*. Missing are the intermediate teeth between the spreading or reflexed corolla lobes (Plate 43,1); the corona is simple, since the exterior corona is greatly reduced; and the inner corona lobes are fused at their base and free only in the upper segments.

Huerniopsis atrosanguinea (N.E. BR.) WHITE et SLOANE (= *Stapelia atrosanguinea* N.E. BR.; = *Caralluma atrosanguinea* N.E. BR.; Color Plate 4,4)

The stems are reclining to upright, branching from the base and partially stoloniferous, 5 to 8 cm long, gray-green with dark red flecks, quadrangular, with sharp, acuminate, horizontal teeth. Flowers appear in groups of 2 to 3, emerging from the middle of new shoots. The corolla tube is bell-shaped, with 5 broadly oval, acute lobes whose upper side is dark purple and papillous; the inner corona horns are very long, upright and bent back at their white tips. *Distribution:* northern Kalahari and Transvaal.

An easily grown plant, its cultivation is the same as for *Huernia*.

Huerniopsis decipiens N.E. BR. (Plate 43,1)

In growth-form, it is similar to *H. atrosanguinea*. Its flowers appear in groups of 2 to 4, open up to 2.5 cm in diameter, with brownish red, sometimes yellow spotted, broadly triangular, pointed corolla lobes, whose upper side is rusty brown, and which has several vibrant, dark-purple club-hairs at its base between the depressions. *Distribution:* Namibia, Botswana, Little Namaqualand.

Pseudolithos (BALLY) BALLY (= *Lithocaulon* BALLY)

One of the most remarkable discoveries of succulent plants of recent decades was made by the Swiss botanist P.R.O. BALLY. In the dry areas of eastern Somalia he found peculiar plants, whose stems resemble those of certain *Trichocaulon* species from South Africa, but whose flowers differed so much from these that a new genus had to be created. Because the plants looked like stones, BALLY chose the generic name *Lithocaulon.*[18]

Pseudolithos cubiforme BALLY (Plate 43,2)

has a spherical, bluntly quadrangular, unbranched, gray-green stem, whose upper surface is covered with flatly pressed, irregularly sized and irregularly arranged, hexagonal leaf pads 2 to 3 mm in diameter. Its flowers appear in multi-flowered umbels, which emerge from special short shoots located on the four angles. The corolla tube is spherical, inflated, ca. 5 mm in diameter, glabrous, and reddish brown inside; the corolla lobes are lineal, ca. 9 mm long, almost upright with reflexed edges, with the upper side pale reddish, densely covered with red hairs, and having 2 to 4 club-hairs at the tip. The corona is cup-shaped and dark red; the inner corona lobes are adpressed to the stigma head.

Pseudolithos migiurtinorum (CHIOV.) BALLY [= *P. sphaericum* (BALLY) BALLY]

differs from the above by its more spherical body and the essentially shorter corolla lobes.

Very rare and difficult to cultivate, it grows best when grafted to *Ceropegia* tubers. Both species seem to be self-fertile, since viable seeds are produced without outside pollination.

The small genus

Pectinaria HAW.

is closely related to *Caralluma* and *Stapelia* but differs from these in the structure of the flowers, whose corolla lobes at first remain attached to each other at the tip, a phenomenon which is known otherwise only in the genus *Ceropegia*. Only later do they detach themselves from each other.

According to N.E. BROWN, *Pectinaria* is the least attractive but at the same time most interesting stapeliad genus—not so interesting because the flowers of all the species are very small and insignificantly colored, but interesting because species such as *P. arcuata, P. saxatilis,* and *P. pillansii* develop subterranean shoots and sometimes, as in *P. pillansii,* develop their flowers below ground.

Pectinaria arcuata N.E. BR. (Plate 43,3)

Its stems are reclining with their tips pushing into the ground and sometimes growing subterraneously, and are indistinctly quadrangular, marked by the leaf pads. The flowers always arise on the under side of the stem, but appear above ground, and are egg-shaped with a tube ca. 3 mm long that is dark red inside, with narrow tips initially fused at the top, and has a creamy white upper side with reddish flecks. *Distribution:* eastern Cape Province (Bedford), under shrubs.

Pectinaria articulata (AIT.) HAW.

A plant with a dwarf growth-form, its stems are 5- to 6-angled and irregularly branched and are divided into fields by the leaf pads. Its flowers appear singly, slightly below the tip of the shoot; the corolla is 6 to 8 mm long with triangular lobes that are fused at the top and somewhat reflexed on the margins; and the tips leave only narrow openings free into the tube. *Distribution:* southwestern Cape Province (Little Namaqualand).

Pectinaria asperiflora N.E. BR.

This plant forms mats with reclining or short, upright, spherical to cylindrical, 6- to 8-angled stems that are covered with spherical, acute podaria. Its flowers appear singly, in form and structure similar to those of *P. articulata,* but the corolla lobes are white on the inside with sprinkles of red, recurved, and are densely covered with large, hair-like papillae. *Distribution:* Cape Land (Laingsburg District).

The most interesting species is

Pectinaria pillansii N.E. BR.,

which has reclining, partially subterranean, quadrangular, toothed stems. Its flowers have a pear-shaped corolla, whose exterior is glabrous and whose interior is covered with transparent papillae. The corolla lobes are stiff and fleshy and fused at the tip, leaving a narrow slit open.

According to observations by PILLANS the flowers are said to develop only under ground; any which set above ground perish. How pollination comes about is not clear; the plant is probably self-fertile. *Distribution:* eastern Cape area (Somerset East).

The species most common in collections is

[18]P.R.O. BALLY: *Lithocaulon* (Asclepiadaceae), a New Genus from Somalia. *Candollea* 17, 1959. Since a fossilized algae from Sardinia had already been described under this name in 1857, *Lithocaulon* BALLY had to be renamed *Pseudolithos. Candollea,* 20, 1965, p. 41

Pectinaria saxatilis N.E. BR. (Plate 43,4),

a dwarf plant growing between rocks or under stone, with partially subterranean, quadrangular, sharply toothed stems. Its flowers occur singly or in groups of 2 to 7, at the base of the stems. The corolla is an acute oval that is blackish purple with a glabrous exterior. The corolla lobes are initially fused at the tip leaving only a narrow slit, later becoming detached and showing long white hairs on the inside. *Distribution:* southeastern Cape Province. Similar is

Pectinaria tulipiflora LUCKH.,

but its flowers are purple-red.

A genus with many species is

Piaranthus R. BR.,

which means "flat flower," so named because the short tube flowers have flatly spread, triangular, acute, usually hairy corolla lobes. The corona is simple; the outer corona is greatly reduced and the inner consists of 5 lobes leaning over the anthers; on their back they bear comb-shaped appendages.

Of the 17 *Piaranthus* species known today (some of which are very closely related) I list the following:

Piaranthus foetidus N.E. BR.

This plant forms mats of egg-shaped or spherical stems that are warty toothed and have 4 to 5 indistinct angles. Its flowers smell strongly of carrion and appear in groups of 2 to 6 near the tips of young shoots, are without a distinct tube, and have acuminate oval corolla lobes, somewhat rolled back at the edges, which are yellowish with red edges. *Distribution:* western Cape Province.

P. foetidus is extremely variable in regard to color of the corolla; several varieties are described.

An interesting species is

Piaranthus globosus WHITE et SLOANE,

whose dense mats of spherical stems resemble little potatoes, the small leaf teeth being their eyes. Its flowers have distinctly bent, yellowish green, red-dotted, hairy corolla lobes rolled at the edges. *Distribution:* unknown.

Piaranthus mennellii LUCKH. (Plate 44,1)

This plant forms tufts and mounds with spherical to elongated, bluntly quadrangular shoots. Its flowers appear in groups of 2 to 6 near the shoot tips and have very short tubes. The corolla lobes are up to 10 mm long and are pale yellow with reddish dots; the upper side has short, white and purple hairs. *Distribution:* Cape Province (Kenhardt District).

Closely related to this is

Piaranthus pallidus LUCKH.

Its stems are reclining, spherical to elongated, bluntly quadrangular, glabrous, and green. Its flowers appear in groups of 2 to 4 near the tips of the stems, with uniformly pale yellow, narrow corolla lobes that are slightly rolled back on the edges; the upper side has velvety hairs. *Distribution:* Namibia (Kenhardt District).

Piaranthus parvulus N.E. BR. (Plate 44,2)

This plant has shoots that are reclining, upright, elongated to ovate, bluntly quadrangular, with 3 to 5 wart-shaped teeth on each edge. Flowers appear in multi-flowered inflorescences (up to 12), opening one after the other, never more than 2 or 3 open at the same time, and are long pedunculated, very small. Corolla lobes are only 4 to 5 mm long, recurved, and straw-yellow; the upper side has velvety hairs. *Distribution:* eastern Cape Province (Laingsburg District).

Piaranthus pillansii N.E. BR.

A plant that grows in mats, it has reclining stems that are elongated to club-shaped, bluntly quadrangular, and green or made reddish by the sun. Flowers occur usually in twos, slightly below the tip of the shoot; the corolla is divided almost to the base into 5 narrowly lanceolate lobes that are up to 16 mm long, rolled back on the edges, and dirty pale yellow, with the upper side having short hairs.

In

var. *inconstans* N.E. BR.

the tips are ochre yellow with dense, bright-red dots; in

var. *fuscatus* N.E. BR.

they are deep, dark red with fine, irregular cross bands.

The flowers have a strong odor like valerian. *Distribution:* eastern Cape Province.

Piaranthus pulcher N.E. BR. (Plate 43,5)

This plant grows in mats with elongated, bluntly quadrangular, sharp-toothed stems. Its flowers are numerous, in umbel-like bundles, with a short, hairy tube and upright lobes reflexed at the end and yellowish green with dark-red dots. *Distribution:* Cape Province (Oudtshoorn, Willowmore, Ladysmith Districts).

Piaranthus punctatus (MASS.) R. BROWN (Color Plate 4,6)

is one of the most beautiful species, whose flowers differ from all the others by its clearly developed corolla tube. The corolla lobes are broadly lanceolate, pointed, with whitish red markings; the upper side has fine, papillous warts. *Distribution:* western Cape Province (Little Namaqualand).

Piaranthus ruschii NEL (Plate 43,6)

is closely related to *P. foetidus,* but differs in its flowers, which have a pleasant, fruity smell. Stems are reclining to upright, spherical, up to 2 cm long, hardly edged, with short-toothed mamillae. Flowers appear singly or in twos near the tip of the

Color Plate 5.

1 (ul) *Caralluma mammillaris*
2 (um) *Huernia hystrix*
3 (ur) *Huernia zebrina*
4 (ml) *Hoodia dregei*
5 (mm) *Stapelianthus madagascariensis*
6 (mr) *Stapelianthus insignis*
7 (ll) *Stapelia flavopurpurea*
8 (lm) *Stapelia longii*
9 (lr) *Trichocaulon kubusense*

shoot; corolla tips are ca. 1 cm long and are greenish yellow with dark purple flecks and dense white hairs. *Distribution:* Namibia (Lüderitz Bay).

Stapelia L.

is the stapeliad genus with the most species. It is divided into a series of sections, which, however, are not always sharply distinguished from one another. Also the numerous described species urgently need to be revised; many of them may be only hybrids, because *Stapelia* inclines to hybridize easily. Therefore the differences between many species may be so slight that definite identification is not always possible. Those who have devoted a lot of time to the genus and have sown seed of their own harvesting know that in every seed bed new forms occur again and again. Not only in cultivation but also in the wild, hybrids are not rare.

The general characteristics of the genus are as follows:

Stems are quadrangular, pubescent or hairy, branching from the base; leaves are reduced to short-lived, deciduous scales (see Plate 34,3); flowers appear usually at the base of the stems, singly or in long-pedunculated cymes (see Plate 34,3), and are highly variable in size, with deeply divided corollas and separated lobes, frequently with a fleshy disc or annulus in the center (in section Orbea). Surrounding the corona, the outer lobes are usually free to the base, rectangular or lanceolate, and are frequently divided at the tip, with the inner corona lying on the anthers or as an elongated horn extending over the anthers, equipped with a wing-like appendage or with a horn on the back (see Figure 12).

The flowers of almost all stapelias (with few exceptions: *S. flavopurpurea*) are distinguished by a penetrating, carrion-like smell, which in no way detracts from the beauty of the flower, for if any stapeliad deserves the name "Star of Honor" it is the stapelias.

Here again I can present only a selection of the most beautiful and most common species.

As I begin with

Stapelia ambigua Mass. (Color Plate 4,7 and Plate 34,3),

I select first one of the "dubious" species, whose flowers show such similarity to those of *S. grandiflora* Mass. that the two species are hard to tell apart. *S. ambigua* belongs in section Stapeltonia (*gigantea-hirsuta* group according to White and Sloane), in which around 35 species are combined, all demonstrating a series of common characteristics: stems are upright and very stout, usually with hairs; the splendid flowers are usually very large and frequently very hairy or with margin hairs (seldom glabrous) and are distinguished by brown-red colorations; the corolla lobes have fine cross markings on the upper side, and the inner corona lobes have a broadly triangular wing on the back.

Of the best known species of this section other than *S. ambigua* are:

Stapelia asterias Mass. (Plate 44,3)

Its flowers are 9 to 11 cm in diameter with star-shaped, flat tips that are dark reddish brown with shiny and fine yellowish cross bands, and are slightly hairy at the base; on their margins the lobes have dense, simple, reddish hairs. In var. *lucida* the corolla lobes are uniformly purple-red.

Stapelia gigantea N.E. Br. (Color Plate 4,8)

has the largest stapelia flowers, which when completely open can reach a diameter of up to 40 cm. Even the buds are striking because of their size; they are as large as a tennis ball with a long point. The corolla is divided almost to the base; the corolla lobes are bright yellow with dense, concentric, somewhat wavy, reddish weals; the hairs are scattered; and the corolla lobes are long, with white hairs. *Distribution:* Natal to Zimbabwe.

Stapelia grandiflora Mass.

Its flowers are similar to those of *S. ambigua,* but somewhat larger, up to 16 cm in diameter, with velvety soft hairs in the throat. The corolla lobes are brownish red with long hairs at the base and glabrous at the darker tips, and with some lighter cross weals; the margins have long, reddish or whitish hairs. *Distribution:* eastern Cape Province and Transvaal.

Stapelia gettleffi Pott (Plate 44,4)

is easily recognized by its foliage; it differs from all others of the same group by its strikingly long, very hairy leaves that remain on the plant clinging to the stem. Its flowers are up to 18 cm in diameter, with purple corolla lobes covered with yellow, diagonal weals, with bright purple hairs at the base and on the margin of the corolla lobes. *Distribution:* Transvaal.

Stapelia hirsuta L. (Plate 44,5)

is a common species that is extremely variable in regard to color and pubescence of its flowers. The typical form has a corolla 10 to 12 cm across, with the upper side having soft hairs and divided beyond the middle; its throat and the base of the corolla lobes are densely covered with long, reddish brown, felt-like, soft hairs. The corolla lobes are dirty reddish yellow from the base to the middle, striped by fine reddish, wavy cross lines, and are uniformly dull red at the tips, with dense hairs on the edge.

Very similar to *S. gigantea* is Transvaal's

Stapelia nobilis N.E.Br.,

which differs from the former by its smaller, more heavily haired flowers, which have a distinct tube.

Even more distinctly developed is the corolla tube of *S. leendertziae* N.E. BR. and *S. wilmaniae* LUCKH., two closely related species differing from each other only in regard to color and hairs of the corolla lobes. The flowers of *S. wilmaniae* (Plate 44,6) have a large, inflated, deep-brown tube, which has short hairs outside, and deep dark-red, warty cross bands inside, with dense purple hairs. The corolla lobes are triangular, ending in a sharp point, recurved, with short hairs in the lower third. In *S. leendertziae* the corolla lobes are completely glabrous. Both species have approximately the same distribution (Transvaal).

Also in section Stapeltonia are the following species, which are less common in cultivation:
Stapelia arnotii N.E. BR., *S. bergeriana* DTR., *S. cylista* LUCKH., *S. desmetiana* N.E. BR., *S. flavirostris* N.E. BR., *S. forcipis* PHILLIPS et LETTY, *S. fuscopurpurea* N.E. BR., *S. gariepensis* PILL., *S. glabricaulis* N.E. BR., *S. immelmaniae* PILL., *S. maccabeana* WHITE et SLOANE, *S. macowanii* N.E. BR., *S. marlothii* N.E. BR., *S. margarita* SLOANE, *S. nudiflora* PILL., *S. peglerae* N.E. BR., *S. pillansii* N.E. BR., *S. plantii* HOOK. f., *S. pulvinata* MASS., *S. schinzii* BRGR. et SCHLCHT., *S. sororia* MASS., *S. tsomoensis* N.E. BR., *S. vetula* SIMS.

An interesting species is

Stapelia engleriana SCHLTR. (Plate 44,7)

It has thick stems up to 30 cm long with slightly toothed ribs and are gray-green or dark green, with much velvety hair. In contrast to most other species, the inflorescences of 1 to 2 flowers appear near the tip. The dark chocolate-colored flowers are characterized by the fact that the broadly triangular, glabrous, heavily wealed corolla lobes roll back completely and lie on the under side of the broad cup-shaped corolla tube. The flowers thus appear completely round and, from above, look like buttons. The corona lobes are upright; those of the outer corona are dark brown and at the tip are briefly 2-lobed; those of the inner corona have 2 horns, are finely warty at the tip, and are yellow with red dots. *Distribution:* Cape Province (Karroo).

S. engleriana belongs to section Clavirostres, to which the following three species also belong:

Stapelia clavicorona VERD.

Its stems are robust, velvety, with distinctly protruding, toothed angles. The flowers are light yellow with fine, red, diagonal lines; their lobes are spread out flat, broadly triangular, with vibrating club-hairs on the margin. The species name comes from the club shape of the inner, 2-horned, dark-purple corona lobes. *Distribution:* Transvaal (Zoutpansberge).

Stapelia herrei NEL (Plate 44,8)

The stems are glabrous, brownish green, and up to 12 cm high. Its flowers occur singly, near the shoot tip, with a distinctly bell-shaped tube and 5 triangular, acute corolla lobes, which are somewhat rolled back on the margins and whose upper side is very rugose. The raised stripes on the corolla lobes are white, and the fields they enclose are deep, dark purple-red. Very similar is

Stapelia neliana WHITE et SLOANE,

which differs from the above by its longer inflorescence pedun-

cle, the larger, wider open flowers, and the less rugose corolla tips.

Both species grow in the desert-like, hot areas of the Richtersveld (Little Namaqualand) and require, therefore, a lot of warmth in cultivation. They grow best grafted.

Stapelia erectiflora N.E. BR., (Plate 45,1 and 3)

is a species that is remarkable in every way—first because the numerous, very long-pedunculated flowers are arranged over the entire length of the stems, secondly because the purple corolla lobes, as in *S. engleriana*, are rolled back so far that the flowers appear to be round and button-like. Its unusual charm, however, comes from a thick, white coat, that covers tube and lobes. N.E. BROWN compares the flowers of *S. erectiflora* to a Turkish fez. The outer, brownish red corona lobes are lineal, bluntly spread, and almost as long as the flower base; the inner corona lobes are simple, i.e., they have no dorsal wing or horn-shaped appendage, a characteristic of section Gonostemon, to which also belong the following species.

Stapelia flavopurpurea MARL. (Color Plate 5,7)

is especially attractive because of its flower color. The flat corolla tube, which is white on the inside with red club-hairs, has 5 narrow, dark-yellow corolla lobes, whose upper side has distinct weals; to this is contrasted the bright carmine-red corona.

S. flavopurpurea and its var. *fleckii* WHITE et SLOANE is one of the few species whose flowers are not distinguished by a penetrating smell of carrion but, on the contrary, have a pleasant smell of honey. *Distribution:* Karroo.

Surely the most interesting flowers are on

Stapelia glanduliflora MASS. (Plate 45,2)

Its short-tubed flower corolla is up to 3.5 cm in diameter and has ovate, pointed, greenish lobes with fine, red dots; on the entire upper side and on the margin it is quite densely covered with club-shaped, white, transluscent hairs, which give the flowers their unusual charm. *Distribution:* eastern Cape Province (Clanwilliam District).

A pretty, small-flowered species also from section Gonostemon is

Stapelia jucunda N.E. BR., (Plate 45,4) [= *Tridentea jucunda* (N.E. BR.) LEACH].

Its stems are upright, forming compact tufts, 4 to 8 cm long, bluntly quadrangular, and glabrous, with tooth-like podaria. Its flowers appear singly or in groups of 2 to 3 on the central shoot segments, with stems ca. 2.5 cm long; the flower corolla is almost flat, somewhat sunken in the middle, ca. 2 cm in diameter, cream colored with red flecks, with moving, purple club-hairs on the margin. *Distribution:* Ceres Karroo and Griqualand.

Further species of the same section are:
Stapelia acuminata MASS., *S. albo-castanea* MARL., *S. ausana* DTR. et BRGR., *S. cinta* MARL., *S. concinna* MASS., *S. deflexa* JACQ., *S. dinteri* BRGR., *S. divaricata* MASS., *S. dwequensis* LUCKH., *S. nouhuysii* PHILLIPS, *S. olivacea* N.E. BR., *S. pearsonii* N.E. BR., *S. stricta* SIMS, *S. surrecta* N.E. BR.

As representatives of section Podanthes (characteristic: inner corona lobes have no appendage lying over the anthers) I list the following:

Stapelia kwebensis N.E. BR. (Plate 45,7).

This plant has stems with short hairs and are quadrangular with rounded ribs and short, upright leaves pressed to the axis. The flowers occur in cymes near the base of new shoots, are short-pedunculate (in var. *longipedicellata* BRGR. flower peduncles are up to 5 cm long), brown or sometimes dark yellowish brown, with short, dish-shaped tubes. The corolla lobes have prominent diagonal weals and are glabrous except for some hairs on the margin, especially near the tip. *Distribution:* Namibia Kalahari, Transvaal.

Stapelia arenosa LUCKH. (Plate 45,5)

Its stems are upright, with 5 blunt angles and short podaria. Flowers usually appear singly, ca. 3 cm in diameter, with their center mounded into a prominently warty but not sharply distinguished ring. The corolla lobes are broadly triangular, acuminate, and dark with raised, net-like, white weals, and with short hairs on the margin. *Distribution:* Cape Province (Clanwilliam District). A very attractive species!

In the same section are:
S. fucosa N.E. BR., *S. irrorata* MASS., *S. juttae* DTR., *S. miscella* N.E. BR., *S. parvipuncta* N.E. BR., *S. portae-taurinae* DTR. et BRGR., *S. rubiginosa* NEL, *S. stultitioides* LUCKH., *S. verrucosa* MASS.

A species remarkable because of its flowers is

Stapelia longii LUCKH. (Color Plate 5,8) [= *Tridentia longii* (LUCKH.) LEACH].

Its stems are reclining, crawling, up to 25 cm long and 6 mm thick, and bluntly quadrangular. Flowers appear singly on stems 2 to 3 cm long; the corolla is ca. 2.5 cm in diameter, without a distinct tube, with the upper side glabrous, shiny, and light brown. The corolla lobes are reflexed, with thick, dark-purple club-hairs at the base. The corona has a striking structure: the outer as well as the inner corona lobes end with a button-shaped spherical knob that is covered with black tubercles, giving the flower a truly bizarre appearance.

Also, the name of section Caruncularia refers to the special structure of the corona. The section includes the interesting

Stapelia longipes LUCKH. [= *Tridentea longipes* (LUCKH.) LEACH]

The stems form thick clumps and are upright and roundish to obtusely quadrangular, with elongated, hardly toothed podaria, and are glabrous and a gray to bluish green. Flowers appear on very long pedicels (up to 18 cm) that are pendulous or lying on the ground, up to 6 cm in diameter, with the upper side very warty, rough, and whitish in the center with red dots. The corolla lobes are uniformly purplish brown, with long purple hairs on the margin of the corolla lobes, especially at the base. *Distribution:* Namaqualand and Namibia.

A very attractive species, it needs a lot of warmth to get it to bloom.

The var. *namaquensis* LUCKH. pictured in Plate 45,8 differs from the type by its considerably larger flowers.

Very closely related to the above and in the same section are: *Stapelia pendunculata* MASS. [= *Tridentea pedunculata* (MASS.) LEACH] and *Stapelia ruschiana* DTR. [= *Tridentea ruschiana* (DTR.) LEACH], whose flowers are also on very long pedicels.

Stapelia rufa MASS. (Plate 45,6),

the "red stapelia," is the only representative of section Fissirostres. Its stems are upright, up to 15 cm long, with fine, soft hairs, and are bluntly quadrangular. Flowers occur in cymes of 4 to 5, opening one after the other, with a short, bell-shaped tube and separated, long-lobed, dark-red, diagonal weals; fine hairs appear at the tips, and longer hairs appear on the margins. Lobes of the inner corona are divided into two upright, soft-haired tips (thus the name Fissirostres). *Distribution:* Cape Province (Karroo).

Stapelia semota N.E. BR. [= *Orbeopsis lutea* (N.E. BR.) LEACH]

has the most northern distribution (up to Tanzania and Kenya) of all the *Stapelia* species; its shoots, because of their long teeth, resemble a *Caralluma* or a *Stultitia*. Flowers are up to 4 cm in diameter, with spreading or recurved, oval-lanceolate acuminate corolla lobes, which are rugose on the upper side, and are uniformly chocolate brown or with yellowish brown markings, and with vibrating purple club-hairs at the margins. The center of the corolla is surrounded by a distinctly pentagonal, chocolate-colored ring. From the highlands of Kenya (Prov. Nairobi) comes a form with pure yellow (var. *lutea*) flowers (Plate 46,1).

S. semota belongs to section Stapelluma, whose members all have stems with long teeth. Also among them are:
S. longidens N.E. BR. (Mozambique),
S. molonyae WHITE et SLOANE (Kenya),
S. woodii N.E. BR. (Natal).

As members of section Orbea (corolla with a distinct ring) we mention the well-known *Stapelia variegata* L. [= *Orbea variegata* (L.) HAW.] (Figure 12) found in every collection. It is not only the first stapelia introduced into Europe, probably in the first half of the 17th century, but it is also an extremely variable species, of which WHITE and SLOANE list no less than 19 varieties—not including the great number of hybrids made with other species in cultivation. Many of them have been described in the literature as actual species, and so there is a great confusion in this area. According to N.E. BROWN, *S. variegata* is the "enfant terrible" among stapelias. The great popularity of *S. variegata* among collectors who are not concerned with systematic problems has many reasons: first it is distinguished by its lush growth, and even with neglect it cannot be killed; also it has very pretty, attractive, striking flowers; finally it is quite willing to bloom and produces flowers continuously during the whole summer.

Here follows a short description (relying on N.E. BROWN) of only the type. I will not go into the numerous varieties, forms, and hybrids.

A plant of mat-like growth-form, it has reclining to upright stems that are 5 to 10 cm long and bluntly quadrangular with distinct teeth. Its flowers appear singly or in cymes of 2 to 5 at the base of young stems on 2 to 5 cm long pedicels. The corolla is 5 to 8 cm in diameter; the annulus is broad, flat, and round or indistinctly pentagonal, is light yellow with reddish flecks, and is slightly rugose. The corolla lobes are broadly triangular and short-acute, spreading or reflexed, pale greenish yellow with dark brown or red flecks, and covered with prominent, warty diagonal weals (Figure 12). Type-locality: Table Mountain near Capetown. Total *distribution:* eastern and western Cape Province.

Closely related to *S. variegata* is

Stapelia lepida JACQ. [= *Orbea lepida* (JACQ.) HAW.]

It differs from the above species by its bi-colored flowers: the ring is whitish with red flecks; the very rugose corolla lobes are sulphur yellow with dark brown flecks and bands.

Habitat and distribution are unknown.

In the same section are also the following species: *S. angulata* TOD., *S. barklyi* N.E. BR., *S. bicolor* BRGR., *S. bijliae* PILL., *S. cupularis* N.E. BR., *S. discolor* TOD., *S. mutabilis* JACQ., *S. maculosa* J. DONN, *S. maculosoides* N.E. BR.

Other species with as many varieties in this section are *S. namaquensis* N.E. BR. and *S. pulchella* MASS.

Stapelianthus CHOUX

is the only stapeliad genus from Madagascar; its six species are scattered throughout the southwestern dry bush areas of the island. In its flower structure there are certain connections to the genus *Huernia,* which are given to developing small "intermediate lobes" in the sinuses of the corolla lobes. Also the flowers have a partially well-developed corolla tube. The main differences between *Stapelianthus* and *Huernia* are in the structure of the corona. In *Huernia* the deeply divided outer corona lobes are spreading, forming a 10-pointed star; in *Stapelianthus,* on the other hand, they are always upright, and the inner corona lobes are short and lie on the anthers.

The *Stapelianthus* species require the same conditions as huernias, but need a little more warmth.

The most widespread and most common species is

Stapelianthus decaryi CHOUX (Plate 46,2).

This plant grows in compact tufts up to 50 cm in diameter; its stems are reclining to upright, branching from the base, gray-green or brownish green, with dark flecks, and are up to 10 cm long and 1 cm thick, with 5 to 6 (–8) ribs. The leaf pads are mounded like mamillae and are quadrangular to hexagonal, with a small, deciduous, soon-falling leaf. A few flowers appear at the base of new shoots, with elongated cylindrical tubes and broadly triangular, reflexed corolla lobes; these, as well as the upper part of the corolla tube are yellowish gray with darker flecks and dense hard papillae, which bear vibrant red hairs. The papilla formation resembles that of *Huernia hystrix;* inter-

mediate lobes are small; the corona is deep purple. *Distribution:* southern Madagascar (Prov. Fort Dauphin).

Stapelianthus madagascariensis (CHOUX) CHOUX (Color Plate 5,5)

Its stems are reclining, spreading, gray-green, with dark red flecks, bluntly hexagonal, with elongated leaf pads and small, deciduous leaves. A few flowers appear at the base of the stem with a short, broadly dish-shaped tube and broadly triangular, acuminate lobes ending in a point, pale yellow with wine red flecks. The upper side of the apex has stiff, red-tipped papillae that are 2 to 3 mm long. The corona is deep dark purple; the outer horns are deeply divided. *Distribution:* southwest Madagascar (from Tuléar to the southern tip of the island).

The very similar

Stapelianthus montagnacii (BOIT.) BOIT. et BERTR. (Plate 46,3)

differs from the above by its somewhat thicker stems, its whitish corolla tube flecked with red, and its whitish corolla lobes with large, merging, carmine-red flecks. The tips, similar to *S. madagascariensis* have hairs; the outer corona lobes are broader and shorter and are divided only in the upper third. *Distribution:* the same as *S. madagascariensis.*

In spite of the similarity in vegetative organs,

Stapelianthus insignis B. DESC. (Color Plate 5,6)

differs from the above two species by its completely different and, for *Stapelianthus,* remarkable flower structure. Stems are decumbent, usually quadrangular, gray-green with red flecks, with downward-pointing, hooked podaria that have a small, lanceolate, deciduous leaf. Flowers usually appear singly at the base of the shoots on short stems; their tube is divided into a bell-shaped tube that is constricted at the base and a flat-spherical segment up to 2 cm in diameter. At the top of the tube between the very short, recurved tips there is only a narrow opening. The whole corolla is completely glabrous, with a gray-green exterior with brownish red flecks; the interior is deep dark purple with a whitish network. The outer corona lobes are very large, lying on the narrowed part of the tube, and are blackish violet. *Distribution:* only from the area from Tuléar and from the extreme southwest (Itampolo).

Stapelianthus pilosus (CHOUX) LAVR. et HARDY (= *Trichocaulon decaryi* CHOUX) (Plate 46,4)

has such a different growth-form from the other species of the genus that CHOUX considered this plant a *Trichocaulon* and described it as *T. decaryi;* however, since the structure of the corona does not differ from the other *Stapelianthus* species, LAVRANOS and HARDY re-named it *Stapelianthus pilosus.*

This plant grows in mats with reclining to upright stems that are up to 15 cm long and ca. 1 cm thick, and which are covered with dense, very small, spiral leaf pads, which are green near the top of the shoot and blend into gray, dry hair tips in the lower segments of the shoot (see Plate 32,4). *S. pilosus* therefore is similar to *Huernia pillansii* (see Plate 42,4). Flowers occur in small numbers at the base of the shoots with a short, cup-shaped tube and broadly triangular, upright, separated or spread lobes and small intermediate tips. The flowers are pale yellow; the exterior has large, wine-red flecks, and the interior has short, pale-yellow papillae with reddish tips. *Distribution:* deciduous forest in southern Madagascar.

S. pilosus, like *Huernia pillansii,* is a slow grower and requires a warm location

A genus with only a few species is

Stultitia PHILLIPS,

whose flowers are distinguished by the formation of a distinctly developed ring.

The two best known, very closely related species are *S. cooperi* and *S. tapscottii.*

Stultitia cooperi (N.E. BR.) PHILLIPS (Plate 46,5)

Stems are upright, up to 5 cm high, bluntly quandrangular, glabrous, with long, conical teeth 5 to 8 cm long, that end in a sharp tip, gray-green with red flecks. Flowers appear singly or in cymes of 2 to 3 at the base of the stems, 3 to 4 cm in diameter; corolla lobes are star-shaped, flattened or recurved, and broadly triangular. The upper side is bright purple with yellowish warts and fine, purple weals; on the margin, especially at the base, are long, mobile club-hairs; and the ring is 8 to 9 mm wide, roundish or bluntly pentagonal, with its upper side densely rugose and purplish red. *Distribution:* eastern Cape Province.

Stultitia tapscottii (VERD.) PHILLIPS (Plate 46,6)

differs from the above especially in its thick, tufted growth-form and in the formation of strikingly long (up to 2 cm), upright, separated leaf pads; the flowers are of similar structure and color as those of *S. cooperi,* with the ring somewhat less distinctly formed. *Distribution:* common in Botswana, Griqualand-West, and Transvaal.

Completely different in flower structure is

Stultitia conjuncta WHITE et SLOANE (Plate 46,7)
[= *Orbeanthus conjunctus* (WHITE et SLOANE) LEACH],

whose flowers have great similarity to those of *Stapelianthus insignis* (see Color Plate 5,6). Its stems are reclining, spreading, up to 15 cm long, bluntly quadrangular, with short teeth, and are gray-green with red flecks. The flowers appear near the tip of the stems with a short basal tube, which abruptly extends into an urceolate corolla and just as abruptly, for the sake of propagation, exposes a small entrance between the very short lobes. The brown ring is visible only by cutting the corolla open and is at the base of the kettle-shaped, expanded flower segment. *Distribution:* northern Transvaal (Zoutpansberge).

Stultitia hardyi R.A. DYER [= *Orbeanthus hardyi* (R.A. DYER) LEACH]

has, in contrast to *O. conjunctus,* not bicampanulate but only campanulate flowers with ovate-acuminate, very shortly united, papillose lobes; the inner corona lobes much exceed the anthers. *Distribution:* Transvaal (Ugllies Poort).

Decabelone DECNE. (= *Tavaresia* WELW.)

[According to A.A. BULLOCK (*Kew Bulletin,* III, 1956) the name *Tavaresia* is invalid and has to be replaced by *Decabelone* DECNE. (1871), but L.C. LEACH, in *Kirkia,* 9 (II:379), 1974, has proved that the genus name *Tavaresia* is correct because it was already described by WELWITSCH in 1854.]

The stems are branched at the base, cylindrical, and gray-green, with many (up to 12) ribs, whose leaf pads, differing from all other stapeliads, have 3 bristly leaf "thorns"—a stouter central one, standing out horizontally, and two shorter, lateral thorns pointed downward (Plate 32,7). The flowers appear in cymes at the base of the stems and are slightly zygomorphic with elongated bell-shaped or funnel-shaped, frequently somewhat bent corolla tube and flare, sharply pointed corolla lobes.

The cultivation of *Decabelone* presents the same problems as in *Hoodia.* It requires a sandy-humusy soil and a warm, sunny location that is airy in the summer. In the winter months very little water should be given. Nevertheless the plant can be kept only a few years. It is best to grow them from seed, which germinates within 24 hours, and then to graft the seedlings to *Stapelia* or, better yet, onto tubers of *Ceropegia woodii* or *C. dichotoma* (Plate 46,8).

The most commonly grown species is

Decabelone grandiflora K. SCHUM. (= *Tavaresia grandiflora* K. SCHUM. Plates 32,7; 46,8),

which has the largest flowers of all the species (Plate 46,8). Its stems are numerous, gathered into groups, upright or nearly so, with up to 14 ribs, and are ca. 20 cm long and 2 cm thick. Its flowers are up to 14 cm long with long bell-shaped tubes that are light yellow with reddish brown flecks, glabrous or with fine papillae, and are somewhat arched; the tips broadly triangular, abruptly constricted into a thorn tip, and the inner side is papillous. *Distribution:* Namibia and northern Transvaal (Limpopo, Salt-Pan).

Rarer in cultivation are:

Decabelone barklyi R.A. DYER (= *Tavaresia barklyi* R.A. DYER)

Similar to *D. grandiflora,* but with smaller flowers, only 5 to 7 cm long. *Distribution:* southeastern Cape Province (Namaqualand to Namibia).

Decabelone elegans DECNE. (= *Tavaresia angolensis* WELW)

The stems are 10 to 15 cm high with only 6 (seldom 8) ribs. The corolla tube is up to 8 cm long and somewhat arched, and the exterior is glabrous and dark yellow with fine red stripes and flecks; the corolla lobes are broadly triangular, sharply pointed, and reflexed, and the upper side is papillous, with short hairs. *Distribution:* coastal area of Angola.

Among the most sought-after stapeliads are the members of the genus

Trichocaulon N.E. BR.,

which is the stapeliad that most resembles cacti. Most species have highly succulent, fleshy, juicy, soft, thick-cylindrical or round, cucumber-like stems, which in many species (*T. alstonii, T. piliferum*) reach a considerable diameter and a length of up to 75 cm. The flowers are small, seldom larger than 1 cm in diameter, and are in multi-flowered inflorescences. The corolla, deeply divided into 5 parts, has a flat wheel-shape or dish-shape; only in *T. annulatum* does it have a distinct ring.

After the leaf pads form, three sections are distinguishable: In the members of section (1) Eutrichocaulon, the "thorny" species, the leaf pads, standing in straight lines and forming ribs, have a short, hard thorn or end in a hair-like tip.

In section (2) Tricholuma the leaf pads, also in ribs, are short spheres, but are not thorny. Here one finds only one species (*T. columnare*).

In the representatives of section (3) Cactoidea, whose stems most closely resemble those of cacti, the leaf pads are in straight lines or arranged irregularly; they are flat, irregularly hexagonal, and have in their middle a tiny, deciduous leaf rudiment.

The thorny species, called "Ngaaps" by the natives (Hottentots), are eaten raw or rolled in sugar, whereas the thornless species have a bitter, slimy sap and are therefore avoided.

The genus has approximately 25 species, which partially are so closely related that a new revision would reduce the number of species considerably. Their distribution area stretches from southern Cape Province to Namibia in dry and stony rock deserts. (*T. decaryi,* described in the literature as being from Madagascar, has already been described on page 84 as *Stapelianthus pilosus.*)

Because of their extreme living conditions (hot, dry), the *Trichocaulon* species present the most difficulties of all stapeliads in cultivation. They require bright and warm places; during the winter months they must be given strict rest, but even in the summer they should get little water. As a potting medium use a loose soil with a lot of pumice bits. It has proved advantageous to sink the pots in pumice, because then you do not need to water the plants themselves but just the pumice, which holds water for a long time. If the plants should nevertheless begin to rot at the base, graft them onto *Ceropegia woodii* tubers or onto thick stapelias, because the re-rooting of cuttings with large cut surfaces exposed is difficult. Growing from seed is easy, but the seedlings must be potted up immediately, since they overwise will be hit by "black death."

Section EUTRICHOCAULON (thorny species)

Trichocaulon alstonii N.E. BR. (Plate 3,4; 6,1)

This plant forms large clumps with numerous, gray-green, multi-ribbed stems that are 3 to 5 cm thick and up to 70 cm long. Its flowers appear in sparse bundles, ca. 1 cm in diameter, with short, bell-shaped tubes and sharp acuminate, glabrous corolla lobes that are yellow on both sides. *Distribution:* western Cape Province (Little Namaqualand, near Numies and Hangpaal) on quartz and granite slopes.

Yellow flowers are found also on *T. flavum* N.E. BR. (Plate 47,1), which, however, has short hairs on the upper side. Vegetatively it is very similar to

Trichocaulon piliferum (L. f.) N.E. BR. (Plate 47,2).

This plant has dark, gray-green stems branching from the base, up to 20 cm tall and up to 5 cm thick with ca. 25 ribs. The mamillae extend into stiff, brown hairs. Flowers appear singly or in groups of 2 to 3 between the ribs, and are up to 18 mm in diameter, with a short, cup-shaped tube and with spread, densely papillous corolla lobes that are dark brownish purple on the upper-side. *Distribution:* southwestern Cape Province (Karroo to Namibia).

An easily recognized and easily grown species is

Trichocaulon pedicellatum SCHINZ (Plate 47,3).

Its shoots are up to 15 cm long, 2 cm thick, cylindrical, multi-ribbed, and gray-green. Its flowers appear in groups of 2 to 5, on long pedicels bent downward and therefore bobbing; the tube is short, with flared tips, which are somewhat reflexed at the margins, and with the upper side dark brownish red with short papillae. *Distribution:* Namibia (Namib Desert).

In the same group are also the following: *T. annulatum* N.E. BR. (flowers with a distinct ring); *T. delaetianum* DTR.; *T. officinale* N.E. BR.; *T. pubiflorum* DTR.; *T. triebneri* NEL; *T. grande* N.E. BR., *T. pillansii* N.E. BR.; *T. rusticum* N.E. BR.

Section TRICHOLUMA

Trichocaulon columnare NEL (Plate 47,4)

is the only representative of this section. Stems rise from a reclining base and are up to 60 cm long, irregularly branched, glabrous, gray to dark green, and cylindrical, with 8 ribs that are divided into short-toothed mamillae. Flowers occur in groups of up to 15, on short pedicels, 4 to 8 mm in diameter, with a short tube and tips ca. 4 mm wide, and are yellowish green on the upper side with red dots and short white hairs. *Distribution:* western Cape Province (Little Namaqualand, Richtersveld).

T. columnare is a relatively easily grown and easily propagated species.

Section CACTOIDEA (HOOK.) N.E. BR. [19] (Plate 47,5)

Stems are thickly cylindrical (spherical in juvenile stage), up to 10 cm tall, branching from the base, thickly covered by broad, flat, more or less hexagonal pads, gray green, and waxy. Flowers appear near the tip of the stem and are small, with cup-shaped tubes and flared corolla lobes, which are pale yellow on the upper side with red flecks and short papillae.

It is widely distributed in western Cape Province (Little Namaqualand).

Closely related to this species is *T. simile* N.E. BR., which is distinguished especially by the distinctly mounded mamillae, which near the tip of the stem have an almost hair-like leaf appendage. In regard to the structure of the corona there are only minor differences.

Also similar is *T. meloforme* MARL. [18] (Plate 32,8) Its flowers are yellow with dark brown flecks, and the lobes of the corolla are uniformly brown.

Trichocaulon keetmanshoopense DTR. [18] (Plate 47,6)

Its stems are thick, cylindrical, up to 15 cm long, forming small groups, violet-gray-green or yellowish brown, with rugose, raised, rounded mamillae. Its flowers are 10 to 14 mm in diameter, flat dish-shaped, without a distinct tube; the corolla lobes are whitish to yellowish green, and reddish brown flecked, with the upper side glabrous. *Distribution:* Namibia.

Trichocaulon kubusense NEL (Color Plate 5,9)

is the "giant" among the cactoid types. While NEL in his diagnosis indicates a length of only 16 cm, I collected specimens in the Richtersveld that were up to 25 cm tall with a diameter up to 6 cm. They are richly branched from the base, forming groups of 10 to 20 columns. The flowers are ca. 1 cm in diameter, with a distinct ring around the corona; corolla lobes are spreading or reflexed, and greenish white with red flecks, with the upper side so densely covered with conical papillae that the flowers appear grayish white. *Distribution:* western Cape Province (Little Namaqualand, the Richtersveld).

T. kubusense, like other species of the same group, frequently tends to form crests on the top of the stems. The largest *T. kubusense* crest found by me had a diameter of 25 cm.

Magnification of the flowers of

Trichocaulon perlatum DTR.

reveals a true, natural work of art. They are basically yellowish green with reddish dots, and the upper side is densely covered with spherical, white papillae, which in the light shine like pearls.

Similar "perlate" flowers are found also on

Trichocaulon truncatum PILL. (Plate 47,7),

which is very closely related to the above and differs only in the structure of the corona.

OTHER STEM SUCCULENT ASCLEPIADACEAE

In the large family of Asclepiadaceae there are stem succulent groups other than the stapeliads to attract the interest of the collector. Of these I name

Brachystelma R.BR.,

a genus from southern and eastern Africa with many species (around 50), whose members are distinguished by large, subterranean, round, flat tubers, that frequently have a depression at the top and roots on the bottom. From the short primary shoot emerge numerous, thin flower shoots that either lie on the ground or stand upright; after the fruit ripens the shoots die back to the base, from which in the following year emerges new growth. The flowers appear singly or in multi-flowered, umbel-like cymes, as in all Asclepiadaceae in terminal position but soon being surpassed by quickly emerging lateral shoots, which themselves end in inflorescences.

Cultivation of these relatively rare plants is similar to that of all tuber-forming, deciduous succulents, i.e., a rest period in their leafless state is absolutely necessary. Although the tubers in their native habitat are completely hidden in the soil, in cultivation they must be raised considerably, so that they can be observed and checked better, thereby avoiding from too much watering.

---

[19] H. HUBER placed *T. cactiforme* N.E. BR., *T. meloforme* MARL., and *T. keetmanshoopense* DTR. into one species, *T. clavatum* (WILLD.) H. HUBER.

From the abundance of species, I describe and picture only a few here, because acquisition of these plants is not easy.

Brachystelma foetidum SCHLTR. (Color Plate 4,2)

is one of those species whose presence at flowering time is revealed at a great distance because of an intensively carrion-like stink. A single, blooming plant can completely "contaminate" a large greenhouse. In spite of the unpleasant smell *B. foetidum* is nevertheless a very decorative plant. Its tubers are hidden deep in the soil, and are up to 15 cm in diameter, flattened, and slightly depressed at the top, with a short, upright stem, from which each year appears upright or reclining, branched, hairy foliage. Its leaf-blades are ca. 1.5 cm long, elliptical to oval, wavy at the margin, with short hairs on both sides, and narrowing into a short petiole. The flowers appear singly or in twos in terminal position and produce an extension in the form of an axil shoot, which in turn produces an inflorescence, etc. The flowers are highly variable in regard to size, color, and markings. The corolla tube is broadly dish-shaped and is white inside, with dark purple bands and flecks; the corolla lobes are dark purple with greenish tips or are uniformly olive-green, narrowly linear with reflexed margins, and are hairy below. *Distribution:* Cape Province to southern Natal, on meadows.

Similar in flower structure is the considerably smaller

Brachystelma coddii R.A. DYER.

From a roundish, depressed tuber only 5 cm in diameter emerge numerous thin, reclining shoots, which in cultivation become up to 20 cm long; they have short-petiolated, oval leaves up to 1.5 cm long and arranged in an alternate or opposite position. The flowers appear singly and have a flat dish-shape with a yellowish tube striped or dotted with red. The tube extends into hairy or glabrous lobes that are 5 to 7 mm long. *Distribution:* Swaziland, on rocky meadows.

One of the most bizarre species is

Brachystelma barberiae HARV. ex HOOK. (Color Plate 4,1).

From a flattened, depressed tube that is up to 20 cm in diameter emerges a thick shoot ca. 10 cm long, which in its leafless state produces a large unbel-like cyme of flowers. In contrast to most other species of the genus, the flowers, smelling sour, appear as little "windows." The lobes of the short, broadly dish-shaped, dark, blackish violet (lighter at the base), striped corolla are greatly elongated and remain united at their tips, so that 5 "windows" are formed, through which pollinating insects fly in and out. Such "window flowers" are found also in the genus *Ceropegia,* which is closely related to *Brachystelma.* The large, long lanceolate leaves that are up to 10 cm long with hairs on both sides appear toward the end of the flowering period. *Distribution:* on grassy slopes and meadows from Transvaal into Transkei.

Window flowers, although considerably smaller, are found also on

Brachystelma pygmaeum N.E. BR. (Plate 47,8),

whose flower form has caused it to be placed also into its own genus, *Dichaelia* (= *D. pygmaea* SCHLTR.). In *B. pygmaeum,* however, one can find window flowers and normally unfolded flowers on the same plant, so that there is no compelling reason to give it its own genus. The formation of windows is caused only by an incomplete unfolding of the corolla lobes. *B. pygmaeum* has flat tubers up to 10 cm in diameter, whose tip produces several thin, leafy shoots. The small, yellowish green, sometimes reddish overlaid flowers are in cymes of 2 to 3; the lobes of the cup-shaped corolla tube are initially united at their tips, but become separated later. This plant is easy to grow and flowers readily. *Distribution:* on grassy slopes in eastern Transvaal.

Ceropegia L.

The genus *Ceropegia,* with its ca. 160 species, is distributed throughout the tropical areas (extreme deserts and rain forests excepted) of the Old World. Its area stretches from South Africa through tropical Arabia to Asia (from India to western China); one species persists on through New Guinea to the northern tip of Australia. Other smaller distribution areas are the Canary Islands, Madagascar, and the neighboring island group of the Comoros. With the richness of species and the size of the area, it is no wonder that there is a great variety of growth-forms and flower forms; they can be only touched upon here. Not all species are succulent in the true sense; some have thin, reclining to creeping or upright, twining shoots with normally developed leaves. They are not interesting in this regard. Numerous species belong to the growth type of tuber succulents, i.e., they have subterranean, rooted tubers, from whose tips develop thin, short, upright or elongated and then usually twining shoots, which die at the end of each growing period.

Another group of ceropegias has highly succulent, upright, reclining to creeping or twining shoots, whose leaves, in alternating swirls can be reduced to tiny scales.

Although the ceropegias may seem unpretentious in regard to their vegetative organs, they are bizarre and magnificent with respect to their flowers. The ceropegia flowers are masterworks of nature as few other plant groups produce and are remarkable in many respects. They differ from the flowers of other Asclepiadaceae in their strikingly elongated corolla tubes, which are often expanded at the base like a kettle; such flowers are also called "kettle flowers."

The bottom of the kettle holds the sexual organs, which structurally are the same as those of the other stapeliads and have already been described in detail on page 65.

Also, in the ceropegias the stamens have appendages in the form of an outer and an inner corona, and the pollen masses of each stamen are united into pollinia.

The five corolla lobes are frequently united at their tips, so that as in *Brachystelma barberiae,* "window flowers" are formed. Above I have already referred to the fact that the window effect is either a permanent or temporary developmental suppression of the corolla tips. This behavior is especially evident in the flowers of *C. dichotoma* and *C. stapeliaeformis.* In the young flowers of these plants, the corolla lobes are united at the tip and are separated only at the base, and so 5 windows are formed; with maturity, however, the tips of the lobes become detached and roll back. In other species, however, these stay constantly united, so that the window effect is retained. Among these window flowers certain very "exotic" flowers appear, such as those of *C. sandersonii* (Plate 49,4), *C. rendallii* (Plate 48,9), and *C. distincta* ssp. *haygarthii* (Color Plate 6,1), which will be described later in more detail.

Remarkable also are the markings and the colorations of the flowers. As these flowers are biologically the same type of carrion flowers as has been evidenced before and give off a carrion-like stink, the predominant colors, as in the other stapeliads, are dirty brown or violet, which entice the pollinating insects (carrion flies).

Many ceropegia flowers are built like the flowers into which an insect slides and is caught: the corolla tube, especially the entrance to the extended kettle, is covered with hairs pointed downward. The structural principle of a fish trap allows the insects to crawl in but prevents their escape. Only after complete pollination do these "trap hairs" wither and allow the insect, laden with pollinia, to leave the flower and seek others.

Cultivation: The cultivation of most ceropegias affords no more difficulty than do the other stapeliads. Twining types should be grown on sticks or wires or grown as hanging plants; during the summer water moderately and provide good air circulation; during the winter, especially for the tuberous types, maintain a rest period. Propagation is accomplished by seed or cuttings.

The revision of the genus by H. Huber[20] has arranged the known species into 21 sections. I can only give a selection here and have chosen especially those species which should interest the hobbyist and have found wide distribution in cultivation.

Ceropegia ampliata E. Mey. (Plate 48,1)

is a twining plant with succulent, glabrous shoots, whose leaves are reduced to deciduous scales. Its flowers usually appear singly, seldom in groups of 2 to 4, and are large and attractive, with a whitish, green-nerved corolla tube that is expanded into a kettle form at the base. The corolla lobes are short, olive green, recurved on the edges, and united at the tips. This is a decorative and easily grown plant. *Distribution:* coastal region of southeastern Africa (Natal) and Namibia.

A no less decorative but very large species is

Ceropegia ballyana Bullock (Plate 48,2).

Its twining shoots are 1 to 2 cm thick, up to 2 m long, glabrous, and fleshy, with large leaves that are longitudinally oval and shiny green. Flowers appear singly or in few-flowered cymes that are up to 10 cm long; the tubes are ca. 2.5 cm long, whitish with darker flecks, and sharply divided from the basal kettle. The corolla lobes are up to 7 cm long, lineal, chocolate brown, hairy on the inside, and twisted corkscrew-like in the upper third. *Habitat:* Kenya (dry forest near Voi).

Easily grown, this plant is easy to propagate from cuttings.

Very close to this species is

Ceropegia robynsiana Werderm. (Plate 48,3),

whose flowers are identical to those of the above species in form and color, with the exception that the kettle is larger and more sharply delineated from the corolla tube, which extends like a funnel toward the tip, and the hairy corolla lobes, united at the tips, are not twisted. *Habitat:* Zaire.

To the same group also belongs *Ceropegia succulenta* Bruce (habitat: Kenya and Uganda), which very closely resembles the above in growth-form and in structure of the flower.

Ceropegia cimiciodora Obermeyer (Plate 49,3)

is a representative of the growth-form of the highly succulent ceropegias with extremely reduced foliage. Its shoots are twining, fleshy, glabrous, and gray-green with olive green flecks. The flowers are numerous, arranged in a spiral, on short, thick inflorescence stalks, unfolding one after the other, so that there is just 1 (sometimes 2) flower open at a time. The flower tube is bent, ca. 5 cm long, kettle-shaped at the base, extending like a funnel toward the opening, and is gray-green with violet flecks. The corolla lobes, in bud, form a 5-pointed star when seen from above; in the mature flower they detach at the tips and bend back; the upper side is pale violet, with hairs on the

[20] "Revision der Gattung *Ceropegia.*" *Memorias da Soc. Broteriana,* vol. XIII, Coimbra, 1957.

margin and on the top. *Distribution:* South Africa (Transvaal). Also of the same growth-form is

Ceropegia stapeliaeformis HAW. (Plate 48,4).

The gray or brownish green flecked, succulent, somewhat warty shoots, with their scale leaves, spread across the ground as do the shoots of many stapeliads (e.g., *Duvalia*), producing roots on their under side, and the growing shoot tip frequently pushes into the ground, grows for a while underground, and then emerges again above the surface. When the plants bloom, the shoots elongate and begin to twine, and can reach a length of up to several meters. Flowers, as in the above species, are arranged in a spiral on thick inflorescence stalks, with cylindrical, gray-green tubes that bear wine-red spots. The tubes are 2 to 4 cm long and extend into a broad funnel near the tip. The corolla lobes are up to 5 cm long and distinctly reflexed, detaching from each other at bloom time and flaring; the upper side has white hairs at the base and is glabrous at the tip and chocolate colored. *Habitat:* eastern Cape Province.

C. serpentina, so described by E.A. BRUCE and found in Transvaal, is considered by H. HUBER to be only a variety of the above. The differences in flower structure are slight; the much longer corolla lobes are twisted in their bud stage; at bloom time the flower opens only on one side, so the corolla lobes appear to be an elongated, twisted tongue.

Ceropegia dichotoma HAW.

is common in cultivation. It is native to the Canary Islands and is a fast grower. Its stems are upright, up to 1 m tall, branching from the base, up to 2 cm thick, cylindrical, gray-green, and clearly segmented. Stem segments are 5 to 10 cm long and are slightly constricted at the nodes. The leaves are lanceolate, falling during the rest period. The flowers appear in multiples in terminal cymes on the upper stalk segments, and are insignificant and yellowish green; the tubes are cylindrical, 1.5 to 2 cm long; and the corolla lobes are lineal, reflexed, attached at the tips before anthesis, and later detached.

Their thick shoots are suitable as grafting stocks for stapliads that are difficult to cultivate.

Similar and also native to the Canary Islands is

Ceropegia drainzii SVENT.,

which is characterized by its insignificant, yellowish white flowers.

Ceropegia fusca C. BOLLE,

another Canary Island species, has stems that when young are dark brown, almost black, and at maturity graying. Its flowers are blackish brown, yellow inside.

Ceropegia dimorpha H. HUMB. (Plate 49,1)

is one of the most interesting ceropegias of all, having relatively small flowers, but whose growth-form is completely different from all other species and which vegetatively resembles a *Caralluma* rather than a *Ceropegia.* It grows in the Isalo Mountains of the southern highlands of Madagascar, where it is hidden between grass in a black humus.

The brownish green, unbranched (or few-branched near the tip) stems, up to 2.5 cm thick and up to 30 cm long, are covered with dense, tooth-like, elongated leaf bases, whose lanceolate-ovate, short-lived, blades are found occasionally on new growth. As soon as the bloom phase begins, the stem elongates (without twining), and the axis diameter suddenly shrinks. The flowers occur in few-flowered cymes. Their light brown corolla tube is short (ca. 1 cm long), has dark brownish violet nerves, and is inflated into a sphere. The distinctly separated, dark purple, lineal corolla lobes remain attached at the tips and have long, violet club-hairs at the margins of the After the seed ripens, the whole elongated inflorescence dies. Branching results from the part of the succulent stem segment near the tip, a behavior that is unique in ceropegias. In this respect *C. dimorpha* is identical to the members of section Eucaralluma.

C. dimorpha is not only a quite unusual species in its blooming stage, but also in its vegetative state; however, it is difficult to grow.

A similar stem dimorphism is also found in the Madagascar species *C. armandii* RAUH and *C. bosseri* RAUH et BUCHLOH, discovered by the author, in which the blooming segments reach a length of several meters and appear as twining shoots.

Ceropegia distincta N.E. BR. (Plate 48,5)

and its subspecies *haygarthii* (SCHULTR.) H. HUBER (= *C. haygarthii* SCHLTR.) (Color Plate 6,1) produce the most remarkable flowers known among the ceropegias. Both are vining plants with thin (3 to 4 cm thick), glabrous, green shoots, which have leaves arranged in alternating opposite position, slightly fleshy, oval-lanceolate, up to 3.5 cm long and 2.5 cm wide. The flowers appear in few-flowered inflorescences, whose axes are pointed downward. By bending upward, the flower stem, which also extends onto the corolla tube (Plate 48,5), causes the flowers to be upright. The bright gray-green tube with wine-red spots and ca. 3.5 cm long thus shows a nearly right-angle bend above the kettle-like extension. The funnel-shaped opening of the tube is divided by a special formation of the corolla lobes into five separate entrance openings ("windows"). The chambering is caused by the corolla lobes being broadened at their base and reflexed so sharply that they protrude like "plates" into the center of the corolla tube. The constricted tips of the corolla lobes on the other hand, fuse into a central column called a stipellum (Color Plate 6,1).

In *C. distincta* this stipellum is short (only a few millimeters) (Plate 48,5); in ssp. *haygarthii,* on the other hand, it is very much elongated and is up to 3 cm long. Since in this plant the corolla lobe ends are again somewhat broadened near the tip and thus open like windows, a small "lantern" borne on a stem is formed, the so-called capitulum, that perches over the flower (Color Plate 6,1).

The distribution area of *C. distincta* is the island of Zanzibar; ssp. *haygarthii* is found in southeastern Cape Province and Natal.

Ceropegia elegans WALL. (Plate 48,6)

Another pretty species is the Indian vining plant *C. elegans,* distinguished by its good growth and willingness to bloom when kept in a warm location. Especially decorative are the large window flowers with their striking markings: the corolla tube, kettle-shaped at the base, has a basic, dirty white color and in the broadly funnel-shaped extended segment has dark violet flecks. The corolla lobes, fused at the top and opening into windows, show the same color pattern and have long, violet hairs on their edge.

Ceropegia radicans SCHLTR. (Plate 48,7)

Shoots are reclining, crawling, and rooting at the nodes; leaves are fleshy, glabrous, broadly elliptical, short tipped, ca. 4 cm long and 2.5 cm wide. Flowers appear in 1- to 3-flowered cymes, with a greenish white, reddish flecked tube that is 6 to 8 cm long and extends into a funnel shape near the tip. The corolla lobes are distinctly reflexed, upright and fused at the tip, and multi-colored: purple-brown at the base, followed by a white diagonal stripe, which is dissolved by a narrow, dark-purple stripe. The upper third of the corolla lobe is shiny green with purple, mobile club-hairs. *Distribution:* southeastern Cape Province.

This is a decorative and easily grown species.

Ceropegia sandersonii HOOK. f. (Plate 49,4)

has very striking, large flowers. It is a widespread winding species in southeastern Africa (from Mozambique to Transvaal), with fleshy leaves 4 to 5 cm long and 3 to 5 cm wide. The flowers are in groups of 2 to 5 on short, thick axes and, when fully developed, have the shape of an open umbrella 4 to 5 cm in diameter. Their corolla tubes are up to 7 cm long, greenish white with dark stripes, cylindrical, and extend toward the tip into a broad funnel shape. The 5 corolla lobes begin from a narrow base and abruptly widen, causing them to fuse into a roof or umbrella covering the entrance to the flower tube. In this way it creates 5 windows as entrance openings to the tube. The tips of the corolla segments, united into the umbrella, are bent inward and form a cone, which extends into the flower and is short, blackish violet, and functions as an odor gland. The roof itself is light green with darker spots underneath and with white, mobile hairs on the margin, which form a fringe on the umbrella. In flowers that are just unfolding, the margin of the umbrella is pointed downwards, but on older flowers it is pointed upward.

C. sandersonii should be in every collection, especially since the plant affords no special problems in cultivation and blooms freely.

Sometimes in collections there are hybrids of *C. sandersonii* crossed with *C. elegans* and *C. radicans*.

Ceropegia rendallii N.E. BR. (Plate 48,9),

has window flowers of similar structure, i.e., umbrella-like, although considerably smaller. It is a representative of the tuberous species. Its vining or upright shoots sometimes reach a length of only 10 cm. The flowers are not larger than 2 cm and are brownish, and the fused corolla lobes are olive green. *Distribution:* Transvaal.

This is a rewarding and interesting species, especially since it requires little space.

Similarly decorative, umbrella-like window flowers are found on

Ceropegia galeata H. HUBER (Plate 49,2),

a vining plant with succulent stems and scale-shaped leaves. Its flowers are very large and are gray-green with numerous brownish violet flecks. The tube at the base is an elongated kettle shape expanding toward the tip, with reflexed, brownish violet margins. The corolla lobes abruptly widen from the narrow base and fuse into an umbrella-like roof, that is short tipped and gray-green with purple flecks; their yellowish margins are bent upward and bear long, fringe-like, mobile, purple hairs. *Distribution:* deciduous forests of Kenya, west of Mombasa.

An actually quite unassuming plant is

Ceropegia woodii SCHLTR. (Plate 48,8)

(considered by H. HUBER as a subspecies of *C. linearis*), a representative of the tuberous species, which is a very effective hanging plant because of its white-marbled, heart-shaped leaves.

From a tube, which can become 5 cm in diameter with good nutrition, emerge numerous, reclining-creeping (in a hanging basket they hang), thin stems with elongated internodes; in the axils of the petiolated, fleshy, heart-shaped leaves, which are light green beneath and dark green with white marbling on the upper side, develop tubers, which are homologous to modified lateral branches and which can serve as vegetative propagation organs. The flowers themselves are small and insignificant and have a short, somewhat bent, brownish tube with dark nerves and a kettle-like base; they also have dark brown, fused lobes with hairs at the margins. *Distribution:* Zambia, Zimbabwe, Transvaal, Natal, Cape Province.

Closely related to *C. woodii* are *C. debilis* N.E. BR. (= *C. linearis* E. MEY. ssp. *debilis*) and *C. linearis* E. MEY. (= *C. linearis* ssp. *linearis*). The latter differs from *C. woodii* by its narrowly linear leaves.

In spite of their unassuming quality, *C. woodii* and *C. linearis* should be in every succulent collection, because the tubers of both species, as stated on page 30, serve as the most important grafting stock for other stapeliads. Both species are grown—if you have a greenhouse—under the benches, since they are quite undemanding and thrive even under unfavorable light conditions. In order to always have enough large tubers on hand, the plants must be fertilized during the growth period (summer). Set the tubers in pots for several weeks before grafting; place them at an angle in order to get sufficient grafting surface. After the tubers have formed new roots, the graft can be carried out as described on page 30, but care must be taken to insure that the tubers do not wither after grafting. To accomplish this, leave them some short foliage, so that nutrition stored in the tubers is not completely drawn off by the scion.

Fockea ENDL.

The genus *Fockea* is represented by a few species from eastern Africa over Angola into the dry areas of South Africa. They are stem succulents, which have a big stem tuber that merges into a thick root and is almost completely hidden in the ground; the tuber produces numerous elongated, vining, leafy stems.

In collecitons we usually find only

Fockea crispa (JACQ.) K. SCHUM. (= *Fockea capensis* ENDL.)

(Plate 49,5 and 6),

from the dry areas of South Africa. Its foliage is thin, creeping or vining, with opposing, elliptical-oval leaves crinkly on the margins. Its flowers are small and insignificant, with greenish, twisted, star-shaped, flattened lobes (Plate 49,6).

FAMILY APOCYNACEAE

In the large family of *Apocynaceae*, the oleander family, there are especially two genera with stem succulent plants, often of huge size—*Adenium* and *Pachypodium*.

The distribution area of the genus

Adenium ROEM. et SCHULT.

is the dry areas of tropical Africa, the island of Socotra, and southern Arabia. So far the following, very closely related species have been described: *A. arabicum* BALF., *A. boehmianum* SCHINZ, *A. coetanum* STAPF, *A. honghei* A.D.C., *A. multiflorum* KL., *A. obesum* BALF., *A. oleifolium* STAPF. *A. socotranum* VIERH., *A. somalense* BALF. f., *A. speciosum* FENZL., and *A. swazicum* STAPF. They are all of approximately the same growth-form and are differentiated by the form and hair arrangement of the leaves and flowers, characteristics which are admittedly subject to great variability. I observed, in Kenya, a large stand of *A. obesum* in which plants with lanceolate and oval-round leaves and flowers that were glabrous as well as pubescent all growing amongst each other; frequently these characteristics change even on one plant. Therefore a revision of the genus must yet determine whether these 11 described species should perhaps be only ecological and geographical varieties of a single species.

As an example I choose

Adenium obesum BALF. (Color Plate 6,4 and Plate 49,7),

which for years has been grown in the Botanical Garden at Heidelberg without difficulty, and every year it develops its splendid flowers. The plant in its youth stage has a regularly formed caudex (up to the size of a soccer ball) which on its top has a "crown" of thin and sparingly branched limbs (Plate 49,7). With age this regular form is lost. The caudex becomes an irregular, thickened body. The whole plant then takes on a shrubby growth-form; in southern Arabia *A. arabicum* (probably identical with *A. obesum*) becomes a large tree up to 5 m tall (Plate 49,8), which resembles the baobab tree. Its leaves,

in a terminal rosette on the ends of the branches which fall during the dry season, are of a slightly fleshy structure. The large, prominent, vivid, carmine-colored to pinkish flowers are found in multiples in short-stalked, terminal inflorescences; its corolla is differentiated into a basal, narrow tube, which contains the ovary, and a broadly bell-shaped segment, which ends in five wide, flared lobes, which in the bud are in a spiral. In the passage into the bell-shaped extension are attached the stamens, which lie over the stigma; the anthers have long, hairy appendages. The ovary consists of two carpels, which ripen into two large, horn-shaped capsules. The seeds are peculiar, since they have hair bundles on both ends. The flowers persist for several weeks.

In its native habitat (eastern Africa) *Adenium* is called "desert rose," a quite justified name, since a single plant in full flower (in Kenya in April) shines in red splatters not unlike a rose shrub in the dry bush, which at that time of year is leafless and desolate.

When the plant is wounded it emits a whitish, very bitter-tasting, and very poisonous sap.

Propagation is best by seed, which germinate very easily. Cuttings, which indeed will take root, normally do not form a caudex. Judging from my experiments, all *Adenium* species are easily grafted to oleander *(Nerium oleander)* and are very willing to bloom.

Adenium can easily be grown along with other succulents, e.g., euphorbias. During the winter, in their leafless state, withhold water for the most part; in the summer water thoroughly. Seedlings will bloom after just 3 to 4 years.

Pachypodium LINDL.

No less interesting succulents are the *Pachypodium* species, the "thick foot" plants, which in growth-form very much resemble the adeniums but differ from them in their thorn cover. The thorns appear in pairs or in threes at the base of the deciduous leaves. Some species, especially the columnar forms, grow rigid in their heavy thorn covering and in their leafless state resemble certain heavily thorned, columnar cacti (Plate 50,1).

In regard to their growth-form there are two distinct groups to consider: tree-like forms and shrubby forms.

The former have a stem sometimes up to 6 m tall, succulent, consisting predominantly of water tissue, and a loose, forked crown of thin lateral branches (Plate 50,5). Branching occurs only after the plant is old enough to bloom and then, because of the terminal position of the inflorescence, always forms at the end of a flowering period. Only *P. namaquanum* remains columnar and unbranched for its whole life, as long as it is not disturbed (Plate 50,1), since flowers appear laterally.

The shrubby types, like *Adenium,* have a basal, sometimes rather large caudex, which has a crown of thin, more or less forked, thorny branches, which during the growing period have a rosette of leaves arranged in a spiral.

The flowers, arranged in more or less long-stalked inflorescences, are quite prominent and resemble those of *Adenium* in structure and shape. Also, in *Pachypodium* the two carpels develop into horn-shaped capsules, which release a great number of brown seeds. In contrast to *Adenium* these have only a single hair bundle to aid in distribution by the wind.

The genus includes 18 species, which occupy two separated areas. One distribution area consists of the dry areas and semi-deserts of South Africa and Namibia, Africa; the second area is the deciduous forests and the central highlands of Madagascar. It is precisely the Madagascar pachypodiums that are of special interest to the hobbyist; through my research trips, I have seen that many of them have found wide distribution in European collections in recent years.

The cultivation of pachypodiums is not so difficult as it seems initially. They require a loose, humusy medium, some bottom heat, more water in their leafy state, and a rest period as soon as the leaves begin to fall. Many of the Madagascar species are suitable for indoor cultivation (see Plate 6,1). With the appropriate cultivation requirements—water even in the winter months if the soil is kept warm—the plants will keep their leaves the whole years. This a very recommendable succulent group!

African species.

Among the tree-like forms are:

Pachypodium leallii WELW. ssp. *leallii* (= *P. giganteum* ENGL.)

Its stems are up to 6 m high, bottle-shaped, and sparingly branched; the leaves are sessile or on short petioles, with lanceolate blades up to 12 cm long and 4 cm wide, and are wavy and pubescent on the margins. Thorns occur always in threes

and are very hard and stout, up to 3 cm long, and shorter on the youngest branches. Its flowers are very large, white, with a pleasant smell; the crown leaves are wavy to curly on the margins. *Habitat:* Namibia.

Pachypodium namaquanum WELW. (Plate 3,3; 50,1),

a characteristic plant of the rocky quartz and granitic slopes of Little Namaqualand, forms stems up to 2 (−3) m high and which, when undisturbed, are completely unbranched (Plate 3,3); only when harmed does it branch. Its stems are thick and bottle-shaped and in its upper segments are covered by the very hard, leather-brown thorns up to 5 cm long. These are found in threes on a mamilla-shaped podarium (Plate 50,1). The hairy, wavy-edged leaves are up to 12 cm long and appear at the beginning of the growing period (in its habitat, September to October) in a terminal rosette. The flowers are numerous, with a very hairy tube that is reddish brown outside and yellowish inside.

Difficult and slow to grow, it needs much warmth.

In its habitat *P. namaquanum* appears in sparse stands in which the tips of all the plants are pointed in the same direction, north. From a distance, and when seen against the evening sky, such stands resemble a group of crouching people; therefore, *P. namaquanum* is referred to by the natives as "half people." A sage relates that the bushmen were driven from their homeland and climbed the slopes to stand watch every evening longingly over their old home. Then they were transformed into plants, pachypodiums, which accordingly all stand with their "heads" leaning to the north.

Among the shrubby species are:

Pachypodium bispinosum (L. f.) DC. (Plate 50,2)

This is a plant with a thick, caudiciform stem base that is mostly hidden in the soil, with numerous, thin, very thorny shoots (thorns in pairs). The leaves are lanceolate and acuminate, with sparse hairs on both sides. The flowers appear in sparse inflorescences, with a wide, dark-purple tube with hair on the inside; corolla lobes are white to purple, with rounded tips. Easily grown from seed, this plant is also easily propagated by cuttings.

Pachypodium leallii WELW. ssp. *saundersii* (N.E. BR.) ROWL. (= *P. saundersii* N.E. BR.) (Plate 50,3)

A sparsely branched shrub, it grows up to 1.5 m high with a caudiciform base and has branches with gray bark and dense thorns (thorns in pairs). Its leaves are on short petioles, with oval-elliptical blades that have hairs on the margins. Inflorescences are sessile, multiflowered; flowers are large, white, with reddish strips. *Distribution:* South Africa (Zululand).

Fast growing in cultivation, it is propagated by seed.

Pachypodium succulentum DC. (Plate 50,4)

In growth-form, this plant is similar to *P. bispinosum,* i.e., with a basal, fleshy napiform root, mostly buried in the soil and merging into a thick caudex. Its branches are numerous, up to 50 cm long, with dense thorns (thorns in pairs), and its leaves are lanceolate, with hairs on both sides. The flowers are small, appearing in few-flowered, sessile inflorescences with narrowly cylindrical, light-purple, hairy tubes; the corolla lobes are narrowly lanceolate and flared, with white margins or with a red central strip. *Distribution:* southern Cape Province (Uitenhage District) and Namaqualand.

Madagascar species

The Madagascar species appear in a considerably larger variety regarding growth-form and flower color. Along with white as a flower color, there are also yellow and pure red, colors which are not found among the African species. The white-flowered Madagascar pachypodiums are predominantly tree-like forms, which grow in the dry areas of the lower altitudes, while the yellow-flowered, shrubby types grow on the near barren shell gneiss and granite peaks of the central highland at altitudes between 1000 and 1500 m.

Among the tree-like forms, which are extraordinarily decorative when young, is

Pachypodium geayi COST. et BOIS (Plate 50,5 and 6)

The columnar, slightly barrel-shaped stem, which can reach up to 1 m in diameter at the base, can reach a height of up to 6 (–8) m, before it begins to branch and form a loose, ideally spherical crown (Plate 50,5). For hobbyists, however, young plants 30 to 50 cm tall are especially attractive. The cylindrical stem, up to 5 cm thick with silvery gray bark, is densely covered with thorns that are from 1.5 to 2 cm long and have fine hairs near the tip of the stem, later glabrous. The thorns are in threes and are perched on warty leaf pads that are dense near the tip of the plant (Plate 50,6). The narrowly lineal leaves are up to 20 (–30) cm long, silvery gray with a usually reddish color at the base, are in a terminal rosette, and are cast off during the dry season; but even in its leafless state *P. geayi* is very decorative and at first glance resembles a heavily thorned columnar cereus. It is particularly suited for growing as a house plant (see Plate 6,1).

In cultivation *P. geayi* will bloom only if planted in the open ground, since it reaches bloom capability only after many years and after forming a large stem several meters high. The flowers themselves are large and white and appear in multiples in short-stalked inflorescences. *Distribution:* dry forests of southwestern Madagascar, preferably on limestone.

The same growth-form is represented also by

Pachypodium lamerei DRAKE (Plate 50,7),

which in habitat forms large trees up to 5 m with a thick, unbranched, succulent stem and a sparsely branched crown. Young plants of this type are also very attractive (see Plate 6,1); they differ from those of *P. geayi* in their vivid green, short-stemmed leaves with lanceolate blades 15 to 20 cm long. In var. *lamerei* the blade has felt-like hairs beneath; in var. *ramosum* both sides are glabrous, and the very stiff, leather-brown thorns, found in threes on a thick leaf pad, are completely glabrous. The large, pure-white or slightly reddish flowers occur in multiples in short-stalked, terminal inflorescences. The fruits are large, thick, horn-like capsules, which release hundreds of seeds.

In its native habitat this beautiful plant is called "Vontaka," meaning "star of the steppe" (but other tree-shaped pachypodiums are also given this name). *Habitat and distribution:* similar to *P. geayi.*

As a young plant it is very good as a house plant.

Also among the tree forms is

Pachypodium rutenbergianum VATKE (Plate 6,2),

whose red-flowered var. *meridionale* H. PICH can form trees more than 10 m tall. In contrast to the two previous representatives, the short, but very stiff, brown thorns appear in pairs at the base of the long-lanceolate, short-petiolated, glabrous leaves. The flowers have reflexed, white or red corolla lobes that are wavy on the margins and occur in multi-branched, short-stalked inflorescences. Seed capsules are long, resembling a Virginia cigar.

P. rutenbergianum is widely distributed in Madagascar and cannot be recommended for cultivation, for it very quickly grows tall without developing a thick stem.

A white-flowered representative of shrubby growth-form and a huge, basal caudex is the species found only in northern Madagascar (Diego-Suarez),

Pachypodium decaryi H. POISS. (Plate 50,8),

rarely found in cultivation. In habitat it forms knotty or barrel-shaped caudexes up to 50 cm high and just as thick, from which emerge a few, nearly thornless branches 1 to 2 m length, which have a terminal rosette of short-petiolated, oval, soft-haired leaves. Its flowers are very large, with an acrid smell (of hawthorn), are pure white, and appear in sessile inflorescences; the crown leaves overlap each other.

P. decaryi has proven very free blooming in cultivation. In the Botanical Garden at Heidelberg even small plants produce many flowers every year.

Northern Madagascar is also the home of the only "pure-red" flowering pachypodium

Pachypodium baroni COST. et BOIS.,

whose growth-form resembles that of *P. decaryi.* Considerably smaller, however, is var. *windsori* H. PICH., which grows in only one location, on the limestone slopes below Windsor Castle north of Diego-Suarez (in the extreme northern part of the island). The plant grows here in the humus-filled rock crevices in association with *Aloe suarezensis.* Old specimens have a caudex with a grayish brown bark and reach about the size of a soccer ball. The caudex elongates into a regenerating, slightly branched primary shoot. The thorny (thorns in pairs) branches bear a rosette of oval, leathery, short-petiolated leaves that are vivid green on the upper side and gray and felt-like beneath. Flowers appear in long-peduncled inflorescences that have a narrow tube with a yellow throat and bright-red, spreading corolla lobes (Color Plate 6,3).

P. baroni var. *windsori* might be one of the most beautiful pachypodiums, which also—even in cultivation—is quite willing to bloom. The specimens in the Heidelberg Botanical Garden bloom every year from May to the end of August.

The yellow-flowered Madagascar species are also very attractive; *Pachypodium rosulatum* BAK., *P. horombense* H. POISS., *P. densiflorum* BAK., and *P. brevicaule* are especially worth mentioning (Plate 51).

With the exception of the latter, all of the species have the same growth-form and have a large, caudex-like, regularly spherical or irregularly formed, gray-barked stem base at maturity, which has a "crown" of more or less regularly branched, short, thick, thorny (thorns in pairs) lateral branches. Every year at the beginning of the growing period these develop a tuft of short-petiolated, lanceolate or oval, gray, felt-like, sometimes glabrous leaves, which are cast off as the rest period begins. Even the thorns disappear on older shoot segments.

The plants can be grown easily from seed. Their development is as follows: the short, at first unbranched primary shoot along with the elongated sprout transforms into a small knot of only water-storing parenchyma. As the plant reaches bloom size (frequently in the 2nd or 3rd year), this knot stops elongating and forms a long-stalked inflorescence; only then does it begin to branch, by developing 2 to 4 axil buds into lateral branches just below the inflorescence base. These lateral branches grow for several years, although the yearly growth is very little, and then, in turn, end with a terminal inflorescence. (Color Plate 6,2). Since these branch again in the same manner as the primary shoot, the course of years sees a system of more or less regularly forked lateral branches (Plate 51,1–4),which all remain quite short but, along with the shoot base, grow very thick. The plant thus loses its regular round form and becomes a misshapen, irregularly formed configuration. Very old plants, especially of *P. horombense* and *P. densiflorum,* can reach a diameter of 1.5 m and a height of up to 1 m (Plate 51,2–4). For the hobbyist and collector, of course, only young plants are of interest.

The three species are vegetatively difficult to distingusih. Only var. *gracilius* H. PERR. of *P. rosulatum* BAK. is easily recognized by its very thin, almost needle-like, reddish brown thorns and the narrowly lineal, glabrous leaves. Only when the long-stalked inflorescences with their bright yellow flowers appear, do the differences between the individual species become more evident. In *P. rosulatum,* including its var. *gracilius* (Color Plate 6,2), the flower corolla has a narrow tube; in the closely related *P. horombense,* on the other hand, the tube is broad. In both species the stamens are enclosed by the corolla tube. In *P. densiflorum* the flowers are considerably smaller, and the stamens, which incline into a sphere, rise out of the very short corolla tube (Plate 51,4).

All three species are clearly mountain plants, which in central Madagascar grow on shell gneiss and granite hills in great stands and climb to 1500 m. Only *P. rosulatum* var. *gracilius*

occupies the lower regions of the wildly cleft Isalo Mountains of sandstone.

All three named pachypodiums afford no great difficulties in cultivation, as long as you give them a bright, warm location. During the summer months water them thoroughly; in the leafless state limit the water.

The most interesting if not the most remarkable succulent of all is

Pachypodium brevicaule BAK. (Plate 51,5 and 6),

which grows in pure quartz rocks in the central highlands of Madagascar and barely rises above its surroundings with its misshapen, flat, bulgy to cow-dung-shaped, silvery gray vegetative body that is up to 60 cm in diameter. During vegetative rest, i.e., in its leafless state, the plant completely resembles the surrounding stone in form and color, and so it can hardly be found (Plate 51,5 and 6). Among the stem succulents *P. brevicaule* is thus a good example of plant mimicry, i.e., of fitting into the surroundings (see also page 136 ff.). Only at flowering time, when the body is covered with hundreds of large, bright yellow flowers, can the plants be seen from a great distance.

The peculiar growth-form of *P. brevicaule* has the same method of branching as the other pachypodiums. After every blooming period, the formation of lateral branching begins, but these remain extraordinarily short; their yearly growth amounts to only a few millimeters. Instead they grow stout and take on a knotty shape. Old plants therefore resemble a heap of discarded potatoes (Plate 51,5). With age the central shoots of such a heap often die, while on the periphery new shoots are produced constantly. In this manner irregularly shaped bodies are formed such as are shown in Plate 51,6 and which resemble a chip of stone more than a living plant.

The large yellow flowers appear sparsely in short-stalked or almost sessile inflorescences.

P. brevicaule is a very slow-growing species, which can be propagated only by seed. Three-year-old seedlings are approximately the size of a pea.

For good growth *P. brevicaule* needs much light and warmth, a slightly acid medium, and little water during the whole year.

In the Itremo Mountains (central Madagascar), where *P. brevicaule* grows along with *P. densiflorum,* hybrids of the two have been found. In regard to their growth-form, they take a middle position between the two parents.

FAMILY PASSIFLORACEAE

When one thinks of passion flowers one usually imagines herbaceous plants with thin shoot axes, which climb with the aid of tendrils and have large, beautifully shaped flowers in bright colors. One needs only to think of the favorite house plant *Passiflor coerulea* or the splendid *P. quadrangularis.* This concept does not entirely represent the succulent passifloras, which belong almost exclusively to the genus

95

Adenia FORSK.

and are found in the dry forests of Africa and Madagascar. They have large, caudiciform, water-storing stem bases, from which emerge upright or pendulous, sometimes thorny branches. In some forms the caudiciform stem base elongates like lianas and climb by their tendrils into the branches of other plants, but other representatives are without tendrils; their succulent shoots remain short. In other groups the succulent organs—roots and shoot bases—are completely buried in the ground and the foliage coming from them is of normal, non-succulent form. The usually single-sexed and dioecious flowers of all succulent passifloras are generally small, insignificant, and hardly decorative.

In collections, even in botanical gardens, these remarkable plants are seldom represented, although their cultivation affords no greater difficulties than other succulents. It is thus difficult to get living plants or seed. Propagation by cuttings from lateral branches is possible, but these do not form a caudex. Typical growth-forms can be produced only from seeds, and these are not commonly available from the usual sources.

Adenia glauca SCHINZ (Plate 52,*1* and *2*)

is very pretty even as a small plant. At maturity it has a large, sometimes above-ground knotty stem base, which continues into a stout, fleshy root. The shoot segment, which continues growth at the tip, each year produces few, slightly branched shoots, which wither after the fruit ripens and which climb by tendrils; the shoots are equipped with large, bluish green, finger-shaped, pinnate leaves. The flowers are small, have a pleasant smell, are yellowish green, and are found in the axils of the foliage. *Distribution:* Transvaal, between rocks.

Similar is *A. digitata* (HARV.) ENGL. (= *A. multiflora* POTT).

Adenia firingalavensis (DRAKE) HARMS (Plate 52,*5*)

is a species widely distributed in the dry forests of Madagascar. It has a bottle-shaped stem base with gray-green bark and is covered with a layer of resin. The lateral branches are whip-like; the plant is therefore called the "whip tree." Its leaves are simple, undivided, with a heart-shaped or frequently 3-lobed blade; the flowers are small, unassuming, and yellowish green.

There are yet other succulent, Madagascar passifloras, but they are too rare to be discussed here.

The east African *A. venenata* FORSK. in its growth-form resembles the Madagascar *A. firingalavensis.* It, too, has a club-shaped, gray-barked stem with whip-like branches, which bear 3- to 5-lobed, dark-green leaves, and climbs by tendrils. The thin shoot segments usually die and are renewed each year.

One of the most bizarre succulents is

Adenia globosa ENGL. (Plate 53,*1–2*),

from the succulent steppes of eastern Africa, called a "plant caricature" by the African botanist VOLKENS. At first sight it seems absurd that this plant should be related to the passion flower. It has neither tendrils nor leaves, but instead it is rigid with thorns; only when the small, insignificant flowers appear, is its relation to the family of passion flowers obvious.

At maturity *A. globosa* in a clearing forms a dense, impenetrable tangle of arching to pendulous, gray-barked branches up to 4 m long; however, if the plant is growing in the under brush of dry forests, the shoots climb into the crowns of the trees.

In the axils of the small, shield-shaped, 3 lobed, short-lived leaves develop the thorns, which are dagger-like and end in a hard, stickery tip. "Woe to the unfortunate one," writes VOLKENS, "who slides down from horse or donkey and falls into this maze of martyrs' tools; he would not get out without severe wounds." If one hacks through the entanglement of thorny branches with a machete, however, then one is astounded to find that these branches emerge from an apical segment of a caudex up to 2 m in diameter and standing far out of the soil. As a young plant, it is regularly round (Plate 53,*1*), with a gray bark and hard warts; in maturity, however, it is deformed and resembles very much a boulder or a block, causing A. ENGLER to refer to is as the "block plant."

Of special morphological interest are the thorns, which give the plant its bizarre appearance and which are normally not present on passion flower relatives. Similar to the Transvaal stem succulent *Adenia spinosa* BURTT-DAVY, the thorns of *A. globosa* are transformed tendrils. *A. spinosa* represents the transition between the two conditions. In it, normal tendrils appear in the leaf axes, but their herbaceous ends die while their bases harden and remain as pseudo-thorns. If the tendrils suberize totally and remain short and stout, then it has the growth-form of *Adenia globosa.*

At the base of the thorns are the insignificant flowers, and the female plants bears spherical fruits (Plate 53,*2*).

According to P.R.O. BALLY, the water content of the stem caudex is so great that it is a source of water for the natives. For this purpose they bore a large hole in the caudex, in which the water from the parenchyma tissue collects and remains fresh for weeks. To prevent it from being used by animals, the hole is stuffed with a wood chock. The plants do not seem to suffer from this treatment.

Closely related to the above species is the recently described *A. pseudoglobosa* VERDC., of which ssp. *pseudoglobosa* is depicted (Plate 53,*3*). It differs from *A. globosa* by its wartless caudex, the much shorter, stiff, upright lateral branches, the longer and narrower thorns, and the considerably larger flowers. *Distribution:* Kenya, near Magadi.

Another quite remarkable, but hardly collected, species is the Namibian

Color Plate 6.

1 (ul) *Ceropegia distincta* ssp. *haygarthii*

2 (um) *Pachypodium rosulatum* var. *gracilius*

3 (ur) *Pachypodium baroni* var. *windsori*

4 (ml) *Adenium obesum*

5 (mm) *Didierea madagascariensis*, branch with male flowers

6 (mr) Branch of *Didierea madagascariensis* with female flowers

7 (ll) *Sarcocaulon rigidum* ssp. *glabrum*

8 (lr) *Sarcocaulon multifidum*

Plate 49.

(ul) *Ceropegia dimorpha* at the type-locality in the Isalo Mountains (southern Madagascar)

(um) *Ceropegia galeata*

(ur) *Ceropegia cimiciodera*

(ml) *Ceropegia sandersonii*

(mr) *Fockea crispa*, young plant

(ll) Flowering shoot of *Fockea crispa*

(lm) *Adenium obesum* in the Tsavo Wild Animal Park (Kenya)

(lr) A 5 m specimen of *Adenium arabicum* in the dry areas near Lodar (southern Arabia)

Plate 50.

1 (ul) *Pachypodium namaquanum*
2 (um) *Pachypodium bispinosum*, flowering shoot
3 (ur) *Pachypodium saundersii*, young plant
4 (ml) *Pachypodium succulentum*, eastern Karroo near Willowmore
5 (mr) *Pachypodium geayi*, the largest specimen in southern Madagascar (ca. 8 m)
6 (ll) Young plant of *Pachypodium geayi* in cultivation
7 (lm) *Pachypodium lamerei* in the dry bush of southern Madagascar
8 (lr) *Pachypodium decaryi*, individual flower

Plate 52.

1 (ul) *Adenia glauca*, young plant

2 (um) Flowering shoot of *Adenia gla.*

3 (ur) *Adenia keramanthus*, shoot wit
        male flowers

4 (ml) Fruiting plant of *Adenia keran
        thus* near Voi (Kenya)

5 (mm) *Adenia firingalavensis* in the d
        bush of western Madagascar

6 (mr) *Gerrardanthus macrorhizus*, flo
        shoot (see 9)

7 (ll) *Momordica rostrata*, shoot wit
        flowers

8 (lm) Caudex (ca. 20 cm in diamet
        an older plant of *Momordica r*

9 (lr) Stem base of an older *Gerrar
        macrorhizus* plant, caudex ca.
        in diameter (see 6)

53.

Adenia globosa, older plant with a caudex of ca. 50 cm
Branch with fruits of *Adenia globosa*, dry

bush near Voi (Kenya)
3 (ml) *Adenia pseudoglobosa* ssp. *pseudoglobosa*,
Magadi Road (Kenya)
4 (mr) *Seyrigia humbertii* (see 6)
5 (ll) *Pyrenacantha malvifolia* in the dry bush

of Kenya (Voi) along with *Aloe secundi-
flora* and *Sansvieria ehrenbergii*
6 (ur) Flowering male branch of *Seyrigia humbertii* (left) and fruiting branch of *Seyrigia multiflora* (right) (see 4)

Plate 54.

1 (ul) *Neoalsomitra podagrica*
2 (um) *Pelargonium carnosum*
3 (ur) *Pelargonium ceratophyllum*
4 (ml) *Pelargonium crassicaule*
5 (mr) *Pelargonium crithmifolium*
6 (ll) *Pelargonium echinatum*
7 (lm) *Pelargonium spinosum*
8 (lr) *Pelargonium klinghardtense*

e 55.

l) *Pelargonium tetragonum*

m) *Sarcocaulon l'heritieri*

r) *Sarcocaulon herrei*, showing thorn formation (see 5)

ıl) *Sarcocaulon mossamedense*

ır) Flowering shoot of *Sarcocaulon herrei* (see 3)

) *Sarcocaulon spinosum*

ı) *Cissus cactiformis* in a dry forest near Voi (Kenya)

) *Cissus rotundifolia* in a dry forest near Maktau (Kenya)

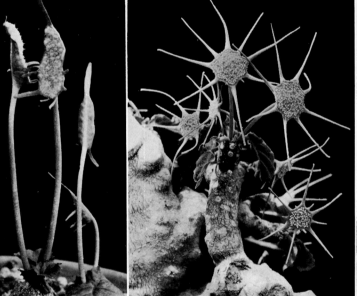

Plate 58.

1 (ul) *Alluaudia procera*, segment of the crown of an older tree in its leafless state

2 (um) Young shoot of *Alluaudia procera* with long-petiolate leaves

3 (ur) Older shoot of *Alluaudia procera* with short-petiolate leaves

4 (ml) *Alluaudia humber* long shoot with developed short-petiolate leaves. ×'s designate growth boundries

5 (mm) *Alluaudiopsis mareriana*. Branches with male (left) female (right) flowers

6 (mr) *Decaryia madagascariensis* near Amnihy, (southwest Madagascar)

7 (ll) *Didiera trollii* near Ampotoka (southwestern Madagascar)

8 (lm) *Didierea madagasiensis*, young plant in leafless state

9 (lr) Young plant of *Didiera madagasiensis* in leafy state

Plate 60.

1 (ul) *Senecio articulatus*
2 (ur) *Senecio kleinia*
3 (ll) *Senecio descoingsii*
4 (lr) *Senecio stapeliiform*
        (right shoot) and
        var. *minor* (left
        shoot)

61.

1) *Aloe ferox* on the Huis River
Pass near Calitzdorp (eastern
Cape Province)

2) *Aloe albiflora*

3) *Aloe bellatula*

4) Stand of *Aloe marlothii* near
Pietersburg (Transvaal)

5 (mm) *Aloe calcairophila*

6 (mr) *Aloe descoingsii*

7 (ll) *Aloe arborescens*, near Graskop
(eastern Transvaal)

8 (lm) *Aloe haworthioides*

9 (lr) *Aloe bakeri*

Plate 62.

1 (ul)   *Aloe parvula*, in the Itremo Mountains
          (central Madagascar) at 1700 m

2 (ur)   *Aloe conifera* near Ambatofinandrahana
          (central Madagascar)

3 (ml)   *Aloe viguieri* in the valley of the Fiherenana
          near Tuléar (southwestern Madagascar)

4 (ll)   *Aloe laeta*

5 (lr)   *Aloe rauh*

Aloe variegata in habitat (Bushman Land near Prieska)

2 (ur) *Aloe variegata* in cultivation

3 (ml) *Aloe claviflora*, Bushman Land near Upington

4 (ll) *Aloe haemanthifolia*

5 (ur) *Aloe aristata*

Plate 64.

1 (ul)   *Aloe albida*
2 (um) *Aloe melanacantha*
3 (ur)   *Aloe krapohliana* near
         Grotderm (the Richters-
         veld)
4 (ml) *Aloe humilis* var. *echinata*
5 (mr) *Aloe ciliaris*
6 (ll)   *Aloe pearsonii*, Hellskloof
         (the Richtersveld)
7 (lml) *Aloe jacksonii*
8 (lmr) *Aloe jucunda*
9 (lr)   *Aloe langistyla*

Adenia pechuelii (ENGL.) HARMS (= *Echinothamnus pechuelii* ENGL.).

It forms spherical stems up to 50 cm in diameter with a white resin crust; the stems cling to cracks in the boulders by means of a long, arrow-shaped root. The caudex produces numerous short, heavily thorned lateral branches that give the plant the appearance of a large hedgehog. A. ENGLER's name for it, *Echinothamnus*, refers to this fact.

Among the succulent adenias without tendrils are the eastern African species

Adenia keramanthus HARMS and *A. volkensii* HARMS.

The former forms gray-barked stems up to 1 m high and up to 10 cm thick, whose branches have heart-shaped leaves all the way around, which have a gray felt-like covering on both sides (Plate 52,2). The fruits, about the size of a chicken's eye, are bright red (Plate 52,4). *Adenia volkensii*, which in its habitat is considered very poisonous, differs from the previous one by its feathery, glabrous leaves.

FAMILY CUCURBITACEAE

The "pumpkin" family of many genera and species is a plant group of many forms. Along with annuals, which include the familiar vegetables, the cucumber *(Cucumis)* and the pumpkin *(cucurbita)* with their sometimes gigantic berry fruits, there are a great number of perennial plants, which climb by tendrils, among which there are several xerophytes from the dry areas of Africa and Madagascar. They belong to the group of leaf succulents as well as stem succulents. Here we are interested only in the latter. Stem succulents are found especially in the little known genera *Corallocarpus* WELW., *Dendrosicyos* BALF. f., *Acanthosicyos* WELW., *Alsomitra* ROEM., *Gerrardanthus* HARV., *Ibervillea* GREENE, *Kedrostis* MEDIC., *Melothria* L., *Momordica* L., *Seyrigia* DERAUDR., *Trochomeriopsis* COGN., etc.

Most of the stem succulent pumpkins have sometimes gigantic caudices, on whose apical end numerous, thin, liana-like branches emerge, which climb into the branches of surrounding trees and bushes. The generally well-known "pumpkins" are formed to a certain degree by the shoot bases. The unisexual and usually dioeceous flowers are small and insignificant; the fruits have various structures.

Here following are only a few, especially attractive species.

Gerrardanthus HARV. ex BENTH. et HOOK

Gerrardanthus macrorhizus HARV. (Plate 52,6 and 9)

is an interesting plant from the dry areas of Kenya and northern Tanganyika, usually growing between boulders. Its gray-green caudex has a thin, broken cork layer, grows above ground, and can reach a diameter of up to 80 cm. The slightly suberized,

liana-like shoots climb with the help of tendrils and become several meters long. Their leaves have a basically heart-shaped, roundish, sometimes 3- to 7-lobed blade with a bright green color or with a silvery upper side. The dioecious flowers are small and insignificant, and their corollas are olive green to dark brown (Plate 52,9). The fruits are small capsules with a lid at the tip, which emits long-winged seeds.

Very decorative and fast growing in cultivation, its caudex can reach a diameter of up to 50 cm in the course of a few years. Unfortunatley the plant, like all other succulent Cucurbitaceae, is very susceptible to attacks from nematodes.

Propagation is only by seed, for cuttings from the liana-like shoots do not form caudexes. To get seed you must have plants of both sexes.

In the same area (Kenya) grows the remarkable

Momordica (TOURN.) L. with

Momordica rostrata A. ZIMM. (Plate 52,7 and 8),

whose thick stem base, however, reaches lesser size than in *Gerrardanthus*. The plant grows preferably in shrubs onto which their slightly woody shoots can climb; the shoots are several meters long and have pinnate leaves in threes. The relatively large flowers are a shiny yellow orange; the fruits at maturity are coral red.

Of the same growth-form is a series of *Corallocarpus, Kedrostis,* and North American *Ibervillea* species.

A quite remarkable Cucurbitaceae is

Neoalsomitra HUTCHINS.

from the Sunda Islands, with

Neoalsomitra podagrica VAN STEENIS (Plate 54,1),

a liana, whose shoot axis is succulent and shows a prominent

97

separation into sharply distinguished yearly growth. Every stem is egg-shaped and with its sharp, hard thorns resembles the fruits of many tropical pumpkin relatives. The thorns are modified leaf petioles. Once the plant reaches bloom, the stem ends begin to elongate greatly and climb with the aid of simple thread-like tendrils. The twining shoot segments, which usually die after the fruit ripens, are thornless and have simple, heart-shaped or three-lobed, pinnate leaves.

One of the most attractive pumpkin relatives is

Dendrosicyos BALF. with

Dendrosicyos socotrana BALF. f.,

the "cucumber tree" from the island of Socotra (Figure 13). Although the plant is not found in cultivation, it should be mentioned in order to show the great variety of growth-forms within the family. In its non-blooming and non-fruiting stage, *D. socotrana* with its barrel-shaped stem up to 1 m thick, up to 6 m tall, and its sparsely branched crown has absolutely nothing in common with normal pumpkin plants and much rather resembles the African baobab tree *(Adansonia digitata)*. Only the flowers and the fruits reveal the family.

Another growth-form is represented by the Madagascar genus

Seyrigia KERAUDR.,

also residents of sparse, dry forests. The following species are known: *S. humbertii, S. multiflora, S. gracilis,* and *S. bosseri.*

Figure 13. A 6-meter-high specimen of *Dendrosicyos socotrana*. (After a water-color by SCHWEINFURTH.)

The prettiest, without doubt, is

S. humbertii KERAUDR. (Plate 53,4 and 6, left),

a liana with thick, potato-like roots. Its quadrangular stems climb with the help of simple, unbranched tendrils and are wrapped in a cloak of white, intertwined hairs; they seem completely leafless, because the tiny, lobed leaves, visible only on new shoots, drop after just a short time. The insignificant, yellowish flowers stand in short-stalked multi-flowered inflorescences; the fruits are coral-red berries.

S. multiflora KERAUDR. (Plate 53,6, right) and *S. gracilis* KERAUDR. differ from the preceding species by the thinner, round, almost glabrous shoots and the richly flowering inflorescences.

FAMILY GERANIACEAE

Stem succulents within the family of crane's bills are found especially in the genera *Pelargonium* and *Sarcocaulon,* which both have their main distribution area in the deserts and semi-deserts of southern Africa.

Especially rich in succulents is the genus

Pelargonium L'HER.,

to which also belong the beloved "geraniums" in their numerous varieties grown as balcony plants *(Pelargonium zonale)*. Although their stems are somewhat fleshy, they are not succulents in the narrow sense of the word, because as everyone knows these plants need a lot of water and prefer semi-shade if they are to show off with their splendid flowers. It is not the same with the highly succulent species from the dry areas. They are definitely xerophytes, which require little water, but much sun and heat and a rest period, which in our climate comes during the summer months, since most of the species unfold their deciduous leaves in the winter. These plants are effective less through their flowers—they are usually small and insignificant—than through their bizarre growth-form. They are small or rather large shrubs with swollen stems, which frequently are enveloped in a thick cork mantle or waxy armour. Some species are known for their thorns or pseudothorns, which have various morphological significance. In *P. echinatum* they are stipules that have transformed into thorns; in *P. spinosum* they are persisitent leaf petioles, and in *P. crithmifolium* they are lignified inflorescences.

Cultivation in a loose, sandy, humusy medium affords no difficulties; propagation is by seed or, in many species, also by cuttings.

Pelargonium carnosum (L.) AIT. (Plate 54,2)

Its stems are gray-green, highly succulent, 4 to 5 cm thick, and sparsely branched. Its leaves appear on short petioles and are lyre-shaped, feathered, not very greatly slit, gray-green, and slightly pubescent to glabrous; the flowers are white, in long-stalked umbels. *Distribution:* Namibia.

Pelargonium ceratophyllum L'HER. (Plate 54,3).

A low, richly branched bush, it has a long, woody, arrow-shaped root and branches 3 to 4 cm thick that are enveloped in a gray-green, waxy armor. Its leaves are flared, very fleshy, pinnate, with few lineal, glabrous to finely hairy leaflets with 3 teeth at the tip. The flowers are white, in long-stalked umbels; these frequently remain attached for a long time but do not form thorns.

A very promising species is

Pelargonium crassicaule L'HER. (Plate 54,4),

a small, richly branched, spherical shrub up to 30 cm tall and 40 cm in diameter, with round branches 2 to 4 cm thick with brown bark. The long petiolated, deciduous leaves appear in a terminal rosette and have a broadly oval, dentate blade that descends the stem somewhat, is wavy on the edge, silvery on the top, and with gray hairs beneath. Flowers appear in groups of 4 to 5 in short-stalked umbels with white corolla petals with red flecks. *Distribution:* Namibia.

Closely related to *P. crassicaule* and perhaps only a form of it is

Pelargonium mirabile DTR.

It differs from the above by its much thinner (about the size of a pencil), more richly branched shoots.

Similar is

Pelargonium cortusifolium L'HER.,

a small dwarf shrub up to 15 cm tall with finger-size, dirty yellowish brown stems made warty or knobby by the leaf petiole bases, which remain attached. Its leaves occur in a terminal

rosette and are long petiolated, with a blade that is covered with silvery gray hairs and is also heart-shaped. The flowers appear in richly branched umbels. *Habitat:* Namibia.

A member of the thorny types is

Pelargonium crithmifolium J.E. SMITH (Plate 54,5),

a boulder-cleft plant of the dry semi-deserts of Namibia and Great Namaqualand. It forms large, richly branched, spherical shrubs almost 1 m tall, whose thick, fleshy, gray-green branches bear a rosette of loosely arranged, petiolated, pinnately lobed, fleshy leaves 8 to 10 cm long. The small, white flowers are in richly branched inflorescences, which after the ripening of the fruit lignify and remain on the plant for several years, giving the plant a very bizarre look.

Pelargonium echinatum CURT. (Plate 54,6)

in its growth-form shows a great similarity to our common pelargoniums. It is a small, low shrub with a few branched, succulent stems, which are covered at maturity by hardened and thorny stipules. In the spring appear long-petiolated leaves with heart-shaped, silvery, pubescent blades on the ends of the shoots. The white or red-flecked flowers are in multiples in umbel inflorescences. *Distribution:* South Africa.

Another very thorny and therefore extremely bizarre species is

Pelargonium spinosum WILLD. (Plate 54,7),

a dwarf bush up to 60 cm tall with glabrous, green branches, which are covered by the stiff, lignified leaf petioles, which are up to 3 cm long and remain as pseudo-thorns while the glabrous, 3- to 5-lobed blade falls. The flowers are white with red strips in stalked umbels of 4 to 6 flowers.

This is a slow-growing plant that is difficult to propagate from cuttings.

A highly succulent species is

Pelargonium klinghardtense R. KNUTH (Plate 54,8),

a characteristic plant of the rock deserts of Namibia and Great Namaqualand (the Richtersveld). It has thick, fleshy, gray-green, sparsely branched stems, which have a rosette of fleshy, bluish gray-green, oval-lanceolate, deeply cut, dentate, deciduous leaves at their tips. Its flowers appear in umbels of 4 to 6 flowers. In cultivation it requires a sunny, warm location and little water.

Pelargonium tetragonum L'HER. (Plate 55,1)

is a fast growing, willing bloomer easily propagated from cuttings. Its stems are 3 to 4 angled and are up to 1 cm thick, glabrous, and pale bluish green with distinctly elongated shoot segments slightly constricted at the nodes. The leaves therefore are far apart with a kidney-shaped to heart-shaped, dentate, lobed, deciduous blade. Flowers are with white or reddish corolla petals with purple nerves. *Distribution:* damp areas of southeastern Cape Province.

99

Remarkable plants are the members of the genus

Sarcocaulon (DC.) SWEET.

They are small (up to 1 m tall), richly or sparsely branched, dwarf shrubs with a long, woody main root. Their succulent stems are enveloped in a thick cork mantle. Because its cells are also impregnated with wax and resin, the plant, even when just removed from the ground, burns like a candle, which gives it the name "candle bush" or "bushman's candle." Since the sarcocaulons inhabit extremely dry, desert-like localities, the cork-wax armor prevents too much loss of water, so that the plants can get along for years without rain. By observing them from the outside you cannot tell whether they are alive or dead, for they can spend years in a state of complete rest. Only when a bit of rain falls in the winter do the short-lived leaves appear. At this time the large flowers appear, which in some species are bright red; the structure of the flowers resembles the native *Geranium* species.

In most species one can observe two different leaf forms: on the long shoots there are long-petiolated leaves, whose blade very soon falls, while the petioles harden and remain for years as thorns (pseudo-thorns) (Plate 55,2 and 5). The sarcocaulons are therefore very thorny plants (the only exception is the thornless *S. multifidum*).

In the axils of the long-petiolated leaves, buds now appear, which grow as short shoots and each year produce a few short-petiolated, not thorny, deciduous leaves. The large white, yellow, or red flowers appear singly on the short shoots. They represent single flowered inflorescences.

Because of the extreme conditions in the habitat, most species are not easy to grow. They require a sunny, warm, location and a light medium. Water only at the beginning of the growing season, which in the northern hemisphere is in the winter months.

The following species are found frequently in cultivation.

Sarcocaulon multifidum R. KNUTH (Color Plate 6,8)

A sparsely branched dwarf shrub, it has short, finger-thick, brown, usually completely thornless branches. Typically the plant has only 2 branches, which grow at right angles and lie on the ground. Sometimes one also finds plants that look like blocks of stone with numerous, short, knotty stems with gray bark. The short-petiolated leaves develop most often only from axil buds at the top of the shoot. They are fine-laciniate and divided 2 to 3 times; their lineal leaflets have much woolly hairs. The flowers occur singly and are long stemmed, up to 3 cm in diameter, with pure white, pink, or bright-red petals with darker bases. *Distribution:* Great Namaqualand and Namibia.

This is a decorative and relatively easily grown species.

Another species with hairy leaflets, but also with thorns, is

Sarcocaulon herrei L. BOL. (Plate 55,3 and 5),

which differs from the above by its upright, heavily thorned, light gray branches about 25 (–40) cm long. Its flowers are white with lemon-yellow flecks at the base. *Distribution:* boulder deserts of the Richtersveld (Great Namaqualand).

All other species have undivided leaf blades that are toothed at least on the margin.

An easily grown, although only slightly succulent, but otherwise very attractive and thorny species is

Sarcocaulon l'heritieri SWEET (Plate 55,2),

a richly branched shrub up to 1 m tall with slender, light gray-green, thin, upright branches. It has long-petiolated leaves of the same shape but almost sessile; its flowers are large, up to 3 cm in diameter, and bright yellow.

Sarcocaulon mossamedense (WELW.) HIERN. (Plate 55,4)

forms upright shrubs 30 to 150 cm tall with thin, slightly branched stems covered with long pedicel thorns. The leaf blade is strikingly large, almost round as a pebble, heart-shaped at the base, and dentate on the margin. Its flowers are large and vivid red.

Sarcocaulon patersonii (DC.) ECKL. et ZEHY.

is a small dwarf shrub, which is quite variable in its growth-form. It has richly branched, thin, horizontally spread branches bent downwards at their tips and covered with thorns 1 to 3 cm long. The leaves are small, narrow, and inverse heart-shaped, with short hairs on the margins. The flowers are smaller than in the other species and are pink. Easily grown, its propagation from cuttings is possible.

Sarcocaulon rigidum SCHINZ (Color Plate 6,7)

is a small, sparsely branched, dwarf shrub with horizontal or upright, thick, yellowish green branches, which are armed with very stiff, brownish thorns. Its short-petioled leaves are narrowly wedge-shaped, two-lobed at the tip or irregularly dentate, and gray-green. The flowers are large and bright red. *Distribution:* Great Namaqualand and Namibia.

The plants that grow in the coastal areas and have hairy sepals are relegated to ssp. *rigidum*, while those from the interior (ssp. *glabrum* REHM) are known for their glabrous sepals (Color Plate 6,7).

S. rigidum, with its thick wax layer, is the actual bushman's candle of the natives. In full bloom it forms a splendid decor in the barren semi-desert. Even in cultivation *S. rigidum* blooms extremely well when treated right.

Of similar growth-form is

Sarcocaulon spinosum (BURM.) O. KTZE. (Plate 55,6), which differs from *S. rigidum* by its longer branches, its very

thick thorns up to 7 cm long, the leaf blades notched at the margin and the yellowish white flowers.

In Great Namaqualand and in the Karroo, *S. spinosum* can appear in great stands.

FAMILY VITACEAE

Everyone should be familiar with the cultivated grapes from the family Vitaceae. From a gnarly stem grow shoots that are initially herbaceous, later woody, with large, lobed leaves and branched tendrils for climbing. These represent modified shoots, the ends of one shoot generation, of which several are formed in one growing season. Instead of tendrils, mature vines produce wine grapes, which frequently reveal a dried tendril fragment at their base.

The extent to which climatic conditions can affect the growth is shown in the following grape species, which have changed their growth-forms so much that their membership in the family can be detected only in the structure of the flower.

The succulent vitaceas belong almost exclusively to the genus *Cissus* (along with the subgenus *Cyphostemma*). They differ from *Vitis* in their 4-flowered, not 5-flowered, inflorescences, which also have no tendrils. (In the subgenus *Cyphostemma* there are no tendrils at all.)

All succulent grapes are decorative, fast-growing plants, which in cultivation, however, develop their growth-form to its fullest when they are planted in the open ground, but then require a lot of room.

Cissus L.

Cissus cactiformis GILG (Plate 55,7)

is a succulent that is distributed in deciduous forests of Somalia through East Africa into northern Transvaal. It well deserves the name "cactus-like grape." The shoots are 3 to 5 cm thick, constricted at the nodes, gray-green, with 5 angles and wavy wings, and are not unlike a segmented cactus, especially since the small leaves in the constricted places are extraordinarily deciduous and are visible only on new shoots. At the nodes appear also panicled inflorescences and simple, unbranched tendrils, with whose help the plant climbs into the crowns of surrounding trees. The fruits have one seed, are black, and because of their bitter taste are not edible.

Of similar growth-form is

Cissus quadrangularis L. (Plate 1,4 right),

a fast-growing species found in all dry forests of Arabia to Angola and in eastern India, the Molucca Islands, and Madagascar. It forms gigantic shrubs and can almost smother its host plants. This species differs from the above by the considerably thinner, sharply quadrangular, narrow-winged, green shoot axes, which are also constricted at the nodes; also different are the relatively large, 3- to 5-lobed leaves. The fruits are also black and inedible.

A richly branched and dense "curtain" is

Cissus rotoundifolia (FORSK.) VAHL (Plate 55,8).

Its distribution area is the coastal savannas of southern Arabia to Mozambique. In contrast to the above species the large, fleshy, bluish green, dentate leaves persist for a long time.

C. rotundifolia is therefore also more of a leaf succulent than a stem succulent. The shoot axes are relatively thin and slightly woody. This is a fast-growing and easily propagated plant.

Of a completely different growth-form are the *Cyphostemma* species from the semi-desert areas of Namibia: *C. bainesii* (HOOK. f.) GILG et BRANDT; *C. betiformsi* CHIOV.; *C. crameriana* SCHINZ, *C. juttae* DTR. et GILG, and *C. uter* B. DESC. from Angola. Because of their unusual growth-form they all belong among the gems of every succulent collection.

Most well known is

Cyphostemma juttae (DTR. et GILG) B. DESC.,

which in habitat (Namibia) forms stems 2 to 3 m high, 1 m thick at the base, soft, watery, and rejuvenating at the point. Its green bark is covered with a thin layer of lighter green, which bursts and peels in papery fragments as the plant becomes thicker.

The large, short-petiolated, fleshy, light gray-green, waxy leaves appear sparsely at the end of the lateral branches at the beginning of the growth period (in the northern hemisphere in the spring). The large, panicled inflorescences are found in terminal position and after ripening of the fruit in the fall are shucked off along with the leaves. The bright red berries are inedible as a result of the high content of tannin. The bitter sap of the stem has been used by natives for producing a poison for arrows.

Propagation is by seed. As a young plant *C. juttae*, with its stout stem, is very attractive and blooms rather early (Plate 56,1).

This species and *C. bainesii*, *C. crameriana*, and *C. uter* all have the same growth pattern.

101

Also, Madagascar is the home of some very remarkable, succulent grapes from the subgenus *Cyphostemma*, but since only a few are in cultivation, I mention them only briefly.

Cyphostemma laza B. DESC. (Plate 56,2)

is one of the most striking phenomena of the dry forests of southwestern Madagascar, with a bottle-shaped, fleshy stem up to 1 m thick at the base and 1 to 2 m long. The stem elongates into whips and produces a few, liana-like lateral branches.

Cyphostemma elephantopus B. DESC.,

as the name suggests, forms thick stem bases like an elephant's foot up to 1.3 m in diameter, with few, climbing thin, lateral branches up to 5 m long.

Others are: *C. cornigera* B. DESC., *C. sakalavensis* B. DESC., and *C. roseiglandulosa* B. DESC.

FAMILY ICACINACEAE

The growth-form of a "block" or "boulder," as I have mentioned on page 96 in regard to some cucurbitaceas, is also represented in some plants of the small family of icacinaceas.

Especially worth mentioning here are the African genera *Pyrenacantha* and *Trematosperma*.

Pyrenacantha WIGHT

An especially striking plant, which belongs to the characteristic species of the dry bush of eastern Kenya, is

Pyrenacantha malvifolia ENGL. (Plate 53,5).

At maturity it forms a caudex up to 1.5 m in diameter, which is semi-spherical or irregularly shaped, with a light gray bark in the rest stage, and seen from a distance the caudex resembles a rock much more than a living plant. At the beginning of the rainy period the caudex end produces several thin, twining shoots, which climb into the branches of surrounding plants, they have heart-shaped, whole leaves. The inflorescences, in spikes, are unisexual and dioecious; they are small and insignificant.

Although the plant is found only rarely in cultivation, its special growth-form and its position as a representative of a slighted family makes it a must in every succulent collection.

In its habitat the juicy flesh of the caudex is relished by elephants and rhinoceroses.

In the bush savannas of Kenya grows

P. vitifolia ENGL. (Plate 56,3).

It also has a very large, but subterranean, hidden stem caudex, from which emerge long, twining shoots whose lobed leaves resemble grape vines.

Trematosperma URB.

A typical boulder plant is also from the same family and is found in Somalia. It is

Trematosperma cordatum URB.

It has the same growth-form as *Pyrenacantha malvifolia* but is said to form knotty, irregular shoot axes up to 3 m in diameter.

FAMILY FOUQUIERIACEAE

Interesting succulents are found also in the small family of fouquierias from northern Mexico to Baja California with its two genera *Fouquieria* and *Idria*. They are heavily thorned bushes *(Fouquieria)* or columnar, unbranched trees *(Idria),* whose long shoots are equipped with deciduous leaves. Their central rib runs far down the shoot axis but hardens and remains as a thorn. In the axil of these thorns appear short shoots, which define the actual assimilation organs.

Fouquieria H.B.K.

The members of the genus *Fouquieria* are richly branched shrubs with very woody branches and are not succulents in the actual sense. Only *F. purpusii* BRANDEG. has stems that are thick at the base, produce new growth at the tip, and are slightly branched.

102

Idria KELLOGG

A true succulent, on the other hand, is

Idria (= *Fouquieria*) *columnaris* KELLOGG (Plate 56,4),

which is among the characteristic plants of the low-precipitation areas of Baja California, where they grow along with other stem succulents such as *Pachycormus* (Family Anacardiaceae) and cacti.

Idria in habitat and when undisturbed forms unbranched columns up to 18 m tall. From a distance the plant appears as a bare, pointed post. It is sometimes referred to as the "telephone pole" plant.

The succulent, spongy stem produces numerous thin, stick-like lateral branches with a short life span, which at maturity are cast off. It is these stick-like branches, which are responsible for assimilation, that give the plant its unusual appearance. With yellowish white flowers at the tip of the plant (Plate 56,4), *Idria* resembles a burning match and in its habitat is also called "el cerillo."

Propagation of this interesting succulent is possible only from seed. Young plants grow very slowly.

FAMILY PEDALIACEAE

Among the less well-known and rare succulents are the pedaliaceas, with the genera *Pterodiscus*, *Sesamothamnus*, and *Uncarina*.

Pterodiscus HOOK.

The *Pterodiscus* species are succulent shrubs with a swollen stem base and thin, herbaceous branches with serrate or laciniate leaves. The large, long-tubed flowers with their broad, 5-lobed angles are found singly in the leaf axils (Plate 56,5).

In *Pterodiscus aurantiacus* WELW. (*Distribution:* South Africa and Namibia), the flowers are vivid orange; in *P. coeruleus* CHIOV. (*Distribution:* Kenya, Somalia), they are bright blue; and in *P. speciosus* HOOK. (*Distribution:* Transvaal, Cape Province), they are purple-violet.

All *Pterodiscus* species require a loamy, sandy soil and a not too cool, bright location. In our climate the growth period comes in the winter, while the plants spend the summer in vegetative rest.

Even rarer than *Pterodiscus* are the members of the genus

Sesamothamnus WELW.

These are thorny, woody plants, richly branched trees, and shrubs with a thick, water-retaining stem base. The long shoots have deciduous foliage, whose thickened petioles remain as pseudo-thorns after the leaf blade falls. In their axils appear short shoots, which yearly produce short-petiolated leaves, which are the actual assimilation organs.

Especially charming are the flowers, which to be sure appear only on old plants, so in cultivation one seldom gets to see them. They are white, yellow, or red and emit a pleasant smell, especially at night. The calyx is small, the corolla tube is a long, narrow cylinder, straight or arched with a bulge or spur at the base. The 5 large corolla lobes are plate-shaped and sometimes have long tassels on the margins (Plate 56,8).

Familiar is

Sesamothamnus lugardii N.E. BR. (northern Transvaal to Namibia).

A shrub up to 2 m tall, it is richly branched with a thick stem base and white flowers (Plate 56,6–7).

Uncarina STAPF

Of the *Uncarina* (= *Harpagophytum*) species, the ones from Madagascar are the prettiest. They are shrubs or small trees up to 3 m tall without thorns and with a thick stem base. Young plants, with their large, dark-green, whole or lobed leaves are highly decorative. The large trumpet-shaped flowers are found in multiples in umbel inflorescences and are usually yellow with dark-violet throats, seldom pale violet. Of special interest are the fruits, which are equipped with long thorns in the shape of a 4-toothed fish hook and which latch onto ones clothing or onto the fur of passing animals, thus providing for

103

distribution of the plant. Only a few species are found in cultivation, e.g., the one depicted on Plate 56,8, U.

decaryi H. HUMB. The fruits are not yet ripe, and so the hook structure of the thorns is not very clear.

FAMILY MORACEAE

Also in the mulberry family, which includes the Mediterranean (also southern German) mulberry and fig trees, there are remarkable plants in the genus

Dorstenia L.

Most dorstenias are herbaceous, sometimes also slightly woody, moisture-loving plants of the tropical rain forests, of which many are cultivated in botanical gardens for their unusual inflorescences. The numerous, small, insignificant flowers are found in dense clusters in a disk or slightly dish-shaped receptacle, which is a star-shaped modification of narrowly lanceolate bracts, giving the whole inflorescence a very unusual appearance. In the dry areas of east Africa, the island of Socotra, and southern Arabia are some species that are completely different in growth-form. They are among the most sought-after and at the same time rarest succulents in collections.

The largest of all succulent dorstenias is the Socotran

Dorstenia gigas SCHWEINF. (Plate 57,*1*; Figure 14),

seldom found in cultivation. It has the shape of a chianti bottle, and the stem can reach a diameter of up to 50 cm. It has a crown of forked branches that produce a tuft of lanceolate leaves in the growing period.

Similar in growth-form is *D. gypsicola* LAVR., discovered by LAVRANOS in Somalia. It has a stem up to 1.2 m tall and very thick.

More common in cultivation is

Dorstenia crispa ENGL. (Plate 57,*2*),

whose var. *lancifolia* ENGL. is common in the undergrowth of dry forests of eastern Kenya (in the vicinity of Voi). It has a club-shaped stem up to 15 cm long, initially unbranched, at maturity branched and then up to 40 cm long, whose surface is covered with warty, spirally arranged scars from the fallen leaves. The stems therefore have a certain similarity to a small pineapple fruit, especially when the plant is growing and then is crowned by a rosette of short-petiolated, long-lanceolate

leaves with dark green surfaces with a silvery sheen. The long-stalked inflorescences are disk-shaped (ca. 2 cm in diameter) and are surrounded by 5 to 7 star-shaped, lineal bracts.

Closely related to this is

Dorstenia foetida FORSK. (Plate 57,*5*)

from the highlands of southern Arabia, growing in rock clefts. In contrast to the above this plant is richly branched, but in extremely sunny locations the lateral shoots remain so short that they, as in *Pachypodium brevicaule*, unite into an irregular, frequently deformed, flat caudex. In cultivation and in shaded locations, the shoots elongate and become up to 15 cm long. As in *D. crispa* the upper surface of young segments are covered with the scars of fallen leaves, whose blade is of a rounder shape. The long-petiolated, chocolate-colored inflorescences are surrounded by thin, bristly bracts.

Figure 14. A 2-meter-high specimen of *Dorstenia gigas*. (After a drawing by SCHWEINFURTH.)

Both species require a loose, sandy, humusy soil, a warm and bright location, and a strict rest period in its leafless state.

Dorstenia hildebrandtii ENGL. (Plate 57,3)

has a fleshy, juicy, above-ground, reddish brown, shiny caudex up to 5 cm in diameter, whose top elongates into a simple or branched, glassy, transluscent, reddish-flecked shoot up to 1 cm thick and 10 to 20 cm long (in cultivation up to 30 cm). The shoot has short-petioled, fleshy, lanceolate leaves arranged in loose order, narrow at both ends, up to 3 cm long, irregularly dentate, wavy at the margins and slightly hairy. Inflorescences appear in the axils and are deep, dark brown, almost round, up to 1.5 cm in diameter, with 5 to 10 lineal, short bracts. *Habitat:* Kenya.

A very interesting species, in cultivation it requires some-what more moisture than the other dorstenias. Unfortunately it does not live long, but it does self propagate.

Similar is *Dorstenia braunii* ENGL. from the same area.

Along with the stem-forming dorstenias there are also about a dozen species from the dry areas of tropical Africa, which have subterranean caudexes of sometimes considerable size (up to 15 cm in diameter). As an example of such a species I cite

Dorstenia bornimiana SCHWEINF. (Plate 57,4),

which is like a miniature version of the well-known alpine violet *(Cyclamen)*. From a small caudex up to 3 cm in diameter appear a few short-petiolated leaves lying on the soil; they resemble the leaves of the alpine violet in shape. The long-stalked inflorescences appear singly or in twos; the receptacle is elongated and surrounded by 2 to 3 lineal bracts.

FAMILY DIDIEREACEAE

Among the oldest plants on earth are the members of the Didiereaceae (named for the French colonel and naturalist GRANDIDIER), a small plant family of only 4 genera and 11 species in all, which inhabits the driest areas of Madagascar (W and SW). Although they are woody plants, trees, and shrubs, one can nevertheless count them among the succulents, since they, especially young plants, store water in considerable amounts in their thick, pulpy bodies, sometimes also in the bark of the shoots or of the roots.

Until just a few years ago the didiereaceas were nearly unknown, with very few collections excepted. Through my research trips to Madagascar so much living material has come to Europe that many representatives are found today in most botanical gardens and even in private collections, especially as their cultivation affords no great difficulties.

The didiereaceas, with the genera *Decaryia* (1 species), *Alluaudiopsis* (2 species), *Didierea* (2 species), and *Alluaudia* (6 species), are thorny plants, of which some so resemble columnar cacti that they are considered such by unthinking lay persons. In contrast to these, however, the flowers of the didiereas are small and insignificant, unisexual, and dioecious. One seldom sees them in cultivation, because the plants must reach a considerable size and a great age before they bloom; however, even just

vegetatively these plants, especially in their youth stages, have such unusual appearances that every succulent collector has to be enthusiastic about them.

Here is a selection of those species that will attract the hobbyist.

Alluaudia DRAKE

As of now six species are recognized: *A. ascendens* DRAKE, *A. comosa* DRAKE, *A. dumosa* DRAKE, *A. humbertii* CHOUX, *A. montagnacii* RAUH, and *A. procera* DRAKE.

When young they are frequently shrub-like; mature plants are frequently tree forms 4 to 10 m tall with a stem 50 cm thick and a more or less richly branched crown, which in *A. comosa* is even a dense mound.

The new shoots have normal, although short-lived leaves (Plate 57,8; Plate 58,2), which are usually arranged in straight lines and frequently sit on a leaf pad (podarium), and so the shoot axis, especially in *A. procera,* shows a tesselation similar to that in many euphorbias and stapeliads (Plate 58,2).

In the axils of these leaves, which are called "long-shoot leaves," appears very early a very strong thorn with a broad foot; it is considered to be the first leaf of the buds forming in the axis of the long-shoot leaves. In most cases these do not grow into long shoots, but their axis is very much shortened and in the course of development is sunk into a hollow between the thorn and the long-shoot leaf. At the end of the growing period the long-shoot leaves fall and leave a scar. At the beginning of a new vegetative period, however, the tip of the short shoot produces 2 leaves, whose blade is in a profile position, giving the plant its remarkable appearance (Plate 58,3). These short-shoot leaves are the real assimilation organs; in habitat they begin to grow in November and fall around the end of February (March). The rest of the year the plants are completely leafless. The short shoots, however, are able to produce new leaves at the beginning of each growing period; they can, however, grow into lateral branches (long shoots), causing branching. Also, the richly branched inflorescences appear on the short shoots.

The individual species are categorized on the basis of their growth-form, the shape of their leaves, and their flowers. The largest species is

Alluaudia ascendens DRAKE (Plate 57,6–7).

It forms trees up to 15 m tall with a thick stem and few, steeply ascending lateral branches. The short-shoot leaf blades are round with a deep notch at the tip. Even young plants show a thick, columnar growth, are completely unbranched, and are densely covered with thorns (Plate 57,8).

Similar in growth-form is

Alluaudia montagnacii RAUH,

whose thorns, however, are stouter than those in the previous species. Both species are highly recommended for the hobbyist; propagation is only by seed.

Alluaudia comosa DRAKE (Plate 57,8)

forms multi-stemmed trees up to 4 m tall with an almost pillow-shaped crown; its main stem branches just above the soil into a V-shape. Young plants are richly branched and very thorny. Propagation is also possible from cuttings.

Alluaudia dumosa DRAKE (Plate 57,9)

differs in growth-form from all other species by its broom-shaped growth and resembles certain euphorbias from the Tirucalli group. A tree up to 6 m tall, it has round, grayish brown, slightly thorny branches. In contrast to all other species of the genus, *A. dumosa* is leafless all year round, because the short shoots produce no leaves and the long-shoot leaves of only a few millimeters are extremely short lived.

A very interesting species, it also will grow from cuttings.

Alluaudia humbertii CHOUX (Plate 58,4)

in youth grows shrub-like, but at maturity forms richly branched trees up to 6 m tall with thin, twig-like branches.

It is fast growing, but as a young plant is hardly attractive;

it can be propagated from cuttings.

Alluaudia procera DRAKE (Plate 58,1-3)

is the most common species in southwestern Madagascar, which often forms dense forests of several square kilometers. When young it grows shrubby, and in maturity it forms trees up to 10 (–15) m tall with a thick stem and a crown of slender, frequently arched branches. Young plants and new shoots are covered with warty, hexagonal, close-set podaria (Plate 58,2), which in their upper third have the stiff, broad-based thorn; short-shoot leaves are long-oval, up to 4 cm long (Plate 58,3). Fast growing, it is easily propagated from seed or cuttings.

From the genus

Alluaudiopsis HUMB. et CHOUX

I have so far identified two species, *A. fiherenensis* HUMB. et CHOUX and *A. marnieriana* RAUH.

Both are richly branched shrubs with woody, thin branches and therefore hardly appeal to the hobbyist. *A. marnieriana*, in contrast to *A. fiherenensis*, has two thorns arranged in pairs and is the only Didiereaceae to have vivid, carmine-red flowers (Plate 58,5).

Decaryia CHOUX

so far is represented by the single species

D. madagascariensis CHOUX (Plate 58,6),

a tree-shrub 4 to 6 m tall. *Decaryia* seems to be a very primitive Didiereaceae, in which a differentiation of the shoot system into long and short shoots has not been carried out. The axil buds in the axils of the long-shoot leaves and flanked by two stiff, hard thorns immediately grow into long shoots, whose axes are bent in a zig-zag, a feature visible on young plants and by which *Decaryia* can be easily recognized.

Propagation by cuttings is possible, although difficult. An easier method is propagation by grafting onto *Alluaudia procera*.

The most interesting didiereaceas are without a doubt the members of the genus

Didierea H. BAILL.,

of which I recognize the two species *D. madagascariensis* H. BAILL. and *D. trollii* CAPURON et RAUH. The two differ particularly in regard to the growth-form of their youth stages. Of all didiereaceas, *Didierea* itself embodies the cactus habit most. (Plate 58,8).

As in *Alluaudia* the shoot system is divided into long and short shoots. The latter appear again in the axils of deciduous, narrowly linear long-shoot leaves; their vegetation points are, however, not sunken into the tissue of the cortex of the long shoot, but sit on an elongated podarium 1 to 3 cm long and have 1 to several whorls of long, stiff thorns (Plate 58,8). Of these the basal one, pointed downwards, can reach a length of up to 10 cm. At the beginning of the growing period the short-shoot tip, which is surrounded by whorls of thorns, produces a bundle of long-linear leaves, which in *D. madagascariensis* is up to 10 cm long, and which represents the actual assimilation organs (Plate 58,9).

As in *Alluaudia* the flowers of *Didierea* also appear on the short shoots and gather into pseudo-umbels, which often cover the long shoots for several meters.

Didierea madagascariensis H. BAILL. (Color Plate 6,5–6; Plate 58,8–9),

is a tree form and reaches a height of 4 to 6 m (Plate 3,5). The short, thick stem merges into numerous, upright branches, which at maturity, especially in the coastal areas, probably

because of the sea wind, frequently approaches a horizontal growth direction. The thorns are very long and stiff, and the leaves are narrowly linear, up to 10 cm long. Young plants are completely unbranched and very decorative.

Propagation is possible only by seed.

Didierea trollii CAPURON et RAUH (Plate 58,7)

differs from *D. madagascariensis* especially in its youth stages. Whereas the former forms an upright, unbranched stem (see Plate, 3,5), in *D. trollii* the primary shoot soon starts to grow horizontally and produces at its base numerous, creeping branches, and so a tangled mesh of prostrate shoots, altogether 1 to 2 m in diameter, results. From the middle of this tangle eventually rise 1 or 2 stout shoots, which form the stems of the older plant. These stems first grow unbranched and in maturity form a crown of horizontally spread lateral branches (Plate 58,7). The thorns are shorter and slenderer than in *D. madagascariensis;* the leaves are obovate and only 1 to 3 cm long.

The distribution area of *D. trollii* joins that of *D. madagascariensis* in the south.

Both species as young plants (even in their leafless state) are quite unusual. Propagation is by seed; *D. madagascariensis* can also be propagated by grafting areoles to *Alluaudia procera*. These then develop into long shoots; in *D. trollii* propagation by cuttings is possible.

All didiereaceas require a sandy, humusy soil, a bright location that is not too cool in the winter, and strict rest in their leafless state. When all these factors are taken into consideration the remarkable plants afford no difficulties in cultivation.

FAMILY CRASSULACEAE

The family of "houseleeks" encompasses predominantly "leaf succulents," i.e., members with fleshy, juicy leaf organs, but in addition there are also definite stem succulents. Of course the transition between the two groups is gradual, and the stem-succulent houseleeks frequently have succulent leaves, even if they are deciduous. The latter belong almost exclusively to the genus *Cotyledon* L.

Cotyledon L.

Cotyledon buchholziana STEPH. et SCHULDT (Plate 59,1)

is a small mini-shrub up to 20 cm and somewhat variable in its appearance; it has cylindrical branches 6 to 12 mm thick with a gray bark. Its leaves are deciduous, in a terminal rosette, and thick cylindrical or ovally flattened; its flowers appear in terminal panicles, and are upright and pink, with recurved

petals. *Distribution:* Namaqualand (the Richtersveld).

Cotyledon paniculata L. f. (= *C. fascicularis* AIT.; Plate 59,3–4),

is widely distributed on stony slopes in the Karroo and Namibia, in large stands. It is generally known as "Botterboom" (butter tree) to the boers. The name comes from the fact that the water-storing shoots are as soft as butter and can be cut with a knife just as easily. *C. paniculata* forms sparsely or richly branched little trees up to 1.5 m tall with a yellowish green stem up to 30 (–50) cm at the base, whose bark, as in *Cyphostemma juttae*, peels in thin layers (Plate 59,2). The slightly fleshy, glabrous or hairy, long-oval, light-green leaves, which are blunt tipped, 6 to 8 cm long, and 3 to 5 cm wide, fall before the appearance of the panicle inflorescences that are up to 60 cm long. The flowers are pendulous or horizontal with a yellow or yellowish red, bell-shaped corolla.

During the greater part of the year *C. paniculata* is leafless; assimilation is taken over during this period by the exterior, green cortex tissue of the shoot axis, which contains chloroplasts. Even as a small plant *C. paniculata* is an attractive

107

phenomenon (Plate 59,3) and a valuable addition to any succulent collection.

Probably the most interesting species is

Cotyledon reticulata THUNBG. (Plate 59,2),

a small shrub up to 50 cm high and distributed scattered from the Great Karroo to Namibia. It has succulent, simple, but frequently branched stems. The deciduous, long-oval, succulent leaves appear as a rosette on the tips of the shoots or on small mamilla-shaped short shoots. The richly branched, panicled, terminal inflorescences are up to 15 cm long and harden after the seed is ripe and remain on the plant for years, a unique behavior for crassulaceas. The upright flowers themselves are small and insignificant; their corolla is yellowish green.

Another remarkable stem succulent is

Cotyledon wallichii HARV. (Plate 59,5 and 7),

a very poisonous dwarf shrub up to 50 cm tall and widely distributed in the Karroo bush of South Africa. Its thick, richly branched stems are covered with persistent and hardened leaf petioles (Plate 59,6), which stay on the plant many years after the shedding of the long, cylindrical, gray-green leaf blades, which are up to 10 cm long and are arranged in a terminal rosette. The greenish flowers appear in long-stalked, panicled, terminal inflorescences.

Even in its leafless state it is extremely attractive and easy to grow.

Very similar and having the same growth-form is *C. dinteri* BAK. f. from Namibia.

Other *Cotyledon* species are introduced in the section on leaf succulents.

FAMILY ASTERACEAE (= COMPOSITAE)

The family of "daisies," with its many growth forms, also has remarkable and interesting succulents. Many of them are leaf succulents, but even among the stem succulents there are noteworthy forms, especially in the genera *Othonna* L. and *Senecio* (TOURN.) L.

Othonna L.

has many species, but not all are succulent; among the stem succulents are the following:

Othonna euphorbioides HUTCHINS. (Plate 59,8)

is a small, succulent, sparsely branched dwarf bush barely 15 cm tall with round branches ca. 2 cm thick and having yellowish gray bark. In the growing season the branches have a tuft of long, linear, gray-green, waxy leaves narrowed at the base toward the petiole. In their axils are thin, simple or branched thorns, which are homologous to the sterile and thorny lateral branches of the inflorescences or the persisting flower peduncle stalks. This unique phenomenon among succulent compositas gives the plant its name, for in its leafless state it resembles certain thorny euphorbias. The flower heads themselves are small, insignificant, and yellow.

A very decorative and rare plant, it casts off its leaves in the summer and grows in the winter.

One of the most unusual and striking species is

Othonna herrei PILL. (Plate 59,6),

a rare, sparsely branched dwarf shrub, known only from Richtersveld (near Stinkfontain and Numies), up to 20 cm tall, and up to 3 cm thick at the base. Its axes are densely covered with cork-like, initially yellow, later dark-brown, warty, tes-

selated leaf pads. The leaves, which unfold in our climate during the winter, are up to 6 cm long and 3 cm wide; their blade is irregularly dentate to notched, wavy on the margins and narrowed at the base towards the petiole. After the blade falls the corky leaf base grows into the already mentioned mamillae. The medium-size, tongue-flowered heads appear in small numbers in a panicled inflorescence.

Cultivation is not so difficult with moderate watering.

Othonna retrofracta JACQ. (= *O. litoralis* DTR.)

is a sparsely branched dwarf shrub from the coastal area of the western Cape area and from Namibia. It grows up to 35 cm tall and has a bottle-shaped main stem, and its leaves appear in a terminal rosette, and are long-oval, 3 to 4 cm long, somewhat fleshy, and bluish green; The flower heads have ligulate flowers, up to 2 or 3 on the same scape. This plant is easy to grow and to flower.

Senecio (including *Kleinia* L. and *Notonia* DC.)

is a genus of many species distributed throughout the entire world and which includes a number of stem succulents.

A frequently cultivated, easily and fast grown species is

Senecio articulatus (L. f.) SCH. BIP. (= *Kleinia articulata* HOW.; Plate 60,1).

This plant has shoots rising from a reclining base, clearly differentiated into sharply divided, cylindrical, gray-green, waxy joints 5 to 15 cm long. Its leaves are remote and long petiolated, and the nerves of the leaf base descend the shoot axis as dark stripes; the leaf blade is somewhat succulent, lobed to pinnatisect, and gray-green. The flower head is small, numerous on elongated scapes with yellowish green tubular flowers. *Habitat:* southeastern Cape Province.

Senecio kleinia (L.) LESS. (= *Kleinia neriifolia* HAW.: Plate 60,2)

is a shrub from the Canary Islands, up to 3 m tall, branching at the end of every flowering period, with cylindrical shoots up to 4 cm thick, gray-green, with dark strips caused by the trailing leaf bases; leaves that are short lived, in a loose rosette on the ends of the shoots, lineal, up to 15 cm long. Flower heads are numerous in a terminal, short-stemmed corymbus and are tubular and yellowish white.

This is a fast-growing, decorative species, which, when planted in the open ground, soon forms a large, untidy bush.

A not very attractive species is

Senecio longiflorus (DC.) SCH. BIP. (= *Kleinia longiflora* DC.).

A sparsely branched bush up to 1 m high it has gray-green shoots 5 to 10 mm thick. The shoots are made somewhat angular by the descending leaf bases with their 3 darker nerves. Leaf blades are long, oval, up to 2 cm long, and deciduous; flower heads are long, cylindrical, in groups of 3 to 5 on a common scape, with whitish or pale violet (= var. *violaceus* E.A. BRUCE et HUTCHINS.) flowers.

The species from Madagascar is considered to be only a variety (var. *madagascariensis* (HUMB.) ROWLEY).

Similar but considerably smaller is

Senecio (= *Notonia*) *descoingsii* H. HUMB. (Plate 60,3).

It reaches only up to 30 cm, has thin shoots ca. 5 mm thick, and has pale yellow, tubular flowers. *Habitat:* southern Madagascar.

Senecio stapeliiformis PHILLIPS (= *Kleinia stapeliiformis* (PHILLIPS) STAPF) (Plate 60,4, right)

forms a lovely convergence to stapeliads (see Plate 6,3). The stems, which at first grow under ground, later upright, are up to 60 cm long and 3 cm thick. Because of the leaves being arranged in 5 to 7 straight lines, the stems are angular to ribbed; the actual leaf blades, as in the stapeliads, are reduced to tiny, thorny scales, while the succulent, reddish brown leaf bases are fused to the shoot axis and descend it. The individual leaf bases are marked off by lighter, green stripes; flower heads are single on elongated, terminal scapes (Plate 60,4), only with tubulars bright-red flowers. *Distribution:* Transvaal into southern Cape Province.

This is an easily grown and easily propagated species.

Essentially smaller is *Senecio gregorii* S. MOORE, considered by ROWLEY to be var. *minor* of *S. stapeliiformis* (Plate 60,4, left).

In contrast to the previous species this senecio has much thinner shoot axes, smaller flower head, and knotty roots.

The monocots discussed in many succulent works, such as the tree form liliaceas *Nolina, Dracaena, Yucca,* as well as *Testudinaria* (family Dioscoreaceae), are not covered in this work, because they are not succulents in the acutal sense of the word, for their stems are very woody and retain water only to a limited degree.

Leaf succulents

If the number of stem succulent plants is extremely large, it is by far exceeded by the number of leaf succulents. Their distribution area is not just the arid and semi-arid zones of the tropics and subtropics; one finds them also in temperate and cooler zones, because many of the native representatives of the crassula family, for instance, our *Sedum* and *Sempervivum* species, are true succulents.

Along with many dicots there are also numerous monocot leaf succulents.

The binding of this book would burst if I were to introduce all of them or even just mention their names. Anyone who is interested in a certain plant group and collects only it would, nevertheless, have to consult literature specializing in that field.

Not mentioned here are the monocot bulbs or the agaves, because these are mostly very large succulents that take up a lot of space and therefore have less attraction for the hobbyist, especially because these are not true succulents. I also do not mention the well-known *Sansevieria* species or the terrestrial, xerophytic bromeliads.

I begin the discussion with the

FAMILY LILIACEAE

Aloe L.

The Liliaceae genus *Aloe* has many species, and not only in cultivation but also in nature it tends strongly toward hybridizing. Its natural distribution area stretches through all Africa, from the extreme south to Arabia. Here it is represented by several hundred species. Also Madagascar is the home of around 50 species showing little relationship to the African species. One finds escapes of aloes in all areas with warm climates, e.g., around the Mediterranean, in the dry areas of South America, and in India.

As a result of the great number of species, *Aloe* appears in many growth-forms: the most common form is the "stemless rosette" lying directly on the ground, i.e., on a short, outwardly barely visible shoot axis, sit numerous, dense, fleshy leaves, usually in a spiral, seldom in just two lines. In many species the base of the short stem tends to off-shoot; the plants appear not as single rosettes but form whole clumps, large tufts, or even compact mounds. Elongation of the shoot axis while the base continues to off-shoot leads to a shrubby growth pattern.

Widely distributed is also the growth-form of the so-called stem rosette plants, i.e., in the course of development an elongated, often meter-long, unbranched stem is formed, which has at its tip a large rosette of living leaves. While the basal rosette leaves gradually die and surround the stem with a thick coat, new leaves are continuously formed at the tip. The sometimes gigantic inflorescences are found in the axils of the uppermost rosette leaves. Examples of such stem-rosette plants are the familiar *Aloe marlothii, A. ferox* (Plate 61,*1–3*), and *A. aculeata* among many others.

Relatively rare is the true "tree-form" growth in this genus. It is exemplified especially in the members of section Dendro-Aloe. The most beautiful examples are *Aloe dichotoma* and *A. pillansii*, depicted in Plate 3,*1–2*. They form gigantic stems (in *A. pillansii* up to 2 m in diameter), which have a more or less richly branched crown. With their impressive size (up to 10 m tall) they

give an almost otherwordly impression (see Plate 3,*2*) and resemble the familiar dragon's blood tree *(Dracaena draco)* of the Canary Islands. Contrasted to these giants are dwarfs of only a few centimeters (*Aloe descoingsii, A. haworthioides, A. minima, A. albida,* etc.). These are the ones that especially attract the hobbyist.

Although most of the species at flowering time are a splendid sight with their shiny red or yellow flowers, they do take up a lot of room in order to show off their typical growth pattern. Many aloes grow quickly and reach maturity in a few years in a nutritious soil.

If you cultivate aloes in pots they should be brought outside in the spring and gradually moved into the sun. The leaves of many species then take on a bright-red color. During the dim winter months water sparingly; be especially careful that no water gets into the rosette, since they are quite susceptible to "heart rot." Especially sensitive are the species from extreme dry areas, such as *A. variegata, A. dinteri,* etc.

Species with "closed" rosettes, i.e., with upright, tightly arranged leaves, e.g., *Aloe aristata,* are very susceptible to mealy bugs and must be constantly treated.

Propagation of aloes generally affords no difficulties. Pupping off-shooting species can be propagated from off-shoots, others by cuttings; only the tree-form species are hard to root and often need several years to form roots.

Easiest of all is propagation by seed, but you should undertake the pollination yourself, because uncontrolled insect pollination generally results in hybrids. Therefore you should use seed of your own or from the natural habitat.

The flowers of almost all species are distinguished by their bright-red or yellow, seldom pure white, color tones and are visited by bees and honey birds. They are typical *Liliaceae* flowers with a usually cylindrical, 6-part perigon, 6 stamens, and a 3-part, superior ovary. The fruits at maturity are self-opening, splitting capsules.

The flowers are never found singly, but appear—often

by the hundreds—in racemose, panicled, or spike-shaped inflorescences sometimes several meters long. You can hardly imagine anything more beautiful than a mass stand in full bloom, for example, of *Aloe ferox, A. marlothii, A. aculeata, A. speciosa, A. rubrolutea,* and *A. striata* among many others, for in habitat the aloes seldom appear singly, but appear frequently in mass stands, sometimes forming actual forests (Plate 61,*1,4,* and 7)

Because many of them have a bitter sap in their leaves, they are hardly ever eaten by animals. From some species (e.g., *A. ferox*) this sap is rendered by cooking and thickened into a resin-like substance, which has medicinal value as a laxative.

In former times every home had at least one pot of the easily grown *Aloe arborescens* (Plate 61,*7*), whose sap was used in the treatment of burns. It therefore became known as the "burn aloe."

Although every species is a beauty—you can really get involved in aloes—for the hobbyist only the small, free-blooming species are to be considered, just from space reasons alone. But even in the Mediterranean area the plants survive outdoors in protected areas, and people there can plant the large species in their gardens.

Madagascar has some very decorative and interesting mini-aloes, of which I list the following:

Aloe albiflora GUILL. (= *Guillauminia albiflora* A. BERTR.) (Plate 61,*2*),

one of the few pure-white-flowered aloes, is a stemless rosette plant producing off-shoots at the base. Their leaves, which are up to 15 cm long, lineal, and pointed with fine teeth on the margin, are gray-green with white flecks. The simple-racemose inflorescences up to 30 cm long and appearing in muiltiples have up to 20 flowers, which unfold one after the other; their white, perigynous petals have a brownish central stripe and are surpassed by the stamens and the pistil. Because of the broad bell-shaped flower, differing from the other species, BERTRAND put *A. albiflora* into its own genus *Guillauminia*. According to G.W. REYNOLDS there is no compelling reason for this. *A. albiflora* requires a loose, humusy soil and a bright location; it is distinguished by a great willingness to bloom and produces its inflorescences almost all year round.

This is a very recommendable species.

Vegetatively little different from the above is

Aloe bellatula REYN. (Plate 61,*3*),

which, however, is distinguished by having pendulous, bright coral-red, long, bell-shaped flowers. It blooms as a 2- to 3-year-old seedling, and is a very pretty and recommendable species, whose cultivation is as above.

Even smaller is

Aloe calcairophila REYN. (Plate 61,*5*),

one of the few Madagascar species with leaves strictly in 2 lines. The rosette leaves are only 3 to 5 cm long with few, narrow, cylindrical, white flowers. The plant grows only on limestone and requires the addition of mortar to the soil.

The smallest Madagascar species is

A. descoingsii REYN. (Plate 61,*6*),

a very much sought-after and extremely rare plant. The rosettes are only up to 3 to 5 cm in diameter, but because of their basal off-shooting, they form clusters up to 30 cm across, in which hundreds of rosettes stand; their highly succulent, short, triangular, dentate, gray-green leaves are found sparsely in a spiral on the short axis. The inflorescences are 10 to 15 cm long, with a very thin scape and ca. 15 upright, bright cinnamon-red, urn-shaped flowers 0.5 cm long, which differ in form from those of the other species. In habitat it grows only on steep limestone slopes.

This is an easily grown and easily propagated plant!

The prettiest species but as rare as the above is

Aloe haworthioides BAK. (Plate 61,*8*),

which grows in black humus on granitic and gneiss cliffs in the central highlands of Madagascar between 1600 and 1800 m. In European collections it was, until a few years ago, totally unknown; the plant was found again on my research trip in 1963 and survived the trip to the Botanical Garden of the University of Heidelberg, from where the plant has found its way into other collections. In its growth-form it resembles more a *Haworthia* from the "setata" group (see page 117) than an *Aloe*. Its numerous, upright, narrow, lineal, long-pointed leaves are covered on both sides and on the margin with long, white, bristly hairs. In all they form a compact rosette of up to 7 cm in diameter. The single, seldom-branched, racemose inflorescences become 10 to 30 cm long and have 20 to 30 flowers in a thick, spike arrangement; their attraction comes less from the formation of the flower corolla than from the greatly surpassing, ribbon-shaped, vivid-orange filaments (Plate 61,8).

It requires humusy soil, some shade, and somewhat more humidity than the other species. In cultivation it blooms from November to December.

Very similar to the above in growth-form is

Aloe parvula BRGR. (Plate 62,*1*),

a small rosette plant, whose striking blue-green, almost violet leaves are less bristly. At flowering time the two species differ by the fact that the usually simple, seldom-branched, racemose inflorescences up to 35 cm long on *A. parvula* have pendulous, bright scarlet flowers of a long, bell shape inflated near the tip. A willing bloomer, its cultivation similar to *A. haworthioides*.

An interesting species, that builds large tufts and is easy to propagate, is

Aloe bakeri SCOTT-ELLIOT (Plate 61,*9*).

It forms elongated stems up to 10 cm long, which have narrow, lineal, sharply dentate, gray or brownish green flecked leaves in a loose rosette. The flowers occur in racemes, and the perigon is red-orange at the base, yellow near the tip.

A rare but extremely attractive species is

Aloe laeta BRGR. (Plate 62,4).

It is almost stemless and forms rosettes maximally up to 20 cm in diameter, whose blue-gray-green, waxy leaves have dense red teeth on the margin. Its flowers appear in a head-like raceme and are pendulous, cylindrical, and carmine red.

A grateful flowerer is

Aloe rauhii REYN. (Plate 62,5),

a plant that forms clusters in habitat and has small rosettes of 10 to 15 cm. The leaves are gray-green with white flecks and are dentate; the flowers appear in long-stalked racemes and are pendulous, carmine red, and inflated toward the tip.

Of the larger Madagascar aloes I cite the following:

Aloe viguieri H. PERR. (Plate 62,3),

whose whitish to gray-green leaves that are up to 40 cm long in thick, usually stemless rosettes remind one of the South African *A. striata* (see Plate 65,2). Flowers are numerous, in elongated racemes, scarlet red, and pendulous.

This species thrives best in a hanging pot in alkaline soil.

Another recommendable species is

Aloe conifera H. PERR. (Plate 62,2),

which even as a seedling is a splendid sight, with its intense blue-green leaves, which become red-violet in the sun and have thorns on both sides. At maturity *A. conifera* usually forms stemless rosettes up to 40 cm in diameter; its flowers are numerous, upright, sessile, short, bell-shaped, and lemon yellow, in a thick, cylindrical spike 15 to 20 cm long.

A very decorative species, it is grown only from seed.

The species mentioned above in no way exhaust the great variety of Madagascar aloes. The most complete collections of the plants are found at this time in the Botanical Garden of the University of Heidelberg and in the Jardin Botanique "Les Cèdres," St. Jean, Cap Ferrat (France). Anyone who is especially interested in the Madagascar species should consult the work by G.W. REYNOLDS, *Les Aloës de Madagascar* (Tananarive, 1958). Also by the same author is a comprehensive, excellent, and well-illustrated book on the South African aloes: *The Aloes of South Africa,* Johannesburg, 1950. Another work, by this now deceased *Aloe* researcher is *The Aloes of Tropical Africa and Madagascar,* 1966.

The African aloes are far better known than those from Madagascar. Many species have been in cultivation for a long time. We have already mentioned that just a few decades ago *Aloe arborescens* was popularly known as the healing or burn aloe and was in every flower box of every farm house. This species is beautiful only in its habitat (see Plate 61,7); in cultivation it is untidy and straggly and therefore has now almost disappeared.

Among the typical "farm house plants" is also the favorite and well-known

Aloe variegata L.,

the "tiger aloe," a plant that is widely distributed in the Karroo of South Africa, but never forms large stands. It appears here and there in groups between bushes and makes a splendid sight at bloom time (Plate 63,1). The short shoot axis 10 to 25 cm long, not visible, has three, frequently somewhat spiraled rows of overlapping, highly succulent, short grisly-edged, small-toothed, gray-green leaves with irregular white flecks. The leaves in cross-section are triangular and are elongated into a sharp point (Plate 63,2). In the axils of the upper leaves appear from winter into spring the inflorescences of ca. 30 cm, which have numerous, long, cylindrical, cinnamon-red, green-nerved flowers.

This very decorative *Aloe* thrives in any room better than in the greenhouse of a botanical garden, for it appreciates the dry room air. In the Botanical Garden at Heidelberg, a specimen of *A. variegata* has been grown for 10 years, and during this time it has received hardly any water but nevertheless blooms every year.

Because of basal off-shooting, propagation affords no difficulties.

One of the small South African species is

Aloe albida (STAPF) REYN. (Plate 64,1),

a member of the section of "grass aloes" (section Graminialoe). It forms small rosettes of 6 to 12 narrow, lineal, dentate, dark green leaves ca. 10 (−15) cm long. Its inflorescences are simple, 10 to 15 cm long, with white, narrow-tubed flowers. *Distribution:* eastern Transvaal.

In the same section are the following mini-aloes:

A. saundersiae (REYN.) REYN.; A. parviflora BAK.; A. myriacantha (HAW.) ROEM. et SCHULT.; A. minima BAK.

They are all known for their dwarf growth-form and for having white flowers (only *A. minima* has dark red flowers); they are rare in cultivation and not easy to grow, requiring humusy soil and rather high humidity.

A species very much favored by hobbyists and therefore common in collections is

Aloe aristata HAW. (Plate 63,5),

which resembles a larger version of *A. haworthioides*. It grows in habitat in the dry Karroo bush as well as on the snow-covered, grassy stony mountain slopes of Lesotho and forms rather large groups of compact rosettes up to 15 cm in diameter. Their numerous, narrow, linear leaves taper into a long, hair-shaped, dry tip, which is bent inward; the leaves overlap so closely that the rosettes appear as a tight ball. In cultivation, especially with a lot of water, the leaves flare out, and the rosettes open so much that the plant loses its typical growth pattern and much of its beauty.

The leaves themselves are gray-green or green with white teeth on the margins; they have, especially underneath, white hairs that have a thick foot and are arranged in rows or bands. The inflorescences are simple or branched, up to 50 cm long, and slightly bent, with red-orange tubes.

112

In the Mediterranean area the plant is propagated by cutting through the rosette axis several times. The numerous axil buds emerge from the rosette leaves and are easy to root.

A. aristata is a favored plant in crossing with species of *Gasteria;* these bi-generic hybrids appear under the name *Gastrolea* (see page 118).

A well-known and favorite, small species from section Humiles (dwarf *Aloe*) is

Aloe brevifolia MILL.,

whose basal off-shooting causes it to grow in rather large groups, and whose compact rosettes have a diameter of up to 8 cm. Their short, long-triangular, blue-green leaves are sharply dentate and have a keel beneath. Inflorescences appear singly or in multiples in the axils of the upper rosette leaves and are up to 40 cm long, with numerous racemose, pale-scarlet flowers.

In the same section are also the following:

Aloe humilis (L.) MILL.,

a highly variable species that forms dense clusters. The small rosettes, 6 to 7 cm in diameter, are formed of linear, lanceolate, gray-green leaves that are up to 10 cm long and bent inwards. The leaves have long teeth on their margins and white, thorny warts at the base, which in var. *echinata* (WILLD.) BAK. (Plate 64,4) extend into fleshy bristles. Inflorescences are 25 to 40 cm long, with pendulous, coral-red flowers in racemes.

An attractive, small species 20 to 30 cm in diameter and frequently appearing singly is

Aloe krapohliana MARL. (Plate 64,3).

Its leaves are numerous, slightly bent upwards, narrow, and lanceolate, with the underside clearly convex. The inflorescences usually appear in multiples, simple or branched, 20 to 40 cm long in a dense raceme, with scarlet-red flowers with greenish tips.

A. krapohliana at bloom time is a splendid plant but not easy to grow. Because of its extremely dry habitat (sand deserts of the Little Namaqualand) it requires sunny, warm locations in cultivation and little water.

A no less decorative species in the same area and equally difficult to grow is

Aloe melanacantha BRGR. (Plate 64,2),

whose tight spherical, usually stemless rosettes up to 30 cm in diameter form rather large masses. Its leaves are numerous, upright, bent inward, up to 20 cm long, dark green to brownish green and have long, stiff teeth on the margins and on the under side along the keel-like central nerve. At the base of the leaf the teeth are white, but they are deep black near the tip; inflorescences are up to 20 cm long, usually unbranched with numerous, initially scarlet-red, later yellow flowers. Flowers in cultivation are rare!

A well-known species from the group of Prolongatae (species with greatly elongated stems) is

Aloe ciliaris HAW. (Plate 64,5),

a plant widely distributed in the undergrowth of forests and bush lands of the dry, eastern Cape area. Its thin stems are up to 5 m long and climb into the tree crowns; the leaves are loosely arranged, up to 15 cm long, with a long sheath at the base and long, white teeth on the margins. Inflorescences are racemose, just below the shoot tip, with bright-red, yellow-tipped flowers.

A fast-growing plant, it blooms well.

Closely related with this are:
A. tenuior HAW., which also exists in a pure-yellow-flowered form, and *A. tidmarshii* (SCHOENL.) MULLER, *A. commixta* BRG., and *A. striatula* HAW.

One of the most remarkable aloes of this group is

Aloe pearsonii SCHOENL. (Plate 64,6),

which grows in the driest area of Namaqualand (the Richtersveld near Numies and above the Hellskloof), but develops such mass stands there that the slopes, even from a great distance, seem bright red from the intense coloring of the leaves.

A. personii is a species whose growth-form differs greatly from all other African aloes. It forms large shrubs that are branched from the base, up to 1 m tall and up to 2 m in diameter. The leaves are triangular in cross-section, up to 9 cm long and 4 cm wide, fleshy, bent back at the tip, dentate, and dark wine red in the dry season. The leaves are arranged in 4 or 5 rows rather densely overlapping, giving the plant its remarkable appearance. Inflorescences appear near the shoot tip and are branched, up to 40 cm long with greenish yellow, sometimes brick-red flowers.

A very interesting plant, but, as is the case with all species of the dry areas, it is not easy to grow and to propagate.

A remarkable *Aloe* from the dry areas of the bushman country is

Aloe claviflora BURCH. (Plate 63,3),

which grows on stony, barren plains, the so-called "flats," sometimes in stands of a square kilometer in size. When young the plant forms compact clusters, which spread on the outer edges; they can be up to 3 m in diameter, almost round. Because the central rosettes of such a cluster die as they age, rings or arcs develop (Plate 62,2), and so the plant is called the "Kraal Aloe" ("claw aloe") by the natives.

The single rosettes, with their short, reclining stem, have a diameter of up to 30 cm; their thick, upright, gray-green leaves have brown teeth on the margins. The diagonally upright or reclining inflorescences are up to 50 cm long and have hundreds of cinnamon-red, later yellow flowers. A cluster in full bloom with dozens of inflorescences all pointing in the same direction is a splendid sight (Plate 63,2).

Aloe haemanthifolia BRGR. et MARL. (Plate 63,4)

is no less interesting; it grows on moist, grassy cliff walls or on inaccessible, steep rocks of deep valleys (Kloofs) of the mountain chain north of Cape Town at altitudes around 1200 m. It is a stemless rosette plant, whose dark green, red-margined leaves are up to 20 cm long and 8 cm wide and are arranged in two rows and cover the short stem (Plate 63,4).

Vegetatively, *A. haemanthifolia* resembles the Liliaceae *Haemanthus,* to which the name refers. Inflorescences appear singly and are unbranched, up to 40 cm long, with numerous, pendulous, pale-scarlet flowers.

A very decorative plant, in cultivation it requires semi-shade, a lot of humidity, and cool temperatures.

Two pretty, small, off-shooting, therefore easily propagated aloes that are also easy to bloom are the following two from Somalia.

Aloe jacksonii REYN. (Plate 64,7)

A plant of dwarf growth-form, it forms rather large mats. The rosette axis (in cultivation) is up to 20 cm long and loosely set with very fleshy leaves. These leaves stand out horizontally from the axis or are somewhat curved back, forming a semicircle in cross-section, are up to 15 cm long and gray-green with white flecks and small, separated teeth on the margins. Inflorescences are simple, unbranched, up to 25 cm long, with strikingly large, pendulous, scarlet-red, waxy flowers inflated toward the tip.

Aloe jucunda REYN. (Plate 64,8)

Its rosettes have a diameter of only 8 to 9 cm; the dark-green, flat-spread, highly succulent leaves have white flecks and stiff, brown teeth on their margins. Its flowers appear in a raceme ca. 30 cm long and pale red.

One of the most splendid small aloes is

Aloe longistyla BAK. (Plate 64,9),

which grows in the dry areas of the Little Karroo and of the eastern Cape area, sporadically in single rosettes. Leaves are upright, 12 to 15 cm long, with a bluish wax, ending in a sharp point, with both sides covered with thorny bristles. The flowers are numerous in a dense raceme, upright, pale brick red, with a style that is exserted far outside the perigon (therefore called the "long-styled *Aloe*").

Aloe peglerae SCHOENL. (Color Plate 8,8),

from the Megalies Mountains near Pretoria on rocky slopes, forms single rosettes up to 30 cm in diameter, which resemble a head of cabbage. Its leaves are up to 25 cm long and are sharp pointed, gray-green, with teeth at the margins and on the central rib on the bases. The tips of the leaves are bent inward and overlap each other like shingles. At bloom time the plants make a splendid sight, when in the middle of the rosette the inflorescences, up to 40 cm long, appear. They have hundreds of short-pedicellated flowers, whose initially bright red, later greenish yellow corolla tubes are far surpassed by the lemon yellow filaments and the pistil.

Unfortunately the plant in cultivation loses its typical growth-form, because the rosette leaves begin to spread out flat in humid air.

A member of the tall, arborescent, stem-rosette plants from section Pachydendron HAW. is

Aloe marlothii BRGR. (Plate 61,4),

which grows in Botswana, Transvaal, Swaziland, and Mozambique on stony hills in rather large stands. Frequently one finds it planted around the villages of the natives.

A. marlothii forms thick, woody stems up to 6 m tall, which are covered almost to the base with the remains of the old, dried leaves. The living leaves form a dense rosette up to 3 m in diameter; their gray to blue-green blades are equipped with stiff, red spines on the margins and on the surface. The inflorescences are richly branched, up to 80 cm tall in panicles, whose branches are more or less spread out horizontally and have hundreds of yellow to yellow-orange flowers.

Of the tree-form aloes, *A. marlothii* is one of the most decorative, which in spite of its size enjoys favor among collectors, for even young plants with their shiny blue-green leaves and the contrasting red spines bring vivid color into a collection.

In the same section are also the following: *A. ferox* MILL. (flowers shiny red; Plate 61,1), *A. africana* MILL. (flowers yellow-orange), *A. aculeata* POLE-EVANS (flowers yellow-red, *A. candelabrum* BRGR. (flowers scarlet red), *A. angelica* POLE-EVANS (flowers yellow), *A. spectabilis* REYN. (flowers red), and *A. thraskii* BAK. (flowers yellow-orange).

Also a favorite *Aloe* is

Aloe plicatilis MILL. (Section Kumara) (Plate 65,1),

which grows on moist slopes and along creek banks of the mountains of the Cape area. In habitat it forms richly branched shrubs up to 2 m tall with smooth, slightly woody shoots. The long, lineal, light blue-green leaves up to 30 cm long and 4 cm wide are arranged in a terminal fan of only 2 rows. The racemose inflorescences have pendulous, scarlet-red flowers.

This is a very decorative species, which, like all smooth aloes, is relatively difficult to propagate from cuttings.

Aloe striata HAW. (Plate 65,2),

a favorite species, is widespread in cultivation and is easily recognized by its bluish white, distinctly longitudinally nerved, red-margined, glabrous leaves and is only to be compared to the Madagascar species *A. viguieri* (see page 112). *A. striata* is especially beautiful at bloom time, when the panicled inflorescences up to 1 m tall unfold; its flowers are numerous and are vivid coral red.

Very closely related to this but considerably rarer (found only in Namibia, in the Richtersveld and Namaqualand) is

Aloe karasbergensis PILLANS,

which differs from the previous species by its indistinctly nerved leaves, which recurve at the tips.

Closely related to *Aloe* is the genus

Lomatophyllum WILLD.,

found only on Madagascar and the Comores (Mauritius).

Vegetatively, as well as in bloom, their members are not distinguishable from *Aloe;* only by the fruit can a distinction be made. In *Aloe* the fruits are dry-skinned capsules that open with long splits; in *Lomatophyllum,* on the other hand, they are fleshy berries that do not open. The genus is represented by about a dozen species, of which only a very few are found in cultivation.

A relatively large species is

Lomatophyllum occidentale H. PERR.,

which has a stemless rosette that off-shoots from the base, with numerous, initially upright, later recurved, dentate leaves sometimes up to 1 m long. Inflorescences appear in multiples, racemose or panicled, with large, pendulous, bright red flowers. *Distribution:* northern and western Madagascar.

Very similar is

Lomatophyllum orientale H. PERR. (Plate 65,3),

whose distribution area is southern Madagascar.

Of the small, stemless species worthy of cultivation I name:
Lomatophyllum citreum GUILL.: rosettes stemless; leaves dark green with white flecks; flowers yellow.
Lomatophyllum prostratum H. PERR.: leaves dark brown; flowers red.

Also closely related to *Aloe* is

Chamaealoe BRGR.,

which is represented by the single species

Chamaealoe africana (HAW.) BRGR. (Plate 65,4)

from southern Cape Province. A plant of dwarf growth-form, it is stemless, off-shooting at the base. Its leaves are numerous, appearing in thick rosettes up to 10 cm across, narrow, lineal, ca. 10 cm long, and dark green with white flecks, with small teeth on the margins. Inflorescences are 15 to 20 cm long, simple, with horizontal, greenish white flowers.

C. africana is a charming, very coveted plant, which requires a loose, humusy soil, a somewhat shady location, and more water than most aloes.

The Liliaceae genus

Haworthia DUV.

also has many species. It is found in South Africa and Namibia. Its members have been cultivated for decades in Europe and enjoy great favor, because their cultivation affords few difficulties. Many species in habitat grow hidden under bushes and under boulders; therefore, they require somewht moister and shadier locations and are sensitive to too much sun. Some species in habitat are hidden in the soil up to the tips of the leaves.

The highly succulent leaves appear in a dense rosette and are overlapping, usually arranged in a spiral, seldom in two rows on short axes equipped with fleshy roots. They frequently have hairs or teeth on the margins and have pearl-like knobs on their leaf blades. The flowers themselves are small and insignificant. They are arrayed in racemose, elongated inflorescences, are whitish, brownish, or greenish in color, and are distinguished by a dorsiventral, 2-lipped structure (Plate 68,1, center).

Like *Aloe* the haworthias tend to form hybrids not only in cultivation but also in habitat, and so a definite classification is very difficult, especially since up to now no modern, comprehensive study of the genus exists.[21]

Propagation is easy. Many species off-shoot willingly at the base and therefore develop compact mats. Most of the non-off-shooting species can be propagated by leaf cuttings: one removes the older rosette leaves carefully, sticks them in pure sand, and within just a few weeks gets young plants.

From the great richness of species I can only list a small selection here. A widely cultivated and highly variable species (nearly 20 recognized varieties and forms) is

Haworthia attenuata HAW. (Plate 68,1, left).

It is distinguished by a mat-like growth of thick rosettes; its long, triangular leaves are up to 7.5 cm long, ending in a sharp tip, and are dark green and equipped with white tubercles on both sides, which frequently merge into lines and cross bands. It is a very easily grown species.

A rare but very beautiful plant is

Haworthia bolusii BAK.

It forms spherical rosettes up to 7 cm in diameter, which in dry periods are completely closed and in rainy seasons are open. The numerous, pale green leaves have keels on the upper part of the under surface; they have dense, white bristles on the margins. The bristles are intertwined, so the plant gives the impression of being woven into a dense cocoon.

In var. *semiviva* V. POELLN. (Plate 66,1) the upper third of the leaf dies during the rest period and remains on the plant as a papery appendage.

This plant is very sensitive to poor drainage.

Similar and difficult to distinguish from the above is *H. arachnoidea* (L.) DUV.

A pretty plant is

---

[21] The reader is referred to the new *Haworthia Handbook* by M.B. BAYER, National Botanic Gardens of South Africa, Kirstenbosch, 1982, with 68 color photographs.

Haworthia cymbiformis (HAW.) DUV. (Plate 66,2),

whose numerous, stemless rosettes form dense mats. The broadly oval, acute, gray-green, somewhat transparent leaves become pale carmine red in intense sun.

In var. *translucens* TRIEBN. et V. POELLN. the leaf tip is free of chloroplasts and therefore completely transparent; only over the nerves are there narrow, green stripes.

A common plant in collections is

Haworthia limifolia MARL. (Plate 66,3),

a rosette plant that off-shoots from the base, and whose broadly triangular, acute, dark green to gray-green leaves roll their margins upward during the dry season. Both sides of the leaf are covered with ca. 15 to 20 diagonal weals, which give the plant its characteristic appearance and to which the plant also owes its name.

A very decorative species with many forms is

Haworthia margaritifera (L.) HAW. (Plate 66,4),

whose rosettes in var. *maxima* (HAW.) UITEW. can reach a diameter of up to 15 cm. The very fleshy, narrowly triangular, pointed, dark-green leaves with a keel on the under surface are equipped on both sides with large, white, pearl-like tubercles.

Among the most remarkable haworthias are
H. maughanii V. POELLN. and *H. truncata* SCHOENL. They are compiled into section Fenestratae, the "windowed" haworthias.

The upright leaves all end at the same height and appear to be hacked off at the top (see Figure 4,1). Because the central water tissue of the leaf stretches right up to the epidermis and has no chloroplasts, the truncated leaf surface is as translucent as frosted glass, thus relegating such succulents to the group of "window-leaf plants" (see also page 20). The chloroplastic assimilation tissue is localized solely on the leaf blade on both sides (see Figure 4,1).

In habitat the plants are buried in the soil up to the windows (Plate 66,5–6; Plate 67,1–2). The entering light therefore can reach the assimilation tissue only by coming through the windows and crossing the central water tissue. The light intensity is thereby greatly reduced. The window phenomenon therefore is conceived of, as already mentioned in the general introduction, as an adaptation against too strong sunlight, which would destroy the chlorophyll. The validity of this light theory will not be discussed here. Let me point out that *H. truncata,* one of the classic examples with window leaves, has been found by me only under dense bushes, i.e., shady places, whereas *H. maughanii* prefers open, stony, barren slopes, thriving there in full sunlight. Nevertheless, both species have the same leaf structure. In

Haworthia maughanii V. POELLN. (Plate 66,5–6)

the rosette leaves are arranged in a spiral on a short, thick axis with fleshy roots. The leaf blades are upright and have the shape of a club with the top lopped off; in cross-section they are round or bluntly triangular (ca. 5 to 10 mm thick). During the dry period the leaves shrivel and the plant withdraws completely into the soil, and it requires a good eye to find it.

Plate 66,5 shows 4 specimens during the dry period in open, stony land near Calitzdorp (eastern Cape Province). Note the hollows in the soil, which have come about as the leaves shrivelled. Plate 66,6 shows a plant in cultivation.

The racemose inflorescences are up to 20 cm long, appear in subterminal position, and have numerous, white flowers with greenish red nerves.

Haworthia truncata SCHOENL. (Plate 67,1–2; Figure 4,1)

In this species the upright-arched, strap-shaped, dark-green leaves are up to 2 cm wide and are arranged in a strictly 2-row fan and also hide in the soil up to the windows (Plate 67,1). Depending on the size of the leaves, I distinguish a large form (forma *crassa* V. POELLN.) and a small form (forma *tenuis* V. POELLN.). The flowers are similar to those of *H. attenuata* (see Plate 68,1, center).

In my climate the plants must be grown above ground, for central Europe does not have the high light intensities of the habitat, but according to my experience, the plant thrives better in semi-shade than in full sun.

Both species can be propagated easily from leaf cuttings.

Windows, although not in such beautiful form, are found also in other haworthias, for example, in

Haworthia obtusa HAW.,

a species of many forms, whose upright, very succulent leaves are triangular in cross-section and end in a tip with no chloroplasts, which therefore acts as a window. The leaves, however, never appear as sharply cut off as in the two species above. The nerves appear in the windows as green lines. In

Haworthia retusa (L.) HAW. (Plate 67,3),

it is the upper side of the leaf, specifically only its upper third, which is transformed into windows as a result of the receding of the assimilation tissue. The leaves are ca. 3 to 5 cm long, roundish at the base, and upright, and the quite succulent, oval-triangular, pointed upper leaf half bends back sharply and functions as a window (Plate 67,3). In habitat the plants again are hidden in the soil up to these windows.

A pretty, very variable species is

Haworthia reinwardtii (S.D.) HAW. (Plate 68, 1, right),

which differs from those discussed above by its elongated (up to 20 cm) axes; these are covered by the initially upright, later incurved, long, triangular, pointed, spirally arranged leaves. The leaves are dark green and, in intensive light, become brownish red to carmine red; they have white, pearl-like tubercles, which in some varieties merge into clear cross bands.

A decorative species, it is easy to propagate because of the basal off-shooting.

Among the stem-forming species is the variable

Haworthia viscosa (L.) HAW. (Plate 68,3).

Because of basal off-shooting, in habitat it forms rather large groups of upright stems 10 to 20 cm long, which are covered with leaves in three, often spiral, rows. These are distinctly folded on the upper side and have a keel beneath; they end in

a thin, sharp tip and the upper surface has fine, rough tubercles.
This is a favorite and easily grown species.
A pretty plant resembling *H. bolusii* is

Haworthia setata HAW. (Plate 4,1).

It forms stemless rosettes up to 5 cm (in var. *gigas* V. POELNN. up to 12 cm) in diameter, which are completely closed in dry weather but open with high humidity (see Plate 4,1). Its leaves are long, lanceolate, end in a sharp tip, and have long, white bristles on their margins.
M.B. BAYER (1976) considers it a synonym for *H. arachnoidea*. (L.) DUV.
Among the frequently collected species is the variable

Haworthia tesselata (SALM) HAW. (Plate 67,4),

a small rosette plant with spirally arranged, flatly spread, very thick, broadly triangular, pointed, dark green to brownish green leaves, whose nerves appear on the upper side as a transparent network. It is therefore referred to popularly as the "net haworthia."

A genus closely related to *Haworthia* is

Astroloba UITEW. (= *Apicra* HAW.),

whose members' growth-form resembles the stem-forming haworthias of the type of *H. viscosa,* but differ from them by their radial, not 2-lipped, zygomorphic flowers (Plate 68,3, right). In collections the genus is relatively rare, although its cultivation affords no greater difficulties than the haworthias. As most species off-shoot from the base, propagation is very simple.

All *Astroloba* species have elongated, upright stems averaging 25 cm long, which are covered by the usually spirally arranged, broadly triangular or narrowly lanceolate leaves, which end in a hard tip.

For cultivation the following species are especially recommendable:

Astroloba aspera (WILLD.) UITEW. (Plate 68,4, left)

Its shoots are up to 15 cm long and its leaves are broadly triangular, pointed, and very warty on the under side and on the margins.

Astroloba bullulata (JACQ.) UITEW.

The stems are 6 to 10 cm long, and the leaves are broadly triangular, acuminate, dark brownish green, and very warty.

Astroloba foliolosa (WILLD.) UITEW. (Plate 68,4, right)

Its rosette stems are slender, up to 35 cm long, and are densely covered with roundish, triangular, smooth, light-green leaves.

Astroloba pentagona (HAW.) UITEW.

The stems are up to 25 cm tall; the leaves are in 5 straight or slightly spiral rows, lanceolate, up to 4 cm long, pointed somewhat rough, and juicy green, with a sharp keel on the under side.

Astroloba spiralis (L.) UITEW.

Its shoots are up to 20 cm tall and are densely covered with overlapping leaves. The leaves are triangular, pointed, and bluish green, with a keel on the under side.

Closely related to *Astroloba* is the genus

Poellnitzia UITEW.,

with the single species *Poellnitzia rubriflora* (L. BOL.) UITEW. (= *Apicra rubriflora*) (Plate 68,2).

It differs from *Astroloba* by its much stouter growth. The upright, elongated, off-shooting shoots are up to 25 cm long and are covered with dense, blue-green, sparsely warty leaves that are arranged in 5 rows. The leaves become up to 4 cm long and are broadly triangular and pointed, with the upper side concave and the under side convex. Inflorescences are up to 35 cm long, with large (up to 2.5 cm) red-orange, cylindrical flowers.

Among the favorite house plants, which once were in every home, and also members of the Liliaceae family is

Gasteria DUV.,

a leaf succulent genus of many species, whose distribution area stretches from southeastern Cape Province to Namibia. They are stemless or short-stemmed rosette plants, whose fleshy, juicy leaves are arranged either in a 2-row fan or in a spiral. Young plants always have leaves in two rows, but when the plants mature they begin to have a spiral leaf arrangement. The inflorescences, which appear in the axils of the upper rosette leaves, are racemes or sparsely branched panicles, which have loosely arranged, usually pendulous flowers typical for the genus: the pale scarlet tube is inflated at the base and narrows into a paler and usually greenish neck (Plate 68,5–8). The fruits are typical Liliaceae capsules.

Cultivation affords no difficulties; therefore, the gasterias belong to the plants which one says cannot be killed. They withstand shade or sun, moisture or dryness, and are not very susceptible to pests.

Propagation, as you can imagine, is simple; many species tend to off-shoot and therefore form rather large mats; others can be propagated easily from leaf cuttings.

Identification of gasterias is not exactly simple, for young plants differ considerably from adult plants, and this genus tends strongly to form hybrids.

One of the largest species is

Gasteria acinacifolia (JACQ.) HAW. (Plate 67,5),

which is not rare in the forests of the southeastern Cape area. The sword-shaped rosette leaves reach a length of up to 35 cm and are rounded at the tip into a triangle; the under side has a keel, and is deep dark green, sometimes with some white flecks.

Among the dwarf gasterias are *G. armstrongii*, *G. brevifolia*, and *G. liliputana*.

G. armstrongii SCHOENL.

in their youth form just 2 rows of leaves and are stemless; their short (up to 4 cm), thick, rounded leaves are pressed to the ground, end in a sharp point, and are warty on the upper side. Although *G. armstrongii* can reach bloom in its distichous stage, it later goes into a spiral leaf arrangement and the leaves elongate. According to recent studies *G. armstrongii* should not be accorded species rank but is only a long-lived youth stage of *G. beckeri* SCHOENL.

Gasteria brevifolia HAW. (Plate 68,6)

Its rosette leaves are usually only in 2 rows, flat spread, up to 15 cm long and 3 to 5 cm wide, thick, tongue-shaped, short tipped, dark green, sometimes with white flecks arranged in crossbands, very warty, rough and with gristle-like teeth on the margins. Inflorescences are 10 to 15 cm long.

Gasteria liliputana v. POELLN. (Plate 68,5),

as a result of generous basal offshooting, forms thick clumps and tufts, whose very small rosettes in youth are distichous; at maturity, however, they have irregularly arranged leaves. The spread, lanceolate, pointed leaf blades are up to 4 cm long and are white spotted with a white, horn-like rim on the margins. The inflorescences are ca. 10 cm long, and the flowers are small and red.

This is a very attractive, willing bloomer.

Probably the prettiest, although rare (in cultivation), species is

Gasteria batesiana ROWLEY (Plate 67,6).

It forms small rosettes with horizontally spread, spirally arranged, broadly triangular to tongue-shaped, pointed, very warty, rough leaves with irregular white bands. In intense light the leaves take on a splendid, golden bronze to dark-olive color.

Gasteria pulchra (AIT.) HAW. (Plate 68,7)

is one of those gasterias, whose leaves have a white marbling on the blade. The numerous, nearly distichous leaves sit on an axis that is 15 to 30 cm long and has off-shoots at the base; they are long-lingulate, short tipped, dirty green (in intense light, reddish green), flat on the upper side, rounded beneath, and have white flecks which merge into irregular crossbands. This spotting gives the plant its special charm and is also found in a number of other species, among which are

Gasteria maculata (THUNBG.) HAW., *G. marmorata* BAK., and *G. trigona* HAW.

One of the favorite gasterias long grown as a house plant is

Gasteria verrucosa (MILL.) DUV. (Plate 68,8),

which has a stemless rosette off-shooting from the base. Its 6 to 10, long-lingulate, gradually pointed leaves are up to 20 cm long and are arranged in a distichous fan and have dense, white warts on both sides, giving it its popular name "warty dwarf aloe."

Under the name

× *Gastrolea* E. WALTH.

are cultivated plants in botanical gardens and collections, which are bi-generic hybrids between *Aloe* and *Gasteria*. As the *Aloe* partner, mostly *Aloe variegata*, *A. aristata*, or *A. striata* are chosen.

Vegetatively the hybrids resemble an *Aloe*, but the flowers in form and color resemble the gasterias.

The two best known and most frequently grown hybrids are: × *Gastrolea bedinghausii* (RADL.) E. WALTH. (hybrid between *Aloe aristata* HAW. and *Gasteria nigricans* HAW.) and × *Gastrolea beguinii* (RADL.) E. WALTH. (hybrid between *Aloe aristata* HAW. and *Gasteria verrucosa* (MILL.) DUV.).

Both look very similiar and clearly reveal their *Aloe aristata* parentage; however, the rosettes are considerably larger and reach a diameter up to 25 cm, with good feeding up to 30 cm. the upright or flared, dark-green leaves are equipped with white warts, which frequently merge into crossbands, and have white teeth on the margins.

Cultivation is the same as for *Aloe* and *Gasteria*.

FAMILY CRASSULACEAE

From this family I have already described (see p. 107) a number of stem succulents, but the leaf succulents represent this family in for greater number; I find them divided into the following genera.

Adromischus LEM.

The genus and its ca. 50 species inhabit the dry areas of Namaqualand and Namibia. They are low-growing rosette plants or small, mini-shrubs that form air roots and have very succulent leaves that fall off at the slightest touch. The leaves fall to the ground, root very quickly, and create new plants (Plate 7,2). Propagation of *Adromischus* species therefore is very easy.

The flowers are in racemose inflorescences; they are small and upright, and their whitish or reddish corollas are spread out into a star-shape (Plate 69,1–5).

Regarding the structure of the flower, there is a close relationship to the members of the Crassulaceae genus *Cotyledon;* many *Adromischus* species therefore are also described as cotyledons.

All *Adromischus* species, relatively unknown among hobbyists, require a loose, humusy soil and bright, warm locations (winter temperatures not below 14° C, 55° F); then they will bloom almost all year.

Adromischus cristatus (HAW.) LEM. (= *Cotyledon cristatus* HAW.; Plate 69,1)

is easily recognized by the short stem wrapped in a thick coat of reddish, tangled aerial roots. The leaf blades are a reverse triangle, on short petioles, inflated, and have short, soft hairs; on the upper margins they are very wavy and therefore appear to be crested. Its flowers are small and greenish to whitish red.

Adromischus festivus C.A. SMITH

is very closely related to the above, but the leaves are less wavy on the margins and are gray-green with dark, wine-red flecks.

Among the stem-forming species with aerial roots is

Adromischus poellnitzianus WERD. (Plate 4,5).

It has shoots up to 5 cm long, wrapped in a thick coat of reddish aerial roots. Its leaves are in a terminal rosette, cylinder-shaped, with a narrow base and slightly wavy at the tip. The inflorescences are up to 40 cm long, and the flowers are upright, with white, red-flecked corollas. *Distribution:* eastern Cape Province (East London).

An easily recognized species is

Adromischus herrei (PARK.) V. POELLN. (= *Cotyledon herrei* BARK.) (Plate 69,2),

from Namaqualand, a clump up to 10 cm tall, whose short axes have shuttle-shaped, pointed leaves 3 to 4 cm long of a striking brownish yellow color. They are covered with a waxy layer and longitudinal lines of short papillae. During the rest period the leaves shrivel and then appear to have longitudinal lines.

Very attractive is

Adromischus maculatus (SALM.) LEM. (Plate 69,3),

from the rocky region of the Karroo. The sparsely branched, thick axes have numerous roundish to spade-shaped leaves that are ca. 4 cm long and 3 cm wide and a gray-green with dark wine-red spots on both sides.

An easily recognized and decorative species is

Adromischus marianae (MARL.) BRGR. (= *Cotyledon marianae* MARL.; Plate 69,4),

growing under bushes and forming mats in the habitat (Clanwilliam Distr.). The short, creeping or ascending axes have upright, lanceolate, gray-green leaves with brownish flecks; the leaves are ca. 8 mm thick, concave on the upper side, very convex beneath, and ca. 10 cm long.

Adromischus schaeferianus (DTR.) BRGR. (= *Cotyledon schaeferiana* DTR., *Cotyledon hoerleiniana* var. *schaeferi* DTR.; Plate 69,5)

is a small species differing from those discussed above. Its distribution area stretches from Little Namaqualand to Namibia, preferring sandy locations.

From an irregularly branched, partially knotty rhizome equipped with fleshy roots emerge thin, short shoots 3 to 4 cm long, which have few, very fleshy, egg-shaped to spherical, glassy, translucent, gray-green to grayish brown leaves with reddish stripes. Flowers appear in sparsely branched inflorescences, relatively large in comparison to the whole plant, with violet-green corollas with red stripes.

A very interesting succulent, in habitat it is buried almost completely in sand and is therefore hard to see.

Of the same growth-form is the southwest African *A. hoerleinianus* (DTR.) V. POELLN. (= *Cotyledon hoerleiniana* DTR.).

Aeonium WEBB et BERTH.

The genus *Aeonium,* represented by many species on the Canary Islands, Cape Verdes, Madeira, and scattered in north Africa, is a rosette plant. The rosettes either lie stemless on the ground or stand at the end of branched or unbranched, slightly woody stems. The yellow, white, or reddish flowers gather into large, panicled, terminal inflorescences. Some species are hapaxanthic, i.e., they die after the seed ripens.

All species are easily grown; they require a bright but cool location and, during the summer, should be placed outside in a shady place.

From the great number of species, I have selected some that are especially suited for growing as house plants.

Aeonium arboreum (L.) WEBB et BERTH.

forms sparsely branched stems up to 1 m tall with terminal rosettes that are up to 20 cm in diameter and have flatly spread, spatulate, short-tipped leaves with hairs on the margins. Its flowers are golden yellow, in panicles 25 to 30 cm long.

An especially beautiful mutation is

var. *atropurpureum* (NICH.) BRGR. (Plate 69,6),

whose rosette leaves are dark purple; in var. *albovariegatum* (WEST.) BOOM they are striped with greenish white, and in var. *luteovariegatum* (WEST.) BOOM the stripes are yellowish white.

Aeonium canariense (L.) WEBB et BERTH. (Plate 69,7)

has large, almost stemless funnel-shaped rosettes, whose spatulate, upright, dark-green leaves are blunt at the tip and have gland hairs on both sides. It flowers are pale-green, in richly branched panicles; the plants die after the seed ripens.

An especially recommendable species is

Aeonium nobile PRAEG. (Plate 69,8),

whose short-stemmed rosettes reach a diameter up to 50 cm; their very fleshy, broadly oval leaves with their hairy margins are arched upward. The plant is especially beautiful at flowering time. From the middle of the rosette emerges a richly branched, panicled inflorescence with hundreds of copper-red flowers. After the seeds ripen the plant dies. Propagation is therefore possible only from seed.

The most attractive *Aeonium* without a doubt is

Aeonium tabulaeforme (HAW.) WEBB et BERTH. (Plate 69,9),

a typical plant from the moist barrancos (gorges) of Teneriffe, where the plant grows on steep lava cliffs. It forms stemless, flat rosettes pressed tight against the substrate. The rosettes have a slightly concave tip, in which the spiral, spatulate leaves with their hairy margins lie tightly overlapping. After some

years of vegetative growth, in the course of which the rosette can reach a diameter up to 50 cm, the shoot tip elongates into a panicle inflorescence up to 60 cm long with hundreds of large, sulphur-yellow flowers. While the inflorescence is forming, the rosette leaves are sucked dry of their nutrition and they die. After the seeds ripen the flowering plant dies but produces offshoots at the base.

Propagation is by seed, but is also possible from cuttings.

If possible they should be grown vertically in shady locations. In a pot they will take on a vertical position by themselves.

A very imposing plant at flowering time is

Aeonium urbicum (C. SM.) WEBB et BERTH. (Plate 70,*1*).

It forms simple or slightly branched shoots up to 1 m tall with a terminal, loose-leafed rosette. The leaves are elongate-spatulate, pointed, with reddish violet margins. The flowers are greenish white and numerous and appear in large terminal, pyramidal inflorescences.

Very closely related to *Aeonium* is

Greenovia WEBB et BERTH.

The best known species is

Greenovia aurea (C. SM.) WEBB et BERTH. (Plate 70,*2*),

whose blue-green, upright leaves form a deep, funnel-shaped rosette, which during the dry season is almost spherical. The inflorescence has dense bracts and branches that give it the shape of a head. After it develops, the rosette dies, but it produces a large number of off-shoots at the base of the mother rosette. The plant thus forms rather large tufts in habitat. Its flowers are large and golden yellow.

Cotyledon L.

Among stem-succulent *Cotyledon* species (see page 107) there are numerous leaf succulents, of which many are suitable as house plants, especially because they can be propagated easily.

A pretty, small species from the Little Karroo (near Ladysmith) is

Cotyledon ladismithiensis V. POELLN. (Plate 70,*4*),

a dwarf shrub up to 20 cm tall, whose thin, slightly woody branches have at their tips rosettes of sessile or short-petiolated, very fleshy leaves that have teeth at their tips and are woolly. Flowers are pendulous, with brownish red, rolled-back petal tips.

A plant that was introduced into Europe in 1670 and has been cultivated since then is

Cotyledon orbiculata L. (Plate 70,3),

a dwarf shrub up to 1.5 m tall, which sometimes appears in mass stands in South Africa from Natal to northern Damaraland and from the Cape peninsula to the mountains of the Karroo. It has a great many leaf shapes, and so a number of varieties have been described. The decussate, snow-white, waxy, red-margined leaves are broad and spatulate (Plate 70,3), short tipped, and narrow near the base; however, they are also lineal or a short-oval shape (var. *oophylla*), flat or cylindrical. The inflorescences are 70 cm long and have in a loosely dichasial arrangement pendulous, red or reddish yellow flowers.

This is a very attractive, fast-growing species. Take care in watering, or you will wash away the white, waxy layer.

One of the favorite leaf succulents present in all collections is

Cotyledon undulata HAW.,

easily recognized by its snow-white, waxy, wavy-margined leaves (Plate 70,5).

C. undulata forms simple or slightly branched stems up to 50 cm long, which like all other species of the genus have 4 rows of roundish, upright leaves, but as a result of asymmetrical growth of the leaf blades, the leaf rows are pressed against each other so tightly that they appear to grow in two rows. In such a case one speaks of a distorted decussation, as is typical for many other crassulaceas (see *Crassula alstonii, C. falcata*, etc.). The terminal inflorescences are ca. 40 cm long and have long-stalked, pendulous flowers in a loosely dichasial arrangement; their yellow-orange petals are rolled back at the tip.

Propagation is by off-shoots and leaf cuttings.

The genus

Crassula L.,[22]

thick-leafed plants in the strictest sense, are distributed almost over the whole world with around 300 species. The highly succulent ones, however, are limited almost exclusively to the dry areas of South Africa; among them are true "gems," which are among the treasures of any succulent collection.

The flowers of the highly succulent species, arranged in richly branched, dichasial inflorescences, are generally small and insignificant. The plants' attractiveness comes solely from their growth-form with their thick, hairy or waxy leaves.

The cultivation of *Crassula* in general affords no great difficulty. The plants require a nutritious, loamy, sandy soil and a location that is not too warm in the winter; especially the highly succulent, rosette types should be given a lot of light during the winter, for otherwise the shoots etiolate and the plants lose their typical shape. Waxy species should not get water on their leaves.

Propagation is easy from leaf or shoot cuttings.

Some species are hapaxanthic and can therefore be propagated only from seed.

A very pretty, small species is

Crassula alstonii MARL. (Plate 70,6).

It grows on the quartz fields of Namaqualand and Namibia and produces sparsely branched, spherical rosettes, in which the grayish white, mussel-shaped, distorted-decussate leaves overlap. Its flowers are small, yellowish green, in loose dichasias.

Among the large, almost tree-like species is

Crassula arborescens (MILL.) WILLD.,

a large shrub or a small tree up to 4 m tall with a thick stem and a richly branched "crown," which grows on dry, rocky slopes, especially in the Central Karroo, and forms rather large stands.

The broadly spatulate to roundish-oval, glabrous, waxy, gray-green, red-margined, fleshy leaves have distinct red dots on their upper side, an important differentiation between it and the similar *Crassula argentea* THUNBG. (= *C. obliqua* SOL.).

Although *C. arborescens* seldom reaches bloom stage, it is especially suitable for growing in the house.

Crassula arta SCHOENL. (Plate 70,7)

forms groups of upright shoots that are up to 10 cm long, densely covered with leaves, and columnar. Its leaves are fleshy, canoe-shaped, triangular, with a blunt keel on the back and ending in a short tip, and are gray-green and with fine, satiny hairs. Its flowers appear in richly branched inflorescences and are insignificant and yellowish green.

A very pretty species, it requires a bright location in the winter; otherwise, the shoot internodes will elongate and the dense leaves will stretch apart.

Crassula brevifolia HARV. (= *C. pearsonii* SCHOENL.; Plate 70,8)

A dwarf shrub very suitable for growing in the house, it has very succulent, oval-round, biconvex, gray-green, red-margined leaves. Its flowers are white, in thick dichasias.

Also the same shape as *C. arta* is

Crassula columella MARL. et SCHOENL. (Plate 71,1),

a plant from dry cliffs of the Richtersveld (Namaqualand), whose 10 cm stems appear quadrangular because the dense leaves are arranged in 4 rows. The leaves are broadly triangular,

---

[22] New literature: TOLKEN, H.R., A Revision of the Genus *Crassula* in Southern Africa, I–II. *Contirbutions from the Bolus Herbarium, Kirstenbosch,* 1977 (not illustrated).

shell-shaped, with a blunt keel on the back, overlapping, light green, densely hairy and slightly warty. The flowers are greenish yellow, in loose dichasias.

A very pretty species, its cultivation is the same as for *C. arta*.

Crassula columnaris THUNBG. (Plate 71,2)

is a remarkable plant, which grows in dry primodial rock flats of the Karroo and Namaqualand. In its vegetative stage it forms egg-size, grayish brown to green spheres. The broad, shell-shaped, hairy-margined leaves lie so closely overlapping that the main axis is not visible. When the plant flowers, the internodes begin to stretch and the leaves come apart. The numerous flowers are in a dense head. After flowering, the plant dies, but not before producing daughter rosettes in the axils of the basal rosette leaves; the new rosettes fall to the ground and take root.

A species that is attractive to hobbyists but which is highly variable and related to *Crassula deceptrix* by all sorts of transitions is

Crassula cornuta SCHOENL. et BAK. f. (Plate 71,3, left).

As in *Crassula arta,* it forms slightly branched stems up to 15 cm long, which are equipped with 4 rows of highly succulent, gray-green, triangularly oval, keeled leaves, that end in a long, horn-like tip: Its flowers are small, cream-colored, in loose to dense inflorescences.

The true *C. cornuta* (Plate 71,3, left) is very rare in cultivation.

Without a doubt one of the gems is

Crassula deceptor SCHOENL. et BAK. f. (= *C. deceptrix* SCHOENL.) (Plate 71,3, right; Plate 5,5).

In habitat it grows exclusively on quartz fields and is so well camouflaged to the environment in form and color that it is hardly discernible. *C. deceptor* is therefore an example of plant mimesis (see p. 136).

Basal branching causes *C. deceptor* to form rather large groups, whose 10 cm long axes are densely covered with fleshy, roundish, triangular, keeled leaves. The leaves are white with wax (there are also pure green forms) and covered with a raised network of papillae (see Plate 5,5).

C. deceptor requires much light; it is especially important to prevent the leaves from being wet so that the waxy layer will not disappear. Between *C. cornuta* and *C. deceptor* there is a gradual series of transitional forms. One such transition is depicted in Plate 71,4.

Among the favorite species is

Crassula falcata WENDL.

It is sold in masses in commercial nurserys and is marketed as *Rochea falcata*. Its common name "sickle leaf" comes from the shape of its fleshy, gray-green leaves. These are found on the thick shoot axis up to 1 m long in distorted decussation (see also p. 121) and because of asymmetrical growth take on a sickle shape with perpendicular margins. Therefore, they seem to be arranged in 2 rows. In habitat these leaf rows are said to point

in a north-south direction, so that the leaves expose only their margins to the severe mid-day sun, as is also the case with many plants referred to as compass plants. This so-called profile placement of the leaves is an adaptation technique and provides protection against strong irradiation from the sun and is designed to prevent too-rapid evaporation. Although the South African botanist R. MARLOTH tried to show that the turning of the leaves and the related asymmetric growth of the leaves of *C. falcata* was a result of the strong light, the plant also retains its typical leaf form and leaf position in the less intense light of the middle-European climate.

C. falcata does not reach its full beauty until it blooms (in the summer), when the large, long-stemmed inflorescences appear. They unfold hundreds of small, shiny-red flowers, which are in a thick corymbus. In habitat (grassy slopes of the southeastern Cape area) the flowering plants are visible from a great distance.

Propagation is by seed, shoot cuttings, and leaf cuttings.

A species suitable for home cultivation and one that forms dense tufts is

Crassula lycopodioides LAM. (Plate 71,5),

the "rat tail" crassula, of which many forms have been described.

C. lycopodioides, distributed on the dry areas of Namaqualand and Namibia on stony, dry slopes, forms richly branched minishrubs up to 30 cm high, whose thin shoots are equipped with 4 rows of small, broadly triangular, overlapping leaves. The very small, insignificant, yellowish-green flowers are found in the leaf axils.

Of the numerous forms, var. *variegata* B. LAMB. is the most beautiful; it is distinguished by having silver-gray, shimmering leaves.

An enlarged version of the above is

Crassula pyramidalis THUNGB. (see Plate 4,6),

a plant of up to 10 cm growing in the Karroo and in Namaqualand on dry, rocky areas. It has the same growth-form as the previous species, but the shoots are less branched and are considerably thicker. In the axils of the densely overlapping leaves are numerous villous hairs, which are capable of absorbing humidity, which precipitates onto the leaf margins in the form of dew. The beautiful, pure-white, pleasantly spicy flowers appear in a terminal, head-like, almost sessile inflorescence. After the seeds ripen the plant dies, but they can be preserved by rooting non-blooming lateral shoots in pure sand.

Closely related to *C. pyramidalis* and perhaps only a variety of it is *C. archeri* COMPT.: the plant is more elegant in all its parts and the quadrangular shoots are thinner and more richly branched than in *C. pyramidalis*.

A very attractive plant is

Crassula marnieriana HUBER et JACOBS. (Plate 71,6)

(considered by the *Crassula* specialist Dr. BOOM to be only a variety of *C. rupestris*), a perennial mini-shrub with reclining to ascending or upright, slightly branched shoots up to 15 cm long, which are equipped with dense, broadly heart-shaped, succulent, gray-green, red-margined leaves. Its flowers are

122

numerous, in short-stalked cymes, smelling distinctly of valerian.

Also considered a mimetic plant is the interesting

Crassula mesembryanthemopsis DTR. (Plate 71,7),

a small rosette plant with fleshy roots, which grows in Namaqualand in gray limestone and with its whitish gray-green rosettes pressed to the ground, fits so well into the environment that in its non-blooming stage it can be detected only by practiced collectors. In Namibia, the rosettes are hidden under the sand, from which protrude only the tips of the club-shaped, triangular leaves. As a result of basal off-shooting, the plant forms dense clusters of numerous rosettes. The small, white flowers appear in almost sessile, head-shaped cymes.

C. mesembryanthemopsis is rare in collections; it blooms in winter and requires a rest period in the summer. Propagation by leaf cuttings is possible.

The above species is not to be confused with

Crassula mesembryanthemoides (HAW.) D. DIETR.,

a dwarf shrub up to 30 cm tall, which with its cylindrical, bristly leaves resembles certain mesembryanthemums from the genus *Trichodiadema* (see p. 155).

Superbly suited as a hanging plant in the home is

Crassula perforata THUNBG. (Plate 71,8),

recognizable by the fact that the fleshy, broadly oval, short-tipped, gray-green, red-spotted, and red-margined leaves are united at the base into pairs and therefore appear to be pierced by the shoot axis; thus the name "pierced succulent."

Very closely related to this but considerably larger is

Crassula rupestris THUNBG.,

found growing on stony, rocky slopes of the Karroo and of Namaqualand and differing from the above by its leaves being united only in a narrow strip at the base and by the fact that it has a more compact inflorescence. In intensive sunlight the whole plant becomes bright red.

Another suitable plant for a hanging pot is

Crassula socialis SCHOENL. (Plate 72,1),

whose small, light-green rosettes with their leaves in 4 rows form a compact tuft. The small, white flowers appear in the winter in clustered cymes.

Among the more rarely grown *Crassula* species is

Crassula teres MARL. (Plate 72,2).

It is very closely related to *C. columnaris* (see p. 122), but differs from it in its almost round columns that are 5 to 10 cm tall, which branch at the base. The gray to brownish gray, broadly dish-shaped leaves are equipped with a translucent margin. According to the South African botanists MARLOTH and SCHOENLAND it is presumably a hybrid between *C. pyramidalis* and *C. columnaris*.

Crassulaceas less well known in Europe are the members of the genus

Dudleya BR. et R.,

from Baja California, among which there are several splendid species suitable for house cultivation; their cultivation is like that of *Echeveria* (see below), with which *Dudleya* is closely related.

One of the most beautiful species is

Dudleya brittonii D.A. JOHANNSEN (Plate 72,3).

The plant is up to 50 cm in diameter, stemless or usually with a short, thick stem supporting its rosette. Its leaves are numerous, lanceolate, narrow near the base, with a sharp point, 7 to 25 cm long, 3.5 to 8.5 cm wide. The outer rosette leaves are spreading, and the inner ones are erect, chalky, waxy, rarely green. The inflorescences are lateral, up to 1 m long, and richly branched; flowers are pale yellow. *Distribution:* Mexico (northern Baja California) on dry, rocky areas.

Very white, mealy leaves are found also on *D. densiflora* (ROSE) MORAN (flowers whitish red) and *D. farinosa* (LINDL.) BR. et R. (flowers yellow).

Do not let water fall on the leaves of the white, frosted species, because the mealy frosting would be washed away. All *Dudleya* species are highly variable and tend to hybridize easily, and so definite identification of the nearly 40 species is very difficult.

Nearly all the members of the many (ca. 100) species of the genus

Echeveria DC.,

are rewarding leaf succulents, whose distribution area stretches from the Mexican highlands to central Peru, Bolivia, and Chile. These are single or clustered perennials, whose spirally arranged, fleshy, glabrous or pubescent, sometimes waxy leaves frequently form compact rosettes.

Wholesale nurseries draw on some of the favorite ones for their long flowering period and for their suitability for planting in dish gardens. Even today in the gardens of the Mediterranean area, *Echeveria* (especially *E. derenbergii*) is used to "carpet" flower beds.

Earlier *Echeveria* was combined with the Old World genus *Cotyledon*, but not only geographical reasons but also the formation of the inflorescences made a separation of the two genera desirable, because in *Cotyledon* the inflorescences are terminal, whereas in *Echeveria* they are lateral and always appear in multiples.

Natural hybrids are unknown, but cultivators have produced a great number of forms for the market, which are superior to native species in beauty and lushness of the bloom.

Cultivation of echeverias afford no difficulties. They require a sandy-humusy, nutritious soil. In the summer they can be put outside in rock gardens. Overwintering requires a bright, cool location (temperatures 6° to 10° C or 42° to 50° F). Do not water the rosette from above, because center rot could result.

Propagation is easy from leaf cuttings. When loose leaves are put into sand they form roots and new plants in a short time.

Here is listed a selection of the most beautiful and most favored species.

Echeveria agavoides LEM. (Plate 72,4)

is an easily recognized species, which is a sort of smaller version of an *Agave*. It forms stout, short-stemmed rosettes, which reach up to 15 cm in height when fed. Its leaves are broadly triangular, pointed, and gray-green (red in strong sun), with short, dark-brown tips. The inflorescences occur in multiples, up to 50 cm long, with surrounding, reddish yellow flowers.

A species frequently used for mass plantings is

Echeveria derenbergii I.E. PURPUS (Plate 72,5),

whose basal off-shooting forms thick carpets of stemless, spherical rosettes up to 6 cm in diameter. Their broadly spatulate, blue-green, waxy, frosted, red-margined leaves end in a sharp, reddish tip. The short flower stems appear in multiples and have large, reddish yellow flowers surrounding the stem.

E. derenbergii is frequently used as a parent in hybrids. *E. derosa* is an especially pretty hybrid between *E. derenbergii* and *E. setosa*. It is also cultivated under the name *E. derenbergii* var. *major*.

Echeveria elegans ROSE (= *E. perelegans* BGR.)

A plant with stemless rosettes, it grows in dense mats because of the numerous "daughter" rosettes on long stolons. Its leaves are numerous, densely rosulate, and the leaf blades are obovate, pointed, 3–6 cm long, very pruinose, and alabaster-white with often reddish and translucent margins. The inflorescences are up to 25 cm tall, and the flowers are 10–12 cm long, with yellow tips. *Distribution:* Mexico (Hidalgo).

Surely the most beautiful *Echeveria* is

Echeveria shaviana E. WALTHER,

a small rosette plant up to 10 cm in diameter with numerous gray-green, quite bluish waxy leaves, whose reddish or whitish margin is very wavy. Inflorescences appear in multiples, up to 30 cm long; flowers are reddish outside, orange inside. *Habitat:* oak forests near Dulces Nombres, 1850 m, Nuevo Leon, Mexico. The plant is also very attractive in its non-blooming stage because of its wavy leaf margins.

Echeveria gibbiflora DC.

It has simple or slightly branched stems up to 50 cm long, which have up to 20 reverse-ovate leaves. In var. *metallica* (LEM.) BAK. the leaves have a beautiful bronze sheen; in var. *carunculata* HORT. they have bumpy protuberances near the base on the upper side; these protuberances give the plant a remarkable look (Plate 72,6).

The inflorescences grow up to 60 cm long and are richly branched; and they have numerous, frosted flowers, which are light red on the outside and yellowish on the inside.

Digressing considerably from the other species in growth-form is

Echeveria harmsii (ROSE) MACBR. (= *Oliveranthus elegans* ROSE: Plate 72,7).

It is not the typical rosette plant, but rather its branched stem is up to 30 cm long and has loosely arranged, slightly pubescent, lanceolate to spatulate, red-margined leaves, which gather into a denser rosette near the tip of the shoot. The 5-angled flowers are cinnabar-red on the outside and yellow inside; they appear sparsely but are very large, up to 3 cm long.

Echeveria leucotricha J.A. PURP. (Plate 72,8),

the "white-haired echeveria," forms loose rosettes 10 to 15 cm in diameter, whose fleshy, lanceolate leaves are somewhat brownish at the tips and covered with white hairs. The inflorescences have leaves on the stems and are up to 40 cm long with bright cinnabar-red flowers.

Hairy echeverias also include *E. pilosa* J.A. PURP. and *E. setosa* ROSE et J.A. PURP. (Plate 73,1), the "bristly echeveria"; it has flat or semi-spherical rosettes up to 15 cm in diameter. The fleshy, spatulate, pointed, blue-green leaves are equipped with white bristles on both sides; the inflorescences appear during the spring and summer, are 10 to 15 cm long, and produce a great number of reddish yellow flowers in a dichasially twisted arrangement. A widely cultivated, favorite species, it is often used for hybrids.

The hairy echeverias must be grown drier than the glabrous species, because they tend to rot easily.

The genus

Kalanchoe ADANS.

includes many (ca. 80) species, which are attractive not only because of their beautiful flowers but also because of their general appearance. They also are well suited to growing in the house. The most beautiful are native to Madagascar, where the genus is widely distributed in an abundance of varying types, which grow not only in extremely dry locations but also in the undergrowth of more humid mountain forests, even as epiphytes (members of the section Kitchingia) on trees in the wetter areas. The distribution area of the genus stretches farther through all of Africa into southern Arabia to the island of Socotra.

The Kalanchoes appear as low-growing perennials barely 10 cm tall, and as shrubs, lianas, or even as small trees up to 3 m tall. Their many leaf forms—simple, lobed, or pinnate—are glabrous or hairy and arranged in alternate opposition to each other.

The upright or pendulous, white, yellow, reddish, or bright-red flowers are seldom single (*K. uniflora*) but usually gather into richly dichasial inflorescences. In contrast to other crassulaceas they are distinguished by their flower organs appearing in fours: they have 4 sepals, 4 petals, 8 stamens, and 4 free (not united) carpels.

Many species produce brood buds on their leaves or inflorescences, which propagate the plant vegetatively (see Plate 7,1). These develop roots already on the mother plant, fall to the ground, and grow into new plants. These species were placed formerly in their own genus *Bryophyllum* ("brood leaf"), which has not been combined with the genus *Kalanchoe* and is considered to be only a section thereof.

Flowering time for the *Kalanchoe* species comes in the winter. They are clearly "short-day" plants. Some of them, including the favorite plant *Kalanchoe blossfeldiana*, are subjected to a short-day treatment to get the flowers to set; thus the flowering time can be postponed or advanced.

All Kalanchoes are fast growers and are easily propagated by shoot or leaf cuttings. They require a deep, humusy soil and a bright, airy location. The glabrous-leafed types can be put outside in the summer. Overwintering requires temperatures that do not fall below 10°C (50°F) if possible; thus they can be grown right along with cacti.

As representatives of the shrub and tree-form species I introduce

Kalanchoe beharensis DRAKE (Plate 73,2)

(named after the village of Behara in southern Madagascar), which is very attractive especially as a young plant. It grows in the dry forests of southwestern Madagascar and forms, in habitat, tree-like shrubs up to 3 m tall, branched from the base. Their woody stems can reach a diameter of up to 15 cm; on younger segments they are covered by large, roundish, triangular scars from the fallen leaves and therefore appear to be knobby. The leaves are on long petioles and have a lobed, notched or toothed blade up to 30 cm long, whose margins, especially at the base of the blade, are distinctly rolled upwards. In the type plant the blade is completely glabrous and waxy; much prettier, however, are the hairy forms, of which the silvery-gray form is the more common one. Even more charming, however, are the forms with brownish red hairs, whose leaves shimmer like liquid bronze against the light. The hairs continue down the leaf petiole and onto the younger segments of the shoot axis. The panicled inflorescences are up to 60 cm long and seldom appear in cultivation; the flowers are small and whitish.

A fast-growing species, which when planted in the open ground, develops into a stately plant within a few years.

Kalanchoe blossfeldiana v. POELLN. (Plate 75,1),

from the Tsaratanana Mountains of northern Madagascar, is a small perennial up to 30 cm tall with glabrous, petiolated, dark-green, red-margined, whole or notched leaves. Flowers are bright red in clustered inflorescences and normally appear in January, persisting for many weeks.

The wild form is probably no longer in cultivation. By horticultural selection and crossing, a large assortment of forms have been developed with a variety of growth-forms and flower colors (even yellow-orange), which can be brought into flower at any time of the year by using techniques of the short day or artificial light, so *K. blossfeldiana* has become a top commerical plant. During the winter the plant should not be kept too warm.

Kalanchoe daigremontiana HAMET et PERR. (Plate 7,1)

is a member of section Bryophyllum. The blade is marbled on the under side; the leaf is long triangular, has a long petiole, and is equipped with notches on the margin, in whose axils small brood buds appear, which quickly develop into little plants and in humid air can develop roots on the mother plant. At the slightest touch the buds fall, root, and grow into new plants. In time, therefore, *K. daigremontiana* can become a nuisance weed. In the winter the 1 meter tall shoot terminates by forming a long-stalked inflorescence; the flowers themselves are insignificant and gray-violet. *Habitat:* dry mountains of southwestern Madagascar.

Differing habitually from all other species is

Kalanchoe jongmansii HAMET et PERR. (Plate 73,3),

whose thin, slightly woody shoots and narrowly linear leaves resemble a small *Hypericum*. The large, yellow flowers appear in small numbers in a loose arrangement in short-stalked inflorescences.

A pretty, small species, which can be grown epiphytically or as a hanging plant, is

125

Kalanchoe manginii HAMET et PERR. (Plate 75,*3*),

from section Bryophyllum. It is a small, shrubby, branched plant with thin, slightly woody shoots up to 30 cm long, which are equipped with small, oval-lanceolate, fleshy, glabrous or slightly hairy leaves up to 3 cm long. The short-peduncled, terminal inflorescences have only a few, pendulous, large, bright-red flowers; numerous brood buds appear near the flowers.

Also among the small species is

Kalanchoe millotii HAMET et PERR. (Plate 73,*4*),

a mini-shrub from the dry areas of southwestern Madagascar, with gray, felt-like, oval, serrate, short-petiolated leaves. Its flowers are numerous, white, and upright.

A plant which is splendid even in its non-blooming stage and unfortunately not often found in collections is

Kalanchoe orgyalis BAK. (Plate 74,*1*),

a richly branched half-shrub, which in habitat (central Madagascar) reaches up to 1.5 m height. The petiolated leaves have a whole, ovate-lanceolate, hairy blade up to 7 cm, which when young is bronze to light chocolate in color. The blade becomes grayish white as it matures. The flowers themselves are small, insignificant, and yellowish.

A slow-growing species, its leaves should not be wet, for that would cause them to become spotted and lose their beauty.

A pretty, small species from the mountains of central Madagascar is

Kalanchoe pumila BAK. (Plate 74,*2*).

It differs from the above species by its very mealy, white, short-petiolated, serrate leaf blades. The plant forms richly branched, low shrubs up to 30 cm tall and produces striking, reddish violet flowers. As in all plants with mealy leaves, these should not be allowed to get wet.

Growing in the underbush of the dry forests of southern Madagascar is

Kalanchoe rhombopilosa MANN et BOIT. (Plate 74,*4–5*),

a small, sparsely branched species up to 30 cm tall, which vegetatively is more like an *Adromischus* than a *Kalanchoe*. The club-shaped, silvery-gray leaves have teeth at their tips and are irregularly spotted with wine-red in the typical form, but there is also a form without flecks and with olive-green and gray-green leaves (Plate 74,*5*). These fall easily but soon produce new roots and plantlets, and so propagation affords no difficulties. Flowers are small, insignificant, and yellowish green.

Kalanchoe scapigera WELW. (= *K. farinacea* BALF. f.) (Plate 74,*6*)

is one of the few species on the island of Socotra (also in Angola); it becomes up to 40 cm tall and has roundish oval, whole, gray-waxy leaves. It flowers are bright red, upright, and numerous, and appear in short-stalked clustered, dichasial inflorescences. This is an attractive although rare species.

A quite remarkable species in regard to growth-form is

Kalanchoe synsepala BAK. (Plate 74,*3*),

from the Madagascar highlands; it has many varieties. The plant forms short but thick, slightly woody stems, which have a few pairs of fleshy, upright, very large, variable flowers. Its leaf blade, which narrows into a broad, fleshy petiole, is broadly oval or long oval; the margins are frequently wavy, red, dentate, or deeply serrate. From the axils of the basal rosette leaves emerge runners that are up to 30 cm long and coming only from an elongated internode; the runners terminate their growth with the formation of a new rosette. At first upright, these new rosettes arch down to the ground, so that the young plants can take root, a behavior unique within the genus. Because of this vegetative behavior *K. synsepala* in habitat always appears in rather large stands. The runner-like stem segments eventually wither, and so the young rosettes are isolated from the mother plant. The long-stalked inflorescences develop in the axils of the upper rosette leaves instead of runners; they have clusters of numerous, upright, white flowers (Plate 74,*3*). The upper segments of the inflorescence scapes are pubescent with glandular hairs, as are the sepals and petals.

Similar in growth-form is

Kalanchoe tetraphylla H. PERR. (Plate 75,*5*),

also from Madagascar but much rarer. It differs from the above by the absence of runners and by the loosely dichasially branched inflorescences with their pendulous, white flowers.

K. tetraphylla does not really deserve its name, because the short, slightly woody stems usually have more than 4, broadly oval, dentate, hairy (glandular hairs) or glabrous leaves.

A plant that is very handsome and also attractive at flowering time is

Kalanchoe thyrsiflora HARV. (Plate 76,*1–3*).

Habitat: South Africa, Transvaal, on rocky slopes. It first forms a stemless rosette of oblique-decussate, very large leaves up to 15 cm long and 7 cm wide, which are rounded at the tip, have a white waxy coating, and frequently have red margins. At flowering time the rosette tip elongates into an inflorescence ca. 1 m long, which is equipped with gradually diminishing leaves (scape bracts). In the axils of the upper bracts appear the flower whorls, which are so compact that they give the appearance of a crested or cylindrical inflorescence, giving it the species name, meaning the "crest-shaped" or "bunched kalanchoe." Flowers are white, with mealy peduncles and urn-shaped calyxes.

After the fruit ripens the plant dies, making propagation possible only from seed.

Very similar to the above species and also hapaxanthic is

Kalanchoe luciae HAMET

from Cape Province to Transvaal. It differs from the above especially in the fact that the flower whorls open up more and the inflorescence is therefore clearly in layers; its flowers are pale yellow.

One of the favorite kalanchoes is the variable species

Kalanchoe tometosa BAK. (Plate 76,2),

from gneiss and granite mountains of central Madagascar at elevations between 1200 and 1600 m. In habitat it is richly branched, up to 80 cm tall; its thick, woody-based, but otherwise herbaceous and densely haired shoots have fleshy, densely felt-like leaves arranged in loose rosettes. The leaves have a variable shape; they are sometimes long, sometimes broadly spatulate, entire or dentate at the tip. In the latter case the teeth are equipped with dark-brown hairs, so the leaf tips appear to have dots on the margins.

In cultivation the plant seldom flowers; in habitat it forms panicles or racemes in a clustered head 60 cm long with yellowish to brownish flowers. *K. tomentosa*, like all felt-like species, requires a bright, sunny location; if it is kept too wet the stems tend to form aerial roots and the shoots etiolate.

Among the most striking species is

Kalanchoe tubiflora (HARV.) HAMET (= *Bryophyllum tubiflorum* HARV., = *B. verticillatum* SCOTT-ELLIOT) (Plate 76,4–5),

from the dry bush of southwestern Madagascar. The plant has a round, simple or sparasely branched, gray-green or pale-red stem up to 80 cm long, which has cylindrical leaves up to 12 cm long and ca. 0.5 cm thick in decussate arrangement (or in whorls of 3 rows). The upper side of the leaf blades have a longitudinal furrow; these are gray-green with dark flecks and show 3 to 7 small teeth on both sides at the tip. In their axils appear brood buds, similar to *K. daigremontiana;* with sufficient humidity the buds take root on the mother plant. When touched these plantlets fall to the ground and continue to grow into new plants. In the fall the main stem ends its growth with the formation of an inflorescence up to 30 cm long with numerous, large, pendulous, bell-shaped, brick-red to reddish violet-gray flowers.

A very pretty species, its mass production of brood buds soon make it a nusiance weed.

Kalanchoe uniflora (STAPF) HAMET [= *Kitchingia uniflora* STAPF; = *Bryophyllum uniflorum* (STAPF) BRGR.] (Plate 77,1)

is one of the epiphytic species of the mountain forests of central Madagascar, which adapts very well in cultivation as a hanging plant. Its reclining to creeping, rooted shoots have fleshy, glabrous, almost sessible, longitudinally oval, notched leaves up to 3 cm long. The large, pendulous, red flowers appear usually singly (but also in threes) in short-stalked inflorescences.

Among the succulent-leaf plants is also the genus

Pachyphytum LINK, KLOTSCH et OTTO,

a Mexican succulent group with the growth-form of ech-

everias. They are also grown the same. They are stemless or short-stemmed rosette plants with thick, fleshy, sometimes waxy leaves; the large, white or reddish flowers appear in initially nodding, later upright, dense inflorescences.

The most beautiful and most well-known species is

Pachyphytum oviferum J.E. PURP. (Plate 77,2),

the "egg" *Pachyphytum,* so called because of the very thick, almost egg-shaped, white, waxy leaves up to 4 cm long and 3.5 cm wide, which are attached to a short stem. The bell-shaped, reddish, yellow-tipped flowers appearing in the spring are in an unbranched cincinnus.

The plant requires a cool winter location and little water during the winter.

Less attractive is

Pachyphytum bracteosum LINE, KLOTZSCH et OTTO (Plate 77,3),

a stemmed rosette plant up to 30 cm tall. Its leaves are thick, fleshy, obovate, upright, short tipped, and white to gray. The inflorescences are up to 30 cm long, and the flowers are bright red, in a cincinnus.

Other species worthy of growing are *P. brevifolum* ROSE: *P. compactum* ROSE; *P. hookeri* (SD.) BRGR; *P. longifolium* ROSE; *P. uniflorum* ROSE; *P. werdermannii* v. POELLN, etc.

The plants cultivated under the name *Pachyveria* HAAGE et SCHMIDT are bi-generic hybrids of *Pachyphytum* and *Echeveria.*

Closely related to *Echeveria* and to *Pachyphytum* is the genus

Graptopetalum ROSE,

of which the beautiful

Graptopetalum filiferum (S. WATS.) WHITEHEAD

is pictured in Plate 77,9 as an example. The stemless rosettes are 5 to 6 cm in diameter and grow in dense mats. Their spatulate, green or brownish leaves are up to 3 cm long and terminate in a long, bristle-like hair tip. The inflorescences are ca. 5 to 8 cm long and are richly branched; the flowers are relatively large, with white petals that are reddish at the tip.

This is a very attractive and easily cultivated species.

Tacitus MORAN

A monotypic species until now represented by the single species *T. bellus* MORAN et MEYRAN, found in

127

northern Mexico (Sierra obscura), and which was found by A.B. LAU in 1972. The plant is very closely related to *Graptopetalum* but differs from it by the wide-open, bright-red flowers. Its leaves are numerous, forming a compact, stemless rosette 3 to 8 cm in diameter, sessile, broadly triangular, short tipped, 2 to 3.5 cm long and 1.5 to 2.8 cm wide, gray-green with reddish-brown margins. The inflorescences are axillary, with few flowers. The flowers are bright carmine red (see Color Plate .8, lower left), up to 3.8 cm wide, and the petals are elliptical oval, 6 to 10 cm wide, and short tipped. The stamens have red filaments. Further study will have to determine whether the differences between it and *Graptopetalum* are sufficient to establish a new genus.

Although the plant was discovered only a few years ago, its easy propagation and its striking flower color have caused it to become widespread in collections.

Propagation is as in *Graptopetalum* and *Echeveria* by leaf cuttings. (Literature: "*Tacitus bellus* R. MORAN and Y. MEYRAN, un nuevo genero y especie de *Crassulaceae* de Chihuahua, Mexico," in *Cactaceas y Succulentas Mexicanas*, vol. XIX, October–December, 1974.)

The genus

Sedum L.,

also known as "fat hen" or "wall pepper," with its ca. 500 species is the largest genus of Crassulaceae. Its main distribution area is on the northern half of the globe in the New World as well as in the Old World. Many species are winter hardy and even native to my area (Germany);[23] therefore, they can be used in rock gardens. The non-hardy, perennial, and highly succulent species come from the dry areas mostly in the New World, especially Mexico. Of these I list only a small selection.

Sedum allantoides ROSE (Plate 77,5)

is a loosely leafed mini-shrub 40 cm tall with roundish leaves that are 2 to 3 cm long and have whitish gray frosting and are slightly flattened and turned upwards on the upper side. The flowers, which appear in dense or loose cymes, are greenish white; flowering time is June and July. *Habitat:* Mexico near Oaxaca.

Sedum bellum ROSE (= *S. farinosum* ROSE),

because of its reclining to hanging shoots and its abundant flowers, is very suitable as a hanging plant. The dense, roun-

dish, oval leaves up to 3.5 cm long and 1 cm wide are frosted with mealiness. The white flowers appear in Janaury and February and are in loose, terminal cymes. *Habitat:* Mexico (Durango).

Another recommended hanging plant is

Sedum morganianum E. WALTH., (Plate 77,7),

a perennial from Mexico with creeping, reclining, densely leafed and therefore sausage-shaped shoots. Its leaves are thick, fleshy, lanceolate, pointed, ca. 2 cm long, arched upwards and lying loosely on the axis, and light grayish green, with a waxy frosting. Its flowers are bright to dark scarlet red.

Even in its non-blooming state it is a very attractive plant.

A species widely spread in cultivation is

Sedum nussbaumerianum BITTER,

a mini-shrub up to 40 cm tall with a loose leaf arrangement. The leaves are lanceolate, pointed, and are arranged at the ends of the shoots in a rosette. They are up to 5 cm long, have a slight keel on the under side, and are yellowish green, but turn brownish with red edges in bright sunlight. *Habitat:* Mexico (Veracruz).

Very closely related is

Sedum adolphii HAMET (Plate 77,6),

which has more lanceolate, blunt-tipped, fleshy leaves.

A very pretty plant resembling *Sedum allantoides* is

Sedum pachyphyllum ROSE (Color Plate 8,7),

a low semi-shrub with upright, later reclining, densely leafed branches. The round to club-shaped leaves are ca. 4 cm long and are arranged in a spiral terminating in a bright-red tip, which also gives the plant the name "booze nose." The red is more intensive as it gets more sunlight. The small, yellow flowers are insignificant and are gathered into a cyme.

Sedum rubrotinctum R.T. CLAUSEN

also has a beautiful red color in its easily broken, cylindrical leaves that are up to 2 cm long and 5 mm thick; in full sunlight the plant becomes a splendid red.

A frequently grown species is

Sedum palmeri S. WATS.,

a small, richly branched semi-shrub with reclining branches, which have at their tips rosettes of spatulate, short-tipped, bluish-green, waxy leaves. The large yellow-orange flowers are in loose cymes and appear in the spring. *Habitat:* Mexico.

Very similar to this is

Sedum compressum ROSE (Plate 75,2),

a small semi-shrub with ascending shoots that are up to 20 cm long. Its leaves are in a loose rosette, ca. 2 cm long, 2 cm wide, longitudinally oval, short tipped, and blue-green. The flowers

[23] These are not considered in this study.

Color Plate 7.

1 (ul) *Lithops turbiniformis* in its natural surroundings near Prieska. Coin is a
South African rand, for comparison of
size.

2 (ur) *Cheiridopsis peculiaris* on slate rocks near
Steinkopf

3 (mul) *Pleiospilus prismaticus,* in the Ceres Karroo

4 (mur) *Conophytum stephanii*

5 (mll) *Conophytum pearsonii*

6 (mlr) *Conophytum velutinum*

7 (ll) *Conophytum ectypum* var. *tischleri*

8 (lr) *Lithops divergens*

Plate 65.

a) *Aloe plicatilis*
b) *Aloe striata*, Meyer-
ingspoort, Long
Mountains (eastern
Cape Province)
c) *Lomatophyllum orientale*
d) *Chamaeloe africana*

Plate 66.

1 (ul) *Haworthia bolusii* var. *semiviva*

2 (ur) *Haworthia cymbiformis*

3 (ml) *Haworthia limifolia*

4 (mr) *Haworthia margaritifera*

5 (ll) *Haworthia maughanii*, in habitat during

the dry season near Calitzdorp. T
is a South African rand

6 (lr) *Haworthia maughanii* in cultivati

ur) *Haworthia truncata* forma *crassa* in habitat near Oudtshoorn, growing under brush

2 (ur) *Haworthia truncata* forma *crassa* in cultivation

3 (ml) *Haworthia retusa*

4 (mr) *Haworthia tesselata*

5 (ll) *Gasteria acinacifolia*, Trapps Valley, near Grahamstown (eastern Cape Province)

6 (lr) *Gasteria batesiana*

Plate 68.

1 (ul)   Left: *Haworthia attenuata*, next to ﬂowers magnified. Right: *Haworthia reinwardtii*

2 (ur)   *Poellnitzia rubriflora*

3 (ml)   *Haworthia viscosa*

4 (mm)   Left: *Astroloba aspera* next to single flowers magnified. Right: *Astroloba foliolosa*

5 (mr)   *Gasteria liliputana*

6 (ll)   *Gasteria brevifolia*

7 (lm)   *Gasteria pulchra*

8 (lr)   *Gasteria verrucosa*

Plate 69.

(ul) *Adromischus cristatus* (inflorescence somewhat shortened)
(uml) *Adromischus herrei*
(umr) *Adromischus* aff. *maculatus*
(ur) *Adromischus marianae*
(ml) *Adromischus schaeferianus*
(mr) *Aeonium arboreum* var. *atropurpureum*
(ll) *Aeonium canariense*, in a barranco on Gran Canaria (Canary Islands)
(lm) Young rosette of *Aeonium nobile*
(lr) *Aeonium tabulaeforme*, in a barranco on Teneriffe (Canary Islands)

Plate 70.

1 (ul) *Aeonium urbicum* on Teneriffe (Canary Islands)

2 (um) *Greenovia aurea*, in a barranco on Gran Canaria (Canary Islands)

3 (ur) *Cotyledon orbiculata*, Little Namaqualand

4 (ml) *Cotyledon ladismithiensis*

5 (mr) *Cotyledon undulata* (Willowmore District)

6 (ll) *Crassula alstonii*, Little Namaqualand near Riethuis

7 (lm) *Crassula arta*

8 (lr) *Crassula brevifolia*

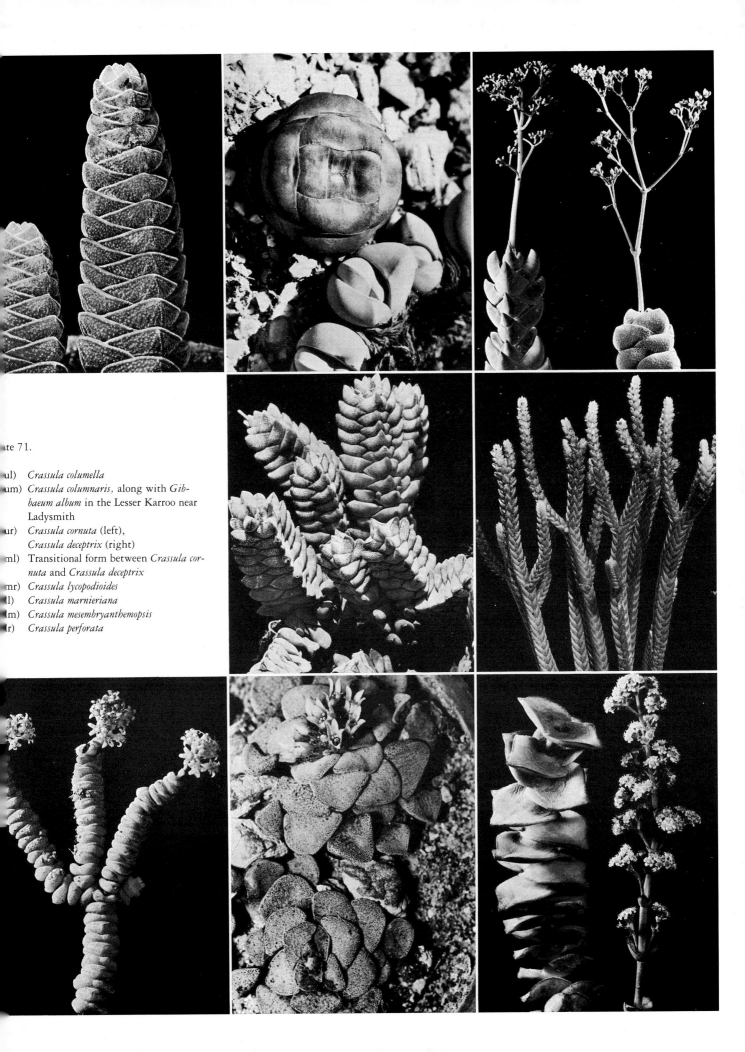

ate 71.

ul) *Crassula columella*

um) *Crassula columnaris,* along with *Gibbaeum album* in the Lesser Karroo near Ladysmith

ur) *Crassula cornuta* (left),
Crassula deceptrix (right)

ml) Transitional form between *Crassula cornuta* and *Crassula deceptrix*

mr) *Crassula lycopodioides*

ll) *Crassula marnieriana*

lm) *Crassula mesembryanthemopsis*

lr) *Crassula perforata*

Plate 72.

1 (ul) *Crassula socialis*
2 (um) *Crassula teres*
3 (ur) *Dudleya brittonii*
4 (ml) *Echeveria agavoides*
5 (mr) *Echeveria derenbergii*
6 (ll)   *Echeveria gibbiflora*
         var. *carunculata*
7 (lm) *Echeveria harmsii*
8 (lr)   *Echeveria leucotricha*

Plate 73.

(l) *Echeveria setosa*
(r) *Kalanchoe beharensis*, in
a dry forest near
Behara (southwest
Madagascar)
) *Kalanchoe jongmansii*
(Photo: J. Marnier-
Lapostolle)
) *Kalanchoe millotii*

Plate 74.

1 (ul) *Kalanchoe orgyalis* (inflorescence some-
        what shortened)
2 (um) *Kalanchoe pumila*
3 (ur) *Kalanchoe synsepala* with runners; above,
        single inflorescence
4 (ll) *Kalanchoe rhombopilosa*, normal form
5 (lm) White form of *Kalanchoe rhombopilosa*
6 (lr) *Kalanchoe scapigera* (= *K. farinacea*)

Plate 75. (facing page

1 (ul) *Kalanchoe bloss*
2 (ur) *Sedum compress*
3 (ml) *Kalanchoe mar*
4 (mr) *Sedum stahlii*
5 (ll)   *Kalanchoe tetra*
6 (lr)   *Villadia imbri*

Plate 76.

1 (ul) *Kalanchoe thyrs*...
plant beginnin...
flower (see 3)

2 (ur) *Kalanchoe tomen*...

3 (ll) Segment of an ...
rescence of *Ka*...
thyrsiflora (see ...

4 (lm) *Kalanchoe tubifl*...
plant with flo...
buds

5 (lr) Flowering *Kal*...
tubiflora

77.

Kalanchoe uniflora (Photo: J. Marnier-
Lapostolle)

2 (um)   Pachyphytum oviferum
3 (ur)   Pachyphytum bracteosum
4 (ml)   Sinocrassula yunnanensis
5 (mm)   Sedum allantoides

6 (mr)   Sedum adolphii
7 (ll)   Sedum morganianum
8 (lm)   Sedum sieboldii
9 (lr)   Graptopetalum filiferum

Plate 78.

1 (ul)   *Senecio antandroi*
2 (um)   *Senecio citriformis*
3 (ur)   *Senecio crassissimus*
4 (ml)   *Senecio ficoides*
5 (mr)   *Senecio decaryi*, near Ihosy
         (central Madagascar)
6 (ll)   *Senecio haworthii* in habitat (the
         Richtersveld near Karrachab)
7 (lm)   *Senecio haworthii* in cultivation
8 (lr)   *Senecio medley-woodii*

79.

) *Senecio mesembryanthe-moides*

·) *Senecio melastomaefolius*

) *Xerosicyos decaryi* near Tuléar (southern Madagascar)

) *Xerosicyos danguyi* with male flowers, near Ampanihy (southern Madagascar)

Plate 80.

1 (ul) *Othonna clavifolia*, in desert sand near
        Grotderm (the Richtersveld)

2 (ur) *Anacampseros alstonii*, old plant (see 4)
3 (ml) *Senecio herreanus*
4 (mr) Flowering *Anacampseros alstonii* (see 2)

5 (ll) *Senecio scaposus*
6 (lr) *Anacampseros albissima* in a quart
        (the Richtersveld)

are yellow-gold, in a short-stalked cincinnus. This plant is a willing bloomer.

Sedum sieboldii SWEET (Plate 77,8)

is an almost winter-hardy plant, which can withstand winters outside in protected places. In the fall the above-ground shoots die; from underground buds come new, reclining shoots in the spring, which are equipped with almost round, sessile, blue-green leaves that are serrate in the upper third. The flowers are pink in dense cymes. *Habitat:* Japan.

In var. *variegatum* hort. the leaves are mottled with yellow.

Let it spend the winter in a cool location; it is well suited as a hanging plant.

An interesting species is

Sedum stahlii SOLMS (Plate 75,4),

which, when given no nutrition and grown in a sunny location, remains short and compact with a bright-red color; when grown in a shady place, however, it etiolates and looses its beauty. Noteworthy is the fact that the small, ovate, dark-brownish red leaves, which are up to 12 mm long, fall at the slightest touch, take root, and produce new plants. The leaves function therefore as propagation organs (brood leaves); the flowers are yellowish, in loose cymes.

× Sedeveria hummellii E. WALTH.,

is a bi-generic hybrid of *Sedum pachyphyllum* and *Echeveria derenbergii.*

The members of the genus

Sempervivium L.,

also known by the various names "roof wort," "house leek," or "stone rose," have their main distribution area in the high mountains of Europe, Asia, and northern Africa. They are perennial, winter-hardy rosette plants, which are especially well suited for rock gardens but should not be grown in the home or greenhouse, because they etiolate and lose their typical growth-form. For this reason they will not be discussed here.

Very similar to the *Sempervivium* species in growth-form are the members of genus

Sinocrassula BRGR.,

distributed from the Himalayas to western China. They are biennial or perennial rosette plants, which formerly were assigned to the genus *Crassula.* They should be grown outside in the summer and overwintered in a cool location.

The best-known species is

Sinocrassula yunnanensis (FRANCH.) BRGR. (Plate 77,4),

a perennial rosette plant that forms dense tufts, and whose half-round leaves are flattened on the upper side, end in a sharp tip, and have finely papillous hair; they are of a dark-green to brownish red color. At flowering time the rosette dissolves and ends in a richly branched inflorescence ca. 20 cm long; the flowers are small and white.

Another common species is

Sinocrassula densirosulata (PRAEG.) BRGR.,

which differs from the above by its narrowly spatulate, pointed, gray leaves with red lines.

The genus

Villadia HAW. [= Altamiranoa (ROSE) E. WALTH.]

is comprised of small, insignificant succulents that resemble native *Sedum* species. They are distributed from Mexico to Peru.

Of the ca. 40 species I cite the following:

Villadia grandyi (HAMET) BAEHNI et MACBR. [= Sedum grandyi HAMET; = Altamiranoa grandyi (HAMET) BRGR.]

A plant of tuft-like growth, it has reclining to ascending stems up to 10 cm long, which are equipped loosely with oval-round, blunt leaves up to 5 mm long. Its flowers are small, white, in few-flowered dichasias. *Habitat:* central Peru.

Villadia imbricata ROSE [= Altamiranoa imbricata (ROSE) E. WALTH.] (Plate 75,6)

forms tufts or carpets with short, sausage-shaped, tightly imbricate shoots up to 6 cm long and branching from the base. Its flowers are small, white to pale red, in upright dichasias.

FAMILY ASTERACEAE
(= COMPOSITAE)

On page 108 I described some succulent members of this family in the stem succulents, *Othonna* L. and *Senecio* (TOURN.) L. These same genera also include a number of leaf succulents, of which the following are representative.

Othonna clavifolia MARL. (Plate 80,*1*)

is from the dry areas of Great Namaqualand and SW Africa. In habitat it is a splendid, reclining plant with a short stem and lateral branches equipped with fleshy, round or short-cylindrical leaves. Because the leaves turn dark wine red in the sun, they give the impression of juicy grapes lying in the sand. In cultivation, especially in the dimmer months, the plant completely looses its growth-form, the shoots elongate, and the leaves become long-cylindrical (up to 4 cm long); therefore, the plant should be grown close under glass. The flowers appear in long-peduncled clusters, yellow.

A striking succulent from the dry bush of southwestern Madagascar is

Senecio antandroi SCOTT-ELLIOT (Plate 78,*1*),

a climbing semi-shrub up to 2 m tall with thin, slightly woody shoots, which are arranged in a loose spiral and have cylindrical leaves up to 12 cm long. Their upper side has faint grooves, and they also have hooked tips, which support the plant in climbing. The flower heads are yellow, in a loose panicle.

Similar and also from Madagascar is

Senecio canaliculatus BOJ. ex DC.

a mini-shrub up to 60 cm tall growing on gneiss and granite hills of the central highlands. It has cylindrical leaves up to 7.5 cm long, which have a furrow on the upper side. Its flower heads are yellow, in a loose panicle.

Senecio citriformis ROWLEY (Plate 78,*2*)

reclines and sprawls, sometimes having upright shoots. Its leaves are thick, fleshy, spherical, pointed, shaped like a lemon, bluish gray, and waxy with prominent nerves. The flowers are cream-colored to yellow, in inflorescences 5 to 15 cm long. *Habitat:* Cape Province.

Senecio crassissimus H. HUMB. (Plate 78,*3*),

a remarkable leaf succulent from Madagascar, is a multi-branched semi-shrub up to 80 cm tall with glabrous, somewhat fleshy branches frequently overlaid with blue-violet. The widely spaced, short-petioled, broadly oval leaves end in a short thorn tip and appear in profile, i.e., their blades are oriented vertically and their narrow margin is directed toward the light. The yellow, numerous heads are arranged in a loose panicle.

There are several forms of *S. crassissimus,* which are distinguished by leaf size and color.

In the South African

Senecio ficoides (L.) SCH. BIP. [= *Kleinia ficoides* (L.) HAW.] (Plate 78,*4*),

a semi-shrub succulent that is up to 1 m tall, the deep bluish green, waxy leaves are also vertical. In this plant, however, the profile is less distinct than in *S. crassissimus,* because the leaves are considerably longer and narrower. The flowers are whitish yellow.

Another species from Madagascar is

Senecio decaryi H. HUMB. (Plate 78,*5*),

a richly branched semi-shrub up to 1.5 m tall with thick branches, which are woody at the base. The leaves are sessile, upright, spatualte, lanceolate-oval, pointed, up to 6 cm long, and grayish green with protruding nerves. The flower heads are numerous in a peduncled, loose, terminal panicle.

A plant found in every succulent collection is

Senecio haworthii (HAW.) SCH. BIP. (Plate 78,*6–7*),

known to hobbyists as *Kleinia tomentosa.* Although the plant was introduced into England more than 150 years ago, its actual habitat is unknown. In 1963 I was able to collect it in rather large stands in Richtersveld near Karrachab on marble-like limestone (Plate 78,*6*). There it forms richly branched shrubs up to 50 cm tall, whose shoots are slightly woody at the base and are equipped with thick, cylindrical, very white-felted leaves, which develop new growth from both ends (Plate 78,*7*). In cultivation it seldom flowers. It requires a bright, sunny location and must be kept completely dry in the winter.

Suitable for dish gardens and hanging pots is

Senecio herreanus DTR. (= *Kleinia gomphophylla* DTR.) (Plate 80,*3*).

Its low, crawling, thin shoots take root on the bottom and bear upright, thick, fleshy, almost spherical, short-tipped leaves that resemble goose berries. On their upper side they have a narrow window without chloroplasts. The nerves protrude as dark green stripes, and the flower heads are small and insignificant. The plant is attractive solely because of its remarkable leaves, which are prettiest when they get a lot of sunlight.

Similar is

Senecio radicans (L. f.) SCH. BIP.,

whose leaves are long and cylindrical.

Senecio medley-woodii HUTCHINS. (Plate 78,*8*)

is distinguished by a white, woolly web on its leaves. Its habitat is Natal. It is a semi-shrub up to 80 cm tall, and its leaves are wedge-shaped and slightly dentate in the top third, with dense, white woolly hairs, but it is glabrous in old age. The flower heads are large, up to 5 cm in diameter, with yellow daisy-like flowers in long-stalked panicles. This plant requires a lot of sun and little water.

A remarkable Madagascar leaf succulent resembling South African mesembs is

Senecio mesembryanthemoides BOJ. ex DC. (Plate 79,*1*),

which in habitat (highlands of central Madagascar between 1500 and 2500 m) forms dense carpets. From a richly branched, fleshy, almost tuberous rhizome emerge numerous thin but short, reclining lateral branches, which bear numerous, spatulate, glabrous leaves that are frequently violet on the under side and dark green above. The leaves are in a dense rosette; the single rosettes join into a compact tuft and have a diameter of 3 to 5 cm each. The flower heads are yellow, single, on a long scape.

This is an easily propagated and easily grown species.

Another leaf succulent from the central Madagascar highlands is

Senecio melastomaefolius BAK. (Plate 79,*2*),

a richly branched semi-shrub up to 60 cm tall. Its branches are densely covered with leaves, and the leaves are thick, fleshy, oval, up to 3 cm long, with the under side having 3 protruding, longitudinal nerves; flower heads yellow in sparse numbers in branched, long-stalked inflorescences.

Further semi-shrubby, Madagascar, leaf-succulent senecios worthy of mention are *S. baronii* H. HUMB.; *S. barorum* H. HUMB.; *S. capuronii* H. HUMB.; *S. leandrii* H. HUMB.; *S. marnieri* H. HUMB.; *S. neobakeri* H. HUMB.; *S. navicularis* H. HUMB.; *S. sakamaliensis* (H. HUMB.) HUMB.; *S. meuselii* RAUH.

Senecio scaposus DC. (Plate 80,*5*)

is a stemless rosette plant with numerous cylindrical leaves sometimes flattened on the upper side, reaching upwards, 5 to 8 cm long. In youth these are covered with a web-like hair coat, which with age disappears. The flower heads are in groups of 1 to 5, yellow, on a short scape.

Very attractive, it should be watered only lightly in winter.

Variety *caulescens* HAW. differs from the type by its forming finger-size, branched stems up to 40 cm long and by its flattened leaves standing out from the axis.

FAMILY CUCURBITACEAE

Leaf-succulent cucumbers are rare in European and American collections. They belong exclusively to the genus

Xerosicyos H. HUMB.

from the dry forests of southwest Madagascar. Four species have been described.

The most common and, at the same time, the prettiest is

Xerosicyos danguyi H. HUMB. (Plate 79,*4*),

a liane, which climbs with the aid of forked, branched tendrils.

It grows up to 5 m long. If the plant finds no support, its shoots arch over; they are woody at the base and have short-petioled, round, short-tipped, thick, fleshy, gray-waxy to green leaves up to 4 cm in size. The small, unisexual flowers appear in umbel clusters emerging from the axils and are yellowish green. The fruits are small capsules that open with a lid; they differ considerably from the normal cucumber fruits.

A very pretty plant, it is easy to propagate from cuttings.

X. perrieri H. HUMB. has considerably smaller, grass-green leaves ending in a sharp tip.

Similar to this is *X. decaryi* GUILL. ex GUILL. ex KER., whose leaves are more longitudinally oval (Plate 79,*3*).

Xerosicyos pubescens M. KER., recently described by M. KERAUDREN, differs from all previously known species by its pubescent leaves and a large, basal stem caudex.

FAMILY PORTULACACEAE

The family of portulacas also has numerous succulents both in the stem-succulent and in the leaf-succulent groups, which belong to the genera *Anacampseros, Ceraria, Portulaca, Portulacaria,* and *Talinum.*

Anacampseros L.,

has representatives of both growth-forms, i.e., stem succulents and leaf succulents. The former are in the section

Avonia, the latter in section Anacampseros.

The members of section Avonia are the so-called white *Anacampseros* species, coveted but not always easy to cultivate. From a short, succulent, sometimes woody stem equipped with fleshy roots and sometimes growing under ground emerge numerous, sausage-shaped or angular shoots, which have small leaves arranged in a spiral. Because these are completely covered by large, tissue-like, silvery stipules, the shoots appear to be completely white and without chlorophyl (see Plate 5,6).

All these species require a porous, sandy-loamy soil, a bright, sunny location, little water during the summer months, and a complete rest during the winter.

The leaf-succulent *Anacampseros* species are low growers with fleshy roots. Their thin shoots have dense, succulent, frequently pubescent leaves, in whose axils are long hairs representing modified stipules; they serve to absorb water (dew or fog) (see Plate 5,4).

Cultivation of these species is much easier than those of section Avonia. They grow fast, require more water in the summer, and can be propagated easily from cuttings.

The inflorescences of all *Anacampseros* species are single or multiple; the large, white or reddish flowers appearing in the summer open in the late evening hours or remain completely closed. Nevertheless they produce seed from self-fertilization.

The genus *Anacampseros* owes its name to the superstition of South African natives, who believe that this little plant can return lost love. They are therefore known also as "love roses."

The distribution area of the genus comprises the dry areas of South Africa and Namibia. One species, *A. australiana* J.M. BLACK, which has been placed in its own section Tuberosa V. POELLN., is found in southwestern Australia.

Section AVONIA

From this section I recognize around 20 species, of which the following are the best known and the most beautiful.

Anacampseros albissima MARL. (Plate 80,6),

native to South Africa and Namibia, is an unqualified quartz plant, which grows only in quartz fields and with its shoots is hardly distinguishable from the environment. Its branches are numerous, thin, cylindrical, and reclining, emerging from a short, fleshy axis equipped with fleshy roots. The stipules are small, pressed tight to the shoot axis, sometimes with brown dots; the flowers are terminal, white, and appear singly or in groups of 2 to 3.

One of the most remarkable species is

Anacampseros alstonii SCHOENL. (Plate 80,2–4).

It forms a body up to 10 cm in diameter, which is fleshy, slightly woody, shaped like an inverted cone, gradually extending into one or more fleshy roots, unsegmented, hidden underground right up to the flat top. On the top surface it has a large number of small, thin, silvery-gray shoots up to 20 mm long, with 4 to 5 angles (Plate 80,2). As it ages the central shoots die, while at the periphery of the axis body, new shoots are continually being formed. The flowers are up to 2 cm in size, single on elongated stalks whitish or slightly reddish (Plate 80,4).

A difficult species, it should not be planted too deep, because otherwise it is easily subject to rot. In habitat the plant is hidden in the ground up to the tips of the shoots.

This plant requires a very sunny, dry, warm location.

Anacampseros herreana V. POELLN. (Plate 81,1)

grows among quartz boulders near Kuboes in Richtersveld (Great Namaqualand). It has a fleshy root, from which emerge few, irregularly branched, thin shoots up to 10 cm long. The bracts, which lie close to the shoot axis, have brown nerves and therefore give the entire plant a brownish appearance.

The natives call it the "beer plant," because beer is brewed from the fleshy roots.

Also a typical plant from the quartz fields is

Anacampseros papyracea E. MEY. (Plate 81,2; Plate 5,6),

probably the prettiest species of the *Avonia* group. Its reclining shoots, also emerging from a very short, fleshy axis, are sausage-shaped and ca. 1 cm thick. The small, dark-green leaves are completely wrapped in the stipules, which are large, like parchment, and lie close to the shoot axis, so that the shoots look as if they were wrapped in waxy paper; the species name refers to this fact. Flowers are whitish green, and single.

Very closely related to this species is

Anacampseros meyeri V. POELLN. (Plate 81,3),

which prefers to grow in clefts in the quartz rocks of Namaqualand; it differs from the above by its sparse, flared bracts giving the 7 cm long shoots a shaggy appearance. Its flowers are single and white.

Also in the same section are:
A. *bremekampii* V. POELLN. (Transvaal)
A. *buderiana* V. POELLN. (Great Namaqualand)
A. *decipiens* V. POELLN. (Transvaal)
A. *dinteri* SCHINZ (the Richtersveld)
A. *fissa* V. POELLN. (Pretoria)
A. *neglecta* V. POELLN. (Great Namaqualand)
A. *ombonensis* DTR. et V. POELLN. (Namibia)
A. *quinaria* E. MEY. (Namibia)
A. *recurvata* SCHOENL. (Namaqualand)

A. rhodesica N.E. BR. (Zimbabwe)
A. ruschii DTR. et V. POELLN. (Great Namaqualand)
A. schmidtii (BRGR) V. POELLN. (the Richtersveld)
A. somaliensis V. POELLN. (Somalia)
A. ustulata E. MEY. (southeastern Cape Province)
A. variabilis V. POELLN. (the Richtersveld)
A. wischkonii DTR. et V. POELLN. (SW Africa)

Section ANACAMPSEROS

These species are less attractive; their leaves are plain green (or in intense light somewhat reddish), but sometimes wrapped in a hairy net.

Anacampseros baeseckei DTR.

is a small plant up to 5 cm tall and branching from the base. Its thin shoots are equipped with dense, shingled, small, wedge-shaped, rounded, white, hairy leaves, in whose axils are long, brownish hairs. Its inflorescences have few flowers, and the petals are carmine red with white margins.

Very similar is

A. densifolia DTR. (Namibia),

which differs from the above by its longer, white bristles, which near the tips of the shoots unite into a white tuft. Its flowers are vivid red-violet.

Fuzzy leaves are found also on
Anacampseros karasmontana DTR. (Namibia). Flowers red-violet.
Anacampseros lanigera BRUCH. (South Africa). Flowers red-violet. (Plate 81,4).
Anacampseros tomentosa BRGR. (Namibia). Flowers red-violet.

Of the species with glabrous leaves I cite:

Anacampseros filamentosa (HAW.) SIMS (Plate 5,4),

a species that is widespread not only in its habitat (Karoo-Namaqualand), but also in collections. It is variable, with stems up to 5 cm long, with fleshy roots and densely arranged leaves that are thick, longitudinally oval to round, end in a short tip, and are loosely hairy. The bristles are very long, white, and twisted; the inflorescences have 3–5 large, red-violet flowers.

Anacampseros lanceolata (HAW.) SWEET.

(Little Karoo and Namaqualand). Its shoots are richly branched; the leaves are numerous, narrowly lanceolate, and short tipped, with the upper side flat and the under side extremely vaulted. The bristles are numerous, white, shiny, and curly, and the inflorescences have 1 to 4 red-violet flowers.

Anacampseros rufescens (HAW.) SWEET.

(southeastern Cape Province and Lesotho). Closely related to *A. filamentosa,* this plant has a fleshy root. Its shoots are richly branched from the base, upright or reclining, and up to 8 cm long, with dense leaves. The leaves are longitudinally oval, pointed, with their blades somewhat recurved, and have the upper side green and the under side reddish brown. The bristles are numerous, whitish yellow, and up to 2 cm long; the flowers

are red-violet.

Native to southeastern Cape Province is

Anacampseros telephiastrum DC. (Plate 81,5),

the largest species of the genus, which at maturity forms rather large tufts. The leaves are in compact rosettes, oval-round to lanceolate, ca. 2 cm long, short tipped, very thick, greenish to brownish. The bristles are wide spreading and short, and the inflorescences are up to 15 cm long, with 1 to 4 large, carmine-red flowers.

A genus little known in Europe is

Ceraria PEARS. et STEPHENS,

The "wax bush," which is represented by few species in the dry areas of South Africa.

Ceraria namaquensis (SOND.) PEARS. et STEPHENS (Plate 82,1–2),

found in Namaqualand and Richtersveld, is a shrub up to 2.5 m tall with many wide-spreading branches and a thick, woody stem base. The rod-shaped branches are equipped with a smooth, light-gray, papery bark. In the axils of the deciduous, small, long-shoot leaves arise short shoots that, as with the Didiereaceae, each year produce 2 to 5 small, wedge-shaped, gray, waxy, succulent leaves that are 3 to 5 mm long (Plate 82,1). These leaves are cast off at the end of each vegetative period. The flowers are unisexual, dioecious, small, appear in panicles, and are white or red (Plate 82,2).

Very attractive, it is not easy to grow; like the following it requires a bright, sunny location. It grows well when it is grafted to *Portulacaria afra.*

Ceraria pygmaea (PILL.) PILL. (Plate 81,6)

is a common mini-shrub in the quartz fields of Richtersveld and has a remarkable growth-form. Like *Anacampseros alstonii* it has an irregular, knotty stem, which is up to 10 cm thick, almost completely buried in the ground, and which merges into a long, fleshy root. The stem bears a large number of very short branches with decussate leaves. The plant thus assumes an almost mound-shaped growth, which is lost in cultivation, however, because of elongation of the shoots. The leaves are very fleshy, wedge-shaped to almost round, with a gray, waxy frosting, becoming bright red-violet in intense sunlight. Flowers appear in groups of 4 to 6, white or reddish, in sessile inflorescences.

Propagation by cuttings is possible, but these do not assume the growth-form of a seedling. Propagation is easy by grafting onto *Portulacaria.*

Portulaca L.

Portulaca grandiflora HOOK. (Plate 82,3)

has become a favorite garden plant in recent years. It is an annual from Brazil, which today appears on the market in many forms with white, yellow, red, or violet, simple or double flowers. Its shoots are reclining or ascending, with short, cylindrical, fleshy leaves. The flowers are up to 4 cm in diameter, in groups of 2 to 4, in terminal inflorescences. The seed is sown early in the spring in sandy, humusy soil, preferably in paper pots; these are then put into the open ground in a sunny location without repotting. In just a few weeks you can then have a beautifully colorful flower carpet.

All other *Portulaca* species are either so unattractive that they are hardly of interest to the hobbyist or they are so rare (e.g., *P. poellnitziana* WERDERM. et JACOBS.) that they are impossible to obtain.

Portulacaria JACQ.

A commonly grown plant reluctant to bloom in cultivation is the "Spekboom" of the Africans,

Portulacaria afra (L.) JACQ. (Plate 82,4),

a shrub with wide-spreading branches, with fleshy, gray-brown, tough stems up to 5 cm thick and sessile, succulent, oval to round, glabrous leaves. The dioecious, pink, very small flowers are found in panicles.

A fast-growing plant, it is easily propagated from cuttings.

More decorative is its yellow form *(foliis variegatis)*, which is also suitable for growing in the home.

In habitat (eastern Transvaal to southwestern Cape area) *P. afra* forms dense populations in the undergrowth of dry forests on stony slopes (Plate 82,4); in tropical and subtropical areas (as close as the Mediterranean) it is suitable as a hedge plant.

FAMILY MESEMBRYANTHEMACEAE (= AIZOACEAE = FICOIDACEAE)

The "mid-day flowers," known among succulent collectors simply as "mesembs," are strictly Old World plants, limited in their natural distribution exclusively to the dry areas of Namibia and South Africa.[24] The common name "mid-day flower" refers to the fact that the first known genera and species do not open their flowers until around noon, i.e., when the sun is at its highest point; but today a whole series of species is known, which are only "night bloomers."

Of all the families, mesembs have the largest number of leaf succulents; as of now over 2000 species are recognized, which are compiled in approximately 150 genera. More species are continuously being described; I have probably gone too far and have conceived the notion of species much too narrowly. A revision of the family will doubtless lead to recognizing some genera as superfluous and they will be combined with others.

The genus *Mesembryanthemum* was established by C. LINNAEUS as early as 1753, and it remained for nearly 160 years the only genus of the family. Around the turn of the century HAWORTH undertook to subdivide them, but for a while it remained as it was. Not until the appearance of the South African botanist N.E. BROWN and the archaeologist G. SCHWANTES from Kiel took on the task of creating a system for the family was a cate-

gorizing established which is still generally valid today. The most recent, comprehensive classification of the family is the work of the famous South African botanist Dr. H. HERRE: *The Genera of the* MESEMBRYANTHEMACEAE, Cape Town, 1971.

Because of their enormous numbers, the mesembs present themselves in a wide variety of growth forms: there are shrubs 1 to 2 m tall, whose woody shoots have succulent leaves but are not really succulents in the strict sense; and there are those remarkable plants that look like pebbles, produce only one pair of highly succulent leaves each year, and are referred to as "living stones." It is these plants that stir up a real collecting mania among hobbyists, but the bushy species, which require a lot of space and become unsightly, attract only a little attention.

The mesembs are exclusively inhabitants of extremely arid regions. They live in the lower areas of southern Africa, the Little and Central Karroo (including Bushman Land), Little and Great Namaqualand as well as the southern Namib desert, in other words areas with yearly

[24] One species, *Delosperma nakurense* (ENGL.) HERRE, grows in the highlands of Kenya; a few annual species are found in northern Africa, Arabia, the Canary Islands, Madagascar, and in the coastal areas of Australia, Chile, Peru, and California.

precipitation under 200 mm or even under 100 mm. Precipitation comes either as winter rain, as in the southern Cape Province area, or as summer rain, which sometimes does not occur at all, as is the case in the regions north of the Cape area, in which, however, wet fogs are not uncommon. The rich lichen vegetation attests to this fact. Often, places in which conophytes grow will be completely covered with lichen thalli (Plate 83,1).

As already indicated in the introduction, all these dry areas are actually sparse in vegetation and have only a scattered covering of plants. Among these, however, especially in the Karroo, the shrubby mesembs play an important role and make up almost 90% of all the vegetation, and so frequently one speaks of a "mesemb steppe." In places it can comprise many square kilometers of flat area. In the dry season such a landscape gives a dry, almost disconsolate impression, but as soon as the first rains come, the picture changes drastically. Overnight the Karroo changes into a blooming garden (Color Plate 1,2–3). As far as the eye can see, there is a sea of colorful flowers. Great and small shrubs of *Lampranthus, Drosanthemum, Aridaria, Delosperma, Ruschia,* etc., are covered with hundreds of silky, shimmering, white, yellow, red, or violet flowers. Between them spread the yellow, white, and blue coloration of many annuals, especially of composites, tuberous, and bulb plants. The flowering Karroo therefore remains in the memory of any Africa traveller and at the time of bloom draws thousands of visitors from the surrounding towns. The splendor lasts only a few weeks, however, and as soon as the rains stop, the annuals wither first, and soon the mesemb bushes again withdraw into their dry, brown coat.

Only relatively few mesembryanthemum genera are distributed over the entire succulent area of South Africa; many, especially the highly succulent ones such as *Lithops, Conophytum, Titanopsis,* etc., have only a small areale distribution and are often found only at one single spot. Their habitats are not the hard, reddish-brown Karroo soil, but rather the quartz fields (see page 16) or clefts in the quartz and primordial rocks (Plate 83,2). It is always surprising to note the meager requirements of these plants, which sit in narrow slits in the rocks and survive with the little water that penetrates to them. For more than three-quarters of the year no water droplets reach them, and they exist during this time exclusively on dew and fog.

Because of the extremely dry locations, the mesembs also demonstrate an abundance of morphological adaptations and forms that serve only to adjust to the supply of water. Mainly water reservoirs are formed; these are provided by the leaves in some species, and also the shoots or the roots in others. Water-storage roots are found in *Aridaria, Delosperma, Ruschia,* and *Trichodiadema* species. In these, the above-ground shoots frequently die during the dry period, and from the surviving root stocks emerge new shoots at the beginning of the vegetative period.

The water content of the leaves can reach 95% of their dry substance, and almost the entire leaf tissue is water-storage parenchyma, with the exception of the peripheral assimilation tissue. The cells, however, do not just hold water but also mucous and rather large amounts of dissolved salts, especially in those species that grow on very salty soil.

The upper surface of the leaves of many species is pebbled with water-filled, bubble-like emergences, whose shiny surface reflects the sunlight and is thus said to protect the plant from the sun. In others, e.g., *Trichodiadema,* the leaves have hairs, which according to MARLOTH are capable of absorbing moisture (fog and dew) from the air, as was already mentioned in the introduction (see also Plate 5,3). Wax coverings and hairy coats reduce the evaporation of water; an effective protection against too much water loss is provided also by the reduction of the entire leaf surface, which is very extreme in *Lithops, Conophytum, Ophthalmophyllum, Dinteranthus, Muiria,* etc. All members of these genera produce each year only a single pair of highly succulent, water-storing leaves (the successive leaf pairs appear in alternating whorls), which are often unified up to a small slit. Thus a narrow canal (Figure 15, Sp) is formed, which bears the shoot tip at its base. Such a leaf pair, along with the very short shoot axis (Figure 15,A) is commonly referred to as the "body." Many such bodies, which themselves often reach a diameter of only a few millimeters, can branch repeatedly and from compact mounds (Plate 83,2–4). At the end of each growth period the old leaves begin to shrivel into a papery skin; they are drained and their nutrients and especially their water are used to form the new leaf pair; but this new pair remains covered by the papery skin during the long dry period and is thus protected against water loss. In the dry period a *Conophytum* mound thus appears to be dead (Plate 83,3–4); but if you remove the dry skin you

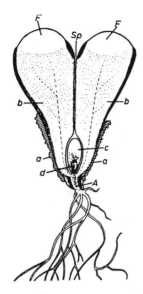

Figure 15. *Lithops salicola*. Longitudinal section of one "body." A = its axis; a = the dried leaf pair from the previous year, b = this year's leaf pair with the window (F) and the split (Sp); c and d are the beginnings of next year's leaf pair.

will find beneath it the green, although small, new leaf organs. As soon as the first rain falls, these begin to swell quickly and begin to grow, breaking the old skin, but the skin remains on the shoot axis for years (Figure 16,1). By counting the number of these collar-like paper hulls you can determine the age of a shoot or of a whole plant (Plate 83,4).

Many highly succulent mesembs, such as *Ophthalmophyllum, Lithops, Fenestraria,* etc., as MARLOTH cited in the example of *Lithops optica,* are hidden in the ground so far that only the end surfaces of the "bodies," i.e., their seemingly hacked-off leaves are visible and these plants, therefore, in their non-blooming stage can hardly be found. So that these leaves can assimilate, "windows" and "inner assimilation surfaces" have been formed. I already referred to this fact in the introduction (see p. 20). The tip of the hacked-off leaf has no assimilation parenchyma, and inside it the central water tissue reaches right up to the epidermis. Thus, as in *Haworthia truncata,* a window is formed which in back light appears to be as clear as glass and through which the light rays fall and reach the assimilation tissue of the leaf surface only by traversing the water tissue. In doing so the light intensity is diminished; the formation of windows is therefore interpreted as a protection against strong sun radiation, as mentioned above.

The most beautiful example of a "window plant" is the "window leaf," *Fenestraria* itself, a rosette plant with a short axis, which bears a rather large number of upright, club-shaped, cylindrical to bluntly triangular leaves, which at their tip have a large triangular window (see Plate 4,3–4). In habitat the plant grows in sandy soil, from which only the window peeps through (see Plate 4,3). Often, even it is completely covered with sand and in its non-blooming stage can be found only if one knows the exact location and has a broom to sweep away the sand. Such window leaves, however, are found in many species of the genus *Ophthalmophyllum* and in *Frithia pulchra* (see Plate 88,6). In these, too, the leaf tip is totally without chloroplasts and is filled with water-storage tissue. Many *Lithops* and also *Conophytum* species do not have such large windows, but have a whole network of mini-windows, i.e., the upper leaf surface is covered by a system of net-like lines, which in the light appear as dark dots, but in penetrating light appear as light stripes or dots. Whether these have the same function as the windows of *Fenestraria* is not yet clear.

The root system of mesembs is generally well developed. It either penetrates in the form of a tap root into the water table, or the roots reach broadly just under the soil surface so that they are able to absorb the smallest trace of moisture coming from fog or dew.

In the discussion of mesembs one must also think of another phenomenon known as "mimesis," "camouflage," or "adaptation." It plays a large role in the highly succulent mesembs. I have already spoken of mimesis in various regards and have given a number of examples. Among the mesembs is the place to investigate this remarkable phenomenon somewhat further, which for a long time was known only in the animal world.

A fine example of mimesis is the chameleon, which can match its surroundings by changing its color and thus escape the sight of its enemies. Among grasshoppers there are species such as the "walking leaf" (Phyllium), which in its resting state is not distinguishable from a dried leaf; "walking sticks" imitate dry branches. From South Africa there are field grasshoppers that are known by older naturalists as "jumping stones" and which match their environment perfectly in form and color; they live in quartz fields, are whitish-bluish color or, in the primordial rock fields, brownish red and can be distinguished from the surrounding stone only when they move. These few examples could be extended many times over.

In the plant kingdom, however, especially among the mesembs, there are excellent examples of mimesis, particularly in the genera *Lithops, Conophytum, Pleiospilos, Lapidaria, Dinteranthus,* etc. They look so much like stones (as the genera names often indicate), that they are simply called "living stones." Like the grasshoppers mentioned above, they match their environment so closely in form and color that in their non-blooming state they can hardly be distinguished, and you must hunt around on your knees in order to find these plants at all. At bloom time, of course, they can be found by their large, white, yellow, or red flowers. Most reports on such "living stones" originate from the botanist BURCHELL from the year 1822, who found *Lithops turbiniformis* in the vicinity of Prieska (Color plate 7,1). He wrote: "When I raised the object, which I at first took to be a peculiarly formed pebble, from the rocky ground, I was surprised that it turned out to be a plant. But in color and shape it bore a striking resemblance to the rocks between which it was growing."

The lithops are prime examples of adaptation to the environment: species from the gray-blue limestone areas have a gray color; others that thrive in red, iron-rich soil, show the color of their surroundings (see Color Plate 7,*a*). It is remarkable, though, that these colors are retained even in cultivation.

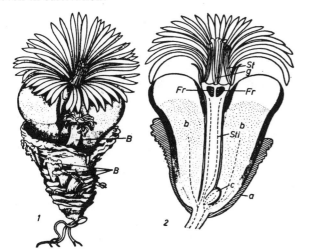

Figure 16. *Lithops olivacea. 1,* A flowering plant with the remains of the old, withered leaves and the dried flower (B) from the previous year. *2,* Longitudinal section of the plant pictured in *1.* a = last year's leaf pair, b = this year's leaf pair, c = the beginnings of next year's leaf pair. Sti = flower stem; Fr = ovaries; g = pistil; St = stamens.

A similar situation exists for *Dinteranthus* species, e.g., *D. pole-evansii.* The plant is white, spherical, and grows only in quartz fields. In shape and color it is identical to the surrounding rocks (Plate 83,5). When we were trying to collect them around Upington (Bushman Land), we took three whole hours to gather a dozen specimens.

The South African botanist MARLOTH should be given credit for detailed observations of mimesis. For example, when writing of *Pleispilos bolusii* from the Little Karroo he says: "The plant generally produces only two leaves, which reach approximately the size of a duck egg. Its top surface is rough like weathered rock and its color is brownish grey with a tinge of green. The leaves are buried half in the soil or in the rocks in which the plant grows; thus it requires a good eye to find them in their non-blooming stage. But in the fall, when their light-yellow flowers of more than 5 cm diameter appear between the leaves, the plant is very striking. But that does not last long, and during the dry season it looks exactly like a piece of rock."

Another striking example of plant mimesis is *Titanopsis calcarea,* which fits into its surroundings so well that it is almost indetectable (Plate 83,6). R. MARLOTH writes about it: "The leaves form a dense rosette and their upper surface, in so far as it is visible, is covered with irregular protruberances or warts, which look exactly like the white pieces of tufaceous limestone, among which the plant grows. No artist could imitate the surface structure and the color of the limestone better and more exactly as nature has done in this case."

Several examples could be cited for the phenomenon of protective coloring and fitting into the environment. I will only mention that almost all succulents with white body color such as *Gibbaeum, Dinteranthus, Argyroderma,* and also some *Crassula* species such as *C. alstonii, C. deceptrix* and the white *Anacampseros* species from the section Avonia are residents exclusively of the quartz fields. Plants with a brown color, on the other hand, such as *Pleispilos bolusii, P. nelii,* etc., are limited in their distribution to the rather brownish primordial stone. The reasons for this are not known, although much has been written about plant mimesis and much more has been speculated.

In general it is thought that this phenomenon is a protection against being eaten by animals. Because of its juiciness and its often pleasant, fresh, tart, sometimes

137

somewhat salty taste, these plants are sought by wild animals such as monkeys, antelopes, hares, and turtles. According to DINTER, *Lithops pseudotruncatella,* to cite just one example, is not only sought by monkeys but it is also found by them. Of the animals introduced by humans I must mention mainly goats and sheep as eaters of these plants whenever they can get to them. They also cause great damage since they trample the plants when they move in great herds across the locales of succulents.

According to POLE-EVANS, a special danger is presented by the non-native ostrich in South Africa: "These birds destroy the majority of the plants, especially mesembryanthema and young aloes. They find every hidden corner of the veldt, and I consider it quite probable that many succulents from these areas will never be seen again."

In addition to animals, however, humans, especially passionate collectors, play perhaps the largest role as destroyers. Since many of the highly succulent mesembs are known only in one location and even there occupy just a very limited area, a number of species have already been destroyed by collectors and can be found only in cultivation. It is therefore a welcome measure that the South African government has begun to take strict action regarding protection of the environment. Only in this way can the unique vegetation of South Africa be kept for posterity.

As reflected in the findings of numerous botanists as well as my own observations, one must refrain from ascribing too much significance to mimesis. The protection received by these plants by their camouflage is not absolute. Animals, especially sheep and goats, find the plants in spite of the rock-like appearance, especially when in times of drought there is no other nutrition in the dry areas. The last word on the phenomenon of mimesis, however, has not been spoken. The Swiss botanist J. SCHITTLER[25] writes: "We ask whether these plants have been given their striking qualities by chance or by a mere whim of nature. Or is there an active attempt to fit into the surroundings on the part of the plants, as LAMARK taught around 1800? Have the mesembs really so much 'inventive spirit,' to outfit themselves and to protect themselves in such a clever way, and have the starving animals of the desert been so stupid to let themselves be fooled for generations by these 'clever' plants? These are obvious but improbable assumptions of human thinking,

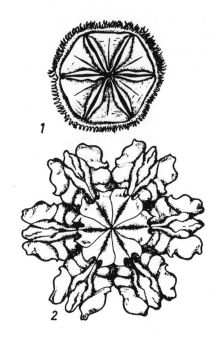

Figure 17. *Gibbaeum velutinum. 1,* Closed capsule; *2,* open capsule (somewhat modified from a drawing by NEL).

which tends to look for simple explanations. But can it not also be that from the endless multiplicity of nature and the abundance of forms developed by plants in the course of many millions of years there have been a few which have survived much better under the given conditions? They survived because they were best adapted and designed for the conditions. They became the victors in the fight for nutrition, light, and space, and were able to preserve their race throughout the history of the earth up to the present day, while many other species disappeared and, if we are lucky, we can observe them as fossils. Even among plants there is a continuous coming and going. No matter how we look at the matter, the living rocks will remain a puzzle to us."

The "flowers" of the mesembryanthemums are distinguished by the very special beauty, size, glowing color (red, yellow, orange, white), and by the silky sheen of their numerous, narrowly lineal to ligulate petals. In their outer form they resemble a composite flower (Figure 16,*1*), as their numerous stamens imitate the disks of the Asteraceae. As mentioned above, the flowers of many of the species open only when the sun is shining full, and during cool, overcast weather they remain closed. They appear

[25] Quoted by H. KRAINZ in *Sukkulenten,* pp. 60/61, Silvia-Verlag, Zürich, 1958.

shortly after the rainy season in such great numbers that frequently hardly anything can be seen of the usually small bodies; often it is precisely the smallest, least attractive species that have the largest and most striking flowers (Color Plate 7,6).

The fruit capsules are woody at maturity and when observed through a strong magnifying glass prove to be real, natural works of art (Figure 17) and according to H. HERRE serve South African goldsmiths as models in the production of gold jewelry.

The number of chambers in the capsule varies (from 2 to many) and is an important characteristic in the identification of individual genera. The capsules open during the rain by means of an ingenious pumping system in the covering of their chambers (Figure 17,2), and as the water enters, the seeds are propelled out of the chamber; during dry weather the capsules remain closed (Figure 17,1). The seeds require 3 to 6 months to mature after the fruit is dry, in order to reach their full germination ability. This time period is identical with the beginning of the rainy period in the native habitats.

THE CULTIVATION AND PROPAGATION OF MESEMBRYANTHEMUMS

Anyone who wants a collection of these highly succulent mesembs must assume the following preconditions:

a. Most of them are "sun plants," which get a great amount of light and warmth in their native habitats. If you can not offer these two factors, you should not try to grow mesembs.

b. Not all the groups can be treated the same; for example, the genera *Lithops, Gibbaeum,* and *Cheiridopsis* and all the leafy species have their growth period, in my climate, in the summer, i.e., they must be watered at this time; the *Conophytum* species and some others, on the other hand, do not acclimatize themselves to this growth cycle but retain their native rhythm; therefore, they have their rest period in the summer and grow from fall to spring. That means that these plant groups must be kept dry in the summer, but should be watered in the winter.

Only after you have made yourself familiar with the peculiarities of the individual genera, have observed the plants carefully, know their rhythm, and are able to give them the required growing conditions, then the cultivation is not only easy, but it will also bring a lot of

pleasure—a bit of truth applicable to all succulents.

Regarding planting mix, mesembs are not particular. They thrive in nearly any mix; but one should avoid using soil that is too rich in nutrients (especially leaf mold), because the plants will become too leggy and not only lose their growth-form but will also be more susceptible to rot and other diseases. The following mix has proven appropriate for cultivation:

1/3 slightly acid potting soil, 1/3 gravel, and 1/3 loam (sandy clay). A bit of pumice or crushed shards will loosen the mix and make it porous. With plants that grow in limestone, such as *Titanopsis calcarea,* it is recommended to mix a little mortar or crushed limestone into the soil. Artificial fertilizer is generally unnecessary; at the most you could add a little Thomas meal but never pure nitrogen fertilizer, for the bodies of the highly succulent species would easily burst and become unsightly if the growth is too fast.

Cover the surface of the soil with stones or pebbles whose shape and color match the appearance of the plants.

The choice of container is based on the size of the plant. Avoid pots that are too large or too small; tall pots should be used only for plants with long, fleshy roots (e.g., *Nananthus*).

Re-potting is necessary only if the plants outgrow their containers, otherwise they can be kept for years in the same pot. The less they are disturbed, the better it is for the plants. After planting them, withhold water for several days in order to prevent rot.

Set the pots side by side on a bench or in the window. It is recommended, however, that you set them in pumice gravel, so that you will not have to water the plants themselves.

A pre-condition for their thriving, however, is, as already mentioned, a sunny, airy, but not drafty location. Mesembs do not like to be overly warm and have humid breezes at the same time, because they will thus lose their typical growth-form.

In the summer they can be set outside, but give care to protect them with a sheet of glass so that strong rain will not damage them. The glass should not be too far above the plants, but at the same time air must be accessible from all sides. For cultivation in the summer, low boxes with windows and open side walls are suitable if they are screened to protect them from birds.

If you take the plants outdoors in the spring (after

nighttime frosts are no longer a danger) then you must gradually get them used to the sun, i.e., after the long winter darkness they must be kept shaded at first in order to prevent sunburn. For this purpose you can paint the glass with white wash; only after the plants are used to the sun can the shading be removed.

If you grow mesembs outside during the summer do not omit watering even of the conophytes, but be stingy with the water, because even in nature they often go for months without a drop of water. Do not be disturbed if the leaves of *Lithops* and *Conophytum* shrivel; it is a completely natural process. Occasional watering during the evening and morning hours is good for the mesembs, because even in habitat they get a little moisture in the form of fog and dew, even in the dry season.

In general the mesembs are not winter hardy, although in habitat in many areas they get some nighttime frosts. In my climate they should be protected from frost at a temperature of $+5°$ to $+10°$ C ($+41°$ to $+50°$ F), but be sure to provide sufficient airing. Watering during this time must be greatly reduced; only those genera such as *Conophytum* and *Gibbaeum*, which are winter growers, need larger amounts of water, provided that the location is not too cool, because otherwise rot could attack.

Propagation of mesembryanthemums can be accomplished from seed or from cuttings. To get seed, however, you need to have two flowering plants of two clones, for most species are self-sterile.

Sow the tiny seed in the spring (March to April). Use a light soil mix, much sand and compost, and sprinkle the seeds over the surface. Water from below. If the seed is mature, germination will take place in a few days. Thin the seedlings soon but only in the fast-growing species; otherwise leave the seedlings undisturbed for as long as possible. The more the young plants crowd each other in the pot, the stronger and more robust they will become, especially if they are soon acclimatized to the direct sun.

Propagation of mesembs by cuttings is also not difficult. Because many species branch and in the course of years form mounds or tufts, you can simply separate a few "bodies" with a sharp knife. After the cut heals stick the cutting in pure, initially dry, later slightly damp sand. After just a few weeks they form roots; but hold off re-potting until a good root system has developed; otherwise there is a danger that the tender roots will be rejected.

Imported plants are to be handled the same way as cuttings. Cut out the old, dried roots and put the plant in pure, dry sand; after a few weeks gradually begin to water. Root formation can be detected when the bodies begin to swell. Sufficient bottom heat encourages root formation.

The best time to receive imports and to get them acclimatized is during the summer months (May to June), for the plants at this time are in a state of rest in their native habitats and still have enough time in our climate to get new roots during the bright, warm season.

Importation of plants in the fall and winter is not recommended, as they can easily perish from rot and would have to be kept completely dry until spring.

PESTS AND DISEASES

If you have your plants constantly under observation, you will in general have few pests and diseases. The most common ailment is root scale. This usually appears when the plants are kept too dry. Its eradication is relatively simple: take the plant out of the soil and powder the roots with a suitable pesticide dust or take the precaution of watering with a pesticide solution during the summer months. Certain species such as *Pleiospilos*, *Titanopsis*, *Nananthus*, etc. are plagued by red spider. An attack is first noticed by a gray coloration of the leaves, and with a magnifying glass the red mites are visible.

In all species whose leaves are fused except for a split (*Conophytum*, *Lithops*, *Pleiospilos*, etc.), colonies of mealy bug or aphids settle on the leaf sheaths. Their eradication, too, is easy.

Much more dangerous than the above ailments from animal pests is the so-called wet rot; most plants fall victim to it. It is recognizable by shoots and leaves turning glassy and weak overnight, and finally by the whole plant collapsing. It is probably a bacterial or fungus disease. As long as only single leaves or shoots are attacked, the infected places can be cleaned out and the plant kept dry and isolated, because this disease can be carried to other plants. Hardened plants are much less susceptible to wet rot than coddled plants and those that get too much nutrition.

Although the above covers the most important points of the care of mesembs, the details cannot be considered as a cure-all. Collectors and hobbyists must get to know their plants through constant observations and treat them accordingly. Only a special cultivation and an intensive study of their life customs will allow these natural works of art to reach their same beauty that is afforded the visitor in the desert landscapes of South Africa.

The following presentation can only offer a selection from the abundance of species and can only give an incentive to the collector. All herbaceous forms are consciously omitted, and of the highly succulent forms, all those that are difficult to grow have been omitted.

Aloinopsis SCHWANT.

Several small rosettes combine into mounds or tufts, which have a long, fleshy root. They are therefore to be cultivated in tall pots. Ca. 16 species.

Aloinopsis luckhoffii (L. BOL.) L. BOL. (Plate 84,1) (= *Titanopsis luckhoffii* L. BOL.; = *Nananthus luckhoffii* L. BOL.)

is a small, tuft-forming rosette plant. Its leaves are upright, up to 2 cm long, with broadly triangular, blunt, thick tip, which is thickly covered with rather regularly arranged, gray-green, wart-like tubercules. The leaf surface resembles that of *Titanopsis,* and its flowers are bright yellow. *Distribution:* Cape Province (Little Namaqualand).

Aloinopsis malherbei (L. BOL.) L. BOL. (= *Nananthus malherbei* L. BOL.) (Plate 84,2)

The rosettes are in multiples with gray-green, upright, club-shaped or spatulate leaves up to 2.5 cm long, which are covered with pearl-like tubercules on the blunt and dentate tip. The flowers are pale brownish to flesh colored. *Distribution:* Ceres Karroo (Calvinia District).

This is a very pretty species.

Aloinopsis peersii (L. BOL.) L. BOL. (= *Nananthus peersii* L. BOL.) (Plate 64,3)

Its rosette leaves are in groups of 2 to 4, flatly spread, elliptical ligulate, pointed, up to 25 mm long and 15 mm wide, very thick, bluish gray-green, with short hairs, and distinctly flecked. Its flowers are single, yellow, up to 2.5 cm. *Distribution:* Great and Little Karroo.

Aloinopsis schooneesii L. BOL. (= *Nananthus schooneesii* (L. BOL.) L. BOL.) (Plate 84,4)

A low rosette plant, it has small, broadly spatulate, very succulent leaves, whose thick, blunt tips are bluntly triangular in cross section and are covered with dark green pustules. Its flowers are yellowish red, glistening with silver. *Distribution:* eastern Cape Province.

Argyroderma N.E. BR.

Because of the whitish gray, smooth, silvery leaf surface this genus is also referred to as "silver skin." It is found exclusively in quartz fields (Plate 84,5). Great stands of them are found in the Knersvlakte, an extensive quartz area of Namaqualand in the Vanrhynsdorp District. From this area there are around 40 species that have been described and which are all very similar and difficult to distinguish from one another; the color of the flowers alone has little taxonomic value in the mesembryanthemums. All argyrodermas are highly succulent and have the same growth-form: as young plants they form simple bodies with one pair of fleshy, semi-egg-shaped leaves fused only at the base and having a wide cleft or a narrow slit between them. The attractive, large, short-peduncled flowers fill almost the entire split (Plate 84,6). After the fruit ripens, branching occurs, and so in undisturbed growth, large clumps arise over the course of many years. The growth period comes in the summer months in my latitude, so during this time they should be watered, but not too much, because the leaves could burst.

The flower color is usually purplish red, red, pink, golden yellow, pale yellow, or yellow, seldom white, and one species can appear in all flower colors, e.g., *A. delaetii* MAASS.

Of approximately 40 species, the *Handbook of Succulent Plants* by H. JACOBSEN (1970) presently lists 10 species.

Bergeranthus SCHWANT.

Ca. 12 species. Growth period in the summer.

As an example I cite

Bergeranthus multiceps (SALM) SCHWANT. (Plate 85,1),

a tuft-forming succulent with many rosettes, whose narrowly lineal, pointed leaves are sharply triangular. Its flowers are long-peduncled, up to 3 cm in diameter, and yellow.

Cheiridopsis N.E. BR.

The members of this genus are highly succulent plants of tuft-like or mounded growth-form. Their short, thick stem axes have 1 to 3 pairs of decussate leaves, whose

141

successive leaf pairs frequently differ in form and size. The basal leaves form only a short sheath, and the successive leaf pairs may be fused to the middle or almost to the tip. These dry up during the dry period into a sleeve-like sheath (the genus name refers to this fact: cheiris = sleeve, opsis = like), which protects the lower leaf organs in the dry period. The leaves themselves are thick, grayish green to whitish, glabrous or slightly hairy, frequently dotted.

The flowers are found singly on every shoot; they are on long stalks and are very large, white, yellowish, reddish, or red.

The growth period is in the summer. The plants require a bright, sunny location and moderate amounts of water. As fall begins they should be kept dry and not too cool over the winter. Ca. 90 species are found mostly in Namaqualand.

One of the most beautiful is

Cheiridopsis candidissima (HAW.) N.E. BR. (Plate 85,2), common and sometimes found in great stands in Namaqualand near Steinkopf and in the Richtersveld. Its shoots unite into compact mounds, with 1 to 3 pairs of whitish gray, boat-shaped leaves 5 to 10 cm long. The flowers are very large (5 to 6 cm in diameter), white to pale pink.

Most species, however, have yellow flowers.

One of the most beautiful species and at the same time an excellent example of mimesis within the genus is

Cheiridopsis peculiaris N.E. BR. (Color Plate 7,2), which occupies reddish brown, clay slate, that has been weathered flat near Steinkopf in Namaqualand. The two basal leaves of the usually single, seldom-grouped rosettes are of the same color and shape. These lower leaves are broadly elliptical up to 5 cm long, almost as wide at the base, with a short tip and lying on the ground; in the light they have the same luster as the surrounding rock. The second leaf pair is much smaller, upright and united up to a small split. This second pair dries during the rest period into a papery tissue, which must be removed in cultivation when new growth begins, for otherwise the next leaf pair cannot develop. The flowers appear singly, on stalks ca. 4 cm long, up to 3.5 cm across, and are yellow.

A difficult species to grow, during the rest period it requires being kept absolutely dry.

Of the small, yellow-flowered species I cite

Cheiridopsis herrei L. BOL. (Plate 85,3); *C. meyeri* N.E. BR.; *C. minima* TISCH.; *C. pillansii* L. BOL.; *C. vanzijlii* L. BOL.

Among the red-flowering species are:

C. carnea N.E. BR.; *C. purpurata* L. BOL.; *C. speciosa* L. BOL.; *C. splendens* L. BOL.

Conophyllum SCHWANT.,

the "conical leaf," is represented by around 25 species predominantly in Namaqualand and is closely related to the genus *Mitrophyllum,* and so both genera are united today into one genus, *Mitrophyllum* SCHWANT. (see p. 150).

Very similar is

Conophytum N.E. BR.

With about 300 species, *Conophytum* is not only one of the richest genera but along with *Lithops* is also one of the most favored genera of mesembs. All species are relatively easy to grow and are suited for growing in the home as well as for commercial production.

The essential aspects of the life of conophytes have been discussed on page 134 ff. They are tiny plants, which at maturity are multi-branched. They have a tuft-like or mound growth-form (Plate 85,5–6). Every shoot (= body) produces only 2 highly succulent leaves each year, which in the spherical forms are united up to a small split (Figure 18,2–4), and in the bilobes, however, have free tips or so-called lobes (Figure 18,1; Plate 85,5–6). The peduncled, white, yellow, pink, red, or violet flower pushes through the split (Figure 18,1–3).

The bodies themselves are spherical, egg-shaped, heart-shaped, or cylindrical; they range in size from a few millimeters to several centimeters. They look like little green marbles, peas, or buttons, and are either puffed at

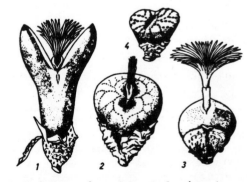

Figure 18. Body shapes of conophytes. *1, Conophytum incurvum; 2, C. truncatum, 3, C. velutinum, 4, C. mundum.*

the tip (Figure 18,*3*), flat (Figure 18,*2*), concave (Figure 18,*4*), notched or bi-lobed (Figure 18,*1*). In many species the leaf surfaces near the split have translucent spots or bumps, which sometimes flow into branched lines or windows (Figure 18,*2,4*).

In some species the growth period begins in May and June, but for most species it begins in the fall and then lasts into the winter. During this time the plants are to be kept moderately moist, well lighted, and airy. In the spring the growth ceases and water should be withheld. The beginning of the rest period is recognized by the fact that the bodies lose their plump shape and become wrinkled; within a few weeks the leaf pair withers into a papery tissue. The nutrients drained from it are used to form the new body, i.e., next year's leaf pair, which in the meantime has grown sufficiently within the dry hull, and so all that is needed is a rain to cause it to break the hull.

During the rest period the conophytes are very unsightly (Plate 83,*3–4*) and with their dry skins resemble more a heap of small stones than a living plant.

In general the conophytes prefer more humid locations than *Lithops* and other highly succulent mesembs (Plate 83,*1*). They grow in clefts in the rocks and among lichens in the fog deserts; only a few species thrive in extremely dry and sunny locations. In their distribution the conophytes therefore stretch much farther into the more humid eastern Cape area than do other highly succulent mesembryanthemums.

For cultivation and propagation refer to the material in the introduction to the family on p. 134.

For many years N.E. BROWN, G. SCHWANTES, A. TISCHER, and L. BOLUS have been concerned with the systematics of the genus and have tried to offer a classification for which the various body shapes, the bloom time, the flower shape and color, and the geographic distribution make up the basis. I can present here only a selection of a typical and decorative forms.

Conophytum bilobum N.E. BR. (Plate 85,*5*),

as the name implies, is a member of the bi-lobes from the subsection *Eubiloba* TISCH. (section Cordiformia (BRGR.) SCHWANT.) with very large bodies, which in maturity join into compact mounds up to 30 cm in diameter in habitat. The bodies are deeply bi-lobed, somewhat compressed laterally, up to 4.5 cm long and 2.5 cm wide, gray to whitish green, with short papillous hairs and reddish-lobed margins. The flowers are up to 3 cm, bright yellow.

In the same group are also the following:

C. albescens N.E. BR.

Its bodies have fine whitish hairs and yellow flowers.

C. elishae (N.E. BR.) N.E. BR.

Its bodies are bluish green with dark spots, and the flowers are yellow.

C. frutescens SCHWANT.

A very large plant, almost a semi-shrub, its stems are up to 10 cm long, upright, slightly branched. Its bodies are up to 3 cm long, dark green, with lighter, translucent spots; the flowers are deep yellow-orange, almost copper.

C. incurvum N.E. BR. (Figure 18,*1*)

has bodies up to 4 cm, somewhat flattened, with upright, somewhat incurved lobes 6 to 8 mm long. The body surface has satin-like hairs, light green with lighter spots; the flowers are yellow and white (var. *leucanthum* (LAVIS) TISCH.).

C. meyerae SCHWANT.

Forms only a few, deeply bi-lobed bodies; the edges of the inner surfaces of the lobes are marked with a line of merging dots; the flowers are yellow.

C. muscosipapillatum LAVIS

has a body up to 4 cm long and 3 cm wide, with fine, satiny hairs, and is gray-green and spotted; the flowers are golden yellow.

C. pole-evansii N.E. BR.

forms mats; its bodies are up to 5 cm long and up to 2 cm wide. The lobes are flared, sharply keeled, red at the edges, otherwise light green; old sheaths are spotted with brown, and the flowers are yellow.

C. stylosum (N.E. BR.) TISCH. (Plate 85,*6*)

forms compact mats with bodies up to 5 cm long, deeply bi-lobed. The lobes have reddish margins and tips, and the flowers are yellow.

The species cited above are only a small selection from the section Cordiformia.

Very beautiful conophytes can be found in the subgenus *Euconophytum*, section Cataphracta SCHWANT. They are all characterized by their forming conical or almost spherical bodies, whose whitish to blue-green leaves are united up to a small slit.

As an example I list

Conophytum labiatum Tisch. (Plate 86,*1*).

Its bodies are round, ca. 1.2 cm high, whitish gray with scattered, dark green spots. The leaves are swollen into lips around the split; the flowers are light yellow.

In the same group are:
C. calculus (Brgr.) N.E. Br; *C. paucipunctum* Tisch.; *C. subrisum* (N.E. Br.) N.E. Br.

Conophytum concavum L. Bol. (Plate 86,*2*)

is a member of the subgenus *Fenestrata* N.E. Br. (section Subfenestrata Tisch.). Its bodies are single or in small groups, inverse egg-shaped, and concave at the tip. The leaves are light green, with fine satiny hairs, and are fused up to a narrow slit; the flowers are white. It grows in quartz fields near Riethuis (Namaqualand).

In the same group are:
C. hallii L. Bol.; *C. pillansii* Lavis.

Conophytum cupreatum Tisch. (subgenus *Fenestrata* N.E. Br., section Pellucida Schwant.) (Plate 86,*3*)

forms small, inverse conical bodies, which unite into a mat, are 10 to 15 mm tall, and are coppery brown. The leaves are united up to a narrow split and on the upper side have dark green windows, which are sometimes set down into the leaf, making the leaf surface appear uneven. The flowers are white and open at mid-day.

Further species:
C. fenestratum Schwant.; *C. pellucidum* (N.E. Br.) Schwant.; *C. terricolor* Tisch.; etc.

Conophytum ectypum N.E. Br. (subgenus *Conophytum*, section Minuscula Schwant.)

is a widely distributed, variable species with a mat-like growth-form (Color Plate 7,*7*), whose small, inverse-cone bodies are 5 to 10 mm, round at the tip and with a small split and remain covered for a long time by the papery tissues of the old leaves. At bloom time the plant makes a splendid show. The pink or bright-yellow (var. *tischleri*, Color Plate 7,*7*) flowers are up to 1 cm and break out in such great numbers that you can hardly see the plant itself.

The species in the Minuscula group are all smaller, have inverse egg-shaped or cylindrical bodies, which are broadly convex on the top and frequently have spots or lines. The relatively large, long-tubed, red or yellow flowers are open all day long.

To this group also belong

C. herrei Schwant.

Plant forms tufts with very small bodies; flowers are bright lilac-red.

C. luckhoffii Lavis

Flowers pinkish purple.

C. minusculum N.E. Br.) N.E. Br.

A very small, tuft-forming species, similar to *C. herrei* (Plate 86,*4*).

C. reticulatum L. Bol.

Its body is small and brownish red, with dark-red spotted leaves, and its flowers are bright carmine red.

C. mundum N.E. Br. (subgenus *Conophytum*, section Tuberculata Schwant.) Plate 83,*1*; Figure 18,*4*

is a mat-forming species with a top-shaped (turbinate) body, 10–12 mm long, truncated at the top. The leaf lobes are nearly circular, fused to a split, and are bright blue-gray-green with many raised translucent spots that are either separated or joined in a line. The flowers are yellowish. This is a beautiful species.

Other species of this group demonstrate similar characteristics. Of these I cite:
C. obcordellum (Haw.) N.E. Br.
Its flowers are white.
C. parvipetalum (N.E. Br.) N.E. Br.
Its flowers are bright pink. Now considered to be a variety of *C. obcordellum*.

Conophytum pearsonii (N.E. Br.) (subgenus *Conophytum*, section Wettsteiniana Schwant.) (Color Plate 7,*5*)

This is a cushion-forming plant with an inverse-conical to spherical or elliptical body, 8–16 mm long and 10–18 mm in diameter, with a nearly smooth surface. The leaves are 2–3 mm long and are fused up to a narrow split. The flowers are large and violet.

This series also contains a large number of species that have broad-conical, distinctive, dark-green bodies with sunken or concave surfaces; the leaves are fused together up to a small split and generally have small or large spots. The long-tubed, day-blooming flowers are large and red, pink, white or yellow.

All species of this series are characterized by many free flowers and, for this reason, are highly esteemed by conophyte growers.

As further examples I cite:
C. flavum N.E. Br.: flowers yellow.
C. globosum N.E. Br.: flowers soft pink.
C. gratum (N.E. Br.) N.E. Br.: flowers red.
C maximum Tisch.: flower lobes—upper surface pink, under side white.
C. ornatum Lavis.: flowers golden yellow, stamens red (Plate 86,*5*).
C. praegratum Tisch.: flowers pink.
C. robustum Tisch.: flowers lilac-rose.
C. wettsteinii (Brgr.) N.E. Br.: flowers violet-purple.

Conophytum pictum (N.E. Br.) N.E. Br. (subgenus *Conophytum*, section Picta Schwant.)

Its body is inverse-conical to elliptical, fused to a split, blue-green, with many dark, partly united spots (Plate 86,*6*). A night bloomer, its flowers are pink.

Further species in this group are:
C. ceresianum L. Bol.: flowers cream colored.
C. minimum (Haw.) N.E. Br.: bodies very small; flowers small, yellowish white.
C. pusillum N.E. Br.) N.E. Br.: plant very small; flowers cream colored.

Conophytum saxetanum (N.E. Br.) N.E. Br. (subgenus

Color Plate 8.

1 (ul) *Lithops aucampiae*
2 (ur) *Argyroderma roseum*

3 (ml) *Lithops otzeniana*
4 (mm) *Fenestraria aurantiaca*
5 (mr) *Dinteranthus pole-evansii*

6 (ll) *Tacitus bellus*
7 (lm) *Sedum pachyphyllum*
8 (lr) *Aloe peglerae* (Megalies Mountains near Pretoria)

81.

1 (ul) Anacampseros herreana

2 (ur) Anacampseros papyracea in a quartz field
(the Richtersveld)

3 (ml) Anacampseros meyeri

4 (mr) Anacampseros aff. lanigera

5 (ll) Anacampseros thelephiastrum

6 (lr) Ceraria pygmaea, in a quartz field near
Sendlingsdrift (the Richtersveld)

Plate 82.

1 (ul) *Ceraria namaquer*
branches with fc
short shoots
2 (ur) Flowering shoot
Ceraria namaque
3 (ll) *Portulaca grandif*
4 (lr) *Portulacaria afra*
dry forest near I
fontein (Transva

Plate 84.

1 (ul) *Aloinopsis luckhoffii*

2 (ur) *Aloinopsis malherbei*, Ceres Karroo near
        Calvinia

3 (ml) *Aloinopsis peersii*, Great Karroo near
        Beaufort West

4 (mr) *Aloinopsis schooneesii*

5 (ll) *Argyroderma* species, Knersvlakte (Lit
        Namaqualand, Vanrhynsdorp Distric

6 (lr) *Argyroderma octophyllum*

Plate 85.

1 (ul) *Bergeranthus multiceps*

2 (ur) *Cheiridopsis candidissima*, near Kamies-
droon (Little Namaqualand)

3 (ml) *Cheiridopsis herrei*, in sand fields near
Swartwater (the Richtersveld)

4 (mr) *Conophyllum grande*, in various stages of
development

5 (ll) *Conophytum bilobum*, near Komaggas
(Little Namaqualand)

6 (lr) *Conophytum stylosum*, quartz slopes near
Stinkfontein (the Richtersveld)

Plate 86.

1 (ul) *Conophytum labiatum*, near Numies (the Richtersveld)

2 (ur) *Conophytum concavum*, in a quartz field near Riethuis (Little Namaqualand)

3 (ml) *Conophytum cupreatum*

4 (mr) *Conophytum minusculum*, plants completely overgrown by lichen and moss

(plateau of the Poison Mountains, Vanrhynsdorp District)

5 (ll) *Conophytum ornatum*

6 (lr) *Conophytum pictum*

Plate 88.

1 (ul) *Dinteranthus vanzijlii*

2 (ur) *Drosanthemum* aff. *hispidum*, Great Kar-
         roo near Beaufort West
3 (ml) *Faucaria tigrina*
4 (mr) *Faucaria tuberculosa*

5 (ll) *Fenestraria rhopalophylla*
6 (lr) *Frithia pulchra*, Megalies Mounta
        near Rustenburg (Transvaal)

Plate 89.

1 (ul) *Gibbaeum album*, Lesser Karroo

2 (ur) *Gibbaeum pilosulum*, completely surrounded by lichens, Lesser Karroo

3 (ml) *Gibbaeum pubescens*, Lesser Karroo

4 (mr) *Gibbaeum velutinum*

5 (ll) *Glottiphyllum linguiforme*

6 (lr) *Glottiphyllum oligocarpum*

Plate 90.

1 (ul) *Lapidaria margaretae*
2 (ur) *Lithops bromfieldii*

3 (ml) *Lithops comptonii* in habitat (Ceres
         Karroo)
4 (mr) *Lithops gracilidelineata*

5 (ll) *Lithops herrei* in a quartz field near
         Sendlingsdrift (the Richtersveld)
6 (lr) *Lithops lesliei*

1.

Lithops localis
Lithops mennellii
Lithops meyeri

4 (mr) *Lithops weberi* in limestone rocks of the Ceres Karroo

5 (ll) *Lithops terricolor,* at the beginning of the dry period; bodies withdrawing into the

soil, Miller Station (Willowmore District, eastern Cape Province)

6 (lr) Flowering plant of *Lithops terricolor* in cultivation

Plate 92.

1 (ul) *Lithops bella*
2 (ur) *Lithops fulleri*

3 (ml) *Lithops karasmontana*
4 (mr) *Lithops optica;* left, a group of forma *rubra*

5 (ll) *Lithops salicola*
6 (lr) *Muiria hortenseae,* in habitat, S Karroo near Riversdale

93.

1   *Monilaria globosa* near Riethuis, (Little Namaqualand)

2 (ur)   *Nomilaria moniliformis* (Knersvlakte, Vanrhynsdorp District)

3 (ml)   *Odontophorus marlothii*

4 (mr)   *Oophytum oviforme,* (Knersvlakte, Vanrhynsdorp District)

5 (ll)   *Ophthalmophyllum lydiae,* Hangpaal near Steinkopf (Little Namaqualand)

6 (lr)   *Ophthalmophyllum pillansii,* entering the dormant stage (Knersvlakte, Vanrhynsdorp District)

Plate 94.

1 (ul) *Ophthalmophyllum praesectum*
2 (ur) *Ophthalmophyllum verrucosum*

3 (ml) *Pleiospilos bolusii*, plant in the dormant stage near Willowmore (eastern Cape Province)
4 (mr) Flowering *Pleiospilos bolusii* near Willowmore (eastern Cape Province)

5 (ll) *Pleiospilos nelii*, with fruit capsule ern Cape Province near Rietbron
6 (lr) *Pleiospilos latifolius* (eastern Cape ince, Prince Albert District)

Plate 96.

1 (ul) *Tischleria peersii*

2 (ur) *Titanopsis primosii*, in limestone near

Kamib (Little Namaqualand)

3 (ml) *Titanopsis schwantesii*

4 (mr) *Trichodiadema densum*

5 (ll) *Vanheerdia divergens*, Ceres Karroo
Polmusfontain

6 (lr) *Vanheerdia primosii*, in limestone r
Springbok (Little Namaqualand)

Conophytum, section Saxetana SCHWANT.) (Plate 87,*3*)

It forms compact mats consisting of several hundred small, green bodies that are 6 to 10 mm long, 2 to 4 mm in diameter, with the top rounded, spherical to oval, with a small, sunken split with hairs. The split is surrounded by several spots, which frequently flow together; the flowers are small and whitish. In cultivation it seldom blooms, and is a night bloomer.

Also in this group are:
C. graessneri TISCH.: flowers creamy white (Plate 83,*2*).
C. hians N.E. BR.: flowers reddish or yellowish white.
C. loeschianum TISCH.: similar to *C. graessneri;* flowers white.

Conophytum stephanii SCHWANT. (subgenus *Conophytum,* section Barbata SCHWANT. (Color Plate 7,*4*)

is one of the most charming and most sought-after conophytes, which grows in clefts of quartz rocks of the Richtersveld, forming rather large mats. The small, round bodies, ca. 7 mm across with a very small split, are densely covered with long, white hairs; the flowers are small, whitish yellow.

In this group are only a few species:
C. depressum LAVIS: flowers yellowish red.
C. fibulaeforme (HAW.) N.E. BR.: flowers pink.
C. pubicalyx LAVIS: bodies very small; flowers reddish.

Conophytum truncatum THUNBG.) N.E. BR. (subgenus *Conophytum,* section Truncatella SCHWANT.) (Figure 18,*2*)

This plant forms loose mats with inverse conical bodies that are up to 1.5 cm long, whose top surface is slightly concave and has a sunken, gray-green to blue-green, short split, with dark spots. Its flowers are yellowish to white and open at night.

In the same group are predominantly night bloomers with distribution more to the east:
Var. *brevitubum* LAVIS: body similar to the above species: flowers pale pink, fragrant (Plate 87,*1*).
C. calitzdorpense L. BOL.: flowers pale red.
C. multipunctatum TISCH.: flowers white.
C. subglobosum TISCH.: flowers white.

Conophytum uvaeforme (HAW.) N.E. BR. (subgenus *Conophytum,* section Ficiformia SCHWANT.) (PLATE 87,*4*)

forms mats, has pear-shaped to spherical bodies that are 10 to 12 cm long and somewhat compressed on the side, and is yellowish to gray-green, with dark dots. Its flowers are whitish yellow, and it is a night bloomer.

Other species of this night-blooming group are:
C. ficiforme HAW.) N.E. BR.: flowers violet-pink; (Plate 87,*2*).
C. odoratum (N.E. BR.) N.E. BR.: flowers bright pinkish red.
C. pardivisum TISCH.: flowers white.
C. translucens N.E. BR. (= *C. uvaeforme* var. *meleagre* (L. BOL.) TISCH.): flowers cream colored.

Conophytum velutinum (SCHWANT.) SCHWANT. (Figure 18,*3*; Color Plate 7,*6*)

is a member of the subgenus *Conophytum,* subsection Ovigera TISCH. Its bodies are roundish oval to egg-shaped, ca. 12 mm long and 8 mm thick, olive green, with fine, velvety hairs. The split is very small, only slightly sunken, and the flowers

are reddish purple.

Also in the same section are:
C. laetum L. BOL.: flowers yellow.
C. meyeri N.E. BR.: flowers yellow.
C. ovigerum SCHWANT.: flowers yellow.
C. tischeri SCHICK.: flowers pale lilac.

A remarkable mesemb is

Dactylopsis N.E. BR.,

which is represented by *D. digitata* (AIT.) N.E. BR., the "finger leaf," from the Knersvlakte, an extensive, very brackish quartz field in the Vanrhynsdorp District, a home of many succulents. As a matter of distribution, *Dactylopsis* is found precisely in very salty places, where it appears in rather large stands.

In its growth-form, *Dactylopsis digitata* differs from all other mesembs by the thick, finger-shaped, cylindrical, soft, gray-green, waxy leaves up to 12 cm long, which emerge from the sheath of the next-oldest leaf (Plate 87,*5*). The sessile, white flowers appear singly. During the dry period the leaves completely shrivel.

A rare and difficult species to grow; it requires a sunny location and in the summer requires complete rest. Even during the winter months water should be sparse. A feeding of table salt in the water, as is often recommended, seems to be unnecessary.

Delosperma N.E. BR.

is a genus of many species, whose members appear as small mini-shrubs or rosette plants with reclining or ascending branches. The cylindrical, 3-angled or almost spherical leaves are frequently covered with short or somewhat elongated papillae; flowers large, white, red, or yellow, single or in multiples in cymes. The growth period is in the summer; during this time the plants can be grown outdoors.

One of the most attractive species is

Delosperma pruinosum (THUNBG.) I. INGRAM [= *D. echinatum* (AIT.) SCHWANT.] (Plate 5,*2*),

a small mini-shrub with richly branched, thin, papillous branches. Its leaves are decussate, egg-shaped to semi-spherical, up to 15 mm long, juicy, and green, thickly covered with long, white papillae, giving the leaves a "stickery" impression. Its flowers are single, short-stalked, and whitish or yellowish, appearing almost through the whole year.

Didymaotus N.E. Br.

A rare plant showing clear characteristics of mimesis is

Didymaotus lapidiformis (MARL.) N.E. BR. (Plate 87,6),

the only member of the genus, which in growth-form resembles *Pleiospilos* (see page 152) and like it has only one pair of large, very thick, rock-like, whitish gray-green leaves colored red by the sun. Its flowers are single, on a stalk and are whitish to red.

In cultivation this is a somewhat difficult species, requiring a bright location and a rest period in the early summer.

Among the favored and sought-after mesembs are also the members of the genus

Dinteranthus SCHWANT.,

of which 6 species are known and whose simple or sparsely branched shoots have 1 to 3 pairs of short, thick, semi-egg-shaped leaves united at the base. *Dinteranthus* is a further, excellent example of mimesis, because the plants, which prefer the quartz fields, with their white, smooth, seldom-dotted leaves resemble the surrounding quartz pebbles so much that in their non-blooming stage they are hard to find (Plate 83,5).

All *Dinteranthus* species are difficult to grow: they require a very bright location and a lot of heat; even during the growing period in the summer only slight amounts of water may be given; otherwise the leaves will burst. In the winter you must shift to a completely dry period. Among the most frequently cultivated species are the following:

Dinteranthus microspermus (DTR. et DERENBERG) SCHWANT.

Plant usually has 1 head, seldom more; leaves are united for up to half their length, with the upper side flat and the under side semi-spherical, and with a suggestion of a keel line, finely pebbled to rough, reddish gray-violet. Its flowers are on a short peduncle and are bright golden yellow. *Distribution:* Namibia.

Dinteranthus pole-evansii (N.E. BR.) SCHWANT. (Color Plate 8,5; Plate 83,5)

These plants usually grow singly. The leaves are united up to half their length, with a narrow slit, and are semi-spherical;

their upper surface is finely granular, whitish gray. The flowers are large, egg-yolk yellow. *Distribution:* Cape Province, Prieska districts.

Dinteranthus vanzijlii (L. BOL.) SCHWANT. (Plate 88,*1*)

has bodies found in multiples, not unlike a *Lithops,* therefore described by L. BOLUS as *Lithops vanzijlii.* Its leaves are united up to a narrow split, with a flattened, gray-green, sometimes reddish spotted and lined tip, and its flowers are orangy yellow. *Distribution:* Bushman Land.

A rare species, it is sensitive to moisture.

Other species are:

D. inexpectatus (DTR.) DTR., *D. puberulus* N.E. BR., and *D. wilmotianus* L. BOL.

Dorotheanthus SCHWANT.

Of all the annual mesembs the members of this genus are the most beautiful, especially

Dorotheanthus bellidiformis (BURM. f.) N.E. BR. (Color Plate 1,*3*),

which is a splendid summer flower for small gardens and is just as well-suited for beds as well as for pots. It is offered on the market in many color varieties with large, white, red, orange, or multi-colored flowers. In dense stands the plant offers a splendid, colorful sight at bloom time (June to August).

Even more beautiful is

Dorotheanthus oculatus N.E. BR.,

in which the bright-yellow flowers have a dark-red spot (eye) at the base. Also the filaments and stigma lobes are a vivid red.

The rich genus

Drosanthemum SCHWANT.

is among the shrubby mesembryanthemums, which in habitat cover dry areas, often by the square kilometer and with their richness of red, yellow, or white flowers afford an undescribable sight (Color Plate 1,*2*).

Although the plants grow easily and are good bloomers in cultivation, they are recommended to collectors who have sufficient room to overwinter them. In the summer they can be put outside.

The opposing, blunty triangular, or cylindrical leaves are densely covered with papillae (Plate 88,*2*), which in the sunlight glisten like the gland hairs of a sun-dew (Drosera), to which the genus name refers.

Species especially recommendable for cultivation are
D. hispidum (L.) SCHWANT. (Plate 88,2) and *D. schoen-landianum* (SCHLTR.) L. BOL.

Faucaria SCHWANT.

All faucarias, when grown in a bright and airy location,
are fast growers and are also appropriate succulents for
growing indoors; their growth period is in the summer.
During this time watering should be generous. In the
early fall the large, bright-yellow flowers unfold and can
appear in such great numbers that the body will be
completely covered with them.

Of the approximately 30 species from the dry areas of
eastern Cape Province,

Faucaria tigrina (HAW.) SCHWANT. (Plate 88,30)

is one of the favorites. Unfortunately it is rare in cultivation in
its pure form, because it is frequently used to make hybrids
with other species, which then are sold under the same name.
Like all other species of the genus, *F. tigrina* is one of the
highly succulent mesembs, whose initially single-headed rosette
later branches to form compact, fleshy-rooted mats, clumps,
or mounds. Every rosette has 2 to 4 pairs of decussate, opposing,
dense, gray-green leaves that are united at the base with short
sheaths; in cross-section they are semi-cylindrical. Their keeled
under side is extended over the leaf tip like a chin. Because the
leaves have prominent (up to 10), recurved teeth ending in a
fine tip, any leaf pair resembles bared, open tiger jaws. The
similarity to tiger jaws is intensified by the white spotting of
the leaves. The large, golden-yellow flowers, as in all other
species, open in the fall.

Similar is *F. felina* (WESTON) SCHWANT., the "cat's jaws,"
whose bright green, indistinctly dotted leaves have only 3 to
5 recurved teeth on their margins. Their under side keel is a
white, cartilaginous strip.

Also a very ferocious-looking species is

F. lupina (HAW.) SCHWANT.,

the "wolf's jaws," whose bright-green, finely dotted leaves have
7 to 9 recurved, hair-fine teeth on their margins. The keel, as
in *F. tigrina,* protrudes like a chin.

An easily recognizable and equally favored species is

Faucaria tuberculosa (ROLFE) SCHWANT. (Plate 88,4)

Their quite thick, broad, rhombic-triangular leaves have three
strong and several thinner teeth on their margins. The upper
side of the leaves is equipped with warty bumps, which give
the plant its typical appearance.

Among the most interesting mesembs are without a
doubt

Fenestraria N.E. BR.,

The "window leaf," which was formly represented by the
two very closely related species *F. aurantiaca* N.E. BR.
and *F. rhopalophylla* (SCHLTR. et DIELS) N.E. BR. Today
these two species are combined into one species, *F. auran-tiaca,* with two varieties, var. *aurantiaca* and var. *rhopal-ophylla* SCHULTR. et DIELS) ROWL.

The former, growing in the sand of the coastal area of
Namaqualand near Port Nolloth and Alexanderbai (also
near Grotderm in the Richtersveld), has golden yellow
flowers 3 to 7 cm in diameter (Color Plate 8,4). The latter
is from South Africa, southern Namibia, and near Lüderitz Bay; its leaves are shorter and more angular, and the
flowers are smaller and white (Plate 88,5).

The essential information on the morphology of *Fenes-traria* has already been presented on page 136, and so the
reader is simply referred to that section. Since it is adapted
to high light intensity and extreme aridity, in cultivation
it requires a bright location. In addition the rosettes
should be planted only up to the root neck, for otherwise
the leaves will rot.

Growth occurs in the summer months, and flowers
appear in August and September, during the summer you
should water only enough to keep the leaves from shri-
veling. In the winter stop watering altogether.

Propagation is accomplished by seed and by leaf cuttings.

Also a typical window leaf plant is

Frithia N.E. BR.,

whose only species, *F. pulchra* N.E. BR. (Plate 88,6),
grows in quartz fields of the Megalies Mountains near
Pretoria. It has the same growth-form as *Fenestraria.*

Its club-like leaves are ca. 2 cm long and are blunt at
the tip, rough, and window-like. Its flowers are solitary,
sessile, carmine red, white in the middle, sometimes
completely pure white.

Cultivation is the same as for *Fenestraria,* but the growth
period is in the winter months, and therefore the plants
should be kept dry in the summer.

Gibbaeum HAW.

This genus, with around 20 species, is limited for the most part to the Little Karroo; only a few species such as *G. heathii, G. gibbosum,* and *G. cryptopodium* are found outside this area. All are highly succulent, have a mound-like or mat-like growth-form, and have short or elongated, but then reclining *(G. geminum),* rooting shoots. Each year the single shoots produce only 1 or 2 or a few pairs of fleshy leaves, which in some species *(G. heathii, G. comptonii)* are united up to a narrow split; in others, however, they are spread far apart. Frequently the blades of a pair are of unequal length, making the split not terminal, but lateral. The stalked, white or violet flowers appear at the beginning of the growth period, from fall to spring. All species, especially the white ones *(G. album),* require a bright location and must be kept completely dry during the rest period (summer).

Recommendable species are as follows:

Gibbaeum album N.E. BR. (Plate 89,*1*)

This plant forms a mound. Its leaves are of unequal length, are dense with white felt, and are united into a crooked, egg-shaped body. Initially, the split is barely visible but later is gaping; the flowers are white.

Gibbaeum cryptopodium (KENSIT) L. BOL.

has few bodies, which are spherical to egg-shaped; its leaves are unequal in length, juicy, fleshy, slightly keeled on the under side, glabrous, and pale green; the flowers are pink.

Gibbaeum dispar N.E. BR.

forms mounds; its bodies are egg-shaped, with two unequal, thick, gray-green, velvety leaves. The flowers are violet red.

Gibbaeum heathii (N.E. BR.) L. BOL.

forms mats, with stout, woody rhizomes. Its bodies are almost spherical, 2 to 3 cm in diameter, with 2 semi-spherical, gray-to-whitish-green leaves, which are united up to one-half of their length, leaving only a narrow split between them. Its flowers are white to slightly pink, appearing in the spring.

Gibbaeum pilosulum (N.E. BR.) N.E. BR. (Plate 89,*2*)

forms mats, with inverse-egg-shaped bodies, about 25 mm in diameter, which are large, semi-glossy, and bright green with sparse white hairs. The split of the two leaves is somewhat lateral, 3 to 4 mm deep; the flowers are violet-red, appearing in December and January.

Gibbaeum pubescens (HAW.) N.E. BR. (Plate 89,*3*)

forms a mat, with short, woody stems, which have 2 to 3 pairs of leaves that are united at the base, flare, appear in alternating lengths, and have white, felt-like hairs. The larger leaves are up to 3 cm long, roundish, and upright, with a crooked keel; the smaller ones are only ca. 1/3 as long. The flowers are violet-red, appearing in February and March.

A very pretty species, in habitat in the quartz fields it forms mass stands (Color Plate 1,*1*).

Gibbaeum velutinum (L. BOL.) SCHWANT. (Plate 89,*4*)

forms mats, with woody branches surrounded by dry leaves. The leaves are extremely flared and unequally long (the larger ones up to 6 cm), with the under side having a crooked keel and the tip protruding like a chin; they are bright green to blue-green, with fine, velvety hairs. The flowers are pinkish violet, appearing in the fall.

Glottiphyllum HAW.,

the "tongue leaf," owes its name to the thick, fleshy, tongue-shaped leaves, which appear in two rows or are decussate on short, forked stems. The very large, shiny-yellow, dandelion-like flowers appear from August to February.

All glottiphyllums (ca. 60) are fast growers and easy bloomers that, when fed too much, will outgrow other plants and crowd them out. Therefore they should not be planted in the open but grown in pots if possible. Only then do they retain their typical growth-form.

Among the best-known species is

Glottiphyllum linguiforme (L.) N.E. BR. (Plate 89,*5*),

which, however, can seldom be found as a pure species; most plants grown under this name are hybrids. The leaves are in two rows, tongue-shaped, up to 6 cm long and 4 cm wide, blunt at the tip and slightly bent outward, soft, fleshy, and bright green.

A small species is

Glottiphyllum oligocarpum L. BOL. (Plate 89,*6*)

Its leaves are in two rows, usually in 2 pairs, pressed flat against the ground, up to 4.5 cm long, blunt at the tip, whitish to olive green, with some raised dots; the flowers are yellow.

In very sunny locations the leaves stay short and acquire a chalky, whitish violet color.

Another small species is

Glottiphyllum parvifolium L. BOL.

Its leaves are in decussate opposition, more or less upright, longitudinal, only 3 to 4 cm long, with a small thorn tip, and with their upper side flat and their under side rounded.

The genus

Lampranthus N.E. Br.

is rich in species that are easily blooming semi-shrubs with upright, flared or reclining branches, which in the summer are suited to being planted outdoors. For small collections this mesembryanthemum group is less suited.

The most frequently cultivated species is

Lampranthus conspicuus (Haw.) N.E. Br.,

which earns its name, "the attractive Lampranthus," justifiably, because of the richness of its large, bright-red flowers. It is a semi-shrub up to 40 cm tall, with semi-spherical, dotted, frequently red-tipped leaves.

To the category of mimetic plants also belongs the genus

Lapidaria Schwant.,

closely related to *Dinteranthus* and represented by the one species, *L. margaretae* (Schwant.), from Namibia (Plate 90,*1*). This is a stemless succulent forming mats at maturity, whose single stems have 3 to 4 pairs of separated, very fleshy leaves united at the base. These are flat on the upper side, greatly billowed and sharply keeled on the under side, triangular toward the tip, and whitish or reddish white. The flowers are very large, golden yellow, and reddish as they fade.

This is a very pretty and rare species!

Lithops N.E. Br.

Recent literature: L. Sprechmann: *Lithops.* Farleigh Dickenson University Press, 1970.

Among the favorite succulents, recommended for all collections, are the numerous species (ca. 80) of the genus *Lithops,* the real "living stones" or "flowering stones." Actually these look so much like pebbles that finding them in nature in their non-flowering state is very difficult, especially since some species occupy an area of only a few square meters.

All *Lithops* species are inhabitants of the dry gravel and sand deserts of South Africa and Namibia. Sometimes they grow in rock clefts or are entirely hidden in loam or sand with only their blunt tips showing; frequently, these leaf tips are beautifully decorated with a network of "windows" (Plate 91,*4–5*). During the dry season they can withdraw completely into the ground. At maturity the shoots (= bodies) can unite to form cushions. As in *Conophytum* each shoot produces, each year, only two semi-cylindrical, blunt-tipped or semi-spherically billowed leaves, which are united up to a more or less narrow split, from which appear the strikingly large, yellow or white flowers (see Figure 16). These appear singly from July to December and are open only at noon.

In general, cultivation of *Lithops* is not difficult if you observe its seasonal rhythm. The growing period is in the summer; during this time the plants should be watered and given a sunny, airy location. Too much water is to be avoided, for otherwise the leaves will burst; the plants then become not only unattractive but also tend to rot easily, because bacteria and fungus spores get into the tissue. From September on, stop watering completely. During the rest period the new leaf pair, i.e., the new body, is formed, and, as in *Conophytum,* the old leaves are drained to a papery tissue (see Figure 16). Wintering should be bright and dry at about + 15°C (+ 59°F).

The planting medium must be porous and not too rich; best is a mix of 2/3 sand, 1/3 loam, and a little humus. When grown too rich the plants grow quickly but completely lose their typical growth-form.

Cultivation is easiest from seed; already after 2 to 3 years you can have flowering-size plants; but propagation from cuttings is also possible.

Yellow-flowered species:

Lithops aucampiae L. Bol. (Color Plate 8,*1*)

Its bodies are ca. 2 cm tall, up to 3 cm in diameter and are clump-forming. The split is ca. 4 mm deep, and the leaf tip surfaces are slightly billowed, sienna brown to yellowish, with olive-green markings consisting of merging dots and lines. This is a very pretty but variable species!

Lithops bromfieldii L. Bol. (Plate 90,*2*)

Its bodies are in multiples, shaped like a top, and 15 mm tall. The split is 3 to 4 mm deep. The leaf tip surfaces are almost flat, with some ochre-brown or dark-olive folds; the furrows are reddish brown amid irregularly distributed windows and forked, blood-red or brownish-red lines. The exterior leaf margins have scalloped, brownish-yellow markings.

Lithops comptonii L. Bol. (Plate 90,*3*)

has bodies single or a few together, up to 4 cm in diameter, with a broad split. The leaf tip surfaces have a large, dark-green, purplish green, or purple window or have numerous small windows. The intermediary "islands" have white dots, and the leaf margins are gray-green with dentate markings.

Lithops divergens L. BOL. (Color Plate 7,8)

Its bodies occur singly or in multiples of 2 or more, with a deeply cut split; the windows are large, transparent, light gray-green, and smooth or finely wrinkled.

Lithops gracilidelineata DTR. (Plate 90,4)

has bodies that occur singly, seldom in twos, shaped like a top. The leaf tip surfaces are circular with a flat split, divided into individual folds by sharp, dark-brown, net-like, etched lines.

This is a very pretty species growing only in quartz gravel; depending on the color of the quartz, the color of the plant bodies also varies from pure white to gray and from bright pink to brick or blood red.

Lithops herrei L. BOL. (Plate 90,5)

forms clumps, and its bodies are conical and brownish green. The leaf tip surfaces are divided by windows into a great many lines and islands, thus appearing wrinkled.

This plant grows only in quartz fields of the Richtersveld (Great Namaqualand).

Lithops lesliei (N.E. BR.) N.E. BR. (Plate 90,6)

has one to four heads, with an inverse-cone shape, are up to 4.5 cm tall and up to 4 cm in diameter, coffee to reddish brown, also olive green. The leaf tip surfaces are slightly billowed, with net-like markings of dark greenish brown surfaces and windows. This is a very variable species!

Lithops localis (N.E. BR.) SCHWANT. (Plate 91,1)

forms clumps; its bodies are inverse-conical, 6 to 12 mm tall, and 10 to 15 mm in diameter. The leaf tip surfaces are somewhat billowed, ochre to red, with numerous violet-green dots.

Var. *terricolor* N.E. BR. (Plate 91,5–6)

This plant has bodies uniting into dense clumps that are up to 2 cm tall and up to 2.2 cm in diameter. The leaf surfaces are flat to slightly convex, brownish to reddish brown, with numerous dark, gray-blue spots.

Lithops mennellii L. BOL. (Plate 91,2)

forms clumps with inverse-conical bodies that are up to 20 mm tall and 25 mm in diameter. The leaf tip surfaces are slightly convex, pinkish brown, wrinkled, with sunken, dark-brown, net-like lines.

Lithops meyeri L. BOL. (Plate 91,3)

also forms clumps with inverse-conical bodies that are up to 30 mm tall, with a wide, deeply cut split. The leaf end surfaces are somewhat convex, bluish green, without markings.

Lithops otzeniana NEL (Color Plate 8,3)

forms dense clumps; its bodies are up to 3 cm tall, brownish green to reddish. The leaf upper surfaces are convex, with

greenish-to-olive-colored, scalloped windows.

Lithops turbiniformis (HAW.) N.E. BR. (Color Plate 7,1)

has bodies that are inverse egg-shaped to conical, up to 25 mm tall, ca. 25 mm in diameter. The leaf tip surfaces are brownish, with warty bumps; between the bumps are dark-brown, branched lines.

This plant grows in red loam, barely standing out from it by virtue of the reddish brown body color.

Lithops weberi NEL (Plate 91,4)

Its bodies occur singly or in multiples and are inverse-conical, up to 15 mm long. The leaf tip surfaces are flat, with some large, gray-green to purple-green or numerous, small, net-like windows. *L. weberi*, because of its bluish gray-green color, is so well matched to the surrounding stones that the plant can be found only by a practiced collector who knows the exact location.

Other yellow-flowered species are:
L. brevis L. BOL., *L. christinae* DE BOER, *L. dorotheae* NEL, *L. fulviceps* N.E. BR., *L. helmutii* L. BOL., *L. hookeri* (BRGR.) SCHWANT., *L. insularis* L. BOL., *L. marginata* NEL, *L. marthae* LOESCH et TISCH., *L. olivacea* L. BOL. (Figure 16), *L. pseudotruncatella* N.E. BR., *L. ruschiorum* N.E. BR., *L. schwantesii* DTR., *L. triebneri* L. BOL., *L. yallis-mariae* N.E. BR., *L. verruculosa* NEL, *L. volkii* SCHWANT., and *L. werneri* SCHWANT. et JACOBS.

White-flowered species are:

Lithops bella (DTR.) N.E. BR. (Plate 92,1)

Its bodies occur in numbers of 1 to 6, ca. 30 mm tall, 22 mm in diameter; in habitat (Namibia) it matches the color of the surrounding granite—brownish yellow to ochre, with darker, somewhat sunken windows.

This is a favorite species that is common in collections.

Lithops fulleri N.E. BR. (Plate 92,2)

forms mats of few heads; its bodies are inverse-conical, up to 15 mm (in cultivation up to 30 mm) in diameter. The leaf tip surfaces are slightly convex, grayish white with dark, brownish, almost violet, branched, sunken windows. Variable in form.

Lithops karasmontana (DTR. et SCHWANT.) N.E. BR. (Plate 92,3)

has bodies that are branched, up to 4 cm long, with a deep, narrow split. The leaf ends are flat to slightly convex, pearl gray with brownish, branching lines. This is a variable species.

Lithops optica (MARL.) N.E. BR. (Plate 92,4)

forms mats with inverse conical bodies that are up to 3 cm tall. The split is deep, and the leaf ends are very convex, gray to muddy colored, with a large, milky window.

L. optica grows in quartz fields near Lüderitz Bay close to the coast in an area that gets frequent fogs.

Among the "gems" of the *Lithops* species and a must for growers is the splendid red forma *rubra* (TISCH.) ROWL., which was discovered in 1923 among quartz shards growing under *Zygophyllum* bushes in a diamond area between Lüderitz Bay and Buntfeldschuh (Namibia). In its structure the red form hardly differs from the type-species; on the other hand its color is dark red, and the large windows are much more prominent. This form was rare up until a few years ago. Since the Dutch *Lithops* specialist Dr. DE BOER succeeded in explaining the inheritance features of the red form and how to create it artificially, the plant has found greater distribution.

Lithops salicola L. BOL. (Plate 92,5)

forms clumps with gray bodies that are inverse-conical, 20 to 25 mm tall, and up to 30 mm in diameter. The leaf tip surfaces are slightly convex, with a large, netted, dark-green to reddish window, whose margin is sinuate.

Lithops villetii L. BOL.

Bodies up to 4.5 cm long, up to 3 cm in diameter with a wide split; leaf ends convex with a large window that is irregularly sinuate on the margins.

More white-blooming species are:
L. erniana LOESCH et TISCH., *L. julii* (DTR. et SCHWANT.) N.E. BR., *L. marginata* NEL, and *L. marmorata* (N.E. BR.) N.E. BR.

The genus

Mitrophyllum SCHWANT.

is so closely related to *Conophyllum* (see page 142) that both genera have been united into one, namely *Mitrophyllum*.

Mitrophyllum means "cap-leaf," so called because of the shape of the first pair of leaves. All species (about 30) are erect, partly more or less richly branched shrubs, 12–70 cm high. The leaves appear in 3 forms (the 3rd form only at flowering time) and so the sterile shoots have 2 pairs of leaves: the first pair form a cap (mitra) or a conus; the second pair is much more smaller and the leaves are united from a quarter up to the entire length to form a sheath enclosing the cone leaves of the following vegetation period. This united leaf pair, appearing in the axil of one cone leaf, persists until the sheath becomes as thin as paper. The third leaf pair, also known as bracts, is the last one of the flowering branch, which has elongated internodes.

The *Mitrophyllum* species are not easy to cultivate. The growing period lasts only few weeks (August to September), and the plants must be kept dry during the long rest period. Propagation by cuttings is difficult.

One of the best-known species is

Mitrophyllum grande N.E. BR. (Plate 84,4) (= *Conophyllum grande* (N.E. BR.) L. BOL.,

which demonstrates the remarkable growth-form. It forms small shrubs with thick, soft stems, on which stubby and elongated internodes alternate. First look at the resting state. This is typified by a conical body up to 20 cm long, 4 to 5 cm at the base; it is wrapped in papery remains of last year's leaf pairs (plant to the left in Plate 85,4). As growth starts this hull is split and the conical body develops a horizontal leaf pair joined only at the base (second plant from the left), whereas the leaves of the following, second pair are upright and united for almost their entire length (plant to the right). From this pair emerges the new growth the next year, during whose formation the second leaf pair is drained and lies over the new leaf pair as a protective, papery hull. Once the plant begins to form flowers, which is rare in cultivation, a third pair of leaves appears, which is separated from the first two by an elongated internode. All three leaf pairs together make up one growth generation. Branching of the plant comes about usually from the axils of the basal leaf pair.

Rare in cultivation and difficult to grow, it requires a very bright, sunny location and absolute rest during the dormant period.

Very similar is

Mitrophyllum mitratum (MARL.) SCHWANT.,

a mat-forming species with thick, soft, slightly woody stems, whose annular nodes become thickened. Cone-leaves are 7–8 cm long, 2–3 cm thick, and the free parts are obtusely trigonus, light-green. Leaves of the second pairs are 10 cm long, light-green, papillose. Flowers are white, and petals are red-tipped. *Distribution:* Little Namaqualand.

Closely related to *Mitrophyllum* is the genus

Monilaria SCHWANT.

Its members are low mini-shrubs with a tuft-like growth-form with short, thick, soft shoots that are often jointed like a string of pearls. Each year's growth comprises two different shapes of leaf pairs: a basal pair of an almost spherical·shape, which is united into a short sheath, followed by a pair of long, half-cylindrical, shiny, papillous leaves united only at the base (Plate 93,1). The latter envelop the next pair of spherical leaves during the rest period. The flowers appear on long stalks and are single, white, yellowish, or red.

Monilaria globosa (L. BOL.) L. BOL. (Plate 93,1)

is a highly succulent, tuft-like species up to 8 cm tall with a short stem covered by leaf remnants and divided into spheres. The basal leaf pair is almost spherical; the leaves of the successive pairs are thick, fleshy, half-cylindrical, up to 3 cm long,

151

and the flowers are large and white. This plant grows only in quartz near Riethuis (Little Namaqualand).

Essentially larger and more richly branched is

Monilaria moniliformis (HAW.) SCHWANT. (Plate 93,2),

which forms rather large stands in the Knersvlakte near Vanrhynsdorp, growing there in quartz fields along with *Argyroderma* and *Dactylopsis digitata*. The leaves of the second leaf pair are long, cylindrical, up to 15 cm long, very soft, and papillous. The flowers are white, on long stalks.

Muiria N.E. BR.

An interesting, highly succulent mesemb is *Muiria hortenseae* N.E. BR. (Plate 92,6), the only species of the genus, which grows on brackish soil in the Little Karroo in the Riversdale district.

The plant forms compact clumps of roundish or slanting egg-shapes of soft, fleshy, gray-green to reddish, densely velvety leaves that are up to 3 cm in size and are united up to a narrow, hardly visible split just below the tip. The flowers occur singly and are pinkish white, barely protruding out of the split.

M. hortenseae is not easy to grow; it requires a bright, warm, dry location. Only during the very short vegetation period (July to September) should it be watered; otherwise the plants should be kept completely dry. With constant, high humidity the bodies begin to split.

Odontophorus N.E. BR.

The members of this genus, with the popular name "teeth plant," form a reclining to upright tuft. Their short, sometimes elongated shoots have 1 to 2 pairs of thick, fleshy, gray-green, warty leaves with 4 teeth on the margins. The stalked, yellow or white flowers appear in the fall and in the spring; the growth period is in the spring and the early summer.

All "teeth plants" (ca. 6 species) are sensitive to stagnant moisture.

As an example I have pictured

Odontophorus marlothii (N.E. BR. (Plate 93,3).

The initially short rosette axis with 2 to 3 pairs of thick, fleshy, gray-green leaves later begins to stretch out. At first it grows upright but later bends toward the ground, and as the internodes become shorter it begins to form new rosettes and develops a mat-like growth-form. The flowers are yellow, appearing

in November.

A very interesting genus resembling *Conophytum* is

Oophytum N.E. BR.,

the "egg plant." There are 3 known species, of which one, *O. nanum* (SCHLTR.) L. BOL., has been put into the genus *Conophytum* by TISCHER.

Oophytum oviforme (N.E. BR.) N.E. BR. (Plate 93,4),

like *Conophytum*, forms rather large tufts, in which numerous, spherical to egg-shaped, olive-green to shiny-purple-red bodies ca. 20 mm long stand close together. The warty-papillous, thick, fleshy leaves are united up to a small split; the flowers appear singly and are very large, with white petals with purple tips.

A very pretty species but a difficult one, because it grows on very brackish soil, usually along with *Dactylopsis digitata*.

Also closely related to the genus *Conophytum* is

Ophthalmophyllum DTR. et SCHWANT.,

the "eye leaf." These are dwarf, usually barely branched succulents, whose cylindrical or inverse-conical bodies, as in *Conophytum* and *Lithops*, are formed from only one pair of fleshy, mostly fused leaves. Their free lobes have a slick, shiny or finely papillous epidermis; they are green, reddish, or purplish red and at the tip show a large translucent window (Figure 4,3).

The flowers, similar to those of *Conophytum*, are white, pink, or reddish violet and appear from September to October. The growth period is in the fall and in early winter.

All ophthalmophyllums (ca. 24) are very sensitive to stagnant humidity; therefore, they should be watered only sparingly and grown in bright locations in porous soil.

Favorite species are:

Ophthalmophyllum friedrichiae (DTR.) DTR.

Its bodies are usually single, cylindrical, up to 3 cm long; its lobes are roundish, smooth, glabrous, and green, with a large window that, at the base, merges into several lighter dots. The flowers are white.

Ophthalmophyllum latum TISCH.

Its bodies occur singly or in pairs and are cylindrical to conical, up to 25 mm tall, bright green to yellow-green, and slightly papillous. The end surfaces of the lobes are somewhat convex, with large windows, and the flowers are white.

Forma *rubrum* TISCH.) ROWL. is the counterpart to *Lithops optica* f. *rubra;* its bodies are distinguished by their vivid purple-red coloring.

Ophthalmophyllum lydiae JACOBS. (Plate 93,5).

Its bodies occur singly or a few together and are up to 25 mm long and ca. 15 mm in diameter, with a narrow split, olive green, finely papillous, and are buried in the ground almost up to the large windows. The flowers are white, and the petals are red tipped. *Distribution:* in quartz fields of Hangpaal near Steinkopf, Little Namaqualand.

Ophthalmophyllum pillansii L. BOL. ex JACOBS. (Plate 93,6)

Currently it is placed by some authors into the genus *Conophytum* (= *C. pillansii* LAVIS).] Its bodies are usually single, ca. 2 cm tall and as thick, light yellowish green, frequently somewhat reddish, with a small, narrow split, buried in the ground up to the large window and during the dry season withdrawing into the soil. Its flowers are purple-red. *Distribution:* in quartz fields of the Knersvlakte near Vanrhynsdorp.

Ophthalmophyllum praesectum (N.E. BR.) SCHWANT. (Plate 94,1)

Its bodies occur in multiples and are cylindrical, up to 3 cm long. The lobes are 3 to 7 mm long, green, feel soft by virtue of fine points, convex at the tip, and with indistinct windows. The flowers are reddish violet.

Ophthalmophyllum verrucosum LAVIS (Plate 94,2)

has bodies that occur singly or in pairs and are cylindrical, with a deep cleft. The tips of the lobes are distinctly warty and have numerous transparent windows.

Other species.

O. australe L. BOL. (Figure 4,2), *O. caroli* (LAVIS) TISCH., *O. dinteri* SCHWANT. ex JACOBS., *O. fulleri* LAVIS, *O. longum* (N.E. BR.) TISCH., *O. maughanii* (N.E. BR.) SCHWANT., *O. pubescens* TISCH., *O. rufescens* (N.E. BR.) TISCH., *O. schlechteri* SCHWANT., *O. schuldtii* SCHWANT., and *O. triebneri* SCHWANT.

Pleiospilos N.E. BR.

Prime examples of mimesis as was mentioned on page 136 are some species of the genus *Pleiospilos,* which in form and coloration imitate the surrounding rock so successfully that it is difficult even for a good observer to distinguish the plants in their non-blooming state. The genus name refers to their similarity to stones; it could be translated as "rock pile."

All species are rosette plants growing singly or in groups with 1–2, seldom 3 or 4 pairs of very fleshy, decussate leaves united at the base and with the under side strongly vaulted, gray-green or dark green with dots

shining through. The flowers are sessile or briefly stemmed, very large, yellow, turning reddish as they fade, appearing from August to October.

The growing period is from May to July; during this time water should be given generously, but later keep the plant dry.

Pleiospilos bolusii (HOOK. f.) N.E. BR. (Plate 94,3–4).

This plant is usually found solitary and is sparsely branched as it matures, with only 1 pair of leaves and a widely gaping split in maturity. The upper side of leaf is flat, and the under side is greatly vaulted and drawn like a chin over the upper side, up to 3.5 cm thick. Its upper surface is smooth or papillous, reddish to brownish green, with numerous, dark-green dots. When the leaves begin to shrivel, the plant can no longer be distinguished from pieces of rock. The flowers are golden yellow, up to 8 cm in diameter. *Distribution:* eastern Karroo (Willowmore District).

Very similar to this is

Pleiospilos simulans (MARL.) N.E. BR.

from the same area. It has bodies that are usually single, with 1 pair of very large leaves that are up to 8 cm long and 7 cm wide, and egg-shaped to triangular, with the upper side somewhat trough-shaped, and the under side keeled and thicker toward the tip. In its natural habitat (eastern Cape Province) they are reddish to brownish green from the sun, and their upper side is heavily dotted, slightly wavy, and pimply. Its flowers are very large, yellow, and slightly fragrant.

Another beautiful example of mimesis is

Pleiospilos nelii SCHWANT. (Plate 94,5)

whose leaves are gray to gray-green, with numerous raised dots, and almost semi-spherical. The leaf upper sides during the rest period are tightly pressed together, giving the plant the appearance of a round, smooth pebble; during the growing period it has a gaping split. The flowers are salmon pink to yellowish. *Distribution:* as above.

Pleiospilos latifolius L. BOL. (Plate 94,63)

A plant of tuft-like growth-form, it has flowering shoots with 2–4 pairs of spread, fleshy, tongue-shaped leaves, whose upper side is flattened, with the under side keeled. The leaves are shiny green with raised dots, up to 8 cm long; the flowers are yellow, with white in the center. *Distribution:* eastern Cape Province.

One of the most beautiful species is

Pleiospilos prismaticus (MARL.) SCHWANT. (Color Plate 7,3)

In the youth stage, it grows singly, branching after bloom. Each body usually has one pair of silvery gray leaves, which become reddish under strong sunlight. The leaves are 3–4 cm long, up to 3 cm wide at the base, and thicker at the tip, with the upper side flat and the under side very convex and equipped with darker dots. The flowers are yellow and are ca. 4 cm in diameter.

A rare plant, it is the most difficult of the species to cultivate. *Distribution:* Ceres Karroo, near Karroopoort.

153

Further noteworthy examples of mimetic plants are found in the genus

Psammophora DTR. et SCHWANT.,

whose 4 species are distributed from the Richtersveld to Namibia. In habitat (but also in cultivation on sunny days) the leaf epidermis emits a sticky sap, to which cling fine sand and dust particles stirred up by the wind. The leaves are therefore encrusted in a thick coat of sand, giving the plant the common name "sand bearer." This covering serves as protection against too much transpiration and against being eaten by animals.

The best-known species is

Psammophora longifolia L. BOL. (Plate 95,1),

from the sand deserts north and south of the Orange River. Its short axes have 2–3 pairs of leaves that are ca. 4 cm long, with the upper side flat and the under side round and slightly keeled. The leaves are brownish gray-green to olive green, and the flowers are white.

Considerably shorter leaves are to be found on *P. herrei* L. BOL. (Richtersveld) and *P. modesta* (DTR. et BRGR.) DTR. et SCHWANT. (the Richtersveld to Lüderitz Bay).

The genus

Rhombophyllum SCHWANT.

has few species (3) and comprises mini-shrubs of densely mat-like growth-form, with long, fleshy roots. Its leaves are decussate, fused by their short sheaths at the base, and keeled on the back with the keel drawn somewhat like a chin over the top of the leaf. The flowers are golden yellow, appearing from June to September.

All rhombophylls are easy to grow and can be propagated by cuttings.

Rhombophyllum dolabriforme (L.) SCHWANT. (Plate 95,2)

is a low semi-shrub, richly branched and reaching 30 cm at maturity. Its branches are pointed upwards and outwards. The leaves are vertically flattened, wedge-shaped near the tip, have a tooth-like tip, and are smooth, grass green with dots showing through. Its flowers appear in 3- to 5-flowered inflorescences.
Similar is

R. nelii SCHWANT.

Its leaves are clearly bilobed at the tip, gray-green, with few

prominent dots.

R. rhomboideum (S.D.) SCHWANT.

is a tuft-building rosette plant, whose 8- to 10-leafed rosettes lie on the ground. Its leaves are up to 5 cm long and rhombic, with the upper side slightly vaulted and the under side keeled. The keel is drawn like a chin over the tip, and the leaves are dark gray-green, with numerous white dots.

Ruschia SCHWANT.,

with its 350 species, is the largest genus of the family. These are either very large or very small shrubs with upright branches, seldom reclining, creeping, or they are mat-forming plants. Along with *Lampranthus, Drosanthemum, Delosperma,* etc., *Ruschia* comprises most of the "Mesemb Steppes" of the dry areas of the Karroo.

The rather large, shrubby species are of little interest to the hobbyist. They can be grown outdoors in the summer, and they grow fast and bloom freely. The dwarf, mat-forming species must be grown under glass even in the summer to protect them from rain.

The red, violet, or white flowers are found singly in the axils or at the tips of the branches or they can appear in multi-flowered inflorescences, which in some species remain on the plant after blooming and thereafter lignify.

From the large number of these plants the following are cited as examples:

Ruschia dualis (N.E. BR.) L. BOL. (Plate 95,3)

is a small, tuft-like species from the brackish quartz fields of the Knersvlakte (Vanrhynsdorp District), which is so unusually rich in rare succulents. Their reclining branches are up to 5 cm long and heavily covered with dead leaves in their lower segments, and have small leaves up to 2 cm long and 5 mm wide that, as in all *Ruschia* species, are united into a sheath surrounding the shoot axis. The free blade segments are whitish gray, flat on the upper side, keeled beneath, with gristly material on the margins. The flowers are sessile and violet-pink.

A very interesting plant worthy of growing.

It so much resembles an *Argyroderma* with its silvery-gray leaves that N.E. BROWN originally described it as *A. duale.*
Also

R. herrei SCHWANT.

(Ceres Karroo and Bushman Land) is a low, mat-forming species as is also

R. pygmaea (HAW.) SCHWANT.,

from the Karroo. Its extremely short shoots bear only 1 or 2 leaf pairs that are united almost to the tip, which wither into a papery hull during the dry season.

As an example of a shrubby type I illustrate

Ruschia perfoliata (MILL.) SCHWANT. (Plate 95,4).

This is a bush up to 50 cm tall with thick branches. Its leaves are united at their short sheaths, flared, up to 1.5 cm long, triangular, ending in a sharp tip, their under side with a keel having 1 or 2 small teeth. The flowers are single and vivid red-violet.

This plant is an attractive and easily grown species.

Schwantesia DTR.

Represented by 10 species in the western part of Cape Province and in Namibia, this genus comprises multi-headed, mat-forming succulents, whose short shoot axes have 2 to 4 pairs of decussate, frequently dentate leaves, which are a bit wider at the tip. Its growth period is from April to October.

The best-known species is

Schwantesia loeschiana TISCH. (Plate 95,5).

This plant forms a compact tuft with leaves that are 25 to 35 mm long, thick, chalky green to bluish white, fused at the base, with the upper side flat, and the under side vaulted and sharply keeled. Its flowers are single, on a short peduncle, yellow, up to 5 cm in diameter. Is designated by ROWLEY as *S. herrei* L. BOL. var. *herrei* f. *major*.

Like all species of the genus it requires a very sunny and dry location.

Stomatium SCHWANT.

A tuft-like or mounding succulents, it has shoots with 4 to 6 pairs of dense, decussate leaves. The leaves are very fleshy, briefly triangular to broadly spatulate or lanceolate, frequently dentate on the edge, with the upper side flat or concave and the under side frequently keeled toward the tip, and sometimes the keel is drawn over the upper side like a chin. The epidermis is dull, pimply, and with translucent warts; the flowers are sessile or on a short stalk, yellow, seldom white, and open at night. These are easily grown plants, whose growth period is in the summer; ca. 40 species.

As an example I have pictured (Plate 95,6) a plant collected from near Beaufort West (Central Karroo). It

closely resembles *S. villetii* L. BOL.

Tischleria SCHWANT.

Tischleria peersii SCHWANT. (Plate 96,1),

the only species of the genus, is a rosette plant forming tufts and having large, golden-yellow flowers.

Its rosette leaves are decussate, united at the base, triangular in cross section, thickened into a club toward the tip, up to 4.5 cm long, and with numerous, notched teeth along the margin. The under side of the leaf is sharply keeled, and the keel is drawn over the upper side like a chin. The genus today is included in *Carruanthus* (SCHWANT.) SCHWANT. ex N.E. BR. and is called *C. peersii* L. BOL.

The members (6 species) of the genus

Titanopsis SCHWANT.

are also favorite mesembryanthemums and are excellent examples of mimesis. They are stemless rosette plants, which gather into rather large clumps. They have diagonally decussate leaves, and their spatulate blade near the tip is either broadened into a wedge or thickened into a club shape. It is covered with variously shaped warts, which run over the edge onto the under side of the leaf; the flowers occur singly, are sessile or with a short peduncle, and are yellow-orange.

The growing season comes in the summer, but water should be given sparingly during this time.

All *Titanopsis* species like a sandy soil and, because they grow in limestone, like lime mortar in the mix.

The most beautiful species and an example of perfect mimesis is the already mentioned

Titanopsis calcaria (MARL.) SCHWANT.,

a small rosette plant with flatly spread, spatulate leaves that are broadened at the tip. With their color and with their irregularly warty surface structure they imitate the surrounding weathered limestone so well that even the trained eye of a collector has trouble distinguishing the plant from the environment (Plate 83,6). *Distribution:* western Cape area.

Native to the same area is the similar

Titanopsis fulleri TISCH.

It differs from the above by the splendid, blue-green, reddish color of its leaves and the more modest formation of warts, which are located primarily on the edges of the leaves.

155

Titanopsis primosii L. BOL. (Plate 96,2)

forms rather large tufts. The rosette leaves are upright, flared, light gray to bluish green, thickened at the tip, blunt, triangular in cross section, and are densely covered with pearl-like, rather regular warts.

This plant grows only in limestone near Springbok (Little Namaqualand).

Very similar and hardly distinguishable from the above is

Titanopsis schwantesii (DTR.) SCHWANT. (Plate 96,3).

(Namibia, Karasberge). The two species are probably identical.

Trichodiadema SCHWANT.

is an interesting mesembryanthemum genus; it contains around 30, predominantly shrubby species, whose semi-cylindrical or cylindrical leaves are equipped with epidermal papillae and have at their tip a tuft of flared bristles (Plate 5,3 and Plate 96,4). The fact that these serve to absorb moisture, according to observations by R. MARLOTH, was mentioned in the introduction. If one observes the plants in their habitat in the early morning after a cool, clear night, then one sees how dew drops condense on the hairs and against the light of the rising sun glisten like a diamond-studded diadem.

One of the favorite of the approximately 30 species is

Trichodiadema densum (HAW.) SCHWANT. (Plate 96,4),

a small, tuft-like dwarf shrub with branches 1 to 15 cm long, which are equipped with cylindrical leaves ca. 20 mm long and 4 to 5 mm thick, which at their tip have a tuft of long bristles. In shape they resemble the mamillae of the cactus genus *Dolichothele*. The flowers appear singly and are carmine red.

A free bloomer, in the summer it can be grown outdoors and can be propagated easily from cuttings.

Vanheerdea L. BOL.,[26]

is an interesting succulent genus, although it is rare in

cultivation. It has 4 species, and its distribution area is in the Ceres Karroo and Little Namaqualand. The plants resemble certain *Gibbaeum* and *Lithops* species.

The largest is

Vanheerdea divergens (L. BOL.) L. BOL. (Plate 96,5).

(Bushman Land, Calvinia District). It grows on brackish-loamy soil and forms compact cushions with a stout, tap root. The cushions are 30 cm in diameter and consist of hundreds of individual bodies. Each body produces each year a pair of gray-green leaves that are up to 6 cm long and 3 cm wide, united at the base; their free lobes are broadened toward the tip, keeled on the back, and finely dentate. The flowers are on a short pedicel, golden yellow, 3 to 4 cm in diameter.

Vanheerdea primosii L. BOL. (Plate 96,6)

(Bushman Land near Gamup and near Springbok). This plant forms dense, flat, mound-like clumps, which resemble those of *Lithops*. The bodies are gray-green, up to 3.5 cm long. The leaves are united up to a flat, slightly gaping split; their blunt end surfaces are slightly concave and are equipped with a dull-green, marbled window. The margins of the upper leaf surface have a few, small teeth, and the flowers are golden yellow, 25 mm in diameter.

This is a very attractive, calcium-loving species.

Vanheerdea roodiae (N.E. BR.) L. BOL.

(Bushman Land near Alwynsfontein). This plant forms compact mounds up to 30 cm in diameter, which in intense sun become a vivid red or yellow-green; the bodies are up to 25 mm long, with blunt, fleshy, semi-spherical, dense leaves with fine hairs. The leaves are united up to a flat split; their margins and the lower, slightly protruding keel have fine hairs. The flowers are on a short stalk and are golden yellow, ca. 25 mm in diameter.

Cultivation is the same as for *Gibbaeum* and *Lithops*.

The growth period is in the spring and early summer.

[26] Although the genus was described by L. BOLUS in the original edition of *Notes Mesembr.*, part III (136, 1938, as *"Vanheerdia,"*) it should be called *"Vanheerdea,"* because it was named after the South African amateur botanist, P. VANHEERDE.

INDEX

Italicized numbers indicate plant or subject is discussed thoroughly. References to illustrations are in parentheses.